The Dimension of Time in WTO Law

# World Trade Institute Advanced Studies



VOLUME 20

The titles published in this series are listed at *brill.com/wtia*

# The Dimension of Time in WTO Law

*A Qualitative and Quantitative Analysis*

*By*

Hsin-Yi Wu

BRILL | NIJHOFF

LEIDEN | BOSTON

The Library of Congress Cataloging-in-Publication Data is available online at https://catalog.loc.gov
LC record available at https://lccn.loc.gov/2026930839

Typeface for the Latin, Greek, and Cyrillic scripts: "Brill". See and download: brill.com/brill-typeface.

ISSN 2405-9331
ISBN 978-90-04-74561-2 (hardback)
ISBN 978-90-04-74562-9 (e-book)
DOI 10.1163/9789004745629



This book is printed on acid-free paper and produced in a sustainable manner.

*This book is dedicated to my supervisors,*
*Professor Peter Van den Bossche,*
*Professor Manfred Elsig,*
*and Professor Ching-Fu Lin.*

# Contents

# Preface

"Time" is an essential element in WTO Law and seems to be pervasive in its legal texts, albeit without sufficient attention and systemic examination paid to so far. This book provides an account of the groundwork with the intention of *observing* and *classifying* time elements (*i.e.*, rules relating to time, or in short temporal rules) and their associated events in the twenty agreements of WTO Law. It aims to establish a prototype for a temporal-event taxonomy and a two-dimensional model for the temporal events association in WTO legal texts. To this effect, it analyzes WTO Law from the point of view of six categories: point in time, timing, frequency in time, period in time, sequence in time, and conceptual expression in time in the agreements examined. It devotes specific attention to *mapping* the establishment, modification, and elaboration of temporal rules under a three-dimensional systemic infrastructure of the WTO. This book seeks to advance our understanding of the theoretical framework of legalization in its four-dimensions, concerning the strength (*i.e.*, precision, obligation, delegation) and the effect (*i.e.*, implementation) of WTO Law. In doing so, it contributes to the disciplines of international law and international relations (IL/IR).

The Dimension of Time in WTO Law is the result of my Ph.D. studies, conducted over a period of more than four years at the World Trade Institute. I have attempted to identify the main threads of the important discussion on "Time and Law" without limiting myself solely to WTO legal texts and documents. However, this book and research do not present a definitive account; rather, they aim to be further developed and refined in the future. I would like to acknowledge the WTO website—particularly its Analytical Index—for providing invaluable resources that greatly supported my research. A considerable part of my work was conducted through consultation of this online documentation established by the WTO.

I am deeply grateful to my supervisors, Professor Peter Van den Bossche, Professor Manfred Elsig, and Professor Ching-Fu Lin, for guiding me into the world of academia and supporting me every step throughout my academic journey, whether abroad in Switzerland or back home in Taiwan. Last but not least, I profoundly thank my family and friends for being there as always.


### Acknowledgement

This Ph.D. research was supported by a grant from the *Swiss Government Excellence Scholarship for Foreign Scholars and Artists* (ESKAS).

# Figures and Tables

## Figures



## Tables

# Abbreviations

| | |
|---|---|
| Anti-Dumping Agreement | Agreement on the Implementation of Article VI of GATT 1994 |
| ATC | Agreement on Textiles and Clothing |
| BOP | Balance-of-Payments |
| CTG | Council for Trade in Goods |
| CTS | Council for Trade in Services |
| Customs Valuation Agreement | Agreement on the Implementation of Article VII of GATT 1994 |
| DG | Director-General |
| DS Report | Dispute Settlement Report |
| DSB | Dispute Settlement Body |
| DSU | Understanding on the Rules and Procedures Governing the Settlement of Disputes |
| GATS | General Agreement on Trade in Services |
| GATT | General Agreement on Tariffs and Trade |
| GPA | Plurilateral Agreement on Government Procurement |
| HWP | Harmonization Work Programme |
| IL | International Law |
| IR | International Relations |
| LDCs | Least-Developed Countries |
| RTAs | Regional Trade Agreements |
| S & DT | Special and Differential Treatment |
| SCM Agreement | Agreement on Subsidies and Countervailing Measures |
| SPS Agreement | Agreement on the Application of Sanitary and Phytosanitary Measures |
| TBT Agreement | Agreement on Technical Barriers to Trade |
| TFA | Agreement on Trade Facilitation |
| TPRB | Trade Policy Review Body |
| TPRM | Trade Policy Review Mechanism |
| TRIMs | Trade-Related Investment Measures |
| TRIMs Agreement | Agreement on Trade-Related Investment Measures |
| TRIPS Agreement | General Agreement on Trade-Related Aspects of Intellectual Property |
| VCLT | Vienna Convention on the Law of Treaties |
| WTO | World Trade Organization |
| WTO Agreement | Marrakesh Agreement Establishing the World Trade Organization |

# Table of Cases

| DS# | Short title | Citation |
|---|---|---|
| 121 | *Argentina—Footwear (EC)* | Appellate Body Report, *Argentina—Safeguard Measures on Imports of Footwear*, WT/DS121/AB/R, adopted 12 January 2000, DSR 2000:I, p. 515 |
| 241 | *Argentina—Poultry Anti-Dumping Duties* | Panel Report, *Argentina—Definitive Anti-Dumping Duties on Poultry from Brazil*, WT/DS241/R, adopted 19 May 2003, DSR 2003:V, p. 1727 |
| 56 | *Argentina—Textiles and Apparel* | Appellate Body Report, *Argentina—Measures Affecting Imports of Footwear, Textiles, Apparel and Other Items*, WT/DS56/AB/R and Corr.1, adopted 22 April 1998, DSR 1998:III, p. 1003 |
| 367 | *Australia—Apples* | Appellate Body Report, *Australia—Measures Affecting the Importation of Apples from New Zealand*, WT/DS367/AB/R, adopted 17 December 2010, DSR 2010:V, p. 2175 |
| 46 | *Brazil—Aircraft (Article 22.6—Brazil)* | Decision by the Arbitrator, *Brazil—Export Financing Programme for Aircraft—Recourse to Arbitration by Brazil under Article 22.6 of the DSU and Article 4.11 of the SCM Agreement*, WT/DS46/ARB, 28 August 2000, DSR 2002:I, p. 19 |
| 22 | *Brazil—Desiccated Coconut* | Appellate Body Report, *Brazil—Measures Affecting Desiccated Coconut*, WT/DS22/AB/R, adopted 20 March 1997, DSR 1997:I, p. 167 |
| 472<br>497 | *Brazil—Taxation* | Appellate Body Reports, *Brazil—Certain Measures Concerning Taxation and Charges*, WT/DS472/AB/R and Add.1 / WT/DS497/AB/R and Add.1, adopted 11 January 2019, DSR 2019:I, p. 7 |
| 70 | *Canada—Aircraft* | Panel Report, *Canada—Measures Affecting the Export of Civilian Aircraft*, WT/DS70/R, adopted 20 August 1999, upheld by Appellate Body Report WT/DS70/AB/R, DSR 1999:IV, p. 1443 |
| 321 | *Canada—Continued Suspension* | Appellate Body Report, *Canada—Continued Suspension of Obligations in the EC—Hormones Dispute*, WT/DS321/AB/R, adopted 14 November 2008, DSR 2008:XIV, p. 5373 |

(*cont.*)

| DS# | Short title | Citation |
|---|---|---|
| 321 | *Canada—Continued Suspension* | Panel Report, *Canada—Continued Suspension of Obligations in the EC—Hormones Dispute*, WT/DS321/R and Add.1 to Add.7, adopted 14 November 2008, as modified by Appellate Body Report WT/DS321/AB/R, DSR 2008:XV, p. 5757 |
| 170 | *Canada—Patent Term* | Appellate Body Report, *Canada—Term of Patent Protection*, WT/DS170/AB/R, adopted 12 October 2000, DSR 2000:X, p. 5093 |
| 170 | *Canada—Patent Term* | Panel Report, *Canada—Term of Patent Protection*, WT/DS170/R, adopted 12 October 2000, upheld by Appellate Body Report WT/DS170/AB/R, DSR 2000:XI, p. 5121 |
| 87<br>110 | *Chile—Alcoholic Beverages (Article 21.3(c))* | Award of the Arbitrator, *Chile—Taxes on Alcoholic Beverages—Arbitration under Article 21.3(c) of the DSU*, WT/DS87/15, WT/DS110/14, 23 May 2000, DSR 2000:V, p. 2583 |
| 207 | *Chile—Price Band System* | Appellate Body Report, *Chile—Price Band System and Safeguard Measures Relating to Certain Agricultural Products*, WT/DS207/AB/R, adopted 23 October 2002, DSR 2002:VIII, p. 3045 (Corr.1, DSR 2006:XII, p. 5473) |
| 511 | *China—Agricultural Producers* | Panel Report, *China—Domestic Support for Agricultural Producers*, WT/DS511/R and Add.1, adopted 26 April 2019, DSR 2019:VI, p. 3297 |
| 339<br>340<br>342 | *China—Auto Parts* | Appellate Body Reports, *China—Measures Affecting Imports of Automobile Parts*, WT/DS339/AB/R / WT/DS340/AB/R / WT/DS342/AB/R, adopted 12 January 2009, DSR 2009:I, p. 3 |
| 454<br>460 | *China—HP-SSST (Japan) / China—HP-SSST (EU)* | Appellate Body Reports, *China—Measures Imposing Anti-Dumping Duties on High-Performance Stainless Steel Seamless Tubes ("HP-SSST") from Japan / China—Measures Imposing Anti-Dumping Duties on High-Performance Stainless Steel Seamless Tubes ("HP-SSST") from the European Union*, WT/DS454/AB/R and Add.1 / WT/DS460/AB/R and Add.1, adopted 28 October 2015, DSR 2015:IX, p. 4573 |

(*cont.*)

| DS# | Short title | Citation |
|---|---|---|
| 431<br>432<br>433 | *China—Rare Earths* | Panel Reports, *China—Measures Related to the Exportation of Rare Earths, Tungsten, and Molybdenum*, WT/DS431/R and Add.1 / WT/DS432/R and Add.1 / WT/DS433/R and Add.1, adopted 29 August 2014, upheld by Appellate Body Reports WT/DS431/AB/R / WT/DS432/AB/R / WT/DS433/AB/R, DSR 2014:IV, p. 1127 |
| 394<br>395<br>398 | *China—Raw Materials* | Appellate Body Reports, *China—Measures Related to the Exportation of Various Raw Materials*, WT/DS394/AB/R / WT/DS395/AB/R / WT/DS398/AB/R, adopted 22 February 2012, DSR 2012:VII, p. 3295 |
| 366 | *Colombia—Ports of Entry* | Panel Report, *Colombia—Indicative Prices and Restrictions on Ports of Entry*, WT/DS366/R and Corr.1, adopted 20 May 2009, DSR 2009:VI, p. 2535 |
| 302 | *Dominican Republic—Import and Sale of Cigarettes* | Panel Report, *Dominican Republic—Measures Affecting the Importation and Internal Sale of Cigarettes*, WT/DS302/R, adopted 19 May 2005, as modified by Appellate Body Report WT/DS302/AB/R, DSR 2005:XV, p. 7425 |
| 415<br>416<br>417<br>418 | *Dominican Republic—Safeguard Measures* | Panel Report, *Dominican Republic—Safeguard Measures on Imports of Polypropylene Bags and Tubular Fabric*, WT/DS415/R, WT/DS416/R, WT/DS417/R, WT/DS418/R, and Add.1, adopted 22 February 2012, DSR 2012:XIII, p. 6775 |
| L616 | *EC—The ACP-EC Partnership Agreement* | Award of the Arbitrator, *European Communities—The ACP-EC Partnership Agreement—Recourse to Arbitration Pursuant to the Decision of 14 November 2001*, WT/L/616, 1 August 2005, DSR 2005:XXIII, p. 11669 |
| 291<br>292<br>293 | *EC—Approval and Marketing of Biotech Products* | Panel Reports, *European Communities—Measures Affecting the Approval and Marketing of Biotech Products*, WT/DS291/R, Add.1 to Add.9 and Corr.1 / WT/DS292/R, Add.1 to Add.9 and Corr.1 / WT/DS293/R, Add.1 to Add.9 and Corr.1, adopted 21 November 2006, DSR 2006:III, p. 847 |

(*cont.*)

| DS# | Short title | Citation |
|---|---|---|
| 27 | *EC—Bananas III (Article 21.5—Ecuador II) / EC—Bananas III (Article 21.5—US)* | Appellate Body Reports, *European Communities—Regime for the Importation, Sale and Distribution of Bananas—Second Recourse to Article 21.5 of the DSU by Ecuador*, WT/DS27/AB/RW2/ECU, adopted 11 December 2008, and Corr.1 / *European Communities—Regime for the Importation, Sale and Distribution of Bananas—Recourse to Article 21.5 of the DSU by the United States*, WT/DS27/AB/RW/USA and Corr.1, adopted 22 December 2008, DSR 2008:XVIII, p. 7165 |
| 299 | *EC—Countervailing Measures on DRAM Chips* | Panel Report, *European Communities—Countervailing Measures on Dynamic Random Access Memory Chips from Korea*, WT/DS299/R, adopted 3 August 2005, DSR 2005:XVIII, p. 8671 |
| 265<br>266<br>283 | *EC—Export Subsidies on Sugar* | Appellate Body Report, *European Communities—Export Subsidies on Sugar*, WT/DS265/AB/R, WT/DS266/AB/R, WT/DS283/AB/R, adopted 19 May 2005, DSR 2005:XIII, p. 6365 |
| 265 | *EC—Export Subsidies on Sugar (Australia)* | Panel Report, *European Communities—Export Subsidies on Sugar, Complaint by Australia*, WT/DS265/R, adopted 19 May 2005, as modified by Appellate Body Report WT/DS265/AB/R, WT/DS266/AB/R, WT/DS283/AB/R, DSR 2005:XIII, p. 6499 |
| 26<br>48 | *EC—Hormones* | Appellate Body Report, *European Communities—Measures Concerning Meat and Meat Products (Hormones)*, WT/DS26/AB/R, WT/DS48/AB/R, adopted 13 February 1998, DSR 1998:I, p. 135 |
| 26 | *EC—Hormones (US)* | Panel Report, *European Communities—Measures Concerning Meat and Meat Products (Hormones), Complaint by the United States*, WT/DS26/R/USA, adopted 13 February 1998, as modified by Appellate Body Report WT/DS26/AB/R, WT/DS48/AB/R, DSR 1998:III, p. 699 |

(*cont.*)

| DS# | Short title | Citation |
|---|---|---|
| 375<br>376<br>377 | *EC—IT Products* | Panel Reports, *European Communities and its member States—Tariff Treatment of Certain Information Technology Products*, WT/DS375/R / WT/DS376/R / WT/DS377/R, adopted 21 September 2010, DSR 2010:III, p. 933 |
| 337 | *EC—Salmon (Norway)* | Panel Report, *European Communities—Anti-Dumping Measure on Farmed Salmon from Norway*, WT/DS337/R, adopted 15 January 2008, and Corr.1, DSR 2008:I, p. 3 |
| 231 | *EC—Sardines* | Appellate Body Report, *European Communities—Trade Description of Sardines*, WT/DS231/AB/R, adopted 23 October 2002, DSR 2002:VIII, p. 3359 |
| 231 | *EC—Sardines* | Panel Report, *European Communities—Trade Description of Sardines*, WT/DS231/R and Corr.1, adopted 23 October 2002, as modified by Appellate Body Report WT/DS231/AB/R, DSR 2002:VIII, p. 3451 |
| 400<br>401 | *EC—Seal Products* | Appellate Body Reports, *European Communities—Measures Prohibiting the Importation and Marketing of Seal Products*, WT/DS400/AB/R / WT/DS401/AB/R, adopted 18 June 2014, DSR 2014:I, p. 7 |
| 315 | *EC—Selected Customs Matters* | Appellate Body Report, *European Communities—Selected Customs Matters*, WT/DS315/AB/R, adopted 11 December 2006, DSR 2006:IX, p. 3791 |
| 315 | *EC—Selected Customs Matters* | Panel Report, *European Communities—Selected Customs Matters*, WT/DS315/R, adopted 11 December 2006, as modified by Appellate Body Report WT/DS315/AB/R, DSR 2006:IX, p. 3915 |
| 219 | *EC—Tube or Pipe Fittings* | Appellate Body Report, *European Communities—Anti-Dumping Duties on Malleable Cast Iron Tube or Pipe Fittings from Brazil*, WT/DS219/AB/R, adopted 18 August 2003, DSR 2003:VI, p. 2613 |
| 316 | *EC and certain member States—Large Civil Aircraft* | Appellate Body Report, *European Communities and Certain Member States—Measures Affecting Trade in Large Civil Aircraft*, WT/DS316/AB/R, adopted 1 June 2011, DSR 2011:I, p. 7 |

(*cont.*)

| DS# | Short title | Citation |
|---|---|---|
| 316 | *EC and certain member States—Large Civil Aircraft* | Panel Report, *European Communities and Certain Member States—Measures Affecting Trade in Large Civil Aircraft*, WT/DS316/R, adopted 1 June 2011, as modified by Appellate Body Report WT/DS316/AB/R, DSR 2011:II, p. 685 |
| 211 | *Egypt—Steel Rebar* | Panel Report, *Egypt—Definitive Anti-Dumping Measures on Steel Rebar from Turkey*, WT/DS211/R, adopted 1 October 2002, DSR 2002:VII, p. 2667 |
| 492 | *EU—Poultry Meat (China)* | Panel Report, *European Union—Measures Affecting Tariff Concessions on Certain Poultry Meat Products*, WT/DS492/R and Add.1, adopted 19 April 2017, DSR 2017:III, p. 1067 |
| 595 | *EU—Safeguard Measures on Steel (Turkey)* | Panel Report, *European Union—Safeguard Measures on Certain Steel Products*, WT/DS595/R and Add.1, adopted 31 May 2022 |
| 156 | *Guatemala—Cement II* | Panel Report, *Guatemala—Definitive Anti-Dumping Measures on Grey Portland Cement from Mexico*, WT/DS156/R, adopted 17 November 2000, DSR 2000:XI, p. 5295 |
| 430 | *India—Agricultural Products* | Panel Report, *India—Measures Concerning the Importation of Certain Agricultural Products*, WT/DS430/R and Add.1, adopted 19 June 2015, as modified by Appellate Body Report WT/DS430/AB/R, DSR 2015:V, p. 2663 |
| 541 | *India—Export Related Measures* | Panel Report, *India—Export Related Measures*, WT/DS541/R and Add.1, circulated to WTO Members 31 October 2019, appealed 19 November 2019 |
| 50 | *India—Patents (US)* | Panel Report, *India—Patent Protection for Pharmaceutical and Agricultural Chemical Products, Complaint by the United States*, WT/DS50/R, adopted 16 January 1998, as modified by Appellate Body Report WT/DS50/AB/R, DSR 1998:I, p. 41 |
| 90 | *India—Quantitative Restrictions* | Panel Report, *India—Quantitative Restrictions on Imports of Agricultural, Textile and Industrial Products*, WT/DS90/R, adopted 22 September 1999, upheld by Appellate Body Report WT/DS90/AB/R, DSR 1999:V, p. 1799 |

(*cont.*)

| DS# | Short title | Citation |
|---|---|---|
| 456 | *India—Solar Cells* | Panel Report, *India—Certain Measures Relating to Solar Cells and Solar Modules*, WT/DS456/R and Add.1, adopted 14 October 2016, as modified by Appellate Body Report WT/DS456/AB/R, DSR 2016:IV, p. 1941 |
| 76 | *Japan—Agricultural Products II* | Appellate Body Report, *Japan—Measures Affecting Agricultural Products*, WT/DS76/AB/R, adopted 19 March 1999, DSR 1999:I, p. 277 |
| 8<br>10<br>11 | *Japan—Alcoholic Beverages II* | Appellate Body Report, *Japan—Taxes on Alcoholic Beverages*, WT/DS8/AB/R, WT/DS10/AB/R, WT/DS11/AB/R, adopted 1 November 1996, DSR 1996:I, p. 97 |
| 336 | *Japan—DRAMS (Korea)* | Panel Report, *Japan—Countervailing Duties on Dynamic Random Access Memories from Korea*, WT/DS336/R, adopted 17 December 2007, as modified by Appellate Body Report WT/DS336/AB/R, DSR 2007:VII, p. 2805 |
| 161<br>169 | *Korea—Various Measures on Beef* | Appellate Body Report, *Korea—Measures Affecting Imports of Fresh, Chilled and Frozen Beef*, WT/DS161/AB/R, WT/DS169/AB/R, adopted 10 January 2001, DSR 2001:I, p. 5 |
| 295 | *Mexico—Anti-Dumping Measures on Rice* | Appellate Body Report, *Mexico—Definitive Anti-Dumping Measures on Beef and Rice, Complaint with Respect to Rice*, WT/DS295/AB/R, adopted 20 December 2005, DSR 2005:XXII, p. 10853 |
| 132 | *Mexico—Corn Syrup (Article 21.5—US)* | Appellate Body Report, *Mexico—Anti-Dumping Investigation of High Fructose Corn Syrup (HFCS) from the United States—Recourse to Article 21.5 of the DSU by the United States*, WT/DS132/AB/RW, adopted 21 November 2001, DSR 2001:XIII, p. 6675 |
| 341 | *Mexico—Olive Oil* | Panel Report, *Mexico—Definitive Countervailing Measures on Olive Oil from the European Communities*, WT/DS341/R, adopted 21 October 2008, DSR 2008:IX, p. 3179 |
| 204 | *Mexico—Telecoms* | Panel Report, *Mexico—Measures Affecting Telecommunications Services*, WT/DS204/R, adopted 1 June 2004, DSR 2004:IV, p. 1537 |

(*cont.*)

| DS# | Short title | Citation |
|---|---|---|
| 538 | *Pakistan—BOPP Film (UAE)* | Panel Report, *Pakistan—Anti-Dumping Measures on Biaxially Oriented Polypropylene Film from the United Arab Emirates*, WT/DS538/R and Add.1, circulated to WTO Members 18 January 2021, appealed 22 February 2021 |
| 479 | *Russia—Commercial Vehicles* | Panel Report, *Russia—Anti-Dumping Duties on Light Commercial Vehicles from Germany and Italy*, WT/DS479/R and Add.1, adopted 9 April 2018, as modified by Appellate Body Report WT/DS479/AB/R, DSR 2018:III, p. 1329 |
| 475 | *Russia—Pigs (EU)* | Appellate Body Report, *Russian Federation—Measures on the Importation of Live Pigs, Pork and Other Pig Products from the European Union*, WT/DS475/AB/R and Add.1, adopted 21 March 2017, DSR 2017:I, p. 207 |
| 475 | *Russia—Pigs (EU)* | Panel Report, *Russian Federation—Measures on the Importation of Live Pigs, Pork and Other Pig Products from the European Union*, WT/DS475/R and Add.1, adopted 21 March 2017, as modified by Appellate Body Report WT/DS475/AB/R, DSR 2017:II, p. 361 |
| 512 | *Russia—Traffic in Transit* | Panel Report, *Russia—Measures Concerning Traffic in Transit*, WT/DS512/R and Add.1, adopted 26 April 2019, DSR 2019:VIII, p. 4301 |
| 371 | *Thailand—Cigarettes (Philippines)* | Appellate Body Report, *Thailand—Customs and Fiscal Measures on Cigarettes from the Philippines*, WT/DS371/AB/R, adopted 15 July 2011, DSR 2011:IV, p. 2203 |
| 371 | *Thailand—Cigarettes (Philippines)* | Panel Report, *Thailand—Customs and Fiscal Measures on Cigarettes from the Philippines*, WT/DS371/R, adopted 15 July 2011, as modified by Appellate Body Report WT/DS371/AB/R, DSR 2011:IV, p. 2299 |
| 371 | *Thailand—Cigarettes (Philippines) (Article 21.5—Philippines)* | Panel Report, *Thailand—Customs and Fiscal Measures on Cigarettes from the Philippines—Recourse to Article 21.5 of the DSU by the Philippines*, WT/DS371/RW and Add.1, circulated to WTO Members 12 November 2018, appealed 9 January 2019 |

(*cont.*)

| DS# | Short title | Citation |
|---|---|---|
| 34 | *Turkey—Textiles* | Panel Report, *Turkey—Restrictions on Imports of Textile and Clothing Products*, WT/DS34/R, adopted 19 November 1999, as modified by Appellate Body Report WT/DS34/AB/R, DSR 1999:VI, p. 2363 |
| 468 | *Ukraine—Passenger Cars* | Panel Report, *Ukraine—Definitive Safeguard Measures on Certain Passenger Cars*, WT/DS468/R and Add.1, adopted 20 July 2015, DSR 2015:VI, p. 3117 |
| 136<br>162 | *US—1916 Act* | Appellate Body Report, *United States—Anti-Dumping Act of 1916*, WT/DS136/AB/R, WT/DS162/AB/R, adopted 26 September 2000, DSR 2000:X, p. 4793 |
| 136 | *US—1916 Act* (EC) | Panel Report, *United States—Anti-Dumping Act of 1916, Complaint by the European Communities*, WT/DS136/R and Corr.1, adopted 26 September 2000, upheld by Appellate Body Report WT/DS136/AB/R, WT/DS162/AB/R, DSR 2000:X, p. 4593 |
| 447 | *US—Animals* | Panel Report, *United States—Measures Affecting the Importation of Animals, Meat and Other Animal Products from Argentina*, WT/DS447/R and Add.1, adopted 31 August 2015, DSR 2015:VIII, p. 4085 |
| 539 | *US—Anti-Dumping and Countervailing Duties (Korea)* | Panel Report, *United States—Anti-Dumping and Countervailing Duties on Certain Products and the Use of Facts Available*, WT/DS539/R and Add.1, circulated to WTO Members 21 January 2021, appealed 19 March 2021 |
| 436 | *US—Carbon Steel (India)* | Appellate Body Report, *United States—Countervailing Measures on Certain Hot-Rolled Carbon Steel Flat Products from India*, WT/DS436/AB/R, adopted 19 December 2014, DSR 2014:V, p. 1727 |
| 406 | *US—Clove Cigarettes* | Appellate Body Report, *United States—Measures Affecting the Production and Sale of Clove Cigarettes*, WT/DS406/AB/R, adopted 24 April 2012, DSR 2012:XI, p. 5751 |
| 406 | *US—Clove Cigarettes* | Panel Report, *United States—Measures Affecting the Production and Sale of Clove Cigarettes*, WT/DS406/R, adopted 24 April 2012, as modified by Appellate Body Report WT/DS406/AB/R, DSR 2012:XI, p. 5865 |

(*cont.*)

| DS# | Short title | Citation |
|---|---|---|
| 384<br>386 | *US—COOL* | Appellate Body Reports, *United States—Certain Country of Origin Labelling (COOL) Requirements*, WT/DS384/AB/R / WT/DS386/AB/R, adopted 23 July 2012, DSR 2012:V, p. 2449 |
| 384<br>386 | *US—COOL* | Panel Reports, *United States—Certain Country of Origin Labelling (COOL) Requirements*, WT/DS384/R / WT/DS386/R, adopted 23 July 2012, as modified by Appellate Body Reports WT/DS384/AB/R / WT/DS386/AB/R, DSR 2012:VI, p. 2745 |
| 449 | *US—Countervailing and Anti-Dumping Measures (China)* | Appellate Body Report, *United States—Countervailing and Anti-Dumping Measures on Certain Products from China*, WT/DS449/AB/R and Corr.1, adopted 22 July 2014, DSR 2014:VIII, p. 3027 |
| 437 | *US—Countervailing Measures (China) (Article 21.5—China)* | Panel Report, *United States—Countervailing Duty Measures on Certain Products from China—Recourse to Article 21.5 of the DSU by China,* WT/DS437/RW and Add.1, adopted 15 August 2019, as upheld by Appellate Body Report WT/DS437/AB/RW, DSR 2019:IX, p. 4931 |
| 345 | *US—Customs Bond Directive* | Panel Report, *United States—Customs Bond Directive for Merchandise Subject to Anti-Dumping/ Countervailing Duties*, WT/DS345/R, adopted 1 August 2008, as modified by Appellate Body Report WT/DS343/AB/R / WT/DS345/AB/R, DSR 2008:VIII, p. 2925 |
| 99 | *US—DRAMS* | Panel Report, *United States—Anti-Dumping Duty on Dynamic Random Access Memory Semiconductors (DRAMS) of One Megabit or Above from Korea*, WT/DS99/R, adopted 19 March 1999, DSR 1999:II, p. 521 |
| 108 | *US—FSC* | Appellate Body Report, *United States—Tax Treatment for "Foreign Sales Corporations"*, WT/DS108/AB/R, adopted 20 March 2000, DSR 2000:III, p. 1619 |
| 2 | *US—Gasoline* | Appellate Body Report, *United States—Standards for Reformulated and Conventional Gasoline*, WT/DS2/AB/R, adopted 20 May 1996, DSR 1996:I, p. 3 |

(*cont.*)

| DS# | Short title | Citation |
|---|---|---|
| 184 | *US—Hot-Rolled Steel* | Appellate Body Report, *United States—Anti-Dumping Measures on Certain Hot-Rolled Steel Products from Japan*, WT/DS184/AB/R, adopted 23 August 2001, DSR 2001:X, p. 4697 |
| 184 | *US—Hot-Rolled Steel* | Panel Report, *United States—Anti-Dumping Measures on Certain Hot-Rolled Steel Products from Japan*, WT/DS184/R, adopted 23 August 2001 modified by Appellate Body Report WT/DS184/AB/R, DSR 2001:X, p. 4769 |
| 177<br>178 | *US—Lamb* | Appellate Body Report, *United States—Safeguard Measures on Imports of Fresh, Chilled or Frozen Lamb Meat from New Zealand and Australia*, WT/DS177/AB/R, WT/DS178/AB/R, adopted 16 May 2001, DSR 2001:IX, p. 4051 |
| 353 | *US—Large Civil Aircraft (2nd complaint) (Article 22.6—US)* | Decision by the Arbitrator, *United States—Measures Affecting Trade in Large Civil Aircraft (Second Complaint)—Recourse to Article 22.6 of the DSU by the United States*, WT/DS353/ARB and Add.1, 13 October 2020 |
| 202 | *US—Line Pipe* | Panel Report, *United States—Definitive Safeguard Measures on Imports of Circular Welded Carbon Quality Line Pipe from Korea*, WT/DS202/R, adopted 8 March 2002, as modified by Appellate Body Report WT/DS202/AB/, DSR 2002:IV, p. 1473 |
| 217<br>234 | *US—Offset Act (Byrd Amendment)* | Appellate Body Report, *United States—Continued Dumping and Subsidy Offset Act of 2000*, WT/DS217/AB/R, WT/DS234/AB/R, adopted 27 January 2003, DSR 2003:I, p. 375 |
| 217<br>234 | *US—Offset Act (Byrd Amendment) (Article 21.3(c))* | Award of the Arbitrator, *United States—Continued Dumping and Subsidy Offset Act of 2000—Arbitration under Article 21.3(c) of the DSU*, WT/DS217/14, WT/DS234/22, 13 June 2003, DSR 2003:III, p. 1163 |
| 268 | *US—Oil Country Tubular Goods Sunset Reviews* | Appellate Body Report, *United States—Sunset Reviews of Anti-Dumping Measures on Oil Country Tubular Goods from Argentina*, WT/DS268/AB/R, adopted 17 December 2004, DSR 2004:VII, p. 3257 |

(*cont.*)

| DS# | Short title | Citation |
|---|---|---|
| 152 | *US—Section 301 Trade Act* | Panel Report, *United States—Sections 301–310 of the Trade Act of 1974*, WT/DS152/R, adopted 27 January 2000, DSR 2000:II, p. 815 |
| 58 | *US—Shrimp* | Appellate Body Report, *United States—Import Prohibition of Certain Shrimp and Shrimp Products*, WT/DS58/AB/R, adopted 6 November 1998, DSR 1998:VII, p. 2755 |
| 236 | *US—Softwood Lumber III* | Panel Report, *United States—Preliminary Determinations with Respect to Certain Softwood Lumber from Canada*, WT/DS236/R, adopted 1 November 2002, DSR 2002:IX, p. 3597 |
| 277 | *US—Softwood Lumber VI* | Panel Report, *United States—Investigation of the International Trade Commission in Softwood Lumber from Canada*, WT/DS277/R, adopted 26 April 2004, DSR 2004:VI, p. 2485 |
| 179 | *US—Stainless Steel (Korea)* | Panel Report, *United States—Anti-Dumping Measures on Stainless Steel Plate in Coils and Stainless Steel Sheet and Strip from Korea*, WT/DS179/R, adopted 1 February 2001, DSR 2001:IV, p. 1295 |
| 344 | *US—Stainless Steel (Mexico)* | Appellate Body Report, *United States—Final Anti-Dumping Measures on Stainless Steel from Mexico*, WT/DS344/AB/R, adopted 20 May 2008, DSR 2008:II, p. 513 |
| 564 | *US—Steel and Aluminium Products (Turkey)* | Panel Report, *United States—Certain Measures on Steel and Aluminium Products*, WT/DS564/R, Add.1 and Suppl.1, circulated to WTO Members 9 December 2022, appealed 26 January 2023 |
| 248<br>249<br>251<br>252<br>253<br>254<br>258<br>259 | *US—Steel Safeguards* | Appellate Body Report, *United States—Definitive Safeguard Measures on Imports of Certain Steel Products*, WT/DS248/AB/R, WT/DS249/AB/R, WT/DS251/AB/R, WT/DS252/AB/R, WT/DS253/AB/R, WT/DS254/AB/R, WT/DS258/AB/R, WT/DS259/AB/R, adopted 10 December 2003, DSR 2003:VII, p. 3117 |

(*cont.*)

| DS# | Short title | Citation |
|---|---|---|
| 381 | *US—Tuna II (Mexico)* | Appellate Body Report, *United States—Measures Concerning the Importation, Marketing and Sale of Tuna and Tuna Products*, WT/DS381/AB/R, adopted 13 June 2012, DSR 2012:IV, p. 1837 |
| 381 | *US—Tuna II (Mexico)* | Panel Report, *United States—Measures Concerning the Importation, Marketing and Sale of Tuna and Tuna Products*, WT/DS381/R, adopted 13 June 2012, as modified by Appellate Body Report WT/DS381/AB/R, DSR 2012:IV, p. 2013 |
| 381 | *US—Tuna II (Mexico) (Article 22.6—US)* | Decision by the Arbitrator, *United States—Measures Concerning the Importation, Marketing and Sale of Tuna and Tuna Products—Recourse to Article 22.6 of the DSU by the United States*, WT/DS381/ARB, 25 April 2017, DSR 2017:VIII, p. 4129 |
| 24 | *US—Underwear* | Appellate Body Report, *United States—Restrictions on Imports of Cotton and Man-made Fibre Underwear*, WT/DS24/AB/R, adopted 25 February 1997, DSR 1997:I, p. 11 |
| 267 | *US—Upland Cotton* | Appellate Body Report, *United States—Subsidies on Upland Cotton*, WT/DS267/AB/R, adopted 21 March 2005, DSR 2005:I, p. 3 |
| 267 | *US—Upland Cotton* | Panel Report, *United States—Subsidies on Upland Cotton*, WT/DS267/R, Add.1 to Add.3 and Corr.1, adopted 21 March 2005, as modified by Appellate Body Report WT/DS267/AB/R, DSR 2005:II, p. 299 |
| 267 | *US—Upland Cotton (Article 21.5—Brazil)* | Appellate Body Report, *United States—Subsidies on Upland Cotton—Recourse to Article 21.5 of the DSU by Brazil*, WT/DS267/AB/RW, adopted 20 June 2008, DSR 2008:III, p. 809 |
| 464 | *US—Washing Machines (Article 21.3(c))* | Award of the Arbitrator, *United States—Anti-Dumping and Countervailing Measures on Large Residential Washers from Korea—Arbitration under Article 21.3(c) of the DSU*, WT/DS464/RPT, 13 April 2017, DSR 2017:VIII, p. 4309 |

(*cont.*)

| DS# | Short title | Citation |
|---|---|---|
| 166 | *US—Wheat Gluten* | Appellate Body Report, *United States—Definitive Safeguard Measures on Imports of Wheat Gluten from the European Communities*, WT/DS166/AB/R, adopted 19 January 2001, DSR 2001:II, p. 717 |
| 322 | *US—Zeroing (Japan) (Article 21.5—Japan)* | Appellate Body Report, *United States—Measures Relating to Zeroing and Sunset Reviews—Recourse to Article 21.5 of the DSU by Japan*, WT/DS322/AB/RW, adopted 31 August 2009, DSR 2009:VIII, p. 3441 |

CHAPTER 1

# Introduction

The World Trade Organization (WTO), established in 1995 succeeding the GATT 1947 as a multilateral rules-based system, has become the central pillar of the international trading system and of global governance in the pursuit of economic prosperity and poverty reduction.[1] Generally speaking, while global governance can be effected through various instruments (*e.g.*, customary international law, embedded norms, and habituated practices),[2] the current WTO is mainly confined to addressing global trade issues by means of "treaties," especially, the *Marrakesh Agreement Establishing the World Trade Organization*, signed on 15 April 1994 and entered into force on 1 January 1995. In other words, the WTO is a forum for its Members to agree by consensus to establish international trade rules among them, and endeavors to solve trade disputes based on those agreed rules. Despite its imperfection and facing many challenges, the WTO has been considered to be highly effective and benefited greatly from its binding rules, according to Bacchus:[3]

> Without the shelter and benefits of binding WTO rules and without a neutral venue for peaceful discussion and dispute resolution, the result would be a worldwide return to the pre-World War II free-for-all of discrimination, high trade barriers, retaliation, and opaqueness that decades of WTO multilateral negotiations and agreements have greatly reduced.

In fact, as indicated by Howse, the critics of global trade governance were not usually motivated by "a reaction against the legal rules of international trade themselves, but the institutional and interpretative behaviour of the official

1 Peter Van den Bossche and Werner Zdouc, *The Law and Policy of the World Trade Organization: Text, Cases and Materials* (4th edition, Cambridge University Press 2017), 80–81.

2 John Gerard Ruggie, 'Foreword' in Thomas G Weiss and Ramesh Thakur (eds), *Global Governance and the UN: An Unfinished Journey* (Indiana University Press 2010), xv. (Global governance is defined "as an instance of the absence of government" at the global level to produce public goods through "the workings of the system of authoritative rules, norms, institutions, and practices by means of which any collectivity manages its common affairs.")

3 James Bacchus, 'The World Trade Organization: Myths versus Reality' (*Cato Institute*, 26 September 2023), https://www.cato.org/publications/world-trade-organization-myths-versus-reality (last visited 27 June 2025).

 | DOI:10.1163/9789004745629_002

guardians of those rules."[4] For this reason, treaties and their legal rules *per se* still play an important role in the global trading regime.

In terms of how treaties derive their regulatory effect, Kennedy emphasized their functions to "constitute [multiple] actors, channel their interactions, and influence their relative powers." He argued that "[a]ll manner of rules, enforced and unenforced, may, as a matter of fact, affect any global transaction."[5] Bilder also acknowledged the functional role of treaties. He fully noticed that the employment of treaties to establish legally binding international obligations frequently involves substantial risks (*e.g.*, the uncertainty of future benefits, the burden of performance, the participation of the parties). However, he still considered that the treaty as a device is particularly helpful to facilitate the arrangement of international affairs due to its reliability, stability, formality, and common framework.[6] To be more specific, Kessler opined that treaties have "a civilizing power on states" due to the fact that they provide "a vocabulary for peaceful dispute resolution" and transform "political disputes in legal claims."[7] In the context of the WTO, for example, the treaties were employed to limit the possibility of political interference with cross-border economic activity.[8] Accordingly, although the treaty itself might not be considered as a first-best instrument for global governance,[9] it still remains one of the most important instruments in use.

Drawing upon the crucial role of "treaties" in global (trade) governance, this book addresses issues concerning the treaties of the WTO (*i.e.*, "WTO Law" as selected in Section 1.2), and undertakes a focused analysis of the mysterious

4 Robert Howse, 'Adjudicative Legitimacy and Treaty Interpretation in International Trade Law: The Early Years of WTO Jurisprudence' in Joseph HH Weiler (ed), *The EU, the WTO, and the NAFTA: Towards a Common Law of International Trade?* (Oxford University Press 2001), 68.

5 David Kennedy, 'The Mystery of Global Governance' in Jeffrey L Dunoff and Joel P Trachtman (eds), *Ruling the World?: Constitutionalism, International Law, and Global Governance* (Cambridge University Press 2009), 55.

6 *See* Richard B Bilder, *Managing the Risks of International Agreement* (University of Wisconsin Press 1981), 6–7 and 14–15.

7 Oliver Kessler, 'The Same as It Never Was? Uncertainty and the Changing Contours of International Law' (2011) 37 Review of International Studies 2163, 2180.

8 Jedediah Britton-Purdy and others, 'Building a Law-and-Political-Economy Framework: Beyond the Twentieth Century Synthesis' (2020) 129 Yale Law Journal 1784, 1805.

9 *E.g.*, the transaction cost of treaties could undermine the willingness of states to sign into an official international agreement. As Pauwelyn et al. stated, concluding a formal treaty may "require huge transaction costs, and once concluded is hard to adapt to changing circumstances," and therefore "is no longer the first-best option to which soft or informal law can only aspire." Joost Pauwelyn, Ramses A Wessel and Jan Wouters, 'When Structures Become Shackles: Stagnation and Dynamics in International Lawmaking' (2014) 25 European Journal of International Law 733, 750–751.

yet pervasive "time elements" embedded in their legal texts (*i.e.*, "temporal rules" as defined in Section 1.3). As a famous quote about "time," "[w]hat, then, is time? If no one ask of me, I know; if I wish to explain to him who asks, I know not."[10] To explore the esoteric issue of "time" in law, it is my contention that what has been neglected in the existing literature is a systemic reflection on what "time elements" in legal texts entail and how they inform our understanding of legal content. This book challenges the assumption that "time elements" are, by definition, technical, and that their formation should be taken for granted or relegated to the background.

It is worthy to note that there has already been an increasing interest in the issues related to "time" in WTO Law. For example, one of the most controversial temporal issues is of that the time-frames under the *Understanding on the Rules and Procedures Governing the Settlement of Disputes* (DSU) are not duly complied with.[11] The criticism was that the dispute settlement proceedings often exceed the standard time-frames (*i.e.*, the 90-day deadline) set by the legal rules. Despite growing awareness of temporal issues, most discussions about "time" tend to arise from specific challenges encountered in WTO practice *ex post* (Section 1.1). In contrast, this book makes a distinct effort to study time elements embedded in WTO legal texts *ex ante* (Section 1.2). It identifies time elements systemically, and defines them under the notion of "temporal rules," a term specifically coined to guide the research undertaken in this book (Section 1.3). This notion can be employed to introduce a new line of thinking that complements the existing theoretical framework of legalization in the disciplines of international law (IL) and international relations (IR) (Section 1.4). All in all, this book explores how the idea of "time" plays out in WTO Law, leading to diverse and interconnected arrangements of legal content. To be more specific, this is a study of time elements embedded in WTO legal texts to manage legal events as well as their functions and developments to influence the governance of the institution (Section 1.5).

Before proceeding any further, the following outlines the general expectations for this book: The research undertaken in this book is not conducted under a vertical approach to provide a concrete solution on how to design or apply particular time elements to address specific challenges, nor to tell whether a given time element really matters under a particular circumstance, although some possibilities will be touched upon. The objectives of this book

10 Saint Augustine, *Confessions XI*, para. 17.

11 *See generally* Louise Johannesson and Petros C Mavroidis, 'The WTO Dispute Settlement System 1995–2016: A Data Set and Its Descriptive Statistics' (2017) 51 Journal of World Trade 357.

are much more under a horizontal approach with the aim of exploring the universe of time elements in WTO Law, tracking their existence and formation, and encouraging continued research in this relatively underexplored area. In other words, this book is a preliminary and groundwork investigation on time elements in WTO Law to address: (1) how they can be identified in legal texts; (2) how they may be associated with legal events; and (3) how they may be changed in practice. Overall, this book puts forward an intellectual theme relating to the role of "time" in (international trade) law discourse.

## 1.1 The Diversity of Temporal Issues in the WTO

How we view the role of time makes a great difference to how we approach temporal issues. In the context of the WTO, most of the discussions on the temporal issues in WTO Law seem to emerge from the challenges related to "time" arising from practice under certain circumstances. These temporal challenges may be wide-ranging and extend beyond the legal rules of the WTO, including (1) the problem of delay, (2) the lack or conflict of time regulation, and (3) the innovation of time management.

First, *the problem of delay* can be found in several occasions and has generated a number of institutional (re)solutions. For example, the delay in completing accession negotiations with least-developed countries (LDCs) gave rise to the adoption of the 2012 accession guidelines by the General Council to facilitate and speed up accession negotiations. These guidelines set out concrete instructions for the WTO Members on how to apply restraint when seeking concessions and commitments from LDCs applying for membership.[12] In addition, the problem of delay has also been discussed in the context of completing dispute settlement proceedings under the DSU. Several proposals for reform were put forward and touched on the strategies for time-saving, *e.g.*, the idea of a permanent panel body,[13] the crucial role of the Secretariat in dispute

---

12 WT/COMTD/LDC/21. *See also* Eric Neumayer, 'Strategic Delaying and Concessions Extraction in Accession Negotiations to the World Trade Organization: An Analysis of Working Party Membership' (2013) 12 World Trade Review 669. (discussing the problems in the selection of the timing and conditions of accession to the WTO, and pointing out the possibility for the existing Members to strategically delay membership on applicant countries.)

13 *See* William J Davey, 'The Case for a WTO Permanent Panel Body' (2003) 6 Journal of International Economic Law 177, 178–179. *See also* Matthew Kennedy, 'Why Are WTO Panels Taking Longer? And What Can Be Done About It' (2011) 45 Journal of World Trade 221. (concerning the unexpected delays in panel proceedings under the DSU, and considering the reasons and possible solutions.)

settlement,[14] and the exceptional nature of the extension.[15] Last but not least, there were also concerns regarding the delay in trade in goods due to customs formalities and procedures (*i.e.*, administrative barriers to trade). To mitigate the effects of delay, the WTO Members concluded negotiations at the 2013 Bali Ministerial Conference and established a new treaty for expediting the movement, release, and clearance of goods, namely, *Agreement on Trade Facilitation* (TFA)—the simplification, modernization, and harmonization of export and import processes—which emerged as an important landmark of the WTO.

Second, *the lack or conflict of time regulation* might also be seen as a cause of ineffective procedures (dispute settlement proceedings, in particular). Some relevant discussions are summarized as follows:

1. No temporal limitation is imposed on making a non-confidential summary of written submissions available in DSU Article 18.2. The problem is that the publication could be too late to be of any practical relevance.[16]
2. No temporal limitation is imposed on submitting evidence to the adjudicators by disputing parties in DSU Article 11. The problem is that the submission could be too late to be consistent with the due process standard.[17]
3. No temporal limitation is imposed on removing authorization for retaliation, the so-called "post-retaliation issue" in DSU Article 22.8. The implied solution is that the authorization could lapse by operation of law (*ipso*

---

14 *See* Joost Pauwelyn and Krzysztof Pelc, 'Who Guards the "Guardians of the System"? The Role of the Secretariat in WTO Dispute Settlement' (2022) 116 American Journal of International Law 534, 560. ("The fact that both panels and the [Appellate Body] now consistently exceed DSU prescribed time-frames may be partly due to a mutually self-reinforcing effect: the Secretariat's involvement in rulings results in a more bureaucratic style where 'no stone is left unturned,' and hypertrophic reports replete with references to earlier rulings. These, in turn, invite longer and more articulate party submissions, which, in turn, call for more detailed and time-consuming examination.")

15 *See* Claus-Dieter Ehlermann, 'The Workload of the WTO Appellate Body: Problems and Remedies' (2017) 20 Journal of International Economic Law 705, 709. (observing that the Members appear to be of the view that extension is only possible if the parties to the dispute reach a consent to do so, or that more detailed reasons should be provided by the Appellate Body in order to be justified under the specific "exceptional circumstances.")

16 *See also* Armin Steinbach, 'The Treatment of Confidential Information in WTO Dispute Settlement Proceedings' (2014) 24 American Review of International Arbitration, https://aria.law.columbia.edu/issues/24-4/the-treatment-of-confidential-information-in-wto-dispute-settlement-proceedings-vol-24-no-4/(last visited 27 June 2025). (examining confidentiality issues in the context of the DSU and the treatment of confidential information in practice.)

17 *See also* Panizzon Marion, 'Fairness, Promptness and Effectiveness: How the Openness of Good Faith Limits the Flexibility of the DSU' (2008) 77 Nordic Journal of International Law 275. (describing how the due process standard can be derived from the DSU to ensure a fair, prompt, and effective dispute resolution.)

*jure*) once substantive compliance has been confirmed through WTO dispute settlement procedures.[18]

4. The conflict between the time-frames for DSU Article 21.5's compliance proceedings and DSU Article 22.6's authorization for retaliation, the so-called "sequencing issue." The problem is that it is not possible to obtain authorization for retaliation within 30 days of the expiry of the "reasonable period of time" for implementation, in cases where the complainant must first refer the disagreement over implementation to a compliance panel, which is expected to take 90 days to issue its report.[19]

Third, *the innovation of time management* can be stimulated by means of law and practice to address the particular issues at hand. For example, the TFA was negotiated to allow developing country Members to self-designate implementation periods of the commitments in order to establish flexibility for them, which is considered as an innovative approach to accord special and differential treatment.[20] In the case of the term-sharing appointment of the Director-General (DG) of the WTO, the difficulty at that time was that the decision on the appointment of the successor to the DG (Mr. Renato Ruggiero) was divisive. The WTO Members were not able to reach an agreement over a year-long effort. To break this deadlock, the Members agreed on the unprecedented arrangement of the term-sharing appointment. It allowed Mr. Mike

18 Appellate Body Report, *Canada—Continued Suspension*, para. 310. ("Although [DSU] Article 22.8 sets forth the resolutive conditions under which the suspension of concessions must cease to apply, it does not identify the procedures to be followed should a dispute arise as to whether one of the conditions has been satisfied.") *See also* Cherie O'Neal Taylor, 'Beyond Retaliation' (2017) 38 Northwestern Journal of International Law & Business 55. (demonstrating the flaws of inadequate post-retaliation regulations in the DSU as well as the manipulation and delay of the disputing parties at the end stage of disputes.)

19 Award of the Arbitrator, *Brazil—Aircraft* (*Article 22.6—Brazil*), fn. 7. *See also* MA Qian, '"Reasonable Period of Time" in the WTO Dispute Settlement System' (2012) 15 Journal of International Economic Law 257. (examining the problems in the determination of the reasonable period of time under the DSU, and suggesting a reform proposal for prompt compliance.)

20 *See* Nora Neufeld, 'The Long and Winding Road: How WTO Members Finally Reached a Trade Facilitation Agreement' (2014) WTO Staff Working Papers, 8, https://www.wto.org/english/res_e/reser_e/ersd201406_e.htm (last visited 27 June 2025). ("[The special and differential] treatment in most WTO agreements focuses on transition periods. While grace periods are still foreseen in the [TFA] mandate, they are but one part of a much more comprehensive flexibilities package, crucially complemented by the introduction of a conditional link between existence of implementation capacity and requirement to undertake a commitment. This novel concept was further expanded by determining that developing [countries] and [LDCs] would not be obliged to implement aspects of a [TFA] when required support for infrastructure was not forthcoming.")

Moore of New Zealand to be appointed for a term of three years beginning on 1 September 1999, and subsequently Mr. Supachai Panitchpakdi of Thailand to serve another three-year term beginning on 1 September 2002.[21] Thereafter, to prevent any future deadlock, the *Decision on the Procedures for the Appointment of* DG was adopted by the Members in 2002 to establish a more comprehensive set of rules and procedures (with explicit time-frames) for the process of future appointments.[22]

When considered together, the issues of time in the WTO can be seen both as *a problem* (*e.g.*, delay or conflict) and as *a solution* (*e.g.*, innovation). Despite these initial observations, temporal issues can still be much more diverse, and their coverage cannot be claimed exhaustive. In addition, various intellectual perspectives on temporal issues can be advanced through different approaches. Recent scholarly interest tends to be *problem- and solution-oriented*, addressing specific cases in practice *ex post*. With this trend in mind, however, this book departs from the *problem-solving* approach and instead adopts a *purpose-finding* orientation by examining temporal issues in legal texts *ex ante*. It is a study of how time elements can be identified and developed within WTO Law.[23]

## 1.2 The Subject Matter of the Research: Twenty Agreements of WTO Law

WTO Law is an ambitious and complex body of international trade rules, which not only contains enforceable rights and obligations for its Members, but also institutional and procedural rules to facilitate the overall functioning

21 WTO News: WTO Member Governments Agree on Director-General Succession, PRESS/131 (22 July 1999), https://www.wto.org/english/news_e/pres99_e/pr131_e.htm (last visited 27 June 2025). (However, it was stressed that "the unprecedented term sharing arrangement did not constitute a precedent for future appointments of the [DG] and agreed to work towards establishing 'a comprehensive set of rules and procedures for such appointments' by the end of September 2000.")

22 WT/L/509, para. 7. ("The appointment process shall start nine months prior to the expiry of the term of an incumbent [DG] with a notification from the Chair to the General Council. The process shall conclude with a meeting of the General Council convened not later than three months prior to the expiry of an incumbent's term, at which a decision to appoint a new [DG] shall be taken.")

23 As Kahn proposed, "[w]e need a form of legal scholarship that gives up the project of reform, not because it is satisfied with things as they are, but because it wants better to understand who and what we are." Paul W Kahn, *The Cultural Study of Law: Reconstructing Legal Scholarship* (University of Chicago Press 1999), 30.

of the WTO.[24] As a whole, WTO Law consists of several multilateral and plurilateral agreements, which are established collectively as a single system under its principal source of the *Marrakesh Agreement Establishing the World Trade Organization* (the WTO Agreement).[25] Within the WTO Agreement, most of the substantive trade agreements can be found in its Annexes 1 and 4, which are: (1) 13 multilateral agreements on trade in goods in Annex 1A; (2) 1 multilateral *General Agreement on Trade in Services* (GATS) in Annex 1B; (3) 1 multilateral *General Agreement on Trade-Related Aspects of Intellectual Property* (the TRIPS Agreement) in Annex 1C; and (4) 2 plurilateral trade agreements in Annex 4. On the other hand, the procedural agreements are placed in its Annexes 2 and 3, namely, the DSU and the *Trade Policy Review Mechanism* (TPRM). If the above-mentioned agreements are enforceable through the WTO dispute settlement mechanism, they are also coined with the term "covered agreements" under the DSU.[26]

It should be noted that Annex 1A of the WTO Agreement contains the *General Agreement on Tariffs and Trade* (GATT 1994), which incorporates by reference the provisions of the GATT 1947 (*i.e.*, its predecessor). In addition, the GATT 1994 includes other six *Understandings on the Interpretation of the Articles of the GATT 1947* and *a Marrakesh Protocol* to annex Members' Schedules of concessions and commitments (Table 1.1 below). Strictly speaking, as confirmed by Article II:4 of the WTO Agreement, although the provisions of the GATT 1947 continue to have legal effect as part of the GATT 1994, the GATT 1994 and the GATT 1947 are "legally distinct." In fact, the GATT 1947 *per se* was terminated on 1 January 1996.[27] However, for the sake of simplicity, other parts of this book

24 Van den Bossche and Zdouc (n 1), 43.

25 MAR Art. II:2: "[T]he agreements and associated legal instruments included in Annexes 1A, 2 and 3 (hereinafter referred to as 'Multilateral Trade Agreements') are integral parts of this Agreement and binding on all Members."; MAR Art. II:3: "Annex 4 (hereinafter referred to as 'Plurilateral Trade Agreements') are also part of this Agreement for those Members that have accepted time, and are binding on those Members."

26 Appellate Body Report, *Brazil—Desiccated Coconut*, p. 13. (The term "covered agreements" was defined to "include the [WTO Agreement], the Agreements in Annexes 1 and 2, as well as any Plurilateral Trade Agreement in Annex 4 where its Committee of signatories has taken a decision to apply the DSU.")

27 *See* PC/12, L/7583. Noting that the GATT 1947 was to become part of the Havana Charter for an International Trade Organization that was negotiated during the United Nations Conference on Trade and Employment held in Cuba from 21 November 1947 to 24 March 1948. As of 1 January 1948, the GATT 1947 was applied through a *Protocol of Provisional Application*. As the Havana Charter never came into force, the GATT 1947 remained provisionally in force until its provisions became part of the GATT 1994.

might not make this legal distinction in all instances, and may use the abbreviation "GATT" to refer to the provisions of the GATT 1947.

Finally, WTO Law has been subject to change over time. One of the original 13 agreements on trade in goods in Annex 1A of the WTO Agreement, the *Agreement on Textiles and Clothing* (ATC), terminated on 1 January 2005 after the expiry of the ten-year transition period of its implementation. Instead, a new agreement was enlisted in Annex 1A, namely, the TFA, which was concluded by the negotiation of the WTO Members in 2013, and entered into force in 2017. In addition, the TRIPS Agreement in Annex 1C of the WTO Agreement was amended to make permanent a decision on patents and public health originally adopted in 2003. This decision was formally built into the TRIPS Agreement and took effect in 2017. Last but not least, only 2 of the original 4 plurilateral agreements in Annex 4 of the WTO Agreement are still in force, which are *Plurilateral Agreement on Trade in Civil Aircraft* and *Plurilateral Agreement on Government Procurement* (GPA). In terms of the GPA, the parties of this agreement initiated a renegotiation, and then adopted a new version of the agreement in 2012 which entered into force in 2021. In sum, there are in total *twenty agreements* of WTO Law which were selected as the subject matter of the research undertaken in this book. These agreements were up to date and still in force to the date of conducting the investigation, including 18 multilateral trade agreements and 2 plurilateral trade agreements as listed in Table 1.1 below.

TABLE 1.1 The subject matter of the research: twenty agreements in WTO Law

| Abbreviation | Full name of agreements |
|---|---|
| MAR | Marrakesh Agreement Establishing the World Trade Organization ("the WTO Agreement") |
| GATT | General Agreement on Tariffs and Trade 1994 (its introduction referred as "GATT 1994")<br>– Incorporating by reference: General Agreement on Tariffs and Trade 1947 ("GATT 1947")<br>– Understanding on the Interpretation of Article II:l(b) of the GATT 1994<br>(other duties and charges) ("Understanding on Art. II:1(b)")<br>– Understanding on the Interpretation of Article XVII of the GATT 1994<br>(state trading enterprises) ("Understanding on Art. XVII") |

TABLE 1.1 The subject matter of the research: twenty agreements in WTO Law (*cont.*)

| Abbreviation | Full name of agreements |
|---|---|
| | – Understanding on Balance-of-Payments Provisions of the GATT 1994 ("Understanding on BOP Provisions") |
| | – Understanding on the Interpretation of Article XXIV of the GATT 1994 (regional trade agreements) ("Understanding on Art. XXIV") |
| | – Understanding in Respect of Waivers of Obligations under the GATT 1994 ("Understanding on Waivers") |
| | – Understanding on the Interpretation of Article XXVIII of the GATT 1994 (concession withdrawal) ("Understanding on Art. XXVIII") |
| | – Marrakesh Protocol to the GATT 1994 ("MAR Protocol") |
| AG | Agreement on Agriculture |
| SPS | Agreement on the Application of Sanitary and Phytosanitary Measures ("the SPS Agreement") |
| TBT | Agreement on Technical Barriers to Trade ("the TBT Agreement") |
| TRIMS | Agreement on Trade-Related Investment Measures ("the TRIMS Agreement") |
| ADP | Agreement on the Implementation of Article VI of GATT 1994 ("the Anti-Dumping Agreement") |
| CV | Agreement on the Implementation of Article VII of GATT 1994 ("the Customs Valuation Agreement") |
| PSI | Agreement on Preshipment Inspection |
| RO | Agreement on Rules of Origin |
| LIC | Agreement on Import Licensing |
| SCM | Agreement on Subsidies and Countervailing Measures ("the SCM Agreement") |
| SG | Agreement on Safeguards |
| TFA | Agreement on Trade Facilitation |
| GATS | General Agreement on Trade in Services |
| TRIPS | General Agreement on Trade-Related Aspects of Intellectual Property ("the TRIPS Agreement") |
| DSU | Understanding on the Rules and Procedures Governing the Settlement of Disputes |

TABLE 1.1 The subject matter of the research: twenty agreements in WTO Law (*cont.*)

| Abbreviation | Full name of agreements |
|---|---|
| TPRM | Trade Policy Review Mechanism |
| CA | Plurilateral Agreement on Trade in Civil Aircraft<br>Including: Protocol (2001) Amending the Annex to the Agreement on Trade in Civil Aircraft<br>Excluding: the List of Harmonized System headings and subheadings in the Annex |
| GPA | Plurilateral Agreement on Government Procurement (2012) |
| Total | 20 Agreements, including 18 multilateral agreements and 2 plurilateral agreements |

## 1.3 The Definition of Temporal Rules: Time Elements in Law

The notion of time is a standard feature of our language and thinking. According to the *Oxford English Dictionary*, "time" as a noun can be defined by its extent (*e.g.*, as a period or quantity), its point (*e.g.*, an occasion or instance), its special and technical use (*e.g.*, grammar tense or rhythmic quality), and in generalized sense (*e.g.*, duration conceived as beginning and ending or indefinite continuous).[28] As such, "time" can be widely perceived and used in the pursuit of different objectives or purposes. In the current context of bringing "time" into law, this research focuses on how to apply the broad notion of "time" to legal texts. Generally speaking, the drafters of law or the negotiators of treaties may inevitably employ time elements in shaping the legal content at hand. In other words, when they are drafting a legal text, it is important for the content to be prescribed and structured in a logical and predictable way. Accordingly, the drafters may use some *temporal words or phrases* to establish a sense of certainty and order for legal texts, such as telling the readers *when* specific rights or obligations would be allowed under which circumstances. Without temporal guidance, the readers may not have clues to let them know when the rights or obligations ought to take place. In this regard, to better study the content of

28 "Time" (*Oxford English Dictionary*, 2012), https://www.oed.com/dictionary/time_n#220292953 (last visited 4 June 2025).

law, it would be crucial to understand how these time elements (*i.e.*, temporal words or phrases) are displayed.

As for how to capture and define time elements in legal texts, this research was inspired by the relevant studies in the field of computer science. Especially, it will be demonstrated in the next Chapter (Section 2.3) that the temporal words and phrases to denote "time" in texts have already been studied intensely in its subfield of *natural language processing* (*e.g.*, in news or medical documents). Drawing upon its well-established definition, the term "temporal expression" has been commonly used to describe the sequence of words in texts that tell us (1) *when* something happened; (2) *how long* something lasted; and (3) *how often* something occurs.[29] Syntactically speaking, temporal expressions can be realized in a myriad of ways and signalled by a wide range of grammatical realizations, for example, prepositions, subordinate relative clauses, adverbs, adjectives, *etc.* Accounts of the temporal expressions vary with regard to the type of the text and the purpose of the research. Among the many possible typologies of temporal expressions across various texts, there is, however, no commonly accepted definition of temporal expressions in the legal domain.

To establish the specific application of the typology in legal studies, this research coins the term "temporal rules" to delimit the denotation of "temporal expressions in legal texts," *i.e.*, the named collection of temporal words and phrases that purports to represent time elements in law. Generally speaking, temporal rules are capable of being used to guide particular legal events, or to evaluate their relationships by reference to one or multiple temporal rules in legal texts. Within this coined term, I suggest and refer to the "rules" to place emphasis not only on the subject matter of legal texts but also on an *internal* perspective of law. As d'Aspremont found, the common understanding of "rules" is to allow us "to escape the necessity to investigate social phenomena behind law-identification processes and to stick to a *purely internal* perspective."[30] It should also be noted that the main purpose of this book is not to provide a settled definition of "temporal rules" in the sense of correctness. Instead, it is to advance the study of time in law by providing an assessment of distinctive temporal rules and a better understanding of their actual employment in the context of WTO Law.

29 Roser Saurí and others, 'TimeML Annotation Guidelines Version 1.2.1' (2006), https://nilsreiter.de/assets/2017-10-01-howto-annotation/timeml-1.2.1.pdf (last visited 5 June 2025).

30 Jean d'Aspremont, 'The Idea of "Rules" in the Sources of International Law' (2014) 84 British Yearbook of International Law 103, 109. (emphasis added)

## 1.4 The Contribution to the Theoretical Framework of Legalization

This research is based on the assumption that temporal rules can play an important role in the legalization of the WTO, and their proper design may facilitate the effectiveness of the institution. To anchor this research in a broader theoretical framework, this book draws upon literature from the disciplines of IL/IR, particularly, the theoretical framework of legalization. When engaging in interdisciplinary studies, one key feature to keep in mind before proceeding further is "the evolution of a disciplinary sensibility," which means a transformation "in the structure of a collective consciousness" for disciplinary turns.[31] For this reason, a brief history of the evolution of IL/IR will be provided beforehand as follows.

After the First World War, IR was born as a distinct discipline and overlapped with IL for the hope of developing new and ideal international institutions under *the concept of the rule of law* to promote world order. However, after the Second World War, it was argued that *the struggle* of *power* still strongly remained, and the "normative limitations" of IL was not effective enough to balance power politics.[32] This challenge inspired the reconceptualization of IL/IR relationship, and then motivated three alternative analytical approaches from a legal point of view: (1) *policy-oriented*—focusing on underlying policy choices of legal doctrines; (2) *process-oriented*—redefining the conception of law from rules to process, *e.g.*, communication, reassurance, monitoring and routinization; and (3) *function-oriented*—reassessing the primary functions of law.[33] Generally speaking, the research approaches back then were mainly the attempts to apply IR theories to the study on IL phenomena. To foster greater possibilities for interdisciplinary studies, it has been encouraged that future

31 John Haskell and Akbar Rasulov, 'International Law and the Turn to Political Economy' (2018) 31 Leiden Journal of International Law 243, 244. (*See also* at 245–246. The authors argued that, strictly speaking, there is no "disciplinary turn" from IL to "political economy" (*cf.*, the relatively well-established IR as a discipline referred in this book) for at least two reasons: (1) "There isn't one single 'correct' or 'naturally given' concept of political economy that is valid for all disciplines."; and (2) "For international lawyers, political economy is basically a 'what' [*e.g.*, the idea that "economic structures and political power are fused together"], not a 'how' [*i.e.*, the discipline that "studies the public management of private rationalities"]; it is something that is just 'out there', not something that you 'do'.")

32 Norman J Padelford, 'Review of Politics among Nations: The Struggle for Power and Peace' (1949) 64 Political Science Quarterly 290, 290.

33 Anne-Marie Slaughter Burley, 'International Law and International Relations Theory: A Dual Agenda' (1993) 87 American Journal of International Law 205, 209.

IL/IR scholarship might consider asking what IL can contribute to IR, and what the joint studies of IL/IR can offer traditional IL scholars and practitioners.[34] In particular, as Hoffmann pointed out, since states want to turn their interests, ideas and gains into law, "a study of the 'legal strategies' of the various units, *i.e.*, of what kinds of norms they try to promote, and through what techniques, may be as fruitful for the political scientist as a study of more purely diplomatic, military or economic strategies."[35]

Following this new urge for IL/IR approaches, in the early 2000s, a special symposium issue of *International Organization* has devoted to studying the causes and consequences of the "legalization" of international politics, *i.e.*, the dynamic process of IL as a particular form of institutionalization characterized by precision, obligation, and delegation.[36] To be more specific, the theoretical framework from Abbott et al. was dedicated to identifying the forms of IL that regulate behavior under three dimensions, each as a continuum, defined as follows: (1) *precision*—"rules unambiguously define the conduct they require, authorize, or proscribe;" (2) *obligation*—"states or other actors are bound by a rule or commitment or by a set of rules or commitments ... in the sense that their behavior thereunder is subject to scrutiny under the general rules, procedures, and discourse of [IL];" and (3) *delegation*—"third parties have been granted authority to implement, interpret, and apply the rules; to resolve disputes; and (possibly) to make further rules."[37] It was argued that the combination of all these three dimensions would provide us a standpoint of comparison in terms of the *strength* of IL, namely, "hard" or "soft" legalization.

For example, statutes or regulations in well-established domestic legal systems were considered as an ideal type of "hard" legalization, while international institutions were less likely to reach the same domestic level.[38] In addition, Dunoff and Pollack acknowledged that different issue areas of law might tend to utilize different approaches of legalization. In the context of *interest-oriented* or *rationalist-oriented* issues (*e.g.*, trade), the hard law approach may be more effective in establishing clear expectations to guide and influence behavior. On the other hand, in the context of *value-oriented* or

---

34 Jeffrey L Dunoff and Mark A Pollack (eds), *Interdisciplinary Perspectives on International Law and International Relations: The State of the Art* (Cambridge University Press 2013), 10 and 33.

35 Stanley Hoffmann, 'The Study of International Law and the Theory of International Relations' (1963) 57 *Proceedings of the American Society of International Law at Its Annual Meeting (1921–1969)* 26, 33.

36 *See generally* Kenneth W Abbott and others, 'The Concept of Legalization' (2000) 54 International organization 401.

37 *Ibid.*, 401.

38 *Ibid.*, 402.

*constructivist-oriented* issues (*e.g.*, human rights), the soft law approach may be preferable for persuading actors to act in a desired manner.[39] Accordingly, in regulating international trade issues, WTO Law has been considered "hard" across all three dimensions of the legalization framework. The WTO in general was observed to administer "a remarkably detailed set of legally binding international agreements" and to operate a dispute settlement mechanism with "significant authority to interpret and apply those agreements in the course of resolving particular disputes."[40]

However, as stated by Abbott et al., the purpose of their three-dimensional legalization framework was to capture "the *overall* legalization of international norms, agreements, and regimes."[41] Therefore, as the authors deliberately noted, their definitions were not intended to address (1) the actual implementation of rules, and (2) the substantive content of rules. They provided the following reasons for excluding these two issues.[42]

(1) *The actual implementation of rules*: The authors first argued that the inclusion of implementation would lead to the impossibility "to inquire whether legalization increases rule implementation or compliance." In addition, with respect to the relevant inquiry related to legalization over time (*i.e.*, "whether international legalization is increasing, or likely to increase, over time"), the authors took no position under the consideration that their "comparative statics approach" was not suitable for conducting this kind of analysis. Nevertheless, they were aware that the issues were "important and intriguing," and agreed that "[e]xploration of legal dynamics would be the logical next step in the research program."[43]

---

39 Dunoff and Pollack (n 34), 41–43.

40 Abbott and others (n 36), 404–405.

41 *Ibid.*, 404. (emphasis added)

42 *Ibid.*, 402. ("Note that we have defined legalization in terms of key characteristics of rules and procedures, not in terms of effects. For instance, although our definition includes delegation of legal authority (to domestic courts or agencies as well as equivalent international bodies), it does not include the degree to which rules are actually implemented domestically or to which states comply with them. To do so would be to conflate delegation with effective action by the agent and would make it impossible to inquire whether legalization increases rule implementation or compliance. Nor does our definition extend to the substantive content of rules or their degree of stringency. We regard substantive content and legalization as distinct characteristics. A conference declaration or other international document that is explicitly not legally binding could have exactly the same substantive content as a binding treaty, or even a domestic statute, but they would be very different instruments in terms of legalization, the subject of this volume.")

43 *Ibid.*, 408. ("On a related set of issues—whether international legalization is increasing, or likely to increase, over time—we take no position. The comparative statics approach that informs this volume is not suitable for analyzing such dynamic phenomena. Yet the

(2) *The substantive content of rules*: The authors considered legal content to be a distinct feature, noting that a non-legal binding document might have identical content to that of a binding treaty. As far as I am aware, no subsequent research agenda has been advanced to engage with the substantive content of rules under the theoretical framework of legalization.

To further explore the research potential related to the second exclusion decision mentioned above, this book proposes a new angle for studying *the substantive content of rules*—through the lens of "temporal rules" embedded in legal texts. In the followings, I will demonstrate (1) what has been done in the existing literature to address the first exclusion decision on *the actual implementation of rules*; and (2) what will be done in this research to deal with the second exclusion decision on *the substantive content of rules*.

### 1.4.1 *What Has Been Done: Legalization over Time (Temporal Dynamics in Legal Practice)*

To address *the actual implementation of rules* and legalization over time (*i.e.*, dynamic process or evolution), a study on "re-conceptualizing legalization" advocated that the temporal dynamics of legalization is not linear and progressive. In other words, more legal precision, obligation, and delegation might not produce more rule of law or effective outcomes.[44] It has been proposed that "implementation" should be built into the theoretical framework of legalization, taking into account its dynamic character and to facilitate the understanding of its three original dimensions. As Carey and Mitchell argued, "[l]egalization theory needs to account for failures or shortcomings in implementation, whether because of institutional erosion or state resistance," and "[t]he law acts with and through politics in a manner that makes any conceptualization of legalization necessary not to exclude politics as antithetical to legal activity."[45]

issues are important and intriguing. We undoubtedly witness increasing legalization in many issue areas.")

44 Henry (Chip) Carey and Stacey M Mitchell, 'Introduction: Re-Conceptualizing Legalization—The Positive and Negative Uses and Effects of International Law' in Henry (Chip) Carey and Stacey M Mitchell (eds), *Legalization of International Law and Politics: Multi-Level Governance of Human Rights and Aggression* (Springer International Publishing 2023), 14. (*See also* at 18. "We can point to the growing density of international legal obligations, followed by examples too numerous to mention, without really knowing whether we have been, are, or will be in a period of greater legalization or de-legalization and whether we are moving closer to rule of law or rule by law.")

45 *Ibid.*, 15.

In terms of how to incorporate this extra dimension of "implementation" into the original legalization framework, it would have a fundamental choice in what the concept of legalization is really explaining, as the authors further indicated:[46]

> If all three variables [*i.e.*, dimensions] were to include implementation, then legalization becomes the same thing nearly or exactly as the international rule of law as a dependent variable. If the implementation is excluded from all three independent variables, the legalization would be one type of law, which some argue does not require enforcement to be law—which is the minority view.

To avoid this dilemma of choice, they derived a new idea that is different from the hard/soft approach of law in the original framework by stating that "the implementation of law can be positive or negative, depending on the character and direction of the implementation." In other words, they assess "the impact of implementation as a *positive* outcome if the rule leads to compliance and *negative* if it permits and/or facilitates non-compliant or illiberal, rule by law."[47] Accordingly, this new approach seems to decouple from the original framework concerning the *strength* of IL (*i.e.*, hard/soft legalization), and establish another criterion concerning the *effect* of IL (*i.e.*, positive/negative legalization).

### 1.4.2 *What Will Be Done: Time in Legalization (Temporal Rules in Legal Texts)*

As the two exclusion decisions mentioned above, *the substantive content of rules* was put forward in tandem with the concern of *the actual implementation of rules*. Abbott et al. decided not to consider the substantive content in their original framework due to its distinct character across different (non-)legal instruments. However, this research argues that the pervasive temporal rules embedded in legal texts may exhibit certain shared characteristics that offer a basis for examining *the substantive content of rules*. Drawing inspiration from emerging literature on "Time and Law," law itself contains diverse but common terminology to underpin legal conception of time (Chapter 2). As Rakoff has already identified, there are four common characteristics of time to be functionally used in the legal system to establish or facilitate the allocation,

46 *Ibid.*, 59.
47 *Ibid.*, 60. (emphasis added)

coordination, rhythm, and texture of law.[48] To be more specific, French regarded "time" as serving six principal functions within the legal framework: (1) time as a measuring device; (2) time as a value unit; (3) time as a delineator of rights; (4) time as an organizer; (5) time as a determinant of what is reasonable; and (6) time as an intrinsic part of basic legal concepts.[49] In line with these functional characteristics of time, this research explores the possibility of "time" (or the coined term "temporal rules") as an important internal element embedded in *the substantive content of rules*, offering a novel approach to enhance theoretical insights into the framework of legalization. This research attempts to uncover the role of "temporal rules" in WTO Law and their potential interconnection with the four-dimensional legalization framework, namely, the *strength* of WTO Law (*i.e.*, precision, obligation, and delegation) and the *effect* of WTO Law (*i.e.*, implementation).

## 1.5 The Orientation of the Research

"Time" seems to be a self-evident experience for most people, and the questioning of which appears to be relatively rare. However, this research is based on the notion that "time" can be crucial in WTO Law, yet it is not fully and systematically examined. This research seeks to provide a detailed groundwork investigation of temporal rules in WTO Law, which may facilitate our understanding of the theoretical framework of legalization. First, by categorizing and producing a preliminary *temporal-event taxonomy* in WTO Law, one may be interested in creating a standardized analytical tool for the substantive content of law. Second, by investigating how temporal rules are *designed* and *applied*, one may be able to understand how important they are to serve as the foundations of legalization. Third, by evaluating how temporal rules are subject to *change* over time, one may be encouraged to consider their fluidity in practice, such as the idea that temporal rules can be established to create not only static expectations but also to enable the dynamic adaptation of law.

Given that "time" is crucial, the objectives of this research must not be overstated and should be defined narrowly. The primary objective is to *observe* and *classify* how temporal rules are embedded and developed in WTO Law at large, and to *suggest* how their employment may have implications for the existing

48 *See generally* Todd D Rakoff, *A Time for Every Purpose: Law and the Balance of Life* (Harvard University Press 2002).

49 Rebecca R French, 'Time in the Law' (2001) 72 University of Colorado Law Review 663, 664–667.

theoretical framework of legalization. This research does not aspire to contribute to the debate about their legal consequences or legal argumentation in WTO Law. It rather relies on preliminary and empirical observations for the attempt to build up a system of thought for the underexplored research area of "Time and Law" (Chapter 2). As Bowker and Star argued, "[i]n a world of imperfect knowledge, any classificatory principle might be good, valid, useful: you will not know what makes a difference until you have built up a body of knowledge that relies, for its units of data, on the classification scheme that you have not yet developed."[50]

While one may still expect legal scholarship to be argumentative or normative, the new data-driven approach of legal studies appears to push forward the equal relevance of empirical or descriptive research, as stated by Alschner et al.: "While counterintuitive findings with important normative implications remain incredibly relevant, journals should not shy away from publishing empirical research where it incrementally adds to or confirms our understanding of the world."[51] Following the empirical approach of legal scholarship, the primary purpose of this research is to offer a scheme of classification based on careful observations rather than an in-depth argumentation.

In addition, this research is a broad effort to investigate and classify the twenty agreements of WTO Law (Section 1.2) with the intention of contributing to future studies beyond the WTO (Section 1.4). Any broad study necessarily involves some generalization and simplification. However, some degree of generalization and simplification is permissible for reasons of economy and necessary to situate the topic within a wider context. As Abbott acknowledged in social science, "[s]caling and clustering may throw away the vast majority of dimensionality, but by doing so they often produce compelling and powerful simplifications of complex data."[52]

It is also worth to note that the fundamental challenges rest on specific classification choices are "how to develop the analogy between the finite number of our exiting examples of things and the indefinite number of things we shall encounter in the future."[53] As Bowker and Star stated, a classification system

50 Geoffrey C Bowker and Susan Leigh Star, *Sorting Things Out: Classification and Its Consequences* (The MIT Press 2000), 276.

51 Wolfgang Alschner, Joost Pauwelyn and Sergio Puig, 'The Data-Driven Future of International Economic Law' (2017) 20 Journal of International Economic Law 217, 229.

52 Andrew Abbott, *Time Matters: On Theory and Method* (University of Chicago Press 2001), 122. ("Much of real science is description. Sociology will not be taken seriously again as a general science of social life until it gets serious about description.")

53 Barry Barnes, David Bloor and John Henry, *Scientific Knowledge: A Sociological Analysis* (University of Chicago Press 1996), 55.

should "grow out of and have to answer to *our common sense*, socially comfortable classifications."[54] Besides, it is also important to pay attention to "the *fluid dynamics* of how classification systems meet up—a plate tectonics rather than a static geology."[55] Accordingly, in order to take into account the "common sense" and "fluid dynamics" of temporal rules in WTO Law, this research had consulted a considerable amount of WTO Jurisprudence and practice before proceeding to categorize temporal rules in WTO legal texts (Section 2.4). The relevant materials were retrieved from the *WTO Analytical Index: Interpretation and Application of* WTO *Agreements* on the WTO website.[56] This Analytical Index provides an article-by-article guide to the interpretation and application of WTO Law, which covers the dispute settlement reports, the decisions or awards of arbitrators, as well as related decisions and other significant actions taken by relevant WTO bodies. This research benefits from this well-established online resource by making use of relevant negotiation history, jurisprudence, and practice to explore and understand temporal rules in a broader context. Although this research examines temporal rules only in the context of the WTO, its contribution may inspire the reflection on the same or similar matter under various fields of legal studies.

To sum up, the following Chapters of this book will provide a groundwork investigation of temporal rules in WTO Law by exploring: (1) how the issue of "time" has attracted intellectual attention in (international) law, and how to establish a new territory for this research (Chapter 2); (2) how temporal rules in WTO Law may be classified into various categories, and their actual distribution in legal texts (Chapter 3); (3) how different types of substantive or procedural events in WTO legal content may be classified, and their association with temporal rules in legal texts (Chapter 4); (4) how temporal rules were established, modified, and elaborated in WTO practice (Chapter 5); and (5) how temporal rules may have implications for the theoretical framework of legalization (Chapter 6). Chapter 7 will conclude.

---

54 Bowker and Star (n 50), 67. (emphasis added)

55 *Ibid.*, 31. (emphasis added)

56 WTO Analytical Index: Interpretation and Application of WTO Agreements, https://www.wto.org/english/res_e/publications_e/ai17_e/ai17_e.htm (last visited 28 June 2025).

CHAPTER 2

# Time and Law

There are different representations of time in various academic disciplines.[1] In psychology, the basic assumption of subjective human time perception is that it has to be related to the occurrence of events as they are perceived and actions taken by the subject. Accordingly, a taxonomy of temporal experiences (*i.e.*, five "elementary time experiences") has been established to represent our time perception, which includes duration, simultaneity/successiveness, sequence, past/present, and future/periodicity.[2] Against these common experiences of time in everyday life, many theoretical physicists, however, have come to an idea of a "timeless reality" and argued that time fundamentally does not even exist. For example, the famous Albert Einstein's theory of relativity was developed on his reconceptualization of time to "spatialize time" into merely one more direction within four-dimensional spacetime.[3] Nevertheless, in philosophy, it could be argued that time still retains its special and important feature to relate events causally and establish the order among them.[4] This debate about time is in line with the so-called "two times problem" between physical and human time, and has drawn scholarly attention to the inquiry into whether time is real, illusory, or both.[5]

Apart from the common experiences and features of time, the notion of "time" seems to play a different role in social settings.[6] According to Felski,

1 For the fundamental questions about time in philosophy, physics, linguistics, and psychology, *see generally* Jeremy Butterfield (ed), *The Arguments of Time* (Oxford University Press 2006).

2 Ernst Pöppel, 'Time Perception' in SM Anstis (ed), *Perception* (*Handbook of Sensory Physiology*), vol 8 (Springer International Publishing 1978), 713–729. For the general theory of time perception, *see generally* Robin Le Poidevin, 'The Experience and Perception of Time' in Edward N Zalta (ed), *The Stanford Encyclopedia of Philosophy* (Summer 2019, Metaphysics Research Lab, Stanford University 2019).

3 *See* Craig Callender, 'Is Time an ILLUSION?' (2010) 302 Scientific American 58, 60–61. ("Spacetime is like a loaf of bread that you can slice indifferent ways, called either 'space' or 'time' almost arbitrarily.")

4 *Ibid.*, 62. ("Time is the direction within spacetime in which good prediction is possible—the direction in which we can tell the most informative stories. The narrative of the universe does not unfold in space. It unfolds in time.")

5 *See generally* Ronald P Gruber, Carlos Montemayor and Richard A Block, 'From Physical Time to a Dualistic Model of Human Time' (2020) 25 Foundations of Science 927, 927–954.

6 For the general sociological theory regarding the relationship between the concept of time and social reality, *see generally* Jiří Šubrt, *The Sociology of Time: A Critical Overview* (Springer International Publishing 2021).

 | DOI:10.1163/9789004745629_003

the conception of time is "enormous complexity" and can exist at many different levels of life and conditions, which is experienced in radically divergent ways.[7] As stated by Singh, "we would perceive the physical world in time, but we would have to constitute the social world, and all its aspect, within time, if it is at all to make a meaningful or purposeful aspect of the social world."[8] In other words, one may have common perception of time in the physical world on the one hand, and have divergent construction of time in the social world on the other hand. For example, with any given social phenomenon, it usually requires to identify specific "social time" as independence of context to understand social structure and interaction.[9] Bowker and Star also recognized the importance of time by stating that "[t]he world must still be cut up into recognizable temporal and spatial units—partly because that is the way the world is and partly because that is the only way that science as we know it can work."[10]

Following the recognition of social time, law in particular has a unique character with respect to the notion of "time." Law itself appears to bridge the passage of social time, as stated by Allott: "Law is a presence of the *social past.* Law is an organizing of the *social present.* Law is a conditioning of the *social future.*" To fix the *present* as a distinction between *past* and *future*, law as a "communicative system within time" considers the *past* as unchangeable and the *future* as changeable in order to create expectation and reduce uncertainty.[11] Despite this heavy interference of time in law, Mawani pointed out that "time is often assumed to exist as though it were a natural phenomenon, unfolding effortlessly and inconspicuously as the backdrop to social and political life."[12] Against this frequent assumption of time as the invisible backdrop, the relationship between "time and law" has increasingly emerged as a significant intellectual theme warranting deeper exploration.

---

7 Rita Felski, *Doing Time: Feminist Theory and Postmodern Culture* (NYU Press 2000), 16–17. (The conception of time is "enormous complexity, including questions of measurement, rhythm, synchronization, sequence, tempo, and intensity. It spans the personal and the public, work and leisure, the instantaneous and the eternal, intimate relations and global structures, everyday life and conditions of extremity.")

8 Chhatrapati Singh, 'The Concept of Time in Law: Basis of Laws of Limitation and Prescription' (1990) 32 Journal of the Indian Law Institute 328, 347.

9 Andrew Abbott, *Time Matters: On Theory and Method* (University of Chicago Press 2001), 123.

10 Geoffrey C Bowker and Susan Leigh Star, *Sorting Things Out: Classification and Its Consequences* (The MIT Press 2000), 98.

11 Philip Allott, 'The Concept of International Law' (1999) 10 European Journal of International Law 31, 32. (emphasis added)

12 Renisa Mawani, 'Law as Temporality: Colonial Politics and Indian Settlers' (2014) 4 UC Irvine Law Review 65, 70.

In this sense, to set the stage for exploring the dimension of time in WTO Law, Section 2.1 seeks to review the trend of academic literature with regard to the issue of time in law in general, and Section 2.2 focuses further on the role of time in the fields of IL and IR in particular. In addition, in order to identify temporal rules in WTO Law, Section 2.3 draws methodological inspiration from the field of natural language processing in computer science for the inquiry of how to conduct temporal and event extraction in legal texts. Last but not least, in order to uncover the "common sense" regarding what temporal rules in WTO Law could be, Section 2.4 provides a preliminary observation from WTO Jurisprudence with the intention of identifying temporal connotations that have been emphasized or raised concerns in practice.

## 2.1 Time in Law

Against the invisible backdrop assumption of time, Greenhouse claimed that law has a temporal dimension which can be mythic, since it is "in time" as a *human product* and also "out of time" as a *systematic promise*.[13] As also explained by Van der Ploeg and Pasquet, time as a "multifaceted notion" simultaneously serves both as the setting within which law must operate in physical time (*cf.*, in time as a human product), and as a notion that law creates through the imposition of legal time (*cf.*, out of time as a systematic promise).[14] Accordingly, this section divides the existing approaches in legal studies that have explored the relationship between "time and law" into two main streams: (1) law is perceived as a *human product* passively embedded or explained in time; and (2) law itself is considered out of time as a *systematic promise* that actively makes or uses time. To be more specific, this section further captures the current trend of legal studies in "time and law" through four lenses: (1) law as a human product embedded in time (*e.g.*, legal culture); (2) law as a human product explained in time (*e.g.*, legal historian); (3) law as a systematic promise that makes time (*e.g.*, socio-legalism); and (4) law as a systematic promise that uses time (*e.g.*, internal-legal-event regulation). In general, this research

13 Carol J Greenhouse, 'Just in Time: Temporality and the Cultural Legitimation of Law' (1989) 98 Yale Law Journal 1631, 1640. ("Law has a mythic dimension, in its self-totalization, its quality of being in time (in that it is a human product) but also out of time (where did it or does it begin or end?) and in its promise of systematic yet permutable meaning.")

14 Klara Polackova Van der Ploeg and Luca Pasquet, 'The Multifaceted Notion of Time in International Law' in Klara Polackova Van der Ploeg, Luca Pasquet and León Castellanos-Jankiewicz (eds), *International Law and Time: Narratives and Techniques* (Springer International Publishing 2022), 5.

posits itself mainly alongside the fourth trend of legal studies, which views temporal rules being used as a systematic promise in WTO Law to regulate legal events inward.

### 2.1.1 *Law as a Human Product Embedded in Time: Linear or Circular*

From a broader cultural perspective, culture differences in the perception of time cause differences in the way we manage time and work. Duranti and Di Prata have identified two common approaches for the perception of time: (1) *monochronic approach*—treating time as linear by emphasizing "schedules, punctuality, and preciseness," and valuing getting things done "on time;" and (2) *polychronic approach*—treating time as being more flexible by emphasizing "interpersonal relationships," and valuing "being" than on "doing."[15] In the field of law, modern legal systems in general are traditionally considered to be developed in Western culture,[16] in which the linear approach of time appears to prevail. According to Greenhouse, law under a linear temporal culture usually embeds with three essential forms of time to establish its certainty, neutrality, and legitimacy: (1) its linear and infinite nature which celebrates the *certainty* of the passage of time; (2) a symbolism of all-times to transcend any particular era which is essential to the *neutrality* of law; and (3) a finite lifetime of judges vested with authorities which becomes a dilemma of the *legitimacy* of the judicial system.[17] For example, to ensure certainty, Wyler and Whelan further pointed out that the linear temporal consideration of law is crucial to strictly apply legal concepts such as the principle of nonretroactivity.[18] However, against the linear approach of time, Mawani has warned that conceptualizing law as only linear and infinite temporality could be problematic and undermine its claims to authority, legitimacy, and universality.[19]

On the flip side of the Western linear temporal culture, as observed by Vanhullebusch, a non-Western temporal culture differs from the Western

15 Giancarlo Duranti and Olvers Di Prata, 'Everything Is about Time: Does It Have the Same Meaning All over the World?', *PMI® Global Congress 2009—EMEA, Amsterdam, North Holland, The Netherlands. Newtown Square, PA: Project Management Institute* (2009).

16 Tilmann Altwicker and Oliver Diggelmann, 'How Is Progress Constructed in International Legal Scholarship?' (2014) 25 European Journal of International Law 425, 431. (The authors pointed out that modern legal systems in general are traditionally considered to be developed in Western societies under the influence of Roman law; on the other hand, "non-Western cultures were and still are less law-centred.")

17 Greenhouse (n 13), 1642–1644.

18 Eric Wyler and Arianna Whelan, 'Lawyers as Creators of Law's Temporal Reality: A Pragmatic Approach to International Law' in Klara Polackova Van der Ploeg, Luca Pasquet and León Castellanos-Jankiewicz (eds), *International Law and Time: Narratives and Techniques* (Springer International Publishing 2022), 32–33.

19 Mawani (n 12), 93.

linear concept of time and embraces the notion of circular time by emphasizing *change* and *continuity*.[20] In theory, he explained the function of time from a Confucian point of view that "[circular] time and timing play an essential part in balancing contradictory positions" which allows "reconciling opposing interests to harmonize relationships that underpin the initial contradictions" (*cf.*, the polychronic approach).[21] In practice, Wyler and Whelan referred to legal pragmatism for its assumption of time to be "cyclical, continuous, and diachronic," and argued that the application of law can be "reciprocal, dynamic, creative and circular" such as the principle of good faith.[22] In sum, law, as a human product, can be seen as grounded in a (Western) linear approach of time to ensure *certainty*, *neutrality*, and *legitimacy*, and/or in a (non-Western) circular approach of time to emphasize *change* and *continuity*.

### 2.1.2 *Law as a Human Product Explained in Time: Synchronic or Diachronic*

From a historian's perspective, history *per se* is a representation of time. According to Gadamer, the historical explanation of social phenomena is important due to the fact that "the great horizon of the past, out of which our culture and our present live, influences us in everything we want, hope for, or fear in the future."[23] In legal studies, the explanation of law in time (*i.e.*, its history) has also been recognized and advanced as a crucial methodological approach. According to Barrozo, time can be situated within two distinct types of explanations of law: (1) *synchronic explanations*—focusing on "time-undilated features of legal phenomena" (*e.g.*, legal doctrine) by exploring whether a phenomenon is temporally placed in the past, present, or future; and (2) *diachronic explanations*—focusing on "time-dilated features of legal phenomena" by exploring how phenomena change over time, such that one phenomenon is partly explained in relation to another situated in the past or future.[24] In other words, law, as a human product, can be explained through a *synchronic* approach, which examines its time-invariant features as they exist

20 Matthias Vanhullebusch, 'China, Confucian Time and International Law: A Normative and Behavioral Account' in Klara Polackova Van der Ploeg, Luca Pasquet and León Castellanos-Jankiewicz (eds), *International Law and Time: Narratives and Techniques* (Springer International Publishing 2022), 283.

21 *Ibid.*, 304.

22 Wyler and Whelan (n 18), 32–33.

23 Hans-Georg Gadamer, *Philosophical Hermeneutics* (University of California Press 2008), 8–9.

24 Paulo Barrozo, 'Law in Time: Legal Theory and Legal History' (2021) 31 Yale Journal of Law and the Humanities 316, 326.

at a particular point in time, and/or through a *diachronic* approach, which examines its time-variant features as they change over time.

### 2.1.3 *Law as a Systematic Promise that Makes Time: Social Construct and Effect*

As mentioned earlier, on the one hand, law can be perceived as a *human product*, embedded within a linear or circular conception of time from a cultural perspective, or explained through a synchronic or diachronic approach from a historian's perspective. On the other hand, law itself can also serve as a *systematic promise*, making or using time. In terms of how law makes time (*i.e.*, to construct the "legal time"), socio-legal scholarship on law's temporalities has flourished in recent years, which addresses the effects of legal time on social ordering. In social settings, legal time is typically understood in relation to the broader notion of social time—that is, as a reflection of the dynamics and transformations of social phenomena. For example, the main theme of the book collection "*Law and Time*" is centered on "making" of legal temporalities towards social justice (*i.e.*, how legal time is made) under the issues of social time, (post)colonial time, labor time, technologies and infrastructures of time, and so forth.[25] To be more specific, Wheatley introduced the idea of "the technologies of temporal indifference" that law adopts to escape time and remain insulated from historical change, which are: (1) *legal analogy*—"creating *nonlinear continuities* that tie dispersed moments into repetitions of preexisting norms and relationships;" and (2) *legal personality*—enabling "the survival and perpetuity of a legal 'person' despite the death or departure of its individual members," which "can be carried through time *indefinitely*."[26] In this sense, legal temporalities and their effects can be reoriented and more broadly understood as forms of *non-linear* time, shaped by legal practices to produce diverse temporal ontologies. In sum, law, as a systematic promise, can itself *construct* legal time, thereby having *effects* on social ordering.

---

25 *See generally* Siân M Beynon-Jones and Emily Grabham (eds), *Law and Time* (Routledge 2019). Drawing on rich contributions of detailed case studies, the temporal effects of law were generally summarized as follows: "(1) law's diverse roles in maintaining linear historicist models of time; (2) law's participation in the materialisation of times; and (3) the unsteady effects of temporal pluralism and 'polytemporalities' in law." *See* Emily Grabham and Siân M Beynon-Jones, 'Introduction' in Siân M Beynon-Jones and Emily Grabham (eds), *Law and Time* (Routledge 2019).

26 Natasha Wheatley, 'Law and the Time of Angels: International Law's Method Wars and the Affective Life of Disciplines' (2021) 60 History and Theory 311, 328. (emphasis added)

### 2.1.4 *Law as a Systematic Promise that Uses Time: Internal-Legal-Event Regulation*

As pointed out by Singh, the concept of time in law seems to be problematic due to its complexity, vested interests, and the lack of internal concern. The character of law is usually externally focused, governing the populace rather than the legal system internally.[27] Building on this line of thought, the understanding of law itself as a *systematic promise* should focus not only on how it makes time to regulate the society *outward* as in the previous section, but also on how it uses time to regulate the legal system *inward*. In order to raise the internal concern of time in law, Singh has proposed at least three types of terminology for considering the legal conception of time to regulate events in law: (1) *prescription*—the duration for the recognition of rights or entitlements (*e.g.*, prescription periods for private property); (2) *limitation*—the time limit for the maintenance of proceedings or cases (*e.g.*, a reasonable time to fulfill a contract); and (3) *evidence*—the time limit for evidence (*e.g.*, the amount of time to be considered relevant as evidence).[28] He further argued that the legal conception of time is not only a matter of public convenience or social order, but also *the basis of justice* which requires to be done within a reasonable time period.[29] Taken together, Singh's legal conception of time provides us a general understanding on the role of time to be used to regulate legal events in law in cases of prescription, limitation, evidence, and justice.

To be more specific, regarding the method of using time in law, Khan presented an analytical model with four principles of temporality that govern how points in time or durations can be used to regulate legal events.[30] First, *temporal triggers*—a point in time can be used to initiate or terminate legal events such as actions, powers, rights, and obligations (*e.g.*, the date of birth for the right to drive), as well as a duration can be used to control unacceptable delays (*e.g.*, the promptness in the prosecution of legal claims). Second, *temporal correlation*—a duration can be used to correlate to change by (1) providing

27 Singh (n 8), 328.

28 *Ibid.*, 335–336.

29 *Ibid.*, 338. ("[T]he very possibility of doing justice demands that it must be done within a reasonable time period, as is the case in criminal trials, certain types of contracts, or the realization of rights or remedies for the suffering, the underprivileged or the victim.")

30 Liaquat Ali Khan, 'Temporality of Law' (2009) 40 McGeorge Law Review 55, 63–65. Noting that the author's categorization for points in time and durations appears to be in a broader sense to cover specific wordings, for example, points in time (*e.g.*, now, before, after, the evening) and durations (*e.g.*, always, awhile, a short time, all night, speedy, reasonable time). The durations were further differentiated into two: a definite duration (*e.g.*, in sunset provisions) and an indefinite/open-ended duration (*e.g.*, in Divine laws).

guidance for legally significant inferences (*e.g.*, perishable within a short duration); (2) deducing causation from temporal proximity (*e.g.*, as compelling evidence of causation); (3) analyzing temporal series to predict trend and effect; and (4) situating events in the timeline to comprehend facts. Third, *temporal inertia*—a duration can be used to measure the resistance to change by (1) preserving fundamental laws to stabilize the system and prevent arbitrariness; (2) setting precedents to safeguard settled expectations; and (3) implementing judicial injunctions to force or prohibit certain actions. Fourth, *temporal cooperation*—a point in time and a duration help facilitate time-sharing cooperation by (1) scheduling numerical or precise time to enforce punctuality (*e.g.*, the reward of compliance), and (2) introducing a flexible concept of time to minimize hardship and promote satisfaction (*e.g.*, fluid work hours).[31] Accordingly, Khan's analytical model of temporality in law offers a more concrete understanding of the types of time applicable to the regulation of legal events and their corresponding purposes.

In sum, law, as a systematic promise, can itself *use* time to regulate legal events *inward*, for example, in cases of prescription, limitation, evidence, or justice, as well as by means of temporal triggers, temporal correlation, temporal inertia, or temporal cooperation. Drawing inspiration from this, this book delves deeper into how time is used in the specific context of WTO Law (Section 6.1).

## 2.2 Time in International Law and Relations

The conception of time in law is equally important in the international arena, though it may differ from—and be more complex than—that in domestic legal contexts. Alter noted that changing IL is far more difficult than altering domestic agreements due to the heterogeneous interests of states and power-influenced voting rules.[32] As also acknowledged by the United Nations, IL is not in a hierarchical relationship *inter se*, and therefore "drawing analogies from the hierarchical nature of domestic legal system is not generally appropriate owing to the differences between the two systems."[33] In terms of

31 *See generally ibid.*, 87–105.

32 Karen J Alter, 'Delegation to International Courts and the Limits of Recontracting Political Power' in Darren G Hawkins and others (eds), *Delegation and Agency in International Organizations* (Cambridge University Press 2006), 327.

33 *United Nation's Report of the Study Group of the International Law Commission*, A/CN.4/L.702, para. 31.

the general issue of time in IL, Higgins found that since IL exists in a horizontal system based on the consent of its members at particular moments, temporal issues may be addressed differently, applied more restrictively, and sometimes even viewed as contradictory.[34] To address the horizontal nature of IL, D'Amato further emphasized the inevitable need for taking into account IR to complement the understanding of IL by stating that "[IL] is a system; its environment is the field of [IR]."[35] With this symbiotic relationship of IL/IR in mind, this section reviews the literature on how "time" has been understood to play a role in the fields of IL and IR, respectively. Reminding that this research grounds its contribution in the theoretical framework of legalization, which spans the joint disciplines of IL/IR (Section 1.4).

### 2.2.1 *The Role of Time in International Law*

The role of "time" in IL can be puzzling and intriguing, albeit the relationship between them remains underexplored. As the book "*International Law and Time*" indicated, IL scholars mainly present IL doctrine "as essentially atemporal," and IL lawyers mostly consider time "as simply a technical problem."[36] In advocating for a deeper understanding of time's role in IL, it recognized "the fundamental significance of time for [IL] as a legal order and as a discipline: the temporalities underpinning rules, concepts, institutions and practices of [IL], as well as the profound temporal assumptions, choices and implications involved in considerations of [IL]."[37] It further noted that "[s]uch intra-disciplinary diversity with respect to 'time' may be disconcerting; however, it opens analytic possibilities and legitimizes a range of topics as areas of inquiry by providing distinct lenses through which to investigate [IL] and time."[38] To illustrate potential topics, six fundamental research questions concerning time and IL are identified as follows: (1) how should IL translate temporal dimensions of social processes in its rules; (2) what IL rules exist

34 Rosalyn Higgins, 'Time and the Law: International Perspectives on an Old Problem' (1997) 46 The International and Comparative Law Quarterly 501, 512.

35 Anthony D'Amato, 'Groundwork for International Law' (2014) 108 The American Journal of International Law 650, 650.

36 Van der Ploeg and Pasquet (n 14), 1–2. *See also* Christian Djeffal, 'International Law and Time: A Reflection of the Temporal Attitudes of International Lawyers Through Three Paradigms' (2014) 45 Netherlands Yearbook of International Law 93, 96. (The author identified three basic "temporal paradigms" of IL lawyers: (1) atemporality: the "eternal and unchangeable" IL; (2) temporality: the "ascertainable and changeable" IL that "endures for a fixed and specified amount of time;" and (3) fluxus: the "unsteady, moving and changing" IL.)

37 Van der Ploeg and Pasquet (n 14), 7.

38 *Ibid.*, 17.

and apply at a particular point in time; (3) how should IL be interpreted and applied in time; (4) what past events should be attributed international legal significance; (5) how may IL as a legal order change over time; and (6) what temporal parameters should IL set out for particular types of conduct within the international domain.[39] Building on these six fundamental research questions, this book proposes that they may be further developed or supported by the four lenses of legal studies on time and law outlined in Section 2.1 which are:

- IL is embedded in time
- IL is explained in time (*cf.*, the research questions (2) to (5))
- IL makes time (*cf.*, the research question (1))
- IL uses time (*cf.*, the research question (6))

Below are selected examples of research concerning the role of time in the field of IL.

First, in line with *IL embedded in time* (*cf.*, Section 2.1.1), IL may be one of the most significant fields where different cultural perceptions of time intersect, yet its current structure is widely viewed as being predominantly influenced and shaped by Western culture (*i.e.*, linear approach of time).[40] As Schramm observed, IL as a discipline, arisen from the signing of the treaties of Westphalia in 1648, is "in fact conceived as a *linear* narrative, illuminating the consubstantiality of time with not only our daily lives, but also with our allegedly impersonal scientific (and professional) endeavors."[41] However, in recent years, this linear temporal representation of IL has been contested. For example, feminist *cyclical* temporality offers new perspectives on the conception of time, aiming toward a more inclusive and "everyday" IL.[42] As a result, IL, rooted in Western traditions, is grounded in a *linear* notion of time; however, a *circular* perspective has emerged as a new way of thinking.

Second, in line with *IL explained in time* (*cf.*, Section 2.1.2), IL can be explained through a *synchronic* approach examining its time-invariant features at a particular point in time; or through a *diachronic* approach examining its time-variant features over time. For example, from a *synchronic* approach,

39 *Ibid.*, 21.

40 Vanhullebusch (n 20), 304.

41 Bérénice K Schramm, 'Interstellar Justice Now: Back to the Future of International Law' in Klara Polackova Van der Ploeg, Luca Pasquet and León Castellanos-Jankiewicz (eds), *International Law and Time: Narratives and Techniques* (Springer International Publishing 2022), 87. (emphasis added)

42 *See generally* Mary Hansel, 'Feminist Time and an International Law of the Everyday' in Susan Harris Rimmer and Kate Ogg (eds), *Research Handbook on Feminist Engagement with International Law* (Edward Elgar Publishing 2019), 379–398.

Salojärvi found that the concept of "human rights" for its meaning to be "always temporal, time-bound, in continuous motion, and can only be identified at a particular moment in time."[43] As for a *diachronic* approach, Orford reflected on law's transfer of meaning over time by emphasizing that IL "is inherently genealogical, depending as it does upon the transmission of concepts, languages and norms across time and space," and "[t]he past, far from being gone, is constantly being retrieved as a source or rationalisation of present obligation."[44] Koskenniemi also recognized past IL as a crucial context for explanation of current IL, especially by examining "how those contexts were formed and to what extent they have persisted to make the world into what it has become today."[45] To be more specific, in the edited book "*Time, History and International Law*," three general methodological approaches have been identified to explore IL and its history in time: (1) history as *narrative* in IL—tracing the development of an IL teleology; (2) history as *argument* in IL—for example, discussing how customary IL has been constructed; and (3) IL *in history*—studying how IL has been engaged in the creation of a history.[46] Under these three methodological approaches, IL can be explained in historical contexts by emphasizing how it has been constructed, developed, and engaged in time. In sum, as Wheatley concluded, "a valid [IL] is never temporally out of place: it is alive, operative, and at home in every new present."[47]

In addition, following the *diachronic* point of view in history, the intellectual interests of time and IL seem to pay relatively more attention on how IL can be applied and interpreted in time (*cf.*, the research question (3)). For example, in terms of how IL can be applied in time, the "intertemporal rule" (*ratione*

---

43 Juhana Mikael Salojärvi, 'Human Rights in Time: Temporalization of Human Rights in Historical Representation' in Klara Polackova Van der Ploeg, Luca Pasquet and León Castellanos-Jankiewicz (eds), *International Law and Time: Narratives and Techniques* (Springer International Publishing 2022), 52. (*See also* at 53. "[A] temporalization that adopts a longer time frame and emphasizes continuity may increase the universal acceptability of human rights, whereas a shorter time frame and a stress on discontinuity may amplify their relativity and political nature.")

44 Anne Orford, 'On International Legal Method' (2013) 1 London Review of International Law 166, 175.

45 Martti Koskenniemi, 'Histories of International Law: Significance and Problems for a Critical View' (2013) 27 Temple International and Comparative Law Journal 215, 238. (*See also* at 216. The author at the same time highlighted the "context-breaking aspect" of IL by stating that "law cannot just be a reflection of the social or historical context. It contains, and must contain, a utopian, context-breaking aspect.")

46 *See generally* Matthew Craven, Malgosia Fitzmaurice and Maria Vogiatzi (eds), *Time, History and International Law* (Brill Nijhoff 2007).

47 Wheatley (n 26), 326.

*temporis*) is a well-known issue in international legal scholarship, which relates to "the delimitation of the temporal sphere of application of norms."[48] Trindade recognized that the origin of this intertemporal rule was due to the possibility of new manifestations of IL and the evolution undergone by rules regarded as "immutable" in the past.[49] In terms of how IL can be interpreted in time, Vidigal pointed out the contentious concept of "evolutionary interpretation" in IL, especially due to the fact that it may be viewed as allowing interpreters to change the law over time without the inference from legal texts.[50] To unfold the meaning of this concept, Kolb understood the definition of the word "evolutionary" to contain two constituent elements which are "time" and "change." As such, he argued that the concept of "evolutionary interpretation" itself is in favor of a "contemporary" understanding of a legal norm to its "original or historical" meaning.[51]

In the specific context of the WTO, the distinction of "evolutionary (factual) application" from "evolutionary (legal) interpretation" was made in response to the criticism of judicial activism. Cook argued that the notion of "evolutionary application" is preferable since it does not change or reject the original meaning of legal norms over time, and it is "merely as a legal hook for justifying its consideration of non-WTO conventions and instruments post-dating the conclusion of the GATT 1947, not as an argument for finding that the meaning of the terms had changed since that time."[52] However, Wyler and Whelan acknowledged that this notion of "application" by emphasizing the ordinary meaning at a given time may not be accepted. Instead, the notion

48 'The Intertemporal Problem in Public International Law' (Institut de Droit International 1975), https://www.idi-iil.org/en/publications/i-le-probleme-intertemporel-en-droit-international-public/ (last visited 28 June 2025).

49 Antônio Augusto Cançado Trindade, 'Time and Law Revisited: International Law and the Temporal Dimension', *International Law for Humankind: Towards a New Jus Gentium* (Brill Nijhoff 2020), 31–32.

50 *See* Geraldo Vidigal, 'Hidden Meanings: Evolutionary Interpretation Between Norm Application and Progressive Development' (2021) 24 Journal of International Economic Law 203, 218.

51 Robert Kolb, 'Evolutionary Interpretation in International Law: Some Short and Less than Trail-Blazing Reflections' in Georges Abi-Saab and others (eds), *Evolutionary Interpretation and International Law* (Hart Publishing 2019), 15–16.

52 Graham Cook, 'The Illusion of "Evolutionary Interpretation" in WTO Dispute Settlement' in Georges Abi-Saab and others (eds), *Evolutionary Interpretation and International Law* (Hart Publishing 2019), 185. (*See also* at 187. For example, the term "natural resources" in GATT Article XX(g) has been interpreted to cover not only "non-living" but also "living" resources such as sea turtles. The author states that "[t]he fact that people in 1947 might not have known that sea turtle was (or would in the future be) the case does not establish a change in the meaning of the term 'natural resources'.")

of "interpretation" may still be preferred without prejudging its projection of time as dynamic.[53] As Van den Bossche also stated, "[t]he generic, *non-static* nature of the terms at issue allowed for their evolutionary interpretation in accordance with the intention of the parties to the agreement."[54]

Finally, to the best of my knowledge, the current trend of IL studies on the issue of time in a theoretical sense appears to focus more on IL as a human product "in time" by considering its dynamic character from a historical approach. IL itself as a systematic promise "out of time" seems to attract relatively less attention, that is, how IL can *make time* and have effects on global ordering (*cf.*, Section 2.1.3), or how IL can *use time* to regulate legal events inward (*cf.*, Section 2.1.4). Nevertheless, a number of studies may have shown the effect of time in IL in a practical sense. For example, Murphy's research regarding the effect of time on a tribunal's jurisdiction has addressed the question on how to clarify "critical dates" to determine the jurisdiction for an investor-state tribunal under a bilateral investment treaty.[55] To address this gap, this research examines how IL can *use time* to regulate legal events inward (*cf.*, the research question (6): what temporal parameters should IL set out for particular types of conduct within the international domain), and provides a preliminary observation and classification in the context of WTO Law (Chapters 3 and 4).

### 2.2.2 *The Role of Time in International Relations*

In the field of IR, the role of time can also be found through different lenses of IR studies, such as IR embedded in time (*i.e.*, its theorical assumptions), IR analyzed in time (*i.e.*, its political analysis), and IR theorizing on time (*i.e.*, its methodology). First, as Hutchings recoginized, IR theorical assumptions are *embedded in time*. For example, temporal assumptions implied in main IR theories can be summarized as follows: (1) (neo)realism—*cyclical time* with recurrence and repetition in international relations; (2) (neo)liberalism—*linear time* toward inevitable, irreversible, and achievable development of man's power and freedom; (3) constructivism—*linear time* toward inevitable global

53 Wyler and Whelan (n 18), 47.

54 Peter Van den Bossche, 'Is There Evolution in the Evolutionary Interpretation of WTO Law?' in Georges Abi-Saab and others (eds), *Evolutionary Interpretation and International Law* (Hart Publishing 2019), 223. (emphasis added)

55 Sean D Murphy, 'Temporal Issues Relating to BIT Dispute Resolution' (2022) 37 ICSID Review—Foreign Investment Law Journal 51, 51. (The "critical dates" include "the date of entry into force of the BIT, the date when the investment was made, the date when the investor acquired the requisite nationality, the date of the alleged breach, the date when the investor first acquired knowledge of the alleged breach and or its loss, and/or the date when the dispute arose.")

government; and (4) critical theories—*linear-progressive time* through economic development or *linear-regressive time* toward decline due to the lack of political alternative to liberal capitalism.[56]

Second, Pierson has prompted us to conduct political *analysis in time* from a historical perspective. "Path dependence" and "increasing returns" were highlighted to justify efforts to "stretch the temporal horizons of political analysis," and to redirect the research questions in order to "contribute to a richer appreciation of the centrality of historical processes in generating variation in political life."[57] For example, in practice, a study on WTO accession examined how GATT accession procedures developed and evolved over time.[58]

Third, IR studies can itself *theorize on time* and provide fresh insights into global politics. The edited book "*Time, Temporality and Global Politics*" has systemically collected several contributions across various case studies (*e.g.*, identity, terrorism, war, gender relations, global ethics and governance) in order to demonstrate how temporal aspects can inform our understanding of world politics.[59] In addition, it recognized the development of IR methodology for theorizing on time, for example, the shift of focus from spatial to temporal phenomena, in particular, the "pace" problem in accelerated modern society.[60] To be more specific, Lawrence et al. explored the relationship between time and institutions to capture the diversity of institutionalization process over time, which are: (1) the pace from its innovation to diffusion and (2) the stability for remaining highly diffused. They demonstrated the temporal effects or consequences of power-based mechanisms by addressing how the relationship of

56 *See generally* Kimberly Hutchings, *Time and World Politics: Thinking the Present* (Manchester University Press 2008), 28–53.

57 Paul Pierson, 'Increasing Returns, Path Dependence, and the Study of Politics' (2000) 94 The American Political Science Review 251, 252. ("[I]ncreasing returns arguments highlight the need to consider hypotheses based on temporal ordering—the possibility that the particular sequencing of events or processes may be a key part of the explanation for divergent outcomes. ... [G]rasping the implications of wide spread path dependence can help orient political scientists to a realistic, which is to say modest, set of aspirations regarding the possibilities for achieving parsimony and predictability in the study of politics.")

58 Hardeep Basra, 'Increased Legalization or Politicalization? A Comparison of Accession under the GATT and WTO' (2012) 46 Journal of World Trade 937, 941. (The author argued that "by recognizing that institutional asymmetry is not new but part of the evolutionary trajectory of the GATT/WTO it better contextualizes the current play of power politics present during WTO accession.")

59 *See generally* Andrew Hom and others (eds), *Time, Temporality and Global Politics* (Bristol: E-International Relations 2016).

60 *Ibid.*, 4–6.

power influences the pace of institutionalization, and how the mode of power (either episodic or systemic) affects the stability of an institution.[61]

In sum, from a general overlook, the approaches of IR studies on the issue of "time" put effort in studying the role of time in its theorical assumptions, its political analysis, and its methodology. This research was inspired by the second lense of IR studies to analyze temporal rules in WTO Law over time (*i.e.*, how they were established, modified, and elaborated through different institutional mechanisms), seeking to contribute reflections on the theoretical framework of legalization (Chapters 5).

## 2.3 Temporal and Event Extraction in Legal Texts

Technological development influences on our ways of producing scholarship on the very topic. In recent years, the exponential growth of computing power and digitization has enabled scholars to analyze vast amounts of information rapidly, opening up an entirely new trend in legal studies (*i.e.*, the so-called "text-as-data approach" or "law-as-data approach").[62] This new trend has also been discovered and developed in the field of international economic law. As Alschner et al. pointed out, "we are entering the data-driven future of empirical international economic law scholarship."[63] Especially, they noted that this new trend of legal studies is particularly beneficial for research areas where theory is lacking or underdeveloped.[64] Building on this line of thought, this research draws methodological inspiration from the "law-as-data approach" to address the underexplored question on how IL can *use time* to regulate legal events through *extracting* temporal rules and legal events in WTO legal texts.

In the field of natural language processing, the development of temporal extraction methods in texts for establishing automatic reasoning systems has been widely studied and applied in several domains, including medical texts, news messages, and historical documents. For example, in the context of news messages, the underlying temporal relations between events are considered to be valuable to produce summaries of developing stories or to "create

61 *See generally* Thomas B Lawrence, Monika I Winn and P Devereaux Jennings, 'The Temporal Dynamics of Institutionalization' (2001) 26 Academy of Management Review 624.

62 *See generally* Michael A Livermore, Daniel N Rockmore and Adam B Badawi (eds), *Law as Data: Computation, Text, and the Future of Legal Analysis* (The Santa Fe Institute Press 2019).

63 Wolfgang Alschner, Joost Pauwelyn and Sergio Puig, 'The Data-Driven Future of International Economic Law' (2017) 20 Journal of International Economic Law 217, 218.

64 *Ibid.*, 221.

timelines." To this end, three basic types of tags are identified to extract a time stamp in news messages as follows: (1) to annotate *temporal* expressions; (2) to annotate *event* expressions; and (3) to indicate the *temporal relations* that hold between times and events. In other words, as Schilder stated, the crucial step of extraction is "to identify what events are being described and to make explicit when these events occurred and which temporal relations hold among them."[65] Apart from news messages, Navas-Loro et al. noted that this temporal extraction method remains relatively unexplored in the legal context, owing to limited temporal resources and the absence of a publicly available temporal gold standard based on legal text corpora.[66]

Nevertheless, some preliminary studies were conducted to capture temporal information in legal texts. Unlike the main purpose of "creating timelines" in news messages mentioned above, Schilder found that temporal information in legal documents is more sophisticated and could contain three functional dimensions: (1) *extrinsic temporal ordering*—law documents and their creation or effective date to offer the history and status of law; (2) *intrinsic temporal ordering*—the event described within the document and placing them onto a time line; and (3) the mining of information about the *participating parties* mentioned in the document, such as companies, law firms, or lawyers.[67] In addition, Schilder and McCulloh identified three types of legal documents for their special applicability of the encoded temporal information: (1) *normative concepts* in statute law; (2) *fact-based narratives* in case law; and (3) *concrete dates* in transactional documents written by lawyers (*e.g.*, contracts, purchase, and sales agreements).[68] Drawing on Schilder's and McCulloh's classification of three types of legal documents, key related studies and observations can be summarized as follows.

First, a study on statute law of the 26 Statute sections of the *United State Code on Aliens and Nationality* has acknowledged that legal texts in general are normally filled with temporal information.[69] According to Schilder's study,

65 Frank Schilder, Graham Katz and James Pustejovsky (eds), *Annotating, Extracting and Reasoning about Time and Events* (Springer International Publishing 2007), 1–2.

66 María Navas-Loro and others, 'TempCourt: Evaluation of Temporal Taggers on a New Corpus of Court Decisions' (2019) 34 The Knowledge Engineering Review 1, 2.

67 Frank Schilder, 'Event Extraction and Temporal Reasoning in Legal Documents' in Frank Schilder, Graham Katz and James Pustejovsky (eds), *Annotating, Extracting and Reasoning about Time and Events* (Springer International Publishing 2007), 61.

68 Frank Schilder and Andrew McCulloh, 'Temporal Information Extraction from Legal Documents', *Annotating, Extracting and Reasoning about Time and Events. Dagstuhl Seminar Proceedings* (2005), 3–8.

69 Ramakrishna Kolikipogu and others, 'A Novel Model for Timed Event Extraction and Temporal Reasoning In Legal Text Documents' (2011) 2 International Journal of Computer Science and Engineering Survey 39, 44.

there are differences of language and function in temporal and event expressions between statute law and case law. In terms of the temporal expression, statute law often contains more *periods of time* or *sets of times* (*i.e., frequency*), instead of *date* expressions found in case law. In addition, the period of time in statute law can sometimes be *open time interval, i.e.*, fully underspecified with respect to the beginning and ending point of the related time. As for the event expression, statute law focuses on *event types* rather than an actual event in fact-based narratives of case law which is similar to news messages. For the relationship between temporal and event expressions, temporal expressions in statute law usually serve as *restriction* by adding time constraints to certain event types.[70]

Second, a study on case law annotated a corpus of 30 legal documents (*i.e.*, court decisions) from the *European Court of Human Rights*, the *European Court of Justice*, and the *United States Supreme Court*. Navas-Loro et al. identified the particularities and importance of temporal information extracted in court decisions, including: (1) to have an effect on the version of the applicable law; (2) to create a chronological order of events; and (3) to assess whether past events may be time-barred.[71] They also demonstrated three different types of temporal information in contexts: (1) in relation to *the legal process*—temporal information regarding the advancement of legal proceedings (*e.g.*, the date of the hearings or decision); (2) in relation to *the case*—temporal information regarding factual events about the case which serves as the basis for a judgment (*e.g.*, the date of entrance); and (3) in relation to *the legal context*—temporal information for legal reference to determine the applicable law and the degree of penalty (*e.g.*, the birth date relating to juvenile offenders).[72]

Third, a study on transactional documents written by lawyers attempted to capture temporal information (*date* expressions in particular) both in numerical (*e.g.*, 30 June 2025) and non-numerical (*e.g.*, today or last year) time in order to provide a model or prototype to discover temporal relationships among available events in the legal text document.[73] To benefit legal practitioners, the temporal extraction method could provide better temporal relationships for decision support by capturing time constraints that may be associated with the extracted events.[74]

70 Schilder (n 67), 62–67.

71 Navas-Loro and others (n 66), 4.

72 *Ibid.*, 7–8.

73 *See* Venkateswrlu Naik. M, Vanitha Guda and Inturi Srujana, 'Reasoning in Legal Text Documents with Extracted Event Information' (2011) 28 International Journal of Computer Applications 8, 9–10.

74 Kolikipogu and others (n 69), 47.

Following the three studies discussed above on temporal extraction across different types of legal documents, this research focuses on extracting temporal information from *treaties* (*i.e.*, WTO legal texts). While there is no available temporal gold standard to conduct temporal extraction, some reflections derived from the existing studies are valuable to take note. First, what is the purpose of conducting temporal extraction? Is it only for practical use (*e.g.*, to create timeline or to retrieve critical information for legal application, judgement, and reference)? Can it also be used to facilitate theoretical thinking as this research proposes? Second, what types of temporal expressions are relevant (*e.g.*, period/frequency/date, (under-)specified, or (non-)numerical)? How many of them can be found (*e.g.*, period and frequency were found to be more than date in statute law)? Third, what are the contexts for these temporal expressions (*e.g.*, legal proceedings, factual case, or legal reference)? What kinds of actual events or event-types can be identified in these contexts? Finally, what is the temporal relations hold between time and events (*e.g.*, serving as restriction or time constraint)?

With these reflections in mind, it leads to the technical problem on the operation of temporal extraction in WTO Law. There are usually three approaches to detect temporal expressions in texts: (1) *the rule-based approach*—to apply manually created rules (*e.g.*, regular expressions) to cover all possible variations of expression of temporal information, which is considered as better performance but inflexible with chance of a missing or erroneous rule; (2) *the machine-learning-based approach*—to apply external machine-learning tools to identify temporal information, which can be more flexible and able to detect unexpected forms but a good pre-trained model is required to ensure its precision and recall of correctly identified items; and (3) *the hybrid approach*—the combination of manually created rules with machine-learning, namely, to create rules of large corpus with machine-learning tools to be manually refined afterwards.[75] Despite the powerful capacity of computerization or automation, the regular temporal expressions in the context of law have not yet been well established. Navas-Loro et al. analyzed several temporal tagging tools against legal documents, and acknowledged the need for tools and guidelines specifically tailored to particularities of the legal domain. They urged for the creation of a temporal-event taxonomy through the combination of temporal information and legal events that would help in a better understanding of legal processes.[76]

75 Navas-Loro and others (n 66), 13–15.

76 *Ibid.*, 22.

Given the absence of a temporal gold standard and relying on personal expertise, this research opts to perform temporal extraction manually through close reading of legal texts (instead of applying software) to gain primary sources of temporal information. As Alschner et al. highlighted, "[d]ecisions on what information to collect, which techniques to select, and what conclusions to draw are all choices that remain squarely with us, humans," and "[t]he most sophisticated computational tools are of little use without knowing what questions to ask."[77] Grimmer and Stewart also emphasized that "the complexity of language implies that automated content analysis methods will never replace careful and close reading of texts."[78] As they further explained, data automation in evaluations should be placed on "helping researchers to assign documents into *predetermined categories*, discover new and useful categorization schemes for texts, or in measuring theoretically relevant quantities from large collections of text."[79] For these reasons, this research examines temporal information (*i.e.*, temporal rules) through careful and close reading of the twenty agreements of WTO Law with the hope to create potential categories for a temporal-event taxonomy in the (international) legal domain for future research or automation.

## 2.4 Temporal Connotation in WTO Jurisprudence

Despite manual annotation of temporal rules as the method for this research, some lessons from the existing annotation tools can be learned. For example, temporal tagging tools usually annotate temporal information in texts through four steps: (1) *identification* (*i.e.*, detection or extraction)—to find temporal expressions and their start and end position in the text; (2) *normalization* (*i.e.*, anchoring)—to interpret temporal expressions to obtain specific instants and intervals represented in a standard format; (3) *classification*—to classify real-world situations (*i.e.*, events) into different categories; and (4) *relation*—to indicate a certain connection between events, times, or a mixture of both.[80] As can be seen, the process of annotation commonly starts from "identification," namely, to "find" temporal information. Bringing it to the context of this research, the first step of manual annotation of temporal information in WTO

77 Alschner, Pauwelyn and Puig (n 63), 223 and 228.

78 Justin Grimmer and Brandon M Stewart, 'Text as Data: The Promise and Pitfalls of Automatic Content Analysis Methods for Political Texts' (2013) 21 Political Analysis 267, 268.

79 *Ibid.*, 270. (emphasis added)

80 Navas-Loro and others (n 66), 1, 2, and 13.

Law would be to *identify* or *find* relevant temporal expressions in legal texts. To generate preliminary observations on relevant temporal expressions, this research has examined WTO Jurisprudence to identify temporal connotations highlighted or contested by WTO Members or adjudicators. In other words, there is a substantial body of WTO Jurisprudence on the issues related to time derived from textual interpretations of WTO Law. These interpretations have led to the general perception that legal provisions may contain specific temporal connotations, which are crucial for understanding the substance of the law and its inner structure. According to the observations of this research, temporal connotations in WTO Law can fall into two types of expressions: (1) the use of *grammatical tense* and (2) the use of *temporal rules*. Appendix 1 offers a summation of the cases.

### 2.4.1 *The Use of Grammatical Tense*

Grammatical tense expresses the location of time in language. In linguistics, Comrie has defined the term "tense" to be "the grammaticalized expression of location in time 'locating' the time of a situation related to the situation of the utterance."[81] Tense plays an important role in analyzing temporal reference to a situation. As Grisot recognized, tense, as a "temporal operator," "applies to the basic form of a sentence, and shifts the evaluated time of that sentence to the past or to the future."[82] In other words, tense "refers directly to temporal entities and expresses temporal relations," and in doing so, "it relates entities to a deictic [center], which is usually the moment of speech (*i.e.*, the now of the speaker)."[83] In the context of legal texts, grammatical tense in legal provisions relates legal events to the *now* of the reader. In this sense, temporal reference of "the moment of reading" or "the now of the reader" seems to be crucial and may cause some problems of vagueness due to the use of different tenses.

Based on the observations on WTO Jurisprudence, the puzzle of grammatical tenses appears to be the use of the *present perfect tense* and the use of the *present tense*. First, in terms of the *present perfect tense*, according to Grisot, there is a puzzle for expressing temporal reference to past time between the simple past tense and the present perfect tense. The simple past tense does not link the past time referred to the present time (i.e., the now of the reader),

81 Bernard Comrie, *Aspect: An Introduction to the Study of Verbal Aspect and Related Problems* (Cambridge University Press 1976), 2.

82 Cristina Grisot, 'The Linguistic Expression of Temporal Reference', *Cohesion, Coherence and Temporal Reference from an Experimental Corpus Pragmatics Perspective* (Springer International Publishing 2018), 35.

83 *Ibid.*, 36.

where the present perfect tense does.[84] In this regard, the present perfect tense implies *temporal continuity* to the present moment. Taking a case in the WTO as an example, Article 4.2 of the Agreement on Agriculture lies down the requirements for Members to convert measures into ordinary customs duties by expressing in the present perfect tense (*i.e.*, "have been required"). The adjudicators argued that the use of the present perfect tense imposes obligations that "came into being in the past, but may continue to apply at present."[85] Besides, this temporal continuity of the present perfect tense may also be emphasized by a passage of time between two legal events. For example, the use of the present perfect tense (*i.e.*, "has not resulted") in the context of finding serious prejudice between the subsidy and the effect in SCM Article 6.2. The adjudicators viewed the present perfect tense as implying that "some time may have passed between the granting of the subsidy and the demonstration of the absence of its effects."[86]

Second, in terms of the use of the *present tense*, Grisot acknowledged the importance of its usage by stating that "an [temporal] operator for the present tense is necessary, because in natural language the present tense is distinguished from the other verbal tenses, and contributes to the compositional treatment of other verbal tenses."[87] The present tense appears to be the center for other tenses and can itself imply *temporal proximity*. For example, Article 2.1 of the Agreement on Safeguards and GATT Article XIX:1(a) use the present tense (*i.e.*, "is being imported") for governing the product to be considered in increased quantities to domestic production. In practice, the adjudicators have drawn on the implication from the present tense to opine that "the increase in imports must have been sudden and *recent*."[88]

As a result, the use of grammatical tense can derive different temporal implications, such as the use of the *present perfect tense* to imply temporal continuity and the use of the *present tense* to imply temporal proximity. It is worth to note that these grammatical tenses may sometimes be interpreted or clarified through the use of temporal rules. Taking the above-mentioned case again as an example, the temporal rule "recent" was employed by the adjudicators in

84 *Ibid.*, 16–17. ("The Simple Past implies a gap between past and present time (i.e. the two moments are disconnected), whereas the Present Perfect implies that the eventuality expressed ... continues at the present time, pointing to the resultative eventuality. ...")

85 Appellate Body Report, *Chile—Price Band System*, para. 206.

86 Appellate Body Report, *US—Upland Cotton*, para. 477. ("The word 'resulted' in this sentence highlights the temporal relationship between the subsidy and the effect, in that one might expect a time lag between the provision of the subsidy and the resulting effect.")

87 Grisot (n 82), 36.

88 Appellate Body Report, *Argentina—Footwear (EC)*, para. 130. (emphasis added)

interpreting the present tense (*i.e.*, "is being imported"). In another case, the adjudicators followed up on this interpretation and employed more temporal rules to clarify the implications of the word "recent" by stating that: "[T]he word 'recent' implies some form of *retrospective* analysis. It does not imply an analysis of the conditions *immediately preceding* the authority's decision. Nor does it imply that the analysis must focus exclusively on conditions *at the very end of the period of investigation*."[89] As such, the correlation between the use of grammatical tense and the use of temporal rule may be an interesting question, but it is beyond the scope of this research.

### 2.4.2 *The Use of Temporal Rules*

While grammatical tense can be relevant temporal information in law, this research focuses on the study of "temporal rules" due to the assumption that they are expressed through common syntactic realizations by means of adverbs, noun phrases, prepositional phrases, and temporal clauses, *etc*. These common syntactic realizations may be identified across different legal content or instruments, which could serve as the common feature of *the substantive content of rules*, used for evaluation and comparison under the theoretical framework of legalization (Section 1.4). With regard to identifying temporal rules in WTO Law through their varied syntactic realizations, this research begins by analyzing WTO Jurisprudence to explore "the types of temporal expressions" that have been emphasized or considered in WTO legal practice. In doing so, it constitutes a general blueprint for categorizing temporal rules in the following Chapter 3. All in all, six expressions of temporal rules and their relevant implications are provided as follows:

First, the *expression of a date or year* (*c.f.*, point in time in Section 3.1.1) is not necessarily well-defined in legal texts, and may permit the relevant authorities to provide further clarification or make a decision. For example, Article 13(b)(ii) of the Agreement on Agriculture uses the term "the 1992 marketing year" to establish the benchmark for granting subsidies. The adjudicators noted that the disputing party subsequently defined this benchmark year "as beginning on 1 July and ending on 30 June of the following year so that, for those products and [the disputing party], the 1992 marketing year did not begin until 1 July 1992."[90]

Second, the *expression of a moment* (*c.f.*, timing in Section 3.1.2) plays a crucial role in triggering rights and obligations, even in the absence of a precise calendar date. For example, DSU Article 5.3 uses the term "at any time" for

89 Panel Report, *US—Line Pipe*, para. 7.204. (emphasis added)

90 Panel Report, *US—Upland Cotton*, para. 7.442.

request of good offices, conciliation, or mediation between the disputing parties. The adjudicators acknowledged that the party referred to this temporal rule to suggest a "procedural possibility" under the provision.[91] In the case of holding additional interim review meeting, DSU Article 15.2 uses the term "[a]t the request of a party" as a temporal trigger. As such, the adjudicators opined that "it is not for [the panel] to decide whether holding an interim review hearing would be useful."[92] It was noted that the disputing party did not request such a meeting; as a result, an interim review meeting did not be held.

Third, the *expression of times* (*c.f.*, frequency in time in Section 3.1.3) can be observed for occasions that are expected to exist or happen repeatedly, although it is not always expressed in numbers. For example, the word "usual(-ly)" is found in Article 5.1(a)(i) and (ii) of the Customs Valuation Agreement, namely, "the commissions *usually* paid or agreed to be paid," "the additions *usually* made for profit and general expenses," and "the *usual* costs of transport and insurance and associated costs."[93] The adjudicators took into account the plain meaning of the word "usual(-ly)" to imply "most often but not concrete," and suggested that "the deductions of the commissions or the additions or the costs of transport ... need not necessarily be tied to a particular unit price for the [greatest aggregate quantity] sale that is being used in the deductive value calculation."[94] Article 7.4 of the Agreement on Safeguards also uses the non-numerical word "regular" in the phrase "at regular intervals" to oblige the progressive liberalization of safeguard measures. The adjudicators identified the word "regular" to mean "recurring or repeated at fixed times, recurring at short uniform intervals," and therefore considered that "regular intervals of liberalization are uniform intervals, that is to say, intervals that are equally separated in time."[95]

Fourth, the *expression of a time-frame* (*c.f.*, period in time in Section 3.1.4), during which a particular occasion is expected to take place, can be found in

---

91 Appellate Body Reports, *China—HP-SSST (Japan) / China—HP-SSST (EU)*, fn. 59. ("The European Union suggested that a 'procedural possibility' that it could envisage would be to invite informally the participants to 'indicate whether or not they would be prepared to voluntarily participate in a short informal meeting'.")

92 Panel Report, *Canada—Continued Suspension*, para. 6.2. *See also* Panel Report, *US—Continued Suspension*, para. 6.2.

93 Emphasis added.

94 Panel Report, *Thailand—Cigarettes (Philippines)*, para. 7.347.

95 Panel Report, *Ukraine—Passenger Cars*, para. 7.362. ("Progressive liberalization that proceeds at equal intervals over the period of application facilitates the adjustment of the domestic industry by exposing it to greater foreign competition following a pattern that allows—and forces—the industry to adjust to each stage of that liberalization, and prepare itself for the next one, at equal time intervals.")

a general term (*e.g.*, "time-frame," "long-term," or "reasonable period") or a numerical term (*e.g.*, "15 months"). For example, in terms of the general term "time-frame" for implementing commitments in GATS Article XX:1(d), the adjudicators defined this term as "a period of time especially with respect to some action or project." They further explained that "[t]he term does not require the setting of a precise date, but it does imply a beginning and an end of a time period."[96] In the case of the word "long-term" for operating costs and losses of export credit guarantee or insurance programmes in Annex I(j) of the SCM Agreement, the adjudicators understood that the use of "long-term" to denote "a period of sufficient duration" to ensure an objective examination of export subsidies.[97] As for the establishment of a "reasonable period of time" in Article 5.7 of the SPS Agreement to review provisional measures, the adjudicators suggested the duration to be decided "on a case-by-case basis and depends on the specific circumstances of each case."[98] Following these examples, a general term for a period may be used in legal texts, which does not specify an exact duration and can be determined based on varying circumstances. However, a general term may also be read in conjunction with a precise duration which serves as a "guideline," *e.g.*, the use of the terms "a reasonable period of time" and "15 months" set forth in DSU Article 21.3(c) for the implementation of recommendations and rulings.[99] The arbitrators viewed the 15-month period as a "guideline," and considered that it is ultimately the relevant "particular circumstances" that influence the determination of a reasonable period of time.[100] Appendix 1 lists more cases regarding the relevant expressions of a time-frame.

---

96 Panel Report, *Mexico—Telecoms*, paras. 7.366 and 7.368. (However, it should still be in line with the objective of the legal provision to "ensure its clarity and precision" without erosion "the practical value of a commitment.")

97 Panel Report, *US—Upland Cotton*, para. 7.832. ("[T]he reference to 'long term' in item (j) to refer to a period of sufficient duration as to ensure an objective examination which allows a thorough appraisal of the programme and which avoids attributing overdue significance to any unique or atypical experiences on a given day, month, trimester, half-year, year or other specific time period.")

98 Appellate Body Report, *Japan—Agricultural Products II*, para. 93.

99 *See also* Panel Report, *US—Section 301 Trade Act*, para. 7.38. ("It is for the WTO or both of the disputing parties, through the procedures set forth in Article 21—not for an individual WTO Member—to determine the reasonable period of time for the Member concerned to implement DSB recommendations and rulings.")

100 Award of the Arbitrator, *US—Offset Act (Byrd Amendment) (Article 21.3(c))*, para. 41. ("The 15-month period is a 'guideline', expressed as a maximum period, and does not represent an average, or usual, period. Rather ... it is ultimately the relevant 'particular circumstances' that influence what is a 'reasonable period of time' for implementation.")

Fifth, the *expression of series of events* (*c.f.*, sequence in time in Section 3.1.5) can be found to arrange occasions to exist or happen *in separation* (*e.g.*, final), *in coincidence* (*e.g.*, coincide or near the same time), or *in tandem* (*e.g.*, at the same time). For example, the use of the word "final" for the determination of customs values in Article 13 of the Customs Valuation Agreement was highlighted to *separate* occasions. The adjudicators observed the function of adding the sequential word as a differentiator by stating that: "[W]hen the drafters intended to distinguish final actions or determinations from provisional actions or determinations, they did specifically add the term 'final'."[101] As for the *coincidence* of occasions, DSU Article 9.3 regulates the "timetable" for the panel process of dispute settlement to examine the complaints related to the same matter. The adjudicators interpreted the "timetable" in relation to the word "harmony" in the same provision to define it as "not require that elements coincide exactly in time." Therefore, they rejected the idea that "'harmonization' requires adoption of identical timetables in multiple proceedings."[102] To be more specific, Article 2.4 of the Anti-Dumping Agreement uses the term "as nearly as possible the same time" to regulate a fair comparison of sales. The adjudicators interpreted this term by combining with the word "comparable" to derive a requirement for "Members to perform numerous average-to-average comparisons based on the shortest possible time periods."[103] As for several occasions happened *in tandem*, in the case of other factors causing injury "at the same time" in Article 4.2(b) of the Agreement on Safeguards,[104] the adjudicators emphasized the mixed situation where several factors are causing injury "at the same time," and ruled that a final determination "can only be made if the injurious effects caused by all the different causal factors are distinguished and separated."[105]

Sixth, the *conceptual expression in time* (*c.f.*, Section 3.1.6) can be found in several contexts to regulate *how fast* occasions are expected to exist or happen

101 Panel Report, *Thailand—Cigarettes (Philippines)*, para. 7.1034.

102 Appellate Body Reports, *EC—Bananas III (Article 21.5—Ecuador II) / EC—Bananas III (Article 21.5—US)*, para. 192. ("[DSU] Article 9.3 may appear to be cast in the way of an obligation, but the word 'harmony' is defined as the combination or adaptation of parts, so as to form a 'consistent and orderly whole'. Quite distinct from 'synchrony', 'harmony' does not require that elements coincide exactly in time. …")

103 Panel Report, *US—Stainless Steel (Korea)*, para. 6.122.

104 SG Art. 4.2(b): "When factors other than increased imports are causing injury to the domestic industry at the same time, such injury shall not be attributed to increased imports."

105 Appellate Body Report, *US—Lamb*, para. 179. For the similar interpretation under Article 3.5 of the Anti-Dumping Agreement, *see also* Appellate Body Report, *US—Hot-Rolled Steel*, para. 223.

in time (*e.g.*, immediate(-ly), prompt(-ly), accelerate), as well as *how long* occasions are expected to last in time (*e.g.*, temporary). In terms of the conceptual expression of "*how fast*," the expression of speediness can be identified as an important condition that must be reconciled with. For example, DSU Article 21.3 makes clear the obligation of "immediate" compliance with the recommendations and rulings. In line with this precondition of "immediate" compliance, the adjudicators interpreted that the right of a reasonable period of time for implementation is "not available unconditionally to an implementing Member."[106] In addition, reading together with DSU Article 21.1 (*i.e.*, "prompt" compliance), the adjudicators noted that "DSU clearly stressed the systemic interest of all WTO Members in the Member concerned complying 'immediately' with the recommendations and rulings of the DSB," albeit with "a certain element of flexibility in respect of time" (*i.e.*, a reasonable period of time).[107] Lastly, in cases of urgency, a request for expedited consideration of the dispute is possible under DSU Article 4.9, which obliges that "panels and the Appellate Body shall make every effort to *accelerate* the proceedings to the greatest extent possible."[108] In practice, the adjudicators might indicate the difficulties for acceleration by stating that "due to other demands on its Members' time, it could not accelerate the timetable prior to the first substantive meeting."[109]

In terms of the conceptual expression of "*how long*," the adjudicators referred to the word "temporary" in the context of suspension of concessions or other obligations in DSU Article 22.8, and considered suspension to be "an abnormal state of affairs that is not meant to remain *indefinitely*."[110] Another example of the interpretation of the word "temporary" can be found in the context of applying export prohibitions or restrictions under GATT Article XI:2(a). The adjudicators also defined the word "temporary" to mean "not permanent" and shall be "lasting or meant to last for a limited time only."[111] Generally speaking, the interpretation of conceptual expressions of time appears to be one of the key concerns related to time in WTO Jurisprudence, which may as a result be considered and denoted as an important category of temporal rules in WTO Law. Appendix 1 offers more cases in WTO Jurisprudence.

---

106 Award of the Arbitrator, *US—Offset Act (Byrd Amendment) (Article 21.3(c))*, para. 40.

107 Award of the Arbitrator, *Chile—Alcoholic Beverages (Article 21.3(c))*, para. 38. ("[A] certain element of flexibility in respect of time is built into the notion of compliance with the recommendations and rulings of the DSB. That element would appear to be essential if 'prompt' compliance, in a world of sovereign states, is to be a balanced conception and objective.")

108 Emphasis added.

109 Panel Report, *Canada—Patent Term*, para. 1.5.

110 Appellate Body Report, *Canada—Continued Suspension*, para. 310. (emphasis added)

111 Appellate Body Report, *China—Raw Materials*, para. 323.

Notably, the broader sense of temporal rules in WTO Law can not only be identified as these six types of expression above, but also be found in the intrinsic characteristic of certain concepts (*e.g.*, imminent threat, emergency action, or unforeseen development). For example, Article 4.1(b) of the Agreement on Safeguards defines the term "threat of serious injury" by stating that, in order to constitute a "threat," the serious injury must be clearly "imminent." The adjudicators further interpreted the use of the word "imminent" to imply that "the anticipated 'serious injury' must be on the very verge of occurring;" in other words, with "a high degree of likelihood that the anticipated serious injury will materialize *in the very near future*."[112] In addition, in the context of the infringement of the applicant's rights in Article 50.3 of the TRIPS Agreement, the adjudicators considered the word "imminent" as a standard of probability by stating that "an 'imminent' event passes a higher threshold than one of mere possibility."[113] The concept of "imminent" therefore seems to contain both a temporal aspect (*i.e.*, in the very near future) and a non-temporal aspect (*i.e.*, a degree of probability). For the sake of simplicity, this research does not denote and categorize the intrinsic temporal aspect of concepts in the following Chapter 3. Instead, it will be considered as an implicit temporal rule that can be derived from the interpretation of the ordinary meaning of specific concepts (*i.e.*, intrinsic meaning by definition in Section 6.2.2).

In sum, there are a wide range of temporal expressions which have been identified and interpreted in WTO Jurisprudence. With these six categorical blueprints and their initial implications in mind, this research is aiming to investigate the use of temporal rules through the denotation of their particular lexical items in WTO legal texts. The basic assumption for this investigation is that certain temporal rules in its expression of time have essentially the same properties whether the wording is used differently. This brings us to Chapter 3, in which we will further explore these properties to define the corresponding categories of temporal rules.

## 2.5 Summary

To foster a better understanding of the issue of "time" in legal studies (WTO Law in particular), this Chapter studies the existing literature regarding "Time and Law" and the WTO Jurisprudence with the intention of establishing a research territory for this book. Beyond legal studies, the notion of "time" in the physical world appears to be fascinating and constantly debated for its (in-)existence

112 Appellate Body Report, *US—Lamb*, para. 125. (emphasis added)

113 Panel Report, *India—Solar Cells*, para. 7.260.

under multiple academic disciplines (*e.g.*, psychology, physics, and philosophy). The role of time in the social world also appears to be highly complex and involve divergent ways of experience and construction. Law, in particular, was considered as a "communicative system" to bridge our past, present, and future to create expectations and reduce uncertainty in a society, albeit that time is often assumed to exist as the invisible backdrop of social life without much attention.

Against this invisible backdrop assumption of time, Section 2.1 reviews the trends of academic literature with regard to the theme of "Time and Law." It captures the existing approaches in legal studies on the issue of time through four lenses: First, law as a human product (from a legal culture perspective) can be embedded in a *linear* approach of time to ensure its certainty, neutrality, and legitimacy, or in a *circular* approach of time to emphasize its change and continuity. Second, law as a human product (from a legal historian's perspective) can be explained through a *synchronic* approach to consider its time-invariant features that place at a particular point in time, or through a *diachronic* approach to consider its time-variant features that change over time. Third, law as a systematic promise (from a socio-legal perspective) can itself *make legal time* and have effects on social ordering. Fourth, law as a systematic promise (from an internal-legal-event regulation perspective) can itself *use time* to regulate legal events inward, for instance, in cases of prescription, limitation, evidence, or justice, and by means of temporal triggers, temporal correlation, temporal inertia, or temporal cooperation. To set the stage for this research, this book positions itself within the fourth lense to explore the use of time in WTO Law (Section 6.1).

Section 2.2 explores the role of time in both IL and IR due to the consideration of their symbiotic relationship and the position of this book within the joint disciplines of IL/IR (Section 1.4). In terms of the role of time in IL, it has been recognized to be fundamentally significant, albeit without sufficient exploration. In this regard, this book also suggests to perceive the trend of IL studies on the issue of time through the four lenses established in Section 2.1. First, *IL embedded in time*—IL as a Western product appears to be traditionally embedded in the *linear* culture of time; however, a *circular* approach has been put forward as a new way of thinking. Second, *IL explained in time*—IL can also be explained through a *synchronic* or *diachronic* approach, relying on historical contexts by emphasizing how IL has been constructed, developed, and engaged in time. In particular, "intertemporal rule" and "evolutionary interpretation" were recognized as topical temporal issues to concern the dynamic character of IL. Lastly, how *IL makes time* and how *IL uses time* are the research themes relatively underexplored. To fill the gap, this book takes the research question on how IL can *use time* to regulate legal events inward in the context of WTO Law (Chapters 3 and 4).

In terms of the role of time in IR, it may also be perceived through different lenses in IR studies, for example: (1) IR theorical assumptions can be embedded in in a linear or circular approach of time; (2) IR analysis can be conducted over time using a historical approach; and (3) IR methodology can itself theorize on time to inform a new understanding of global politics. Taking inspiration from the second lense of IR studies, this research also examines temporal rules in WTO Law over time (*i.e.*, how they were established, modified, and elaborated through different systemic mechanisms) with the hope to provide preliminary insights into the theoretical framework of legalization (Chapters 5).

Section 2.3 draws methodological inspiration from the field of natural language processing in line with the new trend of legal studies, namely, the "law-as-data approach." While no available temporal resource or gold standard has yet been developed for extracting temporal information in legal texts, some preliminary studies on statue law, case law, and transactional documents have provided a number of general reflections worth keeping in mind: (1) what the purpose of conducting temporal extraction is—whether for practical use or theoretical thinking; (2) what types and how many of temporal expressions can be found; (3) what kinds of events or event-types can be identified as contexts for temporal expressions; and (4) what temporal relationships hold between time and events. In terms of the technical operation of extraction, despite the powerful capacity of temporal annotation tools, there is still a need for developing guidelines or categories tailored to the particularities of legal texts, which cannot be fully replaced by automation. For this reason, this research conducts temporal extraction manually through careful and close reading of WTO Law to gain primary sources of temporal information with the hope to establish potential categories for a temporal-event taxonomy in the (international) legal domain.

Before diving into the operation of manual temporal extraction in WTO Law, Section 2.4 provides preliminary observations on WTO Jurisprudence to identify relevant temporal connotations highlighted by WTO adjudicators in practice. These observations set the stage and serve as a blueprint for conducting the investigation and categorization of temporal rules in the following Chapter 3. In WTO Jurisprudence, two types of temporal connotations are commonly seen as controversial, which are the use of *grammatical tense* and the use of *temporal rules*. First, the use of *grammatical tense* may be puzzling and have several temporal implications in practice. For example, the use of *present perfect tense* is seen to imply temporal continuity and the use of *present tense* to imply temporal proximity. In some cases, the adjudicators interpreted the grammatical tense by using temporal rules to underpin its concrete meaning, although the use of grammatical tense and its interaction with temporal rules are beyond the focus of this research.

Second, the use of *temporal rules* can be complicated and realized through different syntactic terms, such as adverbs, noun phrases, prepositional phrases, and temporal clauses, *etc*. In practice, six types of temporal expressions are identified in WTO Jurisprudence with some implications found as follows: (1) the expression of a date or year, which is not always well-defined and may allow the relevant authorities to further decide (*c.f.*, point in time in Section 3.1.1); (2) the expression of a moment, which can trigger certain rights and obligations without setting exact calendar time (*c.f.*, timing in Section 3.1.2); (3) the expression of times, which regulates the recurrence of occasions, either in a numerical or non-numerical term (*c.f.*, frequency in time in Section 3.1.3); (4) the expression of a time-frame, which can be expressed in a general or numerical term (*c.f.*, period in time in Section 3.1.4); (5) the expression of series of events, which arranges the order of occasions to exist or happen in separation, in coincidence, or in tandem (*c.f.*, sequence in time in Section 3.1.5); and (6) the conceptual expression in time, which underlines *how fast* occasions to exist or happen in time and *how long* occasions to last in time (*c.f.*, Section 3.1.6). With these expressions and implications in mind, the following Chapter will proceed to investigate and categorize temporal rules in WTO Law.

CHAPTER 3

# Categorization and Distribution of Temporal Rules in WTO Law

Following the blueprint and implications from Section 2.4, there is a wide range of temporal expressions identified in WTO Jurisprudence. To denote particular lexical items as temporal rules in WTO legal texts and to categorize them by their common properties, some knowledge from the existing annotation tools can be helpful. In the field of natural language processing, the basic guidelines for annotating temporal information in text have been developed. According to the *Instruction Manual for the Annotation of Temporal Expressions*, the main purpose of temporal annotation is to retrieve information denoting in a temporal sense to tell us "*when* something happened, or *how long* something lasted, or *how often* something occurs."[1] These annotation guidelines capture words or numeric expressions that convey a temporal unit or concept, including nouns (*e.g.*, day), time patterns (*e.g.*, 1 January 2025), adjectives (*e.g.*, current), and adverbs (*e.g.*, currently).

Despite the capacity of capturing diverse expressions through annotation tools, some temporal expressions could be considered as non-markable or not able to be normalized in a computer system due to their vagueness, such as subordinating conjunctions (*e.g.*, when), prepositions (*e.g.*, before/after), modifiers (*e.g.*, earlier), idioms (*e.g.*, the last minute), and event-anchored expressions (*e.g.*, the day after the meeting).[2] By acknowledging the potential limitations of annotation tools, non-markable temporal expressions might be relevant in legal texts (WTO Law in particular), which could go beyond the current computational annotation on temporal information. To fill this gap, Section 3.1 attempts to denote temporal rules *manually* by careful and close reading of the twenty agreements of WTO Law (Section 1.2), and groups them into six categories based on the implications from WTO Jurisprudence (Section 2.4). In addition, to discover the distribution of temporal rules in the twenty agreements, Section 3.2 examines *quantitatively* the density of these rules in line with the six categories established.

1 Lisa Ferro and others, 'TIDES 2005 Standard for the Annotation of Temporal Expressions', 39, https://www.ldc.upenn.edu/sites/www.ldc.upenn.edu/files/english-timex2-guidelines-v0.1.pdf (last visited 4 June 2025). (emphasis added)

2 *Ibid.*, 6–10.

 | DOI:10.1163/9789004745629_004

## 3.1 Six Categories of Temporal Rules in WTO Law

While its intention of gap filling, this research is not a pioneering attempt to categorize temporal information in legal studies. Four types of representation have been proposed to categorize temporal information in legal discourse, especially for points in time and durations as follows: (1) absolute temporal references, which refer to points in time, *e.g.*, 6 p.m.; (2) absolute temporal durations, which refer to some certain amount of temporal granularity, *e.g.*, 45 minutes; (3) relative temporal references, which refer to times that are known only by their relative temporal relations to other temporal reference, *e.g.*, when someone is in office; and (4) relative durations, which refer to some uncertain amount of temporal granularity, *e.g.*, less than 3 hours.[3] As such, temporal information in legal discourse may contain not only absolute or numerical expressions, but also relative or uncertain expressions. Bearing these preliminary categories in mind, this section will further expand the representation of temporal information to the six categories of temporal rules in the context of WTO Law. To demonstrate how to denote temporal rules in WTO legal texts, some instructive criteria for the analysis of sentences can be provided as follows.

Article IX:4 of the WTO Agreement (decision-making: granting a waiver):

> A decision by the Ministerial Conference granting a waiver shall state the exceptional circumstances justifying the decision, the terms and conditions governing the application of the waiver, and *the date on*[*Point in Time*] which the waiver shall terminate. Any waiver granted *for a period of more than one year*[*Period*] shall be reviewed by the Ministerial Conference *not later than*[*Sequence*] *one year*[*Period*] *after*[*Sequence*] it is granted, and *thereafter*[*Sequence*] *annually*[*Frequency*] *until*[*Timing*] the waiver terminates. In each review, the Ministerial Conference shall examine whether the exceptional circumstances justifying the waiver still exist and whether the terms and conditions attached to the waiver have been met. The Ministerial Conference, on the basis of the annual review,[4] may *extend*[*Conceptual Expression*], modify or terminate the waiver.

3 B Knight, J Ma and E Nissan, 'Representing Temporal Knowledge in Legal Discourse' (1998) 7 Information & Communications Technology Law 199, 199–200.

4 Noting that the phrase "the *annual* review" is not denoted due to the fact that it is a repeated noun phrase which has been prescribed in the previous sentence, *e.g.*, "[*a*]*ny waiver ... shall be reviewed by the Ministerial Conference ... annually*[*Frequency*], *...*" *See infra*, Section 3.2.

Taking Article IX:4 of the WTO Agreement above as an example, a legal provision can contain several sentences, and each of the sentences can have none to numerous temporal rules conjoined with each other (emphasized in italics). A temporal rule under the same category (with the common property) may itself contain one word (*e.g.*, *after*[Sequence]) to a number of words (*e.g.*, *for a period of more than one year*[Period]). Noting that the full extent of the denoted expressions may sometimes include comparatives (*e.g.*, "more than" in the denotation of *for a period of more than one year*[Period]); however, this research does not attribute specific token to these comparatives for the sake of simplicity.[5] In addition, a temporal rule may also be denoted to anchor on *an event* (*e.g.*, *the date on*[Point in Time] which *the waiver shall terminate*). This anchoring event is crucial to establish the temporal events association in the following Chapter 4. Last but not least, in cases the adjacent phrases contain multiple categories of temporal rules, multiple denotations are created independently (*e.g.*, *thereafter*[Sequence] *annually*[Frequency] *until*[Timing] the waiver terminates). With those instructive criteria in mind, the following subsections will proceed to provide descriptions for each category of temporal rules with lists of examples found in WTO Law. Figure 3.1 below provides a general overview of the categorization of temporal rules. Noting that the primary purpose of this research is to offer a scheme of categorization rather than a complete catalogue. Moreover, there are clearly ways other than that used in this research in which temporal rules might be classified and analyzed.

### 3.1.1 *Point in Time*

According to the definition of "time" in *Oxford English Dictionary*, "point" in time may be "an instant (as the time when a star crosses the meridian), or it may have some duration (as the time for sowing), but the focus of consideration is not on its extent or duration but rather on *the question of when* it occurs, what happens or is done *at that moment*, or how it is characterized."[6] While any unit of time may be taken as a point, the concept of "point in time" used in this research can be indicated by and limited to *calendar time*, either

5 *E.g.*, LIC Art. 3.5(f): "the period for processing applications shall, … , not be *longer than 30 days*[Period] if applications are considered as and when received, i.e., on a first-come first-served basis,…." The phrase *longer than 30 days*[Period] is considered as a single temporal rule which is denoted as a fixed period in time in the following Section 3.1.4. This research did not attribute specific token to the comparative "longer than."

6 "Time" (*Oxford English Dictionary*, 2012), https://www.oed.com/dictionary/time_n#220292953 (last visited 4 June 2025). (emphasis added)

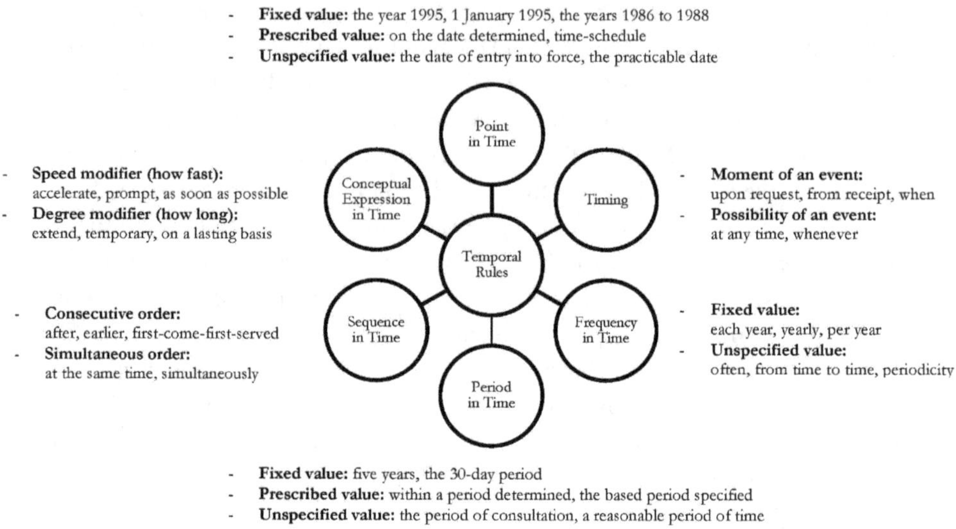


FIGURE 3.1 Six categories of temporal rules

specifying by a numerical value or by a non-numerical term. In WTO Law, three types of point in time can be observed (Table 3.1).

First, it can be fixed in which we are able to confidently identify at the year, month, or day level. There is a wide variety of forms for the expressions of the fixed point in time in legal texts. For example, the date can be expressd using a determiner, such as "year," "month," or "day" (*e.g.*, the year 1995[7]), as well as using (ordinal) numeric patterns (*e.g.*, 1 January 1958[8] and the 10th year[9]) or full names (*e.g.*, this fifteenth day of April one thousand nine hundred and ninety-four[10]). Noting that if both point and duration interpretations of time are possible, the point representation is preferred over the duration

7 AG Art. 1(f): "'implementation period' means the six-year period commencing in the year 1995, except that, for the purposes of Article 13, it means the nine-year period commencing in 1995."

8 GATT Art. XXVII:5: "Before 1 January 1958 and before the end of any period envisaged in paragraph 1 a contracting party may elect by notifying the CONTRACTING PARTIES to reserve the right. ..."

9 AG Annex 5, Para. 7(a): "Thereafter, the level of minimum access opportunities resulting from this formula in the 10th year shall be maintained in the Schedule of the developing country Member concerned."

10 MAR Art. XVI: "DONE at Marrakesh this fifteenth day of April one thousand nine hundred and ninety-four, in a single copy, in the English, French and Spanish languages, each text being authentic."

TABLE 3.1 Temporal rules for point in time in WTO Law

| Types | Temporal Rules | Examples |
|---|---|---|
| Fixed **(F)** | – (in the year) yyyy<br>– (on/at/by) dd/mm/yy<br>– (on) the -th day/(in) the -th year<br>– yyyy to yyyy | – commencing in the year 1995 (AG Art. 1(f))<br>– 1 January 1958 (GATT Art. XXVII:5); this fifteenth day of April one thousand nine hundred and ninety-four (MAR Art. XVI)<br>– on the first day of each three-year period (GATT Art. XXVIII:1); in the 10th year (AG Annex 5, Para. 7(a))<br>– the years 1986 to 1988 (AG Annex 3, Para. 9) |
| Prescribed **(P)** | – on the date (to be) determined/arranged **[by authority]**<br>– **[authority]** (set/state/indicate) the date/deadline<br>– the dates set forth/specified **[in document]**<br>– time-schedule/timetable/deadline | – on the date determined by Ministers (MAR Art. XIV:1)<br>– [panels] set precise deadlines for written submissions (DSU Art. 12.5)<br>– the respective dates set forth in that Annex (GATT Art. I:4); the calendar, financial or marketing year specified in the Schedule (AG Art. 1(i))<br>– time-schedules for the removal of restrictive import measures (Para. 1 of GATT's Understanding on BOP Provisions); timetable for progressive liberalization (SG Art. 12.2) |
| Unspecified **(U)** | – (on/at/by) the date/year (of/on/upon) **[event]**<br>– (any/any given) year/the year in question/(practicable) date/(calendar, financial or marketing) year or day/(fiscal) year/ (working) days or hours/(business) hours/(model) year **[modifier]** | – the date of entry into force of the WTO Agreement (Para. 1(b) of GATT 1994); by the date upon which it enters into force (GATT Art. XXIX:5)<br>– the amount of such payments in any given year (AG Annex 2, Para. 6(b)); from the beginning of the implementation period |

TABLE 3.1 Temporal rules for point in time in WTO Law (*cont.*)

| Types | Temporal Rules | Examples |
|---|---|---|
| | – today/present/past/future/ / recent/current(-ly) **[subjective reference]** | through the year in question (AG Art. 9.2(b)(i))); the [earliest] practicable date (GATT Art. XVI:4); on any working day (LIC Art. 2.2(a)(ii))<br>– today cover a significant proportion of world trade (the Preamble of GATT's Understanding on Art. XXIV); be introduced or currently maintained by that Member (SCM Art. 24.4); their individual present and future development (GATT Art. XXXVII:4); prevent any future breach (TFA Art. 11.1(b)) |

representation (*e.g.*, "the years 1986 to 1988" denoted as point in time[11]). Besides, a non-numerical expression can sometimes be denoted as a fixed expression by referring to the relevant context in legal texts (*e.g.*, "on this date" refers to "15 April 1994" in the previous sentence of the same Article;[12] or "the date of this Agreement" refers to "30 October 1947" in the GATT[13]).

Second, point in time can be prescribed by an authority or documentation to give (various options of) dates. These prescribed dates can not be identified plainly by reading the legal provisions. For example, the decision of the precise date can be delegated to an authority (*e.g.*, "on the date" determined by Ministers;[14] or "precise deadlines" set by panels[15]). It can also make referece to a documentation for the date concerned (*e.g.*, the "respective dates" set forth

11 AG Annex 3, Para. 9: "The fixed external reference price shall be based on the years 1986 to 1988…."

12 Para. 2 of GATT's Understanding on Art. II:1(b): "The date as of which 'other duties or charges' are bound, for the purposes of Article II, shall be 15 April 1994. 'Other duties or charges' shall therefore be recorded in the Schedules at the levels applying on this date."

13 GATT Art. XXVI:1: "The date of this Agreement shall be 30 October 1947."

14 MAR Art. XIV:1: "This Agreement and the Multilateral Trade Agreements annexed hereto shall enter into force on the date determined by Ministers. …"

15 DSU Art. 12.5: "Panels should set precise deadlines for written submissions by the parties and the parties should respect those deadlines."

in that Annex[16]) or to a time-schedule or timetable further established (*e.g.*, "time-schedules" for the removal of restrictive import measures[17]).

Third, point in time can also be unspecified where no precise numerical value is indicated by legal texts or further prescribed by an authority or documention. This unspecified point in time can usually be found to anchor on an event, which requires knowledge about the time of the specific event in order for its value to be fully specified. For example, the phrase "the date of entry into force of the WTO Agreement" is considered as the unspecified point in time that anchors on the event of "entry into force of the WTO Agreement." It needs to be positioned on a date in relation to "entry into force of the WTO Agreement."[18] In addition to the date of an event, the unspecfied point in time can be introduced by modifiers, such as *given*, *practicable*, or *working* (*e.g.*, the payment "in any *given* year;"[19] or "the earliest *practicable* date" for ceasing to grant subsidy[20]).

It should be noted that the unspecified point in time can also anchor on temporal reference of different observers (*i.e.*, the *now* of the observer). According to the theory of deictic time, the present moment of different observers can itself serve as a point in time. In other words, the "now" of the observers is considered as the reference point which derives time as being in the past, present, or future.[21] To this end, this research categorizes subjective temporal reference under the unspecified point in time (albeit not explicitly related to *calendar time*) due to the assumption that the point is being discussed depends on the

16 GATT Art. I:4: "In the case of the contracting parties named in Annex G, the date of April 10, 1947, referred to in subparagraph (a) and (b) of this paragraph shall be replaced by the respective dates set forth in that Annex."

17 Para. 1 of GATT's *Understanding on BOP Provisions*: "Members confirm their commitment to announce publicly, as soon as possible, time-schedules for the removal of restrictive import measures taken for balance-of-payments purposes."

18 Para. 1(b) of GATT 1994: "the provisions of the legal instruments set forth below that have entered into force under the GATT 1947 before the date of entry into force of the WTO Agreement."

19 AG Annex 2, Para. 6(b): "The amount of such payments in any given year shall not be related to, or based on, the type or volume of production (including livestock units) undertaken by the producer in any year after the base period."

20 GATT Art. XVI:4: "Further, as from 1 January 1958 or the earliest practicable date thereafter, contracting parties shall cease to grant either directly or indirectly any form of subsidy on the export of any product. ..." Noting that the term "earliest" is denoted separately under the category of sequence in time. *See infra*, Section 3.1.5.

21 Rafael Núñez and Kensy Cooperrider, 'The Tangle of Space and Time in Human Cognition' (2013) 17 Trends in Cognitive Sciences 220, 221. ("The [McTaggart's] A-series, also called 'tensed' or 'deictic time' here referred to as 'D-time' assumes a specific temporal entity the present moment, 'now' as the reference point and derives temporal categories 'past' and 'future' relative to it.")

person or entity who observes the legal provisions, such as *today*, *current*, or *future* (*e.g.*, customs unions and free trade areas *today*;[22] or subsidy *currently* maintained[23]).

### 3.1.2 *Timing*

This research differentiates "point in time" and "timing" for the perception that timing establishes a temporal focus on *a particular event* without reference to *calendar time* as the above category of point in time. In WTO Law, two types of timing can be identified (Table 3.2). First, timing can indicate the moment of an event in time. In general, the expression of the moment is usually realized by prepositional phrases (*e.g.*, upon, from, and in time of) and temporal clauses (*e.g.*, when, as, and once). For example, Article 12.1(c) of the Agreement on Safeguards obliges Members to immediately notify their safeguard measures "*upon* taking a decision to apply or extend a safeguard measure." The WTO adjudicators have paid attention to this special moment of "taking a decision" and clarified the timing of notification by stating that "the relevant triggering event is the 'taking' of a decision," and therefore the key is "whether a 'decision' has occurred, or has been 'taken', and not on whether that decision has been given effect."[24] In this sense, the identification of a specific moment (*e.g.*, *upon* taking a decision) can be important in the context of law to understand when certain obligations are expected to be undertaken (*e.g.*, notification). Noting that the moment of an event can also be found in temporal range expressions introduced by certain prepositions which indicate the starting or ending points of timing (*e.g.*, *from* receipt of the request of the Committee;[25] and *until such time as* the Ministerial Conference has appointed a DG[26]).

In terms of the temporal clause (*e.g.*, a when-clause), it brings into focus a temporal referent which is associated with the event in the main clause.[27] Taking Paragraph 4 of GATT's *Understanding on Article XXVIII* as an example,

---

22 The Preamble of GATT's Understanding on Art. XXIV: "customs unions and free trade areas have greatly increased in number and importance ... and today cover a significant proportion of world trade."

23 SCM Art. 24.4: "The PGE may be consulted by any Member and may give advisory opinions on the nature of any subsidy proposed to be introduced or currently maintained by that Member."

24 Appellate Body Report, *US—Wheat Gluten*, para. 120. (emphasis added)

25 RO Art. 9.2(c)(ii): "The Technical Committee shall complete the above work within one year and three months from receipt of the request of the Committee."

26 MAR Art. XVI:2: "the Secretariat of GATT 1947 shall become the Secretariat of the WTO, and the [DG] to the CONTRACTING PARTIES to GATT 1947, until such time as the Ministerial Conference has appointed a [DG]...."

27 Marc Moens and Mark Steedman, 'Temporal Ontology and Temporal Reference' (1988) 14 Computational Linguistics 15, 23.

TABLE 3.2 Temporal rules for timing in WTO Law

| Types | Temporal Rules | Examples |
|---|---|---|
| Moment (M) | – at (the time of)/by/upon/on[a] /(for) such time/times in/in time of/the timing of **[event]**<br>– (as) from/since/until (such time as) /to (the point of)/ through **[range]**<br>– when/as/once **[clause]** | – at the request of any Member (MAR Art. XIII:4); at the time of the selection (ADP Art. 6.10); by the end of the relevant period (MAR fn. 4); upon acceptance (MAR Art. X:2); in time of war or other emergency (GATS Art. XIV bis:1(b)(iii)); the timing of implementation of the provisions (TFA Art. 13.2)<br>– from receipt of the request (RO Art. 9.2(c)(ii)); since previous negotiations (GATS Art. XIX:3); until such time as the Ministerial Conference has appointed a DG (MAR Art. XVI:2); to the point of first sale (AG Art. 1(b))<br>– when a tariff concession is modified or withdrawn (Para. 4 of GATT's Understanding on Art. XXVIII); as [any significant changes] occur (Para. 11 of GATT's Understanding on Art. XXIV); once [measures] have been agreed upon (GATT Annex I, Ad Art. XXIV, Para. 11) |
| Possibility (P) | – at any time/at any point in time<br>– whenever | – at any time give notice to the Executive Secretary (GATT Art. XXVI:5(b)); be requested at any time by any party to a dispute (DSU Art. 5.3); be accepted at any later point in time (RO Annex II, Para. 3(d))<br>– whenever the General Council has made specific recommendations (Para. 13 of GATT's Understanding on BOP Provisions) |

a *E.g.*, upon/on + [acceptance/accession/approval/agreement/determination/entry into force/establishment /expiration/notification/receipt/reference/request/sponsorship].

the event in the main clause (*e.g.*, the Member ... shall be deemed to have an initial negotiating right) can refer to the focused temporal referent (*e.g.*, when a tariff concession is modified or withdrawn).[28] While one may not consider the meaning of "when" primarily temporal in the clause, it has been argued that the conjunction "when" still has "a single sense-meaning, reflecting its role of establishing a temporal focus."[29] Besides, other generic expressions of the moment of an event (*e.g.*, the time of, for such time, and the timing of) can also be found to represent the timing at which an event happens or ends (*e.g.*, the timing of implementation of the provisions[30]).

Second, timing can indicate the possibility of an event in time and imply that the event may happen repetitively. Instead of establishing a specific moment, the temporal expressions introduced by *at any time* and *whenever* emphasize that the event may occur at any or every point while something is happening (*e.g.*, *at any time* give notice to the Executive Secretary[31]). As mentioned in Section 2.4, the WTO adjudicators acknowledged the use of "at any time" for request of good offices, conciliation, or mediation in DSU Article 5.3 to suggest a "procedural possibility" under the legal provision.

However, it should be noted that *when/as/whenever/upon* are not denoted as the temporal rules of timing to establish the specific moment or possibility of an event, if they are conjoined by adjectives or nouns to indicate general "status." For example, the expressions of status include the adjectives *necessary, possible, or (im)practicable,* and the nouns *need, cause,* or *justification* (*e.g.*, *whenever* possible,[32] *as* the need arises,[33] or *upon* good cause

28 Para. 4 of GATT's Understanding on Art. XXVIII: "When a tariff concession is modified or withdrawn on a new product ..., the Member possessing initial negotiating rights on the tariff line where the product is or was formerly classified shall be deemed to have an initial negotiating right in the concession in question."

29 Moens and Steedman (n 27), 16. (However, "the *when*-clause predicates something more than mere temporal coincidence, that is, some contingent relation such as a causal link or an enablement relation between the two events.")

30 TFA Art. 13.2: "The extent and the timing of implementation of the provisions of this Agreement shall be related to the implementation capacities of developing and least-developed country Members."

31 GATT Art. XXVI:5(b): "Any government ... may at any time give notice to the Executive Secretary that its acceptance shall be effective in respect of any separate customs territory or territories so excepted."

32 SCM Annex VI, Para. 8: "Enquiries or questions put by the authorities or firms of the exporting Members and essential to a successful on-the-spot investigation should, whenever possible, be answered before the visit is made."

33 SPS Art. 12.7: "The Committee shall review the operation and implementation of this Agreement three years after the date of entry into force of the WTO Agreement, and thereafter as the need arises."

shown[34]). While these expressions of status may also give rise to temporal emphasis in legal provisions, this research focuses on capturing the "event" for the purpose of establishing temporal events association in the following Chapter.

### 3.1.3 *Frequency in Time*

Frequency in time conveys the number of times (*i.e.*, how often) an event that happens within a particular period or the indication of the repetition of an event in time. In WTO Law, two types of frequency in time can be observed (Table 3.3). First, frequency can be fixed in which one can identify the number of times introduced by noun phrases containing a quantifier such as "each" or "(once) every" with a time unit (*e.g.*, once every six months[35]), as well as adverbial numbers (*e.g.*, *twice* in the five-year period[36]). It is often possible to discern the numerical time-frame in which these sets of times occur. Besides, frequency can also be found in adjectives and adverbs derived from time units (*e.g.*, on a *yearly* basis[37]) and other expressions (*e.g.*, screen time per theatre *per year*[38]). Second, frequency can be unspecified and introduced by vague quantifiers which do not refer to a specific number of times (*e.g.*, *often*,[39] *regular*,[40] or *from time to time*[41]). The generic expression is also found to ask for the number of times with which the event is repeated (*e.g.*, *the frequency with which* applications for a subsidy are refused or approved[42]).

---

34 ADP Art. 6.5: "Any information which is by nature confidential ... which is provided on a confidential basis by parties to an investigation shall, upon good cause shown, be treated as such by the authorities."

35 TBT Annex 3, Para. J: "At least once every six months, the standardizing body shall publish a work programme containing its name and address, the standards. ..."

36 SG Art. 7.6(b): "such a safeguard measure has not been applied on the same product more than twice in the five year period immediately preceding the date of introduction of the measure."

37 Para. 9 of GATT's *Understanding on BOP Provisions*: "On a yearly basis, each Member shall make available to the Secretariat a consolidated notification. ..."

38 GATT Art. IV(a): "Screen quotas ... shall be computed on the basis of screen time per theatre per year or the equivalent thereof. ..."

39 DSU Art. 2.3: "The DSB shall meet as often as necessary to carry out its functions within the time-frames provided in this Understanding."

40 SG Art. 7.4: "In order to facilitate adjustment in a situation where the expected duration of a safeguard measure ..., the Member applying the measure shall progressively liberalize it at regular intervals during the period of application."

41 GATT Art. XVI:5: "The CONTRACTING PARTIES shall review the operation of the provisions of this Article from time to time with a view to examining its effectiveness. ..."

42 SCM Fn. 3: "In this regard, in particular, information on the frequency with which applications for a subsidy are refused or approved and the reasons for such decisions shall be considered."

TABLE 3.3 Temporal rules for frequency in time in WTO Law

| Types | Temporal Rules | Examples |
|---|---|---|
| Fixed (F) | – each year/(once) every ... years or months/(times) in the ... period<br>– monthly/yearly/annual(-ly) / on an (annual/yearly) basis<br>– per (year/annum)/once | – at least once every six months ... publish a work programme (TBT Annex 3, Para. J); a safeguard measure ... not be applied ... more than twice in the five-year period (SG Art. 7.6(b))<br>– on a yearly basis ... make available ... a consolidated notification (Para. 9 of GATT's Understanding on BOP Provisions); the annual average market exchange rate (AG Attachment to Annex 5, Para. 3)<br>– screen time per theatre per year (GATT Art. IV(a)); each person may be reappointed once (DSU Art. 17.2) |
| Unspecified (U) | – often/always/regular(-ly)/ periodic(-ally)/usual(-ly)/ sporadic<br>– from time to time/on a regular-basis /at regular intervals<br>– the frequency/periodicity (with which/of) | – meet as often as necessary (DSU Art. 2.3); provide periodically information (ADP Art. 8.6)<br>review the operation of the provisions ... from time to time (GATT Art. XVI:5); progressively liberalize [the safeguard measure] at regular intervals (SG Art. 7.4)<br>– information on the frequency with which applications for a subsidy are refused or approved (SCM fn. 3); the periodicity of consultation (Para. 7 of GATT"s Understanding on BOP Provisions) |

### 3.1.4 *Period in Time*

Period in time represents a length of time when an event occurs (*i.e.*, how long). In WTO Law, three types of period in time can be observed (Table 3.4). First, period in time can be fixed in a numerical value describing how long an event lasts. This fixed period in time is often expressed by (1) the time units introduced by *for* to indicate the exact amount of time an event lasted (*e.g.*,

TABLE 3.4 Temporal rules for period in time in WTO Law

| Types | Temporal Rules | Examples |
|---|---|---|
| Fixed (F) | – [for/in/within/during] (a period (term) of) ... days/months/years<br>– [during] the ...-day | – for a period of more than 5 years (GATS Annex on Art. II Exemptions, Para. 3); within 20 days of the establishment of the panel (DSU Art. 1.2); sixty days' notice of such suspension (GATT Art. XVIII:21)<br>– an extension of the 30-day period (ADP Art. 6.1.1); the expiration of the ninety-day time limit (GATT Annex I, Ad Art. XVIII, Para. 21) |
| Prescribed (P) | – [within] a period/at intervals (specified/established/proposed /prescribed/agreed/selected / contemplated/determined) **[by authority]**<br>– the period/time-frame (specified/envisaged/covered) **[in document]** | – within a period specified by the CONTRACTING PARTIES (GATT Art. XXX:2); within such period as the CONTRACTING PARTIES may prescribe (GATT Art. XII:4(d)); at such intervals as shall be determined (AG Art. 18.2)<br>– during the base period, specified in the relevant tables of supporting material (AG Art. 1(a)(i)); the period covered by each such document of publication (CV Art. 9.1) |
| Unspecified (U) | – [during/over/within/throughout] the period/time-frame /time limit/term/duration of **[event]**<br>– [during/within/over/in/for] a **[modifier]** period/length/time/interval | – throughout the period of consultation (GATT Art. XIX:3(b)); the time-frame for delivery of goods or services (GPA Art. VII:2(e)); the term of the contract (GPA Art. II:8(a)); the term of protection of a work (TRIPS Art. 12)<br>– the selection of a representative period for any product (GATT Art. XIII:4); the realistic time required for production (GPA Art. X:8); allow a reasonable interval between the publication ... and its entry into force ... (SPS Annex B(2)) |

*for* a period of 5 years[43]) or (2) the time units introduced by, such as *in, within,* and *during,* to indicate that the time of an event is included in a specified time-frame (*e.g.*, within 20 days of the establishment of the panel[44]). The noun phrases of a period can also be found (*e.g.*, the 30-day period[45]). Noting that a non-numerical expression can be referred to a fixed period through reading the relevant context (*e.g.*, the "implementation period" in the Agreement on Agriculture is principally referred to "the six-year or nine-year period commencing in the year 1995."[46]).

Second, period in time can also be prescribed by an authority or documentation and its precise duration can not be plainly identified in legal provisions. In other words, the precise duration can be delegated to an authority to further decide (*e.g.*, within a period specified by the CONTRACTING PARTIES[47]). It can also make referece to a documentation for the precise duration (*e.g.*, during the base period specified in the relevant tables of supporting material[48]).

Third, period in time can be unspecified by means of non-numerical temporal expressions which refer to a duration by conceptualizing an event as a single unit (*i.e.*, for the duration of the entire event or during the entire event).[49] In other words, the conceptual duration can be defined by the temporal extent of an event instead of by numerical values (*e.g.*, *throughout the period of* consultation[50] or *the term of* the contract[51]). Besides, the unspecified period

---

43 GATS Annex on Art. II Exemptions, Para. 3: "The Council for Trade in Services shall review all exemptions granted for a period of more than 5 years."

44 DSU Art. 1.2: "… where the parties to the dispute cannot agree on rules and procedures within 20 days of the establishment of the panel,…."

45 ADP Art. 6.1.1: "Due consideration should be given to any request for an extension of the 30 day period. …"

46 AG Art. 1(f): "'implementation period' means the six-year period commencing in the year 1995, except that, for the purposes of Article 13, it means the nine-year period commencing in 1995."

47 GATT Art. XXX:2: "… any contracting party which has not accepted it within a period specified by the CONTRACTING PARTIES shall be free to withdraw from this Agreement. …"

48 AG Art. 1(a)(i): "with respect to support provided during the base period, specified in the relevant tables of supporting material incorporated by reference in Part IV of a Member's Schedule; and. …"

49 Javier Valenzuela and Daniel Alcaraz Carrión, 'Temporal Expressions in English and Spanish: Influence of Typology and Metaphorical Construal' (2020) 11 Frontiers in Psychology 1, 7.

50 GATT Art. XIX:3(b): "contracting party shall … be free to suspend, upon the taking of the action and throughout the period of consultation, such concessions or other obligations as may be necessary to prevent or remedy the injury."

51 GPA Art. II:8(a): "where the term of the contract is 12 months or less, the total estimated maximum value for its duration."

can also be conjoined to vague modifiers, such as *representative*, *realistic*, or *reasonable* (*e.g.*, a *representative* period[52]).

### 3.1.5 *Sequence in Time*

Sequence in time refers to a "series of ordered temporal events," which is different from period in time concerning the "temporal magnitude" of events.[53] In WTO Law, two types of sequence in time can be observed (Table 3.5). First, sequence can be in a consecutive order in which the events are following one after another. To describe the ordered events in time, it has been argued that "the order of events within a sequence, in which one event precedes ('is earlier than') or follows ('is later than') another one, regardless of the point in time from which this may be observed."[54] In other words, the sequential time concerns "the relation of one temporal landmark to another, with no mandatory anchoring to the present moment."[55] This consecutive sequence is often introduced by (1) prepositions, such as *before* or *after* (*e.g.*, *after* instituing or intensifying such restrictions or *before* doing so[56]); (2) adjectives (adverbs) or their comparative/superlative forms (*e.g.*, *formerly* a part of the Ottoman Empire;[57] or not *earlier* than six months, nor *later* than three month[58]); and (3) generic expressions in the order in which the event happens (*e.g.*, on a *first-come first-served* basis[59]). Second, sequence can be in a simultaneous order to emphasize the events happening or existing at nearly or exactly the

---

52 GATT Art. XIII:4: "the selection of a representative period for any product and the appraisal of any special factors affecting the trade in the product shall be made initially by the contracting party applying the restriction."

53 Núñez and Cooperrider (n 21), 221.

54 Andrea Bender and Sieghard Beller, 'Mapping Spatial Frames of Reference onto Time: A Review of Theoretical Accounts and Empirical Findings' (2014) 132 Cognition 342, 346. Noting that this statement is derived from the McTaggart's B-series description of events.

55 Núñez and Cooperrider (n 21), 221.

56 GATT Art. XVIII:12(a): "Any contracting party applying new restrictions or raising the general level of its existing restrictions …, shall immediately after instituting or intensifying such restrictions (or, in circumstances in which prior consultation is practicable, before doing so) consult with the CONTRACTING PARTIES…."

57 GATT Art. I:3: "The provisions of paragraph 1 shall not apply to preferences between the countries formerly a part of the Ottoman Empire. …"

58 GATT Annex I, Ad Art. XXVIII, Para. 1.3: "Not earlier than six months, nor later than three months, prior to 1 January 1958, or to the termination date of any subsequent period, a contracting party wishing to modify or withdraw any concession embodied in the appropriate Schedule, should notify the CONTRACTING PARTIES to this effect."

59 LIC Art. 3.5(f): "the period for processing applications shall, … , not be longer than 30 days if applications are considered as and when received, i.e. on a first-come first-served basis. …"

TABLE 3.5 Temporal Rules for Sequence in Time in WTO Law

| Types | Temporal Rules | Examples |
| --- | --- | --- |
| Consecutive (C) | – before/heretofore/after/ thereafter<br>– previous(-ly)/subsequent(-ly) /formerly/ sequentially/historically / retroactive(-ly)/prospective /consecutive/successive / early (earlier, earliest)/later (latest) /sooner/first/next/ last/final(-ly)<br>– on a first-come first-served basis/in the early stages/at an early (appropriate) stage/ in (good) time /(as far) in advance as practicable | – before resorting to further action (DSU Art. 4.5); after instituting or intensifying such restrictions (GATT Art. XVIII:12(a))<br>– with retroactive effect (TFA Art. 3.4); for two consecutive calendar years (SCM Art. 27.6); not earlier than six months, nor later than three months (GATT Annex I, Ad Art. XXVIII, Para. 1.3)<br>– on a first-come first-served basis (LIC Art. 3.5(f)); in the early stages of development (GATT Art. XVIII:1); have notified in good time (SCM Art. 12.6) |
| Simultaneous (S) | – at (as nearly as possible/ about) the same time<br>– simultaneous(-ly)/ concurrently | – the terms ... shall be terminated at the same time (TRIMS Art. 5.5); such value closely approximates to one of the following occurring at or about the same time (CV Art. 1.2(b))<br>– simultaneously informing the Member concerned (Para. 4 of GATT's Understanding on Art. XVII); the provisions of this Article may be invoked, if ..., but not concurrently (AG Art. 5.1(a)) |

same time. It is ususally introduced by the expressions, such as *at the same time*[60] or *simultaneously*.[61]

60 TRIMS Art. 5.5: "The terms of such a TRIM shall be equivalent in their competitive effect to those applicable to the established enterprises, and it shall be terminated at the same time."

61 Para. 4 of GATT's Understanding on Art. XVII: "If the matter is not satisfactorily resolved it may make a counter-notification to the Council for Trade in Goods, for consideration

### 3.1.6 *Conceptual Expression in Time*

Conceptual expression in time adds special temporal meaning to an event, which has not yet been covered by the above-mentioned five categories. In WTO Law, two types of conceptual expression in time can be observed (Table 3.6). First, conceptual expression can be related to speed which represents "how fast" the event should happen. This speed modifier can be expressed by (1) verbs to arrange for the event to go faster (*e.g.*, *accelerate* the [dispute settlement] proceedings[62]); (2) adjectives or adverbs, such as *immediate(-ly)*, *prompt(-ly)*, and *timely*, to indicate that the time of the event should happen or be done without delay (*e.g.*, request an *immediate* meeting;[63] or enter *promptly* into further negotiations[64]); and (3) relevant phrases introduced by the expressions of ability, such as *as [adjective/adverb] as + possibility* or by prepositions, such as *in/on … manner/basis* (*e.g.*, as soon as possible[65] or in an expeditious manner[66]).

Second, conceptual expression can be related to degree which refers to "how long" the event should last. This degree modifier can be expressed by (1) verbs to arrange for the event to go longer or shorter, such as *extend, delay, and shorten* (*e.g.*, *extend* the periods established;[67] or this period may … *be shortened*[68]); (2) durative expressions introduced by *short* and *long* (*e.g.*, as *short* a period as possible[69] or unforeseen *short-term* requirements[70]); (3) other adjectives or

by the working party set up under paragraph 5, simultaneously informing the Member concerned."

62 DSU Art. 4.9: "In cases of urgency …, the parties to the dispute, panels and the Appellate Body shall make every effort to accelerate the proceedings to the greatest extent possible."

63 CA Art. 9.6.1: "Any Signatory may upon such notification request an immediate meeting of the Committee."

64 GATT Art. II:5: "… the two contracting parties, together with any other contracting parties substantially interested, shall enter promptly into further negotiations with a view to a compensatory adjustment of the matter."

65 TBT Art. 5.2.2: "… the competent body transmits as soon as possible the results of the assessment in a precise and complete manner to the applicant so that corrective action may be taken if necessary. …"

66 ADP Art. 10.4: "… any cash deposit made during the period of the application of provisional measures shall be refunded and any bonds released in an expeditious manner."

67 DSU Art. 12.10: "In the context of consultations involving a measure taken by a developing country Member, the parties may agree to extend the periods established in paragraphs 7 and 8 of Article 4."

68 TBT Annex 3, Para. L: "This period may, however, be shortened in cases where urgent problems of safety, health or environment arise or threaten to arise."

69 ADP Art. 7.4: "The application of provisional measures shall be limited to as short a period as possible, not exceeding four months. …"

70 LIC Art. 3.5(g): "The period of licence validity shall not preclude imports from distant sources, except in special cases where imports are necessary to meet unforeseen short-term requirements."

TABLE 3.6 Temporal rules for conceptual expression in time in WTO Law

| Types | Temporal Rules | Examples |
|---|---|---|
| Speed (S) | – accelerate<br>– immediate(-ly)/prompt(-ly)/rapid(-ly) /expeditious(-ly), expediting, expedited/timely/readily/speedy<br>– as soon as (practicable/possible) /as expeditiously as possible /as promptly as possible /as quickly as possible / as rapidly as possible /without (undue) delay<br>– in an expeditious manner / in a timely fashion /on an accelerated basis | – make every effort to accelerate the proceedings (DSU Art. 4.9)<br>– request an immediate meeting of the Committee (CA Art. 9.6.1); enter promptly into further negotiations (GATT Art. II:5)); provide timely opportunities for all interested parties to see all information (ADP Art. 6.4)<br>– transmits as soon as possible the results of the assessment (TBT Art. 5.2.2); provide for expedited shipments ... as rapidly as possible (TFA Art. 8.2(b))<br>– be refunded and any bonds released in an expeditious manner (ADP Art. 10.4); make its decisions or recommendations in a timely fashion (GPA Art. XVIII:6(f)) |
| Degree (D) | – extend/prolong/delay/postpone/ shorten<br>– short(-er)/long(-er) / short-term/mid-term/long-term<br>– provisional(-ly)/temporarily / indefinitely/permanently<br>– on a lasting basis /on a permanent basis /in the long run / in a relatively short period /in the very short term /within a reasonably short time | – extend the periods established (DSU Art. 12.10); delay application of the provisions of this Agreement (CV Art. 20.1); this period may ... be shortened (TBT Annex 3, para. L)<br>– as short a period as possible (ADP Art. 7.4); have long constituted an economic unit (GATT Art. XXIV:11); that time may be shorter or longer (DSU Art. 21.3(c)); unforeseen short-term requirements (LIC Art. 3.5(g))<br>– be applied provisionally to the fullest extent (Para. 1(b)(ii) of GATT 1994); be temporarily exported for manufacturing, processing, or repair abroad (TFA Art. 9.2(c)); be renewable indefinitely (TRIPS Art. 18) |

TABLE 3.6 Temporal rules for conceptual expression in time in WTO Law (*cont.*)

| Types | Temporal Rules | Examples |
|---|---|---|
| | | – maintaining or restoring equilibrium in their balance of payments on a sound and lasting basis (GATT Art. XII:3(a)); citizenship, residence or employment on a permanent basis (GATS Annex on Movement on Natural Persons, Art. 2) |

adverbs, such as *provisional(-ly)*, *temporarily*, and *indefinitely*, to indicate that the time of the event should or should not last for long (*e.g.*, be applied *provisionally*;[71] or be renewable *indefinitely*[72]); and (4) relevant phrases introduced by prepositions, such as *in/on … manner/basis* (*e.g.*, on a lasting basis[73]).

## 3.2 The Distribution of Temporal Rules in WTO Law

Before proceeding to demonstrate the quantitative results regarding the distribution of temporal rules in WTO Law, it needs to be noted that some information close to temporal rules are not denoted under certain instances for the sake of simplicity, which includes: (1) temporal expressions in (sub-)titles of the Agreements/Articles, *e.g.*, the title of Article 11 of the Anti-Dumping Agreement "*Duration* and Review of Anti-Dumping Duties and Price Undertakings;" (2) references to (the date of) documentation, *e.g.*, the Decision of *5 April 1966* (BISD 14S/18) in DSU Article 3.12; (3) references to the relevant parts of the legal content in texts, *e.g.*, "the paragraph *immediately* above" in GATT Annex I, Ad Article I:1; and (4) the noun phrases which contain repeated temporal information that has been denoted in other parts of the texts, *e.g.*,

71 Para. 1(b)(ii) of GATT 1994: "… Part II of GATT 1947 shall be applied provisionally to the fullest extent not inconsistent with legislation existing on the date of the Protocol."

72 TRIPS Art. 18: "The registration of a trademark shall be renewable indefinitely."

73 GATT Art. XII:3(a): "Contracting parties undertake, in carrying out their domestic policies, to pay due regard to the need for maintaining or restoring equilibrium in their balance of payments on a sound and lasting basis. …"

the *provisional* measure in Article 6 of the Agreement on Safeguards[74] and the *semi-annual* reports in Article 25.11 of the SCM Agreement.[75] While these four instances may also shed some light on the role of time in legal texts to clarify legal substance and structure, this research limits the focus to temporal rules in relation to specific legal events. For reference, Appendix 2 provides a list of non-denoted temporal information in the twenty agreements of WTO Law.

To demonstrate the relevance of temporal rules in WTO Law, the reflection of their density in legal texts could provide a primary indication of their importance, which means that temporal rules may be relevant whereas they could be found to appear frequently throughout the texts. As a result, this research intends to quantify temporal rules in order to examine how many or how dense of them are actually embedded in WTO Law. In this regard, the density of temporal rules is an indicator on the number of times a temporal rule appears in the legal text compared to the total content (as a percentage of the overall word count, including footnotes). In other words, if the legal text has 100 words and 5 temporal rules appears to be denoted, the density of temporal rules is 5 %. This calculation is commonly used in text mining as a means to determine how important a given phrase is to a document. As can be seen in Table 3.7 below, the overall density of temporal rules in WTO Law is about 2 % (1.94 %), which means that 3,741 temporal rules appear within the total number of 193,046 words on the twenty agreements of WTO Law. While there is no set number of words for each temporal rule, one may have general expectations that one temporal rule as a single unit could be identified within 50 words of the legal content in WTO Law as a whole. Nevertheless, the density of temporal rules can be different depending on the nature of the content in each agreement. For example, the Agreement on Safeguards contains the highest density of temporal rules (3.67 %) compared to the other agreements, in particular the SPS Agreement with the lowest density (1.03 %). This means one may

74 SG Art. 6: "… a Member may take a provisional safeguard measure pursuant to a preliminary determination. … The duration of *the provisional measure* shall not exceed 200 days. …" Noting that the temporal rule "provisional" has been denoted in the former part of the Article, and therefore the "provisional" in the noun phrase "the provisional measure" is not denoted repeatedly in the later part.

75 SCM Art. 25.11: "Members shall also submit, on a semi-annual basis, reports on any countervailing duty actions taken within the preceding six months. *The semi-annual reports* shall be submitted on an agreed standard form." Noting that the temporal rule "on a semi-annual basis" has been denoted in the former part of the Article, and therefore the "semi-annual" in the noun phrase "the semi-annual reports" is not denoted repeatedly in the later part.

TABLE 3.7 The density of temporal rules in WTO Law

| Ranking | Agreement in WTO Law | Number of temporal rules | Word count of legal texts* | Density of temporal rules |
|---|---|---|---|---|
| 1 | SG | 138 | 3,759 | 3.67 % |
| 2 | DSU | 341 | 11,544 | 2.95 % |
| 3 | LIC | 78 | 2,797 | 2.79 % |
| 4 | AG | 255 | 10,110 | 2.52 % |
| 5 | TPRM | 28 | 1,142 | 2.45 % |
| 6 | RO | 104 | 4,523 | 2.30 % |
| 7 | TFA | 310 | 13,623 | 2.28 % |
| 8 | GPA | 259 | 11,513 | 2.25 % |
| 9 | ADP | 246 | 11,704 | 2.10 % |
| 10 | CA | 67 | 3,249 | 2.06 % |
| 11 | SCM | 409 | 20,346 | 2.01 % |
| 12 | GATT | 664 | 35,302 | 1.88 % |
| 13 | TRIMS | 25 | 1,441 | 1.73 % |
| 14 | PSI | 58 | 3,574 | 1.62 % |
| 15 | TRIPS | 238 | 14,942 | 1.59 % |
| 16 | MAR | 73 | 4,768 | 1.53 % |
| 17 | TBT | 109 | 8,688 | 1.25 % |
| 18 | GATS | 143 | 11,958 | 1.20 % |
| 19 | CV | 140 | 12,648 | 1.11 % |
| 20 | SPS | 56 | 5,415 | 1.03 % |
| Total | 20 Agreements | 3,741 | 193,046 | 1.94 % |

* Footnotes of the legal texts are included in the word count.

encounter a temporal rule per 25 words in the Agreement on Safeguards and per 100 words in the SPS Agreement, approximately.

To the best of my knowledge, there are no benchmarks or guidelines, if possible, to govern how densely temporal information should or should not appear in legal texts. Despite this uncertainty, some insights from the distribution of temporal rules within each of the twenty agreements of WTO Law may provide a preliminary impression to explore the relevance of temporal rules to specific legal content. For this reason, Table 3.8 below further indicates the distribution of the six categories of temporal rules found in each agreement. In general, *period in time* is most frequently found in the twenty agreements

TABLE 3.8 The distribution of the six categories of temporal rules in WTO Law

| Agreement (# of rules) | 1. Period | 2. Sequence | 3. Timing | 4. Point | 5. Concept | 6. Frequency |
|---|---|---|---|---|---|---|
| 1. SG (138) | 37.0 % (51) | 21.0 % (29) | 7.2 % (10) | 14.5 % (20) | 17.4 % (24) | 2.9 % (4) |
| 2. DSU (341) | 38.1 % (130) | 19.9 % (68) | 17.6 % (60) | 13.2 % (45) | 9.7 % (33) | 1.5 % (5) |
| 3. LIC (78) | 35.9 % (28) | 12.8 % (10) | 14.1 % (11) | 21.8 % (17) | 11.5 % (9) | 3.8 % (3) |
| 4. AG (255) | 34.5 % (88) | 20.8 % (53) | 10.2 % (26) | 26.3 % (67) | 3.1 % (8) | 5.1 % (13) |
| 5. TPRM (28) | 14.3 % (4) | 17.9 % (5) | 10.7 % (3) | 7.1 % (2) | 10.7 % (3) | 39.3 % (11) |
| 6. RO (104) | 18.3 % (19) | 22.1 % (23) | 28.8 % (30) | 6.7 % (7) | 15.4 % (16) | 8.7 % (9) |
| 7. TFA (310) | 20.6 % (64) | 25.8 % (80) | 15.8 % (49) | 16.8 % (52) | 18.1 % (56) | 2.9 % (9) |
| 8. GPA (259) | 34.0 % (88) | 15.4 % (40) | 18.5 % (48) | 16.2 % (42) | 11.6 % (30) | 4.2 % (11) |
| 9. ADP (246) | 25.2 % (62) | 22.8 % (56) | 22.4 % (55) | 13.4 % (33) | 14.2 % (35) | 2.0 % (5) |
| 10. CA (67) | 4.5 % (3) | 17.9 % (12) | 19.4 % (13) | 34.3 % (23) | 16.4 % (11) | 7.5 % (5) |
| 11. SCM (409) | 27.6 % (113) | 19.3 % (79) | 19.8 % (81) | 15.2 % (62) | 13.7 % (56) | 4.4 % (18) |
| 12. GATT (664) | 17.3 % (115) | 23.9 % (159) | 16.9 % (112) | 28.3 % (188) | 10.4 % (69) | 3.2 % (21) |
| 13. TRIMS (25) | 36.0 % (9) | 20.0 % (5) | 12.0 % (3) | 16.0 % (4) | 8.0 % (2) | 8.0 % (2) |
| 14. PSI (58) | 12.1 % (7) | 19.0 % (11) | 20.7 % (12) | 15.5 % (9) | 29.3 % (17) | 3.4 % (2) |
| 15. TRIPS (238) | 25.2 % (60) | 20.6 % (49) | 21.8 % (52) | 19.3 % (46) | 11.8 % (28) | 1.3 % (3) |
| 16. MAR (73) | 27.4 % (20) | 17.8 % (13) | 31.5 % (23) | 12.3 % (9) | 5.5 % (4) | 5.5 % (4) |
| 17. TBT (109) | 16.5 % (18) | 17.4 % (19) | 44.0 % (48) | 3.7 % (4) | 14.7 % (16) | 3.7 % (4) |

TABLE 3.8 The distribution of the six categories of temporal rules in WTO Law (*cont.*)

| Agreement (# of rules) | 1. Period | 2. Sequence | 3. Timing | 4. Point | 5. Concept | 6. Frequency |
|---|---|---|---|---|---|---|
| 18. GATS (143) | 20.3 % (29) | 20.3 % (29) | 24.5 % (35) | 20.3 % (29) | 10.5 % (15) | 4.2 % (6) |
| 19. CV (140) | 15.0 % (21) | 26.4 % (37) | 30.0 % (42) | 8.6 % (12) | 11.4 % (16) | 8.6 % (12) |
| 20. SPS (56) | 19.6 % (11) | 12.5 % (7) | 37.5 % (21) | 5.4 % (3) | 19.6 % (11) | 5.4 % (3) |
| Total (3741) | 25.1 % (940) | 21.0 % (784) | 19.6 % (734) | 18.0 % (674) | 12.3 % (459) | 4.0 % (150) |

as a whole, which represents about a quarter of all temporal rules (25.1 %). It is followed by *sequence in time* (21.0 %), *timing* (19.6 %), *point in time* (18.0 %), *conceptual expression in time* (12.3 %), and *frequency in time* (4.0 %). However, the distribution of the categories varies considerably among different agreements. As a result, it is difficult to draw an effective conclusion. Given this difficulty, the pattern of the results seems to demonstrate that the agreements with a higher density of temporal rules contain more *periods in time* (*e.g.*, the Agreement on Safeguard, the DSU, the Agreement on Import Licensing, and the Agreement on Agriculture as the top four in dense), and the agreements with lower density contain more *timings* (*e.g.*, the SPS Agreement, the Customs Valuation Agreement, the GATS, the TBT Agreement, and the WTO Agreement as the bottom five in dense). Some explanations might be provided as follows.

First, the legal content of those agreements with more *periods in time* tends to establish "temporal magnitude," including how long a measure is allowed to be taken, how long a procedure is expected to be completed, and how long a period can be considered as comparable to make measurements. For example, the Agreement on Safeguards provides for economic emergency exceptions and allows WTO Members to adopt "safeguard measures" in extraordinary situations where a surge in imports causes (or threatens to cause) serious injury to the domestic industry. To strike a balance for allowing these exceptional situations, several durations regarding the application of safeguard measures are set out as restrictions in Article 7 of the Agreement on Safeguards.[76] As for period in time for procedural issues, DSU contains legal provisions that establish the proceedings for the dispute settlement between WTO Members. To ensure the effectiveness of the system, several requirements for the proceedings are prescribed with time-limits, such as the durations for the disputing parties to reach an agreement or the durations for WTO Members to adopt dispute settlement reports.[77] The Agreement on Import Licensing also comprises a number of time-limits for procedures of import licensing, such as the durations for submitting import licence applications or the durations for processing the applications.[78] In terms of period in time for measurements, the Agreement on Agriculture states the base periods for calculating or determining the level of support for an agricultural product, such as the durations for the calculation of the cumulative amounts of budgetary outlays for export subsidies or the durations for the determination of the eligibility of decoupled income support.[79]

Second, the legal content of those agreements with more *timings* tends to establish "temporal focus," including when notification shall take place, when legal provisions shall be applied, and when actions shall take effect. For example, the TBT Agreement aims to deal with the unnecessary trade-restrictive impact of technical regulations and standards by promoting the harmonization of national regulation on the basis of international standards or rules. To acknowledge the existence of the relevant regulation, timing for its notification seems to be crucial, such as when to notify the proposed technical

76 *E.g.*, SG Art. 7.1 allows WTO Members to apply safeguard measures "only for such period of time" as may be necessary to prevent or remedy serious injury and to facilitate adjustment, and the period shall "not exceed four years," unless it is extended.

77 *E.g.*, DSU Art. 1.2 obliges WTO Members to agree on rules and procedures "within 20 days" of the establishment of the panel, and DSU Art. 16.4 requires WTO Members to adopt the report "within 60 days" after the date of circulation of a panel report to the Members.

78 *E.g.*, LIC Art. 1.6 specifies "at least 21 days" for "a reasonable period" for the submissions of import licence applications, and LIC Art. 3.5(f) envisages, in a general case, that "the period for processing applications" shall "not be longer than 30 days."

79 *E.g.*, AG Art. 9.2(b)(i) requires WTO Members to calculate the cumulative amounts of budgetary outlays for export subsidies from the beginning of "the implementation period" through the year in question, and AG Annex 2, Para. 6(a) requires to determine the eligibility for decoupled income support by clearly-defined criteria such as income, status as a producer or landowner, factor use or production level in "a defined and fixed base period."

regulation or when to provide the copies of the proposed regulation.[80] In the case of the application of legal provisions, the Customs Valuation Agreement contains various provisions prescribing several approaches to determine the customs value of the imported goods. To ensure its practical use, timing for the sequential order of application of legal provisions with regard to how to determine the customs value can be found, such as when to reverse the order of application of Articles or when to use the specific provisions.[81] To ascertain the validity of actions, the WTO Agreement as the principal source of WTO Law consists of provisions in related to the amendment and withdrawal undertaken by WTO Members. It underlines the timing of when amendments or withdrawal shall take effect.[82]

In addition to *period in time* and *timing*, the distribution of other categories of temporal rules may also be observed from the nature of the content in each agreement. For example, *frequency in time* appears to play an important role in regulating the repeated procedures for trade policy review in TPRM.[83] The focus of this research is, however, not to analyze the nature or the particular function of each and every agreement in details, but provides a general understanding that temporal rules do appear with diversified forms in WTO Law. Following the observation of a quarter of temporal rules in the form of *period in time*, it is worth to note that *period in time* as a unit and category of temporal rules does not often stand alone in texts, and usually conjoins with other categories in order to be adjunct to relevant anchoring events in a broader context. For example, DSU Article 16.4 obliges the panel report to be adopted "[w]ithin 60 days after the date of circulation of a panel report to the Members." In this Article, the *period* "within 60 days" is followed by the *sequence in time* "after" and the *point in time* "the date of circulation of a panel report." In other words,

80 *E.g.*, TBT Art. 2.9.2 obliges WTO Members to notify the proposed technical regulation "at an early appropriate stage, when" amendments can still be introduced, and TBT Art. 2.9.3 obliges to provide the copies of the proposed regulation "upon request."

81 *E.g.*, CV Art. 4 allows WTO Members to reverse the order of application of Articles 5 and 6 "at the request" of the importer, and CV Annex 1, General Note, Para. 2 prescribes to use the provisions of the next Article in the sequence "when" the customs value cannot be determined under the provisions of a particular Article.

82 *E.g.*, MAR Art. X:2 states that amendments shall take effect only "upon acceptance" by all Members, and MAR Art. XV states that withdrawal shall take effect "upon the expiration" of six months from the date on which written notice of withdrawal is received.

83 *E.g.*, TPRM Para. C(ii) requires "periodic" review for the trade policies and practice of all Members, or to be subject to review "every three/five/seven years" for different trading entities.

the temporal magnitude of 60 days for adopting the report is put into a consecutive order by sequence and finally anchors on the unspecified date of circulation of the report. This suggests that the retrieval of *period in time* for a specific event may ultimately lead us to the inquiry of the relevant events in context, which creates certain temporal events nexus worth to be discovered in the following chapter (Chapter 4). This might also explain the pattern that the WTO agreements with a higher density of temporal rules seem to contain more *periods in time*.

Furthermore, Figure 3.2 below reports the distribution of the subtypes under the six categories of temporal rules. While one may consider temporal expressions in numbers (*i.e.*, fixed values) as the most attractive information to be retrieved, the results of denotation in the context of WTO Law suggests that temporal rules without numerical expressions could also have important roles to play. Given the possibility to express time in fixed values, *point* (18.0 %), *period* (25.1 %), and *frequency* (4.0 %) *in time* in total account for less than a half of temporal rules (47.1 %). On the other hand, *timing* (19.6 %), *sequence in time* (21.0 %), and *conceptual expression in time* (12.3 %) together as non-numerical expressions account for another 52.9 %. These non-numerical expressions can be highly correlated to the arrangement of events, *i.e.*, 93.6 % of *timing* appear to establish the temporal focus on events (*i.e.*, the moment), and 95.2 % of *sequence in time* to establish the consecutive order among events. In addition, the distribution of the subtypes of the *point/period/frequency in time* also represents the relevance of non-numerical expressions: 62.3 % of *point in time* are unspecified values, which means they may require additional knowledge about the time of specific events or the temporal reference of particular observers. Despite the fact that more than half of *period or frequency in time* are in numbers (*i.e.*, 54.5 % of *period* and 65.3 % of *frequency*), the other amount of prescribed or unspecified values can not be neglected. Last but not least, besides positioning the "event" as a crucial element for non-numerical temporal rules, the appearance of the prescribed and unspecified values in time seemingly underpins the potential involvement of WTO Members or the Bodies of the WTO to determine or elaborate on the usuage of temporal rules in a systemic context. As a result, these quantitiative observations could draw our attention to the need to go beyond the identification of temporal rules in isolation, and further proceed to demonstrate how they interact with legal events in WTO Law (Chapter 4) and how they are developed through different systemic mechanisms in WTO practice (Chapter 5). For reference, Appendix 3 provides the detailed statistics on the distribution of temporal rules in each agreement of WTO Law.

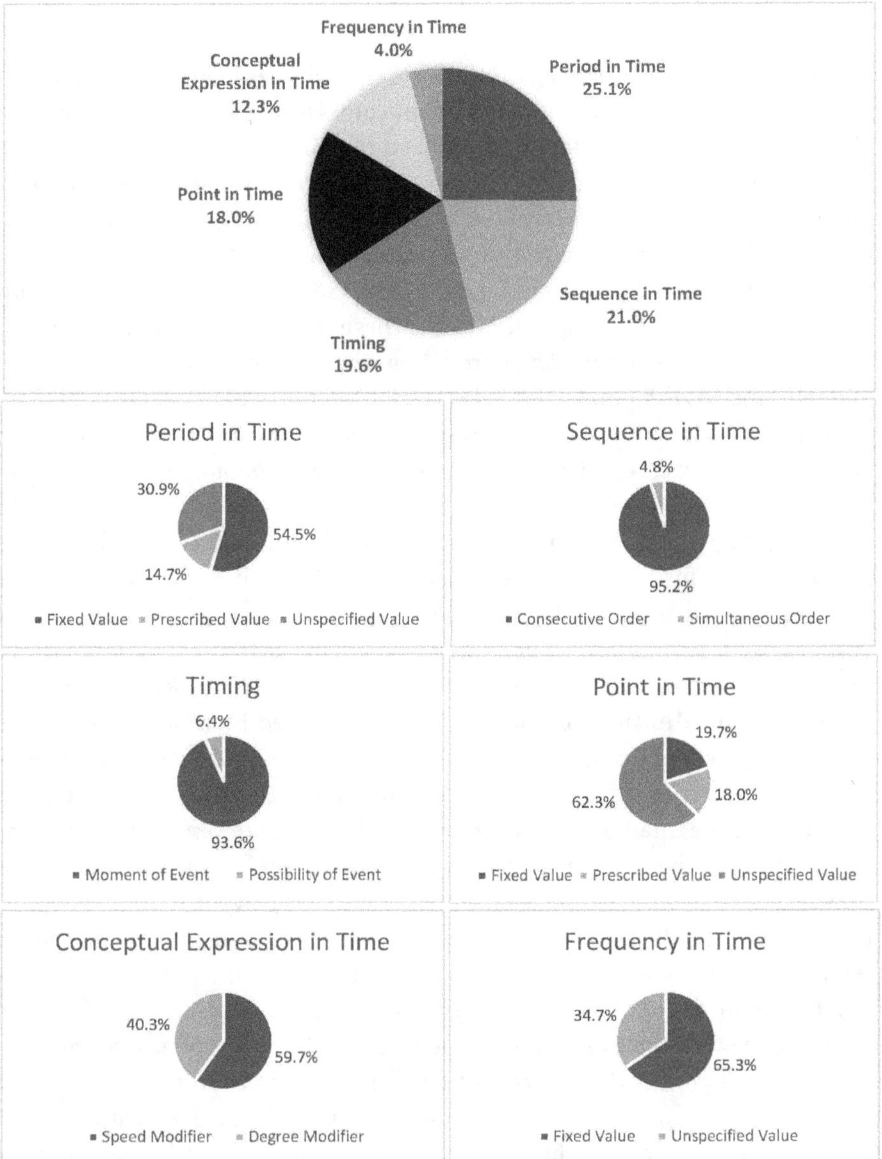


FIGURE 3.2 The distribution of (sub-)categories of temporal rules in WTO Law

## 3.3 Summary

Following the implications regarding the temporal rules in WTO Jurisprudence in Section 2.4, it is noticed that WTO adjudicators have expressed some doubts about the meaning of certain temporal expressions in legal texts, which may imply the salience of time in WTO Law. To provide a general investigation of temporal rules in WTO legal texts, this Chapter takes a step to denote them by careful and close reading of the twenty agreements of WTO Law (Section 1.2), and further classifies them into six categories (Section 3.1). It also statistically examines the density and distribution of these temporal rules denoted in the agreements with the intention of providing empirical evidence on the features and relevance of temporal rules in WTO Law (Section 3.2).

Section 3.1 manually classifies temporal rules in the twenty agreements of WTO Law into six categories, which are *point in time, timing, frequency in time, period in time, sequence in time*, and *conceptual expression in time*. Generally speaking, the representation or characteristic of temporal rules in the six categories can be further summarized as follows: (1) with a *fixed* value, which refers to explicit numerical expressions, *e.g.*, 1 January 1995, annual, or five years; (2) with a *prescribed* value, which refers to implicit time that is delegated to third parties (an authority or documentation) to decide, *e.g.*, on the date determined by Ministers or within a period specified by the CONTRACTING PARTIES; (3) with a *unspecified* value, which refers to time that is known only by specific events or associates with vague modifiers, *e.g.*, the date of entry into force of the Agreement or a reasonable period; (4) with *the moment of an event*, which refers to the particular time of a specific event, *e.g.*, upon acceptance; (5) with *the possibility of an event*, which refers to the event that may happen repetitively, *e.g.*, at any time or whenever; (6) with a *consecutive* order, which refers to temporal sequence that the events are following one after another, *e.g.*, before or earlier; (7) with a *simultaneous* order, which refers to temporal sequence that the events are happening or existing at the same time, *e.g.*, simultaneously; (8) with a *speed* modifier, which represents how fast the events should happen, *e.g.*, immediate or as soon as possible; and (9) with a *degree* modifier, which represents how much time the events should last, *e.g.*, temporary or on a lasting basis. Taking into account all these diverse representations of temporal rules, this researsch suggests consideration should also be given to "non-numerical expressions" of time, which might lead to the inquiry of a particular "event" (Chapter 4) and the "authority" involved (Chapter 5).

Section 3.2 quantitatively reflects on the density of temporal rules, namely, how frequently they are found in WTO Law. The results demonstrate that the overall density of temporal rules in WTO Law is about 2 % (*i.e.*, 1.94 %; 3,741 temporal rules/193,046 textual words, including footnotes), which means approximately one temporal rule can be denoted within 50 words of the legal texts. Given this general ratio for the entire WTO Law, the density varies depending on the nature of legal content in each agreement, such as the highest in the Agreement on Safeguards (roughly one per 25 words) in comparison to the lowest in the SPS Agreement (roughly one per 100 words). As for the distribution of the six categories of temporal rules, the results indicate around a quarter of temporal rules in WTO Law are *period in time* (25.1 %) which is followed by *sequence in time* (21.0 %), *timing* (19.6 %), *point in time* (18.0 %), *conceptual expression in time* (12.3 %), and *frequency in time* (4.0 %). This pattern of the results seemingly suggests that the agreements with a higher density of temporal rules contain more *periods in time*, and the agreements with lower density contain more *timings*. One of the reasons behind could be due to the fact that *period in time* does not often stand alone in a sentence and usually combines with several categories of temporal rules to form certain temporal events nexus in context. Furthermore, the results of the investigation of the subtypes of each categories suggest that the "non-numerical expressions" of temporal rules cannot be neglected. For example, *timing, sequence in time, and conceptual expression in time* together as intrinsically non-numerical expressions account for more than half of the total temporal rules (52.9 %). Despite the potentiality for the other three (namely, *point in time, period in time, and frequency in time*) to be expressed in numbers with fixed values, 62.3 % of *point in time* are unspecified, a slightly more than half (54.5 %) of *period in time* are fixed, and less than two thirds (65.3 %) of *frequency in time* are in numbers. As a result, this research suggests that the study on temporal rules should pay close attention to the relevant legal events associated with them (Chapter 4), and their potential development in a systemic context (Chapter 5). With these empirical implications in mind, the following Chapter will first proceed to categorize and examine the relevant legal events in WTO Law.

CHAPTER 4

# Temporal Events Association in WTO Law

Following the empirical implications from the previous Section 3.2, there are strong bonds between the temporal rules and relevant events in legal texts. Similar to the introduction in Chapter 3, to denote the relevant legal events, some knowledge regarding the extraction of "events" from the existing studies and annotation tools may be noteworthy. First, to single out "events" in a philosophical sense, it has been argued that some "elements" of time may be considered independently as "objective temporal facts" in addition to the subjective passage of time.[1] These "objective temporal facts" in the context of natural language sentences are generally described as the "events."[2] Second, researchers in linguistics have made a distinction between the properties of events by classifying verbs into verb classes under the so-called "lexical aspect" or "Aktionart." At the conceptual level, to individuate events based on verb classes, Vendler's influential scheme of classification distinguishes verbal predicates into four different types, which are non-dynamic *states*, open-ended *activities*, near-instantaneous *achievements*, and close-ended *accomplishments*.[3] Generally speaking, two properties are crucial in categorizing events: (1) *telicity*: whether an event has a natural stopping point, and (2) *dynamicity*: whether an event appears in the progressive.[4]

---

1 MM Schuster, 'Is the Flow of Time Subjective?' (1986) 39 The Review of Metaphysics 695, 697. ("Objective temporal facts are seen as having nothing to do with tenses or with pastness, presentness, or futurity; rather they have to do with one element being earlier or later than another.")

2 *See* Stig W Jørgensen, 'Carol Tenny & James Pustejovsky (eds.): Events as Grammatical Objects. The Converging Perspectives of Lexical Semantics and Syntax. CSLI Publications, 2000. ISBN 1-57586-205-0' (2001) 24 Nordic Journal of Linguistics 241, 241–245.

3 Susan Rothstein, 'Verb Classes and Aspectual Classification', *Structuring Events: A Study in the Semantics of Lexical Aspect* (John Wiley & Sons, Ltd 2004), 6. The four types of verbal predicates are further defined as follows: (1) *states*: non-dynamic situations (*e.g.*, understand); (2) *activities*: open-ended processes (*e.g.*, run); (3) *achievements*: near-instantaneous events (*e.g.*, recognize); and (4) *accomplishments*: processes with a natural endpoint (*e.g.*, build a house).

4 *Ibid.*, 7 and 11–12. Noting that a *telic* event moves towards an endpoint where are determined by the nature of the event (*e.g.*, read the book). An *atelic* event can go on indefinitely (*e.g.*, run). Although the properties of *telic* events may be imprecise and require contextual determination, the description of the *telic* event can still entail that there is a point at which the event is over (*e.g.*, run to Paris). On the other hand, a *dynamic* event asserts that "an eventuality of a particular kind is 'in progress' or going on" (*e.g.*, read or run), and a *non-dynamic* event

 | DOI:10.1163/9789004745629_005

Third, at the operational level, the concept of events is nevertheless varied and may consist of different definitions and strategies under different annotation purposes and approaches. In other words, different annotations can be made in the same sentence as to the number and extent of the events concerned. For example, according to the *TimeML Annotation Guidelines*, the "events" are defined as a cover term for situations that happen or occur, or those describe states or circumstances in which something obtains or holds true. Syntactically speaking, the events are typically verbs, although they may be expressed by means of nominalizations (*e.g.*, consideration), adjectives (*e.g.*, ready), predicative clauses (*e.g.*, would be prepared), or prepositional phrases (*e.g.*, on board).[5] In line with its coverage of all the potential syntactical expressions, the Guidelines classify seven types of events, such as reporting, perception, aspectual, *etc.*[6] However, these seven types of events may be generic and not suitable to adapt to the legal domain. To this end, a preliminary study on

contains stative predicates (*e.g.*, sit) and near instantaneous achievements which are over as soon as they have begun (*e.g.*, notice).

5 Roser Saurí and others, 'TimeML Annotation Guidelines Version 1.2.1' (2006), 2, https://nilsreiter.de/assets/2017-10-01-howto-annotation/timeml-1.2.1.pdf (last visited 5 June 2025). *See also* Georgiana Puşcaşu and Verginica Barbu Mititelu, 'Annotation of WordNet Verbs with TimeML Event Classes' in Nicoletta Calzolari and others (eds), *Proceedings of the Sixth International Conference on Language Resources and Evaluation* (LREC'08) (European Language Resources Association (ELRA) 2008). (From statistics extracted from TimeBank, "the annotated extent of an event is in 64.5 % of the times a verb, in 28 % of the cases a noun, 3.4 % of events are adjective, 0.3 % prepositions, while 3.8 % are assigned a part-of-speech category called OTHER (these events are, in most cases, numeric expressions or adverbs).")

6 *Ibid.*, 'TimeML Annotation Guidelines Version 1.2.1', 9–15. (The seven types of events are defined as follows: (1) REPORTING: the action of a person or an organization declaring something, narrating an event, or informing about an event (*e.g.*, report, explain, state); (2) PERCEPTION: the physical perception of another event (*e.g.*, see, behold, hear); (3) ASPECTUAL: different facets of event history (*e.g.*, initiation, continuation, termination); (4) LACTION: an intentional action introduces an event argument describing an action or situation from which we can infer something (*e.g.*, try to monopolize, delay a strike, agree to lend); (5) LSTATE: states that refer to alternative or possible worlds (*e.g.*, feel, hope, believe); (6) STATE: states describe circumstances in which something obtains or holds true (*e.g.*, shortage, injuries, be); and (7) OCCURANCE: all the many other kinds of events describing something that happens or occurs in the world (*e.g.*, eruption, cost, spend).) *See also* 'TimeML Markup Language for Temporal and Event Expressions', https://timeml.github.io/site/index.html (last visited 5 June 2025). ("TimeML is a robust specification language for events and temporal expressions in natural language. It is designed to address four problems in event and temporal expression markup: (1) time stamping of events (identifying an event and anchoring it in time); (2) ordering events with respect to one another (lexical versus discourse properties of ordering); (3) reasoning with contextually underspecified temporal expressions (temporal functions such as 'last week' and 'two weeks before'); and (4) reasoning about the persistence of events (how long does an event or the outcome of an event last).")

ten court decisions from the European Court of Justice has attempted to identify linguistic and legal information required for legal events.[7] In this study, Navas-Loro and Santos observed that the "event in the legal domain is used as a fine grained structure, and also combined with others (entity, relation, event, temporal expression, value)."[8] They have provided six differential criteria to serve as a starting point for conducting legal event extraction, including: (1) the jurisdiction and language used; (2) the type of document; (3) the level of abstraction; (4) the agents involved; (5) the features of the event; and (6) the purpose of annotation.[9] While these six criteria were given in the context of *case law* studies (*i.e.*, court's judgements) with the intention of capturing the "factual" events of cases rather than the "normative" events in law (*i.e.*, legal texts),[10] those criteria may be helpful to clarify the target and limitation of legal information that this research attempts to denote in this Chapter. Accordingly, the background of this Chapter to extract legal events in WTO legal texts can be summarized as follows.

- **Jurisdiction and language used:** multilateral/plurilateral treaties, English as an official language
- **Type of document:** international trade law (*i.e.*, the twenty agreements of WTO Law)
- **Level of abstraction:** normative concepts
- **Agents involved:** WTO Members, the Bodies of the WTO
- **Features of the event:** only temporal rules related
- **Purpose of annotation:** to establish temporal events association (Section 4.1)

---

7 *See generally* María Navas-Loro and Cristiana Santos, 'Events in the Legal Domain: First Impressions', *Proceedings of the 2nd Workshop on Technologies for Regulatory Compliance co-located with the 30th International Conference on Legal Knowledge and Information Systems (JURIX 2017) (TeReCom)* (Zenodo 2018).

8 *Ibid.*, 49.

9 *Ibid.*, 51–52. (The six criteria are further explained as follows: (1) multi-jurisdictionality and multilinguism: common law or civil law jurisdictions, the languages expressed or translated; (2) document-dependency such as legal or corporate documents, domestic or international legislation, underlying domains (*e.g.*, civil, criminal, or business); (3) level of abstraction: from a specific argument to a general consideration of the case; (4) agents and role such as the applicant, a judge, or the court; (5) temporal, contextual and spatial features such as chronological events within court proceedings; (6) scenario or application-based: the purposes of annotation (*e.g.*, to predict judicial decisions or to detect legal argumentation).)

10 Noting that the judgements were analyzed only the constituent sections, namely, the preamble, background of the case, consideration on the questions referred, and final ruling. Navas-Loro and Santos discarded the sections of legal context and cost attribution as no legal events are put forth.

In addition, based on Navas-Loro's and Santos's experience of their initial analysis, some difficulties have been identified while processing the legal documents, such as (1) the challenge of legal terminology: non-conventional meanings or several interpretations; (2) the variety of event-aware information: identity-related event (*e.g.*, the litigant parties), location-event (*e.g.*, the place of the national court), date-related event (*e.g.*, the date of request), and domain-related event (*e.g.*, consumer protection); and (3) the internal structure of the documents (*e.g.*, at a paragraph level of decision or in the summary).[11] To cope with these potential difficulties, this research considers to (1) focus on the general categorization of *event-types* to avoid the interpretation of a specific event; (2) denote only *temporal rule*-related events; and (3) document legal provisions at a sentence level.

To sum up, legal event extraction can be considerably distinct and complex, and currently no consensual definition or standard representation for legal events in law has yet been established. To fill this gap, this Chapter attempts to denote and categorize events in the twenty agreements of WTO Law (Section 1.2) to understand what types of events are commonly associated with temporal rules, which may contribute to the creation of a temporal-event taxonomy in the legal domain. In the following sections, Section 4.1 establishes a two-dimensional ("2-D") model to analyze the association between the temporal rules and *event-types*. Section 4.2 and Section 4.3 denote the relevant events *manually* and categorize them into eight types of substantive events and eight types of procedural events, respectively. Finally, Section 4.4 examines the temporal events association *quantitatively* to demonstrate how they are actually distributed in WTO Law.

## 4.1 The Two-Dimensional Model for Temporal Events Association

The strong bonds between the temporal rules and events can be simply due to the fact that the contextual relation of events frequently involves temporal adjacency. In a syntactical sense, Dowty highlights that the relations between the events is often indicated "explicitly through definite time adverbials,

11 *Ibid.*, 53–54. Noting that Navas-Loro and Santos also present other observations which may be more relevant in the context of *case law* study, such as: (1) the background of the case including the relevant events, arguments and facts of the parties; (2) the reference to the juristic positions of the former courts; (3) the interpretative issue alleged by the parties for the same event; and (4) the negation and factuality for the event.

temporal subordinate clauses, or certain tense combinations."[12] As a result, the relationship of events can usually be identified through reading certain temporal syntactical items in the textual context carefully. It should be noted that, as mentioned in Section 2.4, this research focuses on the use of temporal rules and leaves the use of grammatical tenses intact.

As for how to represent the temporal relations of events, various models have been established to capture temporal information in sentences in the field of natural language processing. For example, there is a model of representing thirteen possible relationships of events by capturing their *temporal hierarchy* in reference intervals (*e.g.*, whether the events are simultaneous, overlapping, or sequential in time).[13] In addition to the *temporal hierarchy*, other types of temporal relationship of events can be identified in language at the semantic level, *e.g.*, *temporal inclusion* (or subevents), *temporal precedence* (or causality), *temporal ordering* (or narrative sequence), and *temporal inference* (or event co-reference).[14] Nevertheless, as argued by Marsic, "[w]hile temporal relations make explicit in text via mechanisms such as tense, grammatical aspect or temporal adverbials can be automatically identified, the types of semantically implicit temporal relations mentioned above pose real challenges to automatic systems due to the world knowledge required for their identification."[15] In this sense, temporal relations of events can be highly complex and may be considerably difficult to be denoted by annotation tools.

In consideration of how challenging and complicated the temporal *relation* of specific *events* could be, I would like to make a distinction and aim to establish the *association* of general *event-types*, namely, "temporal events association" conjoined by temporal rules in a more conceptual sense. In other words, the focus of attention is on the fact of two *event-types* being involved with or connected to each other through the adjacency of temporal rules. The understanding of this general temporal association of *event-types* matters due to the research question of this book to theoretically explore the possibility of "temporal rules" to serve as important internal elements in the content of WTO Law (Section 1.4). This temporal events association may provide a valuable analytical tool for the knowledge of the role of time in relation to the nature of legal content. Prior to the close and careful investigation and categorization of

12 David R Dowty, 'The Effects of Aspectual Class on the Temporal Structure of Discourse: Semantics or Pragmatics?' (1986) 9 Linguistics and Philosophy 37, 37.

13 *See generally* James F Allen, 'Maintaining Knowledge about Temporal Intervals' (1983) 26 Communications of the ACM 832.

14 Georgiana Marsic, 'Syntactically Motivated Task Definition for Temporal Relation Identification' (2012) 53 Traitement Automatique des Langues 23, 26.

15 *Ibid.*

the events in WTO Law, I will firstly establish a two-dimensional (2-D) model to evaluate the temporal events association under sentence structure in legal texts.

Generally speaking, there are primarily two approaches established in linguistics regarding how to analyze sentence structure in texts, which are (1) the *root verb* of the superordinate or subordinate clause at the sentence level, and (2) the *constituent* of a sentence by the phrasal node, as Ma et al. argued, "constituency embraces analysis of underlying structure and transformations, accounting for numerous phenomena such as subject-verb inversion in interrogatives," which "permit[s] a powerful structured analysis of syntactic relationships."[16] Since the sentences in legal texts can be lengthy and contain several legal events within different parts of a sentence, this research denotes the relevant events not only by capturing *root verbs* at the sentence level, but also by identifying certain *constituents* at phrasal level that appear in close proximity to the corresponding temporal rules. To demonstrate how to denote the events in WTO legal texts in two dimensions more clearly, some instructive criteria are provided as follows.

TABLE 4.1 The two-dimensional model for temporal events association

| Sentence | Temporal rule | Main event | Supporting event |
|---|---|---|---|
| ① | the date on[Point in Time] | state[EXPRESSION] | terminate[EFFECT] |
| ② | for a period of more than one year[Period] | be reviewed[REVIEW] | granted[ORDER] |
| | not later than[Sequence] | be reviewed[REVIEW] | is granted[ORDER] |
| | one year[Period] | be reviewed[REVIEW] | is granted[ORDER] |
| | after[Sequence] | be reviewed[REVIEW] | is granted[ORDER] |
| | thereafter[Sequence] | be reviewed[REVIEW] | terminates[EFFECT] |
| | annually[Frequency] | be reviewed[REVIEW] | terminates[EFFECT] |
| | until[Timing] | be reviewed[REVIEW] | terminates[EFFECT] |

16 Megan Ma and others, 'Deconstructing Legal Text: Object-Oriented Design in Legal Adjudication' (2020) MIT Computational Law Report, 8, https://law.mit.edu/pub/deconstructinglegaltext/release/1 (last visited 5 June 2025). The authors explained the analysis of sentence structure as follows: (1) sentence level (*i.e.*, dependency trees), which "begins with the root verb of the superordinate clause and branches out from there, with subordinate verbs arranging substructures;" and (2) phrase structure (*i.e.*, constituency relations), that "each 'constituent' (or, individual element) in a sentence is headed by its own phrasal node."

TABLE 4.1 The two-dimensional model for temporal events association (*cont.*)

| Sentence | Temporal rule | Main event | Supporting event |
|---|---|---|---|
| ③ | This sentence contains typical events (e.g., review, examine), but does not refer to temporal rules. | | |
| ④ | extend[Conceptual Expression] | extend[MODIFICATION] | N/A |

Article IX:4 of the WTO Agreement (decision-making: granting a waiver):

① *A decision by the Ministerial Conference granting a waiver shall state*[EXPRESSION] *the exceptional circumstances justifying the decision, the terms and conditions governing the application of the waiver, and the date on*[Point in Time] *which the waiver shall terminate*[EFFECT].

② *Any waiver granted*[ORDER] *for a period of more than one year*[Period] *shall be reviewed*[REVIEW] *by the Ministerial Conference not later than*[Sequence] *one year*[Period] *after*[Sequence] *it is granted*[ORDER], *and thereafter*[Sequence] *annually*[Frequency] *until*[Timing] *the waiver terminates*[EFFECT].

③ *In each review, the Ministerial Conference shall examine whether the exceptional circumstances justifying the waiver still exist and whether the terms and conditions attached to the waiver have been met.*

④ *The Ministerial Conference, on the basis of the annual review,*[17] *may extend*[Conceptual Expression] [*extend*[MODIFICATION]], *modify or terminate the waiver.*

Table 4.1 above takes Article IX:4 of the WTO Agreement denoted in Section 3.1 as an example. Based on the general observations of this research, the temporal rule in the second column (as highlighted in grey) can be associated with the relevant events in two dimensions, which are (1) the main event in the third column (as highlighted in yellow) as the high-level context, and (2) the supporting event in the fourth column (as highlighted in green) as the low-level anchor. This two-dimensional temporal events association occurs regardless of the relative ordering of temporal rules and events in the sentence.

First, to establish the main event for a temporal rule in the sentence (*i.e.*, the first dimension), this research relies mainly on the identification of *root or central verb*(*s*) situated in the sentences (*e.g.*, state[EXPRESSION], in the sentence ①, be reviewed[REVIEW] in the sentence ②, and extend[MODIFICATION] in the sentence ④). In principle, only the sentences that contain temporal rules are denoted (*e.g.*, the sentence ③ is intact). It should be noted that a temporal rule can be associated with more than one main event and be denoted in duplicate. For example, in GPA Article XXI:3, the temporal rule annually[Frequency] is denoted twice with its two main events, namely, review[REVIEW] and

17 Noting that the phrase "the *annual* review" is not annotated due to the fact that it is a repeated noun phrase which has been prescribed in the previous sentence, *e.g.*, "[*a*]*ny waiver ... shall be reviewed by the Ministerial Conference ... annually*[Frequency]*. ...*" *See supra*, Section 3.2.

inform[NOTIFICATION], respectively.[18] Due to the scheme of categorization of this research, a temporal rule itself can sometimes be considered as the main event (*e.g.*, the temporal rule extend[Conceptual Expression] itself is also highlighted as the main event extend[MODIFICATION] in the sentence ④).

Second, to establish the supporting event on which temporal rules anchor (*i.e.*, the second dimension), this research relies mainly on phrase structure to identify *event-constituent*(*s*) for each temporal rule in the sentence. The set of relevant constituents of events for temporal rules is more diverse and can be identified in various syntactical forms. Based on the observation in WTO Law, each temporal rule is usually linked to one specific event-constituent (*e.g.*, the date on[Point in Time] which the waiver shall terminate[EFFECT] in the sentence ①), although two event-constituents can also be found in some cases. For example, in GPA Article XXII:14, the temporal rule at the time[Timing] is denoted twice with the two supporting events, namely, accepts[ACCEPTANCE] and accedes[INSTITUTION], respectively.[19] In addition, each event-constituent can be anchored by

18 GPA Art. XXI:3: "The Committee shall annually[Frequency]: a. review[REV] the implementation and operation of this Agreement; and b. inform[NOT] the General Council of its activities. ..." Other examples of double counting can be found in SPS Art. 11.2 ("establish an advisory technical experts group[INS], or consult[DIS] the relevant international organizations"); PSI Art. 2.16 ("either issue a Clean Report of Findings[DEC] or provide a detailed written explanation[EXP]"); TRIPS Arts. 22.3 and 23.2 ("refuse[ACC] or invalidate[EFF] the registration of a trademark"); and GPA Art. XXII:8(b)(vi) ("be reviewed[REV] and updated[MOD] periodically"). Noting that the temporal rules in GATT Art. XIX:1(a) and (b) could also be denoted in duplicate based on the categories established in this research, such as: "the contracting party shall be free, in respect of such product, and to the extent and for such time[Timing] as may be necessary to prevent or remedy such injury, to suspend the obligation[APP] in whole or in part or to withdraw or modify the concession[MOD]." However, the temporal rule "for such time[Timing]" did not be double-counted due to the consideration that the subsequent GATT Art. XIX:2 appears to refer to the prospective events (*i.e.*, suspend the obligation[APP] or withdraw or modify the concession[MOD]) as the general "action pursuant to the provisions of paragraph 1 of this Article." To this end, this research simplified the denotation for GATT Art. XIX:1(a) and (b) by classifying the two prospective events as a single event under MODIFICATION (*i.e.*, *suspend the obligation ... or to withdraw or modify the concession*[MOD]).

19 GPA Art. XXII:14: "This Agreement shall not apply as between any two Parties where either Party, at the time[Timing] either Party accepts[ACC] or accedes[INS] to this Agreement, does not consent to such application." Other examples of double counting can be found in SPS Annex B, Para. 5(b), TBT Arts. 2.9.2 and 5.6.2 ("when amendments can still be introduced[MOD] and comments taken into account[EXP]"); TBT Annex 2, Para. 4, DSU Art. 13.1 and Appendix 4, Para. 4 ("[b]efore ... seeks such information[NOT] or advice[INS]"); as well as CA Arts. 9.3.1 and 9.7.1 ("the governments which have accepted[ACC] or acceded[INS] to it", "its acceptance[ACC] or accession[INS] to this Agreement", or "either accepts[ACC] or accedes[INS] to this Agreement").

multiple temporal rules (*e.g.*, not later than[Sequence] one year[Period] after[Sequence] it is granted[ORDER] in the sentence ②).

It should also be noted that the same event-constituent can simultaneously serve as the main event for one temporal rule and the supporting event for another temporal rule. Taking a provision in GATT Annex I as an example, the event-constituent "Article III has been modified[MODIFICATION]" is considered as the supporting event for the temporal rule "after[Sequence]" which is preceded by the main event-constituent "[t]he cross-reference. … shall only apply[APPLICATION]."[20] On the other hand, the same event-constituent "Article III has been modified[MODIFICATION]" can also be highlighted as the main event for the temporal rule "by[Timing]" which is followed by the supporting event-constituent "the entry into force[EFFECT] of the amendment."[21] As a rule of thumb, the denotation of events should appear in close proximity to the corresponding temporal rules.

The following subsections will proceed to categorize the *event-types* (either as the main event or the supporting event) that are found to be associated with temporal rules in WTO Law. In line with the formalistic convention in the *TimeML Annotation Guidelines*,[22] the following categories of the *event-types* will be in upper case (e.g., DEFINITION). The primary purpose of this research is to offer a scheme of categorization rather than a complete catalogue. There are clearly ways other than that used in this research in which the *event-types* might be classified and analyzed.

## 4.2 Eight Types of Substantive Events

To begin with how to classify substantive events in this section in comparison with procedural ones in the following section, it should be acknowledged the common concept of "substantive" WTO Law contrasted with "procedural" one. Substantive WTO Law usually refers to legal provisions concerning the rights and obligations of WTO Members under the WTO agreements, rather than dealing with legal processes by which the substantive law is created, applied

---

20 GATT Annex I, Ad Art. II, Para. 2(a): "The cross-reference, in paragraph 2 (a) of Article II, to paragraph 2 of Article III shall only apply[APP] after[Sequence] Article III has been modified[MOD] by the entry into force of the amendment. …"

21 *Ibid.*: "The cross-reference, in paragraph 2 (a) of Article II, to paragraph 2 of Article III shall only apply after Article III has been modified[MOD] by[Timing] the entry into force[EFF] of the amendment. …"

22 *See* 'TimeML Annotation Guidelines Version 1.2.1' (n 6). Noting that the terms are used in upper letters when they denote the *class concepts* of event-types.

and enforced. In terms of the general content, most of substantive WTO Law can be found in the thirteen multilateral agreements such as on the GATT, the GATS, and the TRIPS Agreement. From the perspective of law, this distinction between "substantive" and "procedural" law can be important due to the fact that substantive law often derives direct legal consequences for WTO Members and therefore has the higher potential to influence the outcome of legal disputes, albeit this distinction is not always clear. With this in mind, the purpose of this research is not to provide a clear distinction of the "substantive" and "procedural" events in the sense of appropriateness.

Instead, it is to establish the *event-types* for temporal rules in a syntactical sense with the intention for a better understanding of temporal events association in WTO legal texts. As a result, the concept of "substantive events" is used broadly in this research to denote stative eventualities which do not usually occur in the progressive or develop gradually over time as a process. The subject of the substantive events is not limited to the rights and obligations of WTO Members. It widely contains the employment of legal provisions and the function of the Bodies of the WTO. It should be noted that the conceptual umbrella of "substantive events" or "procedural events" is only used for the sake of convenience rather than correctness, and therefore it can be and will be abandoned in Section 4.5 of this Chapter.

As mentioned above, since verbal events are most frequently encountered, this research focuses on the identification and classification of events expressed mainly by means of (nominalized) verbs. However, it does not follow that every occurrence of the verb in question necessarily expresses the same concept or meaning. In other words, an identification and analysis of the substantive (or procedural) events in WTO legal texts may reveal a certain degree of inconsistency in the sense that the same verb in different contexts could be classified under different event-types. Despite the possibility of inconsistency, the task of categorization is conducted with the assumption that the core properties of the event-types can be captured by certain lexical terms in general and refined by reading carefully through the context in particular.

In addition, one might argue that the scheme of categorization for events in the context of WTO Law might be arbitrary or trivial. In this regard, the aim of this research is to provide a preliminary contour for the underexplored research territory and to generate some insights based on the investigation of potential event-types associated with temporal rules at a conceptual level. It needs to be noted that the choice for the classification was influenced or limited by my knowledge and experience, and therefore one should be aware of the possibility of misinterpretation. Nevertheless, the statistics seem to indicate that the chances of 95 % for interjudge agreement could be expected in

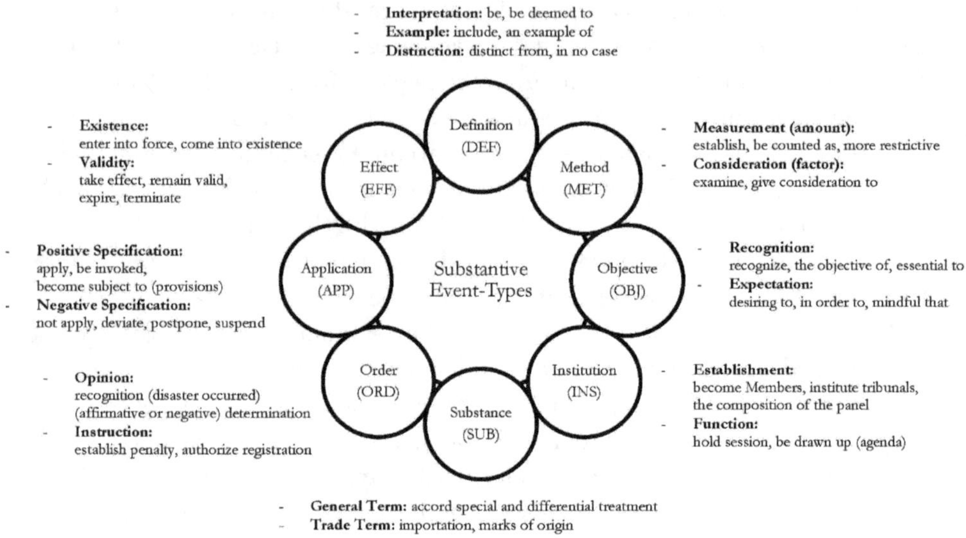


FIGURE 4.1 Eight types of substantive events in WTO Law

nominal scaling, and a substantial part of the disagreemnts is a concequence of marginal discrepancies.[23] For this reason, relying on close and careful reading of the twenty agreements of WTO Law, this section proposes eight types of substantive events and provides criteria and examples in details as follows (Figure 4.1). The criteria and examples in the following subsections are representative not exhaustive.

### 4.2.1 *Definition (DEF)*

DEFINITION as an event-type prescribes or clarifies the meaning or coverage of a specific legal term by means of (1) providing an interpretation, (2) listing an example, or (3) making a distinction (Table 4.2). As has been observed in treaties, the functional aim of drafting definitions (or use of terms) is relevant to the operation and application of the purposes of the agreement. Their legislating force can be affected by creative attribution of the meaning through negotiation and transference of the meaning from the context of reference.[24] In this sense, DEFINITION may be seen as one of the most critical event-types in the legal domain. First, the interpretation prescribes circumstances in which

23 Jacob Cohen, 'A Coefficient of Agreement for Nominal Scales' (1960) 20 Educational and Psychological Measurement 37, 44.

24 Evangelos Raftopoulos, *International Negotiation: A Process of Relational Governance for International Common Interest* (Cambridge University Press 2019), 160–163.

TABLE 4.2 The event-type of DEFINITION in WTO Law

| Criteria | Phrases | Examples |
|---|---|---|
| Interpretation | – be/have (the same meaning) / become/represent/constitute /permit/mean/cover/amount<br>– be deemed to /be limited to /be presumed (not) to /be considered (not) to /be interpreted as /be defined as /be recognized as /be taken (as/ to) /be treated as | – the date of this Protocol is 15 April 1994 (Para. 9 of GATT's Marrakesh Protocol); [the schedule] shall become a Schedule to GATT 1994 (MAR Protocol Art. 1); the term "reasonable measures" would permit a contracting party to eliminate the inconsistent taxation (GATT Annex I, Ad Art. III:1)<br>– be deemed to have an initial negotiating right (Para. 4 of GATT's Understanding on Art. XXVIII); be interpreted as referring to the rest of the producers (ADP Art. 4.1(i)); be recognized as use of the trademark (TRIPS Art. 19.2) |
| Example | – include (including) /contain (containing) /consist of<br>– an example of/for example / such as/e.g. /(take) the form of | – include a complete description of ... (GPA Art. X:7); contain at least the following information ... (GPA Art. VII:3); consist of ... the provisions of the legal instruments (Para. 1(b) of GATT 1994)<br>– an example of such restrictions would be the case where ... (Note to Art. 1 Para. 1(a) (iii) of CV Annex I); clearly-defined criteria such as income, status ... (AG Annex 2, Para. 6(b)); such measures should take the form of tariff increases (SG Art. 6) |

TABLE 4.2 The event-type of DEFINITION in WTO Law (*cont.*)

| Criteria | Phrases | Examples |
|---|---|---|
| Distinction | – distinct from /differ from / except for<br>– in no case /in (exceptional/ special) cases /as a general rule | – [the GATT 1994] is legally distinct from ... (MAR Art. II:4); those procedures differ from their own (TBT Art. 3.1); except for time-periods specifically prescribed in this Article (SCM Art. 4.12)<br>– in no case shall the proceedings exceed 90 day (DSU Art. 17.5); exceed 10 years only in exceptional cases (Para. 3 of GATT's Understanding on Art. XXIV); as a general rule not exceed nine months (DSU Art. 20) |

a legal term holds true or is considered to be true. For example, the interpretation can be introduced by the verbs *be* and *have* to prescribe a legal term as true (*e.g.*, The date of this Protocol *is* 15 April 1994[25]), or by the verb phrases, such as *be deemed* and *be presumed*, to prescribe a legal term considered to be true (*e.g.*, *be deemed* to have an initial negotiating right[26]). Second, the example lists circumstances that are typical of the coverage of a legal term. For example, the verbs *include*, *consist*, and *contain* are employed to provide examples (*e.g.*, such documentation shall *include* a complete description[27]), or the norm phrases, such as *an example of* and *the form of*, can also be found (*e.g.*, *an example of* such restrictions[28]). Third, the distinction differentiates circumstances in which legal terms are comparable. For example, the verbs *distinct*, *differ*,

25 Para. 9 of GATT's Marrakesh Protocol.

26 Para. 4 of GATT's *Understanding on Art. XXVIII*: "... the Member possessing initial negotiating rights on the tariff line where the product is or was formerly classified shall *be deemed* to have an initial negotiating right in the concession in question."

27 GPA Art. X:7(f): "such documentation shall *include* a complete description of ... f. where there will be a public opening of tenders, the date, time and place for the opening. ..."

28 Note to Art. 1, Para. 1(a)(iii) of CV Annex I: "*An example of* such restrictions would be the case where a seller requires a buyer of automobiles not to sell or exhibit them prior to a fixed date which represents the beginning of a model year."

and *except* may signal the difference between the legal terms or the extent of a specific one (*e.g.*, [the GATT 1994] be legally *distinct* from [the GATT 1947][29]), or the norm phrases, such as *in no case*, *in exceptional cases*, and *as a general rule* (*e.g.*, *In no case* shall the proceedings exceed 90 days.[30]).

### 4.2.2 *Method* (*MET*)

METHOD as an event-type clarifies (1) the basis in the process of measurement or (2) the factors that should be taken into consideration in the process of judgement (Table 4.3). Those relevant processes can include evaluation, assessment, calculation, valuation, determination, *etc*. First, the measurement focuses on setting a benchmark or comparing a value that corresponds to the amount, degree, or quality of a measure.[31] For example, the measurement can be introduced by the active verbs, such as *establish*, *assess*, and *set*, to provide the basis for conducting a measurement (*e.g.*, *establish* appropriate amortization and depreciation periods[32]), or by the passive verbs, such as *be counted*, *be calculated*, and *be computed* (*e.g.*, *be counted as* a part of the initial period[33]). The adjectives or comparatives, such as *higher*, *more restrictive*, and *equal to*, can also express a difference in size, degree, or quality of a measure (*e.g.*, be *more restrictive* than it was[34]). Second, the consideration refers to particular factors or facts that are required to be thought about when making a judgement. For example, the verbs *examine* and *consider* are commonly employed to introduce the factors or facts (*e.g.*, *examine* any known factors[35]), or the verb phrases, such as *give consideration to*, *pay regard to*, and *bear in mind*, are also found (*e.g.*, *give* sympathetic *consideration to* granting requests[36]).

---

29 MAR Art. II:4: "The [GATT 1994] ... *is legally distinct from* the [GATT], dated 30 October 1947,...."

30 DSU Art. 17.5: "*In no case* shall the proceedings exceed 90 days."

31 *E.g.*, level, rate, margin, percent, per capita, average, amount, price, value, quantity, share, mark-up, incidence, price, volume, type, factor, trend, or data.

32 ADP Art. 2.2.1.1: "... in particular in relation to *establishing appropriate amortization and depreciation* periods and allowances for capital expenditures and other development costs."

33 SG Art. 6: "The duration of any such provisional measure shall *be counted* as a part of the initial period and any extension referred to in paragraphs 1, 2 and 3 of Article 7."

34 SG Art. 7.4: "A measure extended under paragraph 2 shall *not be more restrictive than* it was at the end of the initial period, and should continue to be liberalized."

35 ADP Art. 3.5: "The authorities shall also *examine any known factors* other than the dumped imports which at the same time are injuring the domestic industry. ..."

36 TFA Art. 17.4: "The Committee shall *give sympathetic consideration to* granting requests for extension taking into account the specific circumstances of the Member submitting the request."

TABLE 4.3 The event-type of METHOD in WTO Law

| Criteria | Phrases | Examples |
| --- | --- | --- |
| Measurement | – establish, select (period) /exceed (amount)/assess (effect) /require (quota)/ set (level) /apportion, reflect, ascertain (value) /determine (proportion) /maintain and restore (equilibrium) /apply (classification or rate)<br>– be counted/be calculated /be computed/be determined /be adjusted/ be constructed /be compared/be classified /be based (basis or grounds)<br>– more restrictive/equal to /higher/greater/lower/ less /larger/maximum | – establish appropriate amortization and depreciation period (ADP Art. 2.2.1.1); exceed the amount of the trade actually affected (Para. 6 of GATT's Understanding on Art. XXVIII); maintaining or restoring equilibrium in their balance of payments on a sound and lasting basis (GATT Art. XII:3(a))<br>– be counted as a part of the initial period (SG Art. 6); be limited to what is necessary (TBT Art. 5.2.7); be determined by comparison with a comparable price of the like product (ADP Art. 2.2); be based on import statistics (Para. 2 of GATT's Understanding on Art. XXIV)<br>– not be more restrictive than it was (SG Art. 7.4); collect a duty equal to the difference (GATT Annex I, Ad Art. XXIV: 9); has had … a larger share in the market of … than (GATT Annex I, Ad Art. XXVIII: 1.4) |
| Consideration | – examine (factor) / consider (fact) /judge (condition) /explore (possibility) /elaborate (criterion) /prioritize (request)<br>– [take into/give/accord] consideration to /[pay/ have] regard to /[give/ require] attention to / take into account /bear in mind /give priority to | – examine any known factors (ADP Art. 3.5); consider this fact as a potential mitigating factor (TFA Art. 6.3.6); judged in the light of the conditions of trade (GATT, Annex I, Ad Art. XXVIII, Para. 1.6)<br>– give particular consideration to the special situation (TFA Art. 20.4); pay due regard to the proportion prevailing during a previous representative period (GATT Art. XI: 2); bear in mind the special difficulties (TBT Art. 12.9); give appropriate priority to perishable goods (TFA Art. 7.9.2) |

### 4.2.3 *Objective* (OBJ)

OBJECTIVE as an event-type illustrates the goals of the agreements or rules by means of (1) giving recognition or (2) setting expectation (Table 4.4). In principle, this event-type may be frequently found in the preamble of treaties which constitutes the "immediate context for the interpretation" and serves as a "final negotiating storage" of the given regime.[37] In the context of the WTO, the adjudicators have referred to the preamble of the WTO Agreement, and held that "[a]s this preambular language reflects the intentions of negotiators of the WTO Agreement, we believe it must add colour, texture and shading to our interpretation of the agreements annexed to the WTO Agreement."[38] In this sense, OBJECTIVE may also be referred as one of the most critical event-types in the legal domain.

First, the recognition emphasizes the awareness or acceptance of some rules or goals to be important. For example, it can be introduced by the verbs, such as *recognize* and *note* (or their -ing or -ed form), to indicate the purposes of the rules (*e.g.*, *recognize* that customs duties often constitute serious obstacles to trade[39]), or by the noun phrases, such as *the objective of* and *the purpose of* (*e.g.*, *the first objective of* the dispute settlement mechanism[40]). The adjective phrases, such as *be essential to* and *be necessary to*, can also signal the need to achieve a goal (*e.g.*, *essential to* the effective functioning of the WTO[41]). Second, the expectation expresses hope for some rules to be conducted in a particular way or lead to a certain result. For example, the (modal) verbs, such as *desire*, *intend* and *can*, are employed to introduce a wish or express possibility for a particular action (*e.g.*, *desiring to* provide for the speedy, effective and equitable resolution of disputes[42]), or by the phrases, such as *in order to* and *with a*

---

37 Raftopoulos (n 24), 160.

38 Appellate Body Report, *US—Shrimp*, para. 153. *See also* Max Hulme, 'Preambles in Treaty Interpretation' (2016) 164 University of Pennsylvania Law Review 1281, 1342. ("[T]he VCLT provides the preamble with two routes in which to exert its influence: first, as an integral part of the holistic textual analysis of the treaty, and second, as the standard repository for statements of object and purpose.")

39 GATT Art. XXVIII bis: 1: "The contracting parties *recognize that* customs duties often constitute serious obstacles to trade;…."

40 DSU Art. 3.7: "… *the first objective of* the dispute settlement mechanism is usually to secure the withdrawal of the measures concerned if these are found to be inconsistent with the provisions of any of the covered agreements."

41 DSU Art. 3.3: "The prompt settlement of situations … *is essential to* the effective functioning of the WTO and the maintenance of a proper balance between the rights and obligations of Members."

42 The Preamble of the PSI: "*Desiring to* provide for the speedy, effective and equitable resolution of disputes between exporters and preshipment inspection entities arising under this Agreement. …"

TABLE 4.4 The event-type of OBJECTIVE in WTO Law

| Criteria | Phrases | Examples |
|---|---|---|
| Recognition | – recognize/note/understand/consider **[(-ing/-ed) that …]**<br>– the objective of /the purpose of /a need to/ need for<br>– be essential to /[be/become] necessary (to/ for) /be appropriate for / prove unnecessary | – recognize that customs duties often constitute serious obstacles to trade (GATT Art. XXVIII bis:1); noting that sanitary and phytosanitary measures are often applied on the basis of bilateral agreements or protocols (the preamble of the SPS)<br>– the first objective of the dispute settlement mechanism (DSU Art. 3.7); for the purpose, *inter alia*, of the prompt review and correction of administrative action relating to customs matters (GATT Art. X:3(b))<br>– the prompt settlement of situations … is essential to the effective functioning of the WTO (DSU Art. 3.3); where imports are necessary to meet unforeseen short-term requirements (LIC Art. 3.5(g)) |
| Expectation | – desire/intend/aim / expect/ensure/can **[(-ing/-ed) at/to/for/ that …]**<br>– in order (to/that) /with a view to /so as to<br>– mindful that | – desiring to provide for the speedy, effective and equitable resolution of disputes (the preamble of the PSI); the procedures set out above are not intended to prevent the authorities of a Member from proceeding expeditiously (ADP Art. 6.14); expeditious arbitration … can facilitate the solution of certain disputes (DSU Art. 25.1)<br>– in order to allow time for producers … to adapt their products and methods of production (SPS Annex B, Para. 2); with a view to expediting the release of goods upon arrival (TFA Art. 7.1.1)<br>– mindful that such programmes must be carried out without [delays] (the preamble of the PSI) |

*view to* (*e.g.*, *in order to* allow time for producers ... to adapt their products and methods of production[43]). The adjectives, such as *mindful*, also give attention to the future conduct of certain actions (*e.g.*, *mindful that* such programmes must be carried out without [delays][44]).

### 4.2.4 *Institution* (*INS*)

INSTITUTION as an event-type relates to (1) the establishment or (2) the function of the (bodies of) organization or governmental authorities (Table 4.5). The level of institution can contain the core entities (*e.g.*, Ministrial conference and the Secretariat of the WTO) and subsidiary entities (*e.g.*, Dispute Settlement Body of the WTO).[45] First, the establishment focuses on the creation of the organization or entities. For example, the membership of the (bodies of) organization can be introduced by the verbs, such as *become*, *be*, and *accede* (*e.g.*, *become* original Members of the WTO[46]). To create certain entities, the verbs, such as *institute*, *establish*, and *choose*, can be found to introduce or compose a system (*e.g.*, *institute* judicial, arbitral or administrative tribunals or procedures[47]).[48] The noun phrases, such as *the composition of* and *the accession of*, can also signal the significant members within the entities (*e.g.*, *the composition of* the panel[49]). Second, the function refers to the duty or task in which the entities work or operate. For example, the active verbs, such as *hold*

---

43 SPS Annex B, Para. 2: "Members shall allow a reasonable interval between the publication of a sanitary or phytosanitary regulation and its entry into force *in order to* allow time for producers in exporting Members, and particularly in developing country Members, to adapt their products and methods of production to the requirements of the importing Member."

44 The Preamble of the PSI: "*Mindful that* such programmes must be carried out without giving rise to unnecessary delays or unequal treatment. ..."

45 The WTO is generally structured as follows: (1) Ministerial Conference (the top-level decision-making body) meets every two years; (2) General Council (also as Trade Policy Review Body and Dispute Settlement Body) meets several times a year; (3) the Goods Council, Services Council and TRIPS Council report to the General Council; and (4) numerous specialized committees and working groups or parties for individual agreements or issue areas. *See* the WTO official website, https://www.wto.org/english/res_e/booksp_e/anrep_e/anrep19_chap10_e.pdf (last visited 8 June 2025).

46 MAR Art. XI:1: "The contracting parties to GATT 1947 as of the date of entry into force of this Agreement, ... shall *become original Members* of the WTO."

47 GATT Art. X:3(b): "Each contracting party shall maintain, or *institute* as soon as practicable, judicial, arbitral or administrative tribunals or procedures. ..."

48 *E.g.*, a Council, a committee, a technical expert group, the panel, subsidiary bodies, or enquiry points.

49 SCM Art. 7.4: "*The composition of the panel* and its terms of reference shall *be established* within 15 days from the date when it is established."

TABLE 4.5 The event-type of INSTITUTION in WTO Law

| Criteria | Phrases | Examples |
|---|---|---|
| Establishment | – become/be/accede/sign **[members]**<br>– maintain/institute/establish /compose/choose **[(members of) entities]**<br>– the composition of/the accession of **[(members of) entities]** | – become original Members of the WTO (MAR Art. XI:1); cease to be a Party to this Agreement (GPA Art. XXII:13); become party to an arbitration proceeding (DSU Art. 25.3)<br>– institute ... judicial, arbitral or administrative tribunals or procedures (GATT Art. X:3(b)); establish an advisory technical experts group (SPS Art. 11.2); the Members of the panel shall be chosen (PSI Art. 4(c))<br>– the composition of the panel (SCM Art. 7.4); the accession of the Government of Japan to the General Agreement (GATT Annex H) |
| Function | – meet/hold (session)/hold (office) /make available (assistance) /remind (member)/establish (list) / exercise (responsibilities)<br>– (agenda) be drawn up / (statements) be translated into /(meeting) be convened /(issue) be placed on /(schedule) be presented to | – hold dedicated session (TFA Art. 21.4); make available technical assistance (TPRM Para. D); remind a Member if that Member has not notified (TFA Art. 16.4)<br>– a provisional agenda for each session shall be drawn up (CV Annex II, Para. 12); speeches or statements made in any of these three languages shall be immediately translated into the other official languages (CV Annex II, Para. 22) |

and *meet*, can oblige the entity to perform its duty (*e.g.*, the Committee shall *hold* a dedicated session[50]).[51] The passive verbs or phrases, such as *be drawn up* and *be translated into*, appear to focus on the work required to be conducted by the entity (*e.g.*, a provisional agenda shall *be drawn up*[52]).

### 4.2.5 *Substance* (*SUB*)

SUBSTANCE as an event-type mainly introduces rights or obligations for WTO Members to take certain actions, either (1) in general terms or (2) in trade terms (Table 4.6). There is a wide variety of (trade) measures which could be considered as rights or obligations for the Members. First, the general term refers to the wordings that the Members are allowed or obliged to perform certain actions, which does not directly make a reference to trade by a plain reading of the text. For example, it can be introduced by the general verbs, such as *accord*, *provide*, and *contribute*, to require the Members to take certain actions not necessarily limited to a specific trade measure (*e.g.*, *accord special and differential treatment* to least developed countries[53]).[54] Second, the trade term focuses more directly on the wordings of conducts related to trade,[55] which can be denoted by the (nominalized) verbs, such as *import*, *sale*, and *purchase* (*e.g.*, at the time of *importation*[56]), or by the special nouns or noun

50 TFA Art. 21.4: "The Committee shall *hold* at least one dedicated session per year."

51 *E.g.*, maintain or include (lists), devise (arrangements), provide (assistance), suspend (work), designate (officials), carry out or exercise (functions), sponsor (negotiations), seek or provide (advice), initiate, determine, or publish (programme), suggest or retain (names of governmental and non-governmental individuals), invite (interested parties), prepare (a factual report), administer (requirement), take (note), serve on (an expert review group), or assist in (preparing the documentation).

52 CV Annex II, Para. 12: "A provisional agenda for each session shall *be drawn up* by the Secretary-General."

53 GPA Art. V:1: "As provided for in this Article and on request, the Parties shall *accord special and differential treatment* to [least developed countries]."

54 *E.g.*, use (standards), apply (restrictions), introduce or take (measures), maintain (requirements), exercise (restraint or direction over [another person]), protect or make (work), take place (use), carry out (invention), or pursue (the right of action).

55 *E.g.*, market, product, payment, fee, duty, charge, expenditure, profit, expense, subsidy, tax, refund, bond, allowance, contract, royalty, guarantee, licence, invoice, provision, commission, cash deposit, purchase order, order confirmation, consumption, production, competition, start-up operation, commercial exploitation, investment, procurement, shipment, automatic import licensing, customs clearance, customs convoy, customs escort, customs union, aircraft repair and maintenance services, trademark, geographical indication, layout-designs, patent, tendering, auction.

56 GATT Art. IX:3: "Whenever it is administratively practicable to do so, contracting parties should permit required marks of origin to be affixed at the time of *importation*."

TABLE 4.6 The event-type of SUBSTANCE in WTO Law

| Criteria | Phrases | Examples |
|---|---|---|
| General Term | – accord (treatment) /undertake or prevent (acts) /apply or eliminate (restrictions) /introduce (limitation) / adopt or maintain (measures) /allow or process (application) /safeguard (interests) | – accord special and differential treatment (GPA Art. V:1); preventing the following acts (TRIPS Art. 14.1); eliminate [any restrictions applied] (GATT Art. XVIII:11); introduce such a [reciprocal and proportionate] limitation (Para. 3(d) of GATT 1994); adopt or maintain [transitional measures] (GPA Art. V:3) |
| Trade Term | – import/export/produce / purchase/sale<br>– affix (marks of origin) / settle (contract) /impose or levy (duty) /form (customs union) /abolish (subsidies) /require or release (security) | – at the time of importation (GATT Art. IX:3); for purchases made under exceptionally advantageous conditions (GPA Art. XIII:1(g)); when sold for export to the country of importation (CV Art. 1.1)<br>– marks of origin to be affixed (GATT Art. IX:3); a contract settled before the additional duty is imposed (AG Art. 5.3); the formation of such a customs union or of such a free-trade (GATT Art. XXIV:5(c)) |

phrases, such as *marks of origin, goods*, and *production* (*e.g.*, *marks of origin* to be affixed[57]).

### 4.2.6 *Order* (ORD)

ORDER as an event-type refers to (1) the opinion or (2) the instruction from the (bodies of) organization, governmental authorities, or private entities (Table 4.7). First, the opinion represents a judgment of the issue concerned. For example, it can be introduced by the (nominalized) verbs along with conjunctions, such as *recognize that*, *find that*, and *determine that*, to confirm a belief or situation (*e.g.*, a formal *recognition* by government authorities *that* a natural

57 GATT Art. IX:3: "Whenever it is administratively practicable to do so, contracting parties should permit required *marks of origin to be affixed* at the time of importation."

TABLE 4.7 The event-type of ORDER in WTO Law

| Criteria | Phrases | Examples |
|---|---|---|
| Opinion | – recognize/determine/ find /rule/consider/judge /render/satisfy [+ **that/whether/how ...**]<br>– make (affirmative or negative) determinations / give advisory opinions on / make appropriate recommendations on | – a formal recognition by government authorities that [a disaster occurred] (AG Annex 2, Para. 8(a)); the authorities determine that the countervailing duty is no longer warranted (SCM Art. 21.2); it is subsequently found that there has been no infringement or threat of infringement of an intellectual property right (TRIPS Art. 50.7)<br>– affirmative or negative [determinations], may be made (ADP Art. 6.8); give advisory opinions on the nature of any subsidy proposed to be introduced or currently maintained by that Member (SCM Art. 24.4) |
| Instruction | – establish (penalty)/ fix (timetable) /grant (waiver)/set (deadlines) / accord (sufficient time) /award (contract)/ appoint (persons)/assign (responsibilities)<br>– authorize (to effect registration) /recommend (to withdraw) /order (to desist)/request (to bring forward review) | – establish a penalty for that person (TFA Art. 6.3.6); fix the timetable for the panel process (DSU Art. 12.3); any waiver granted for a period of more than one year (MAR Art. IX:4)<br>– authorize [the United Nations] to effect registration of this Agreement (GATT Art. XXVI:7); recommend that the subsidizing Member withdraw the subsidy (SCM Art. 4.7); order a party to desist from an infringement (TRIPS Art. 44.1) |

or like disaster ... has occurred or is occurring[58]), or by the noun phrases, such as *make determinations, give opinions* and *make recommendations* to introduce

58 AG Annex 2, Para. 8(a): "Eligibility for such payments shall arise only following *a formal recognition by government authorities that* a natural or like disaster (including disease outbreaks, pest infestations, nuclear accidents, and war on the territory of the Member concerned) has occurred or is occurring;...."

a statement that expresses an (dis-)agreement or thought (*e.g.*, preliminary and final *determinations, affirmative or negative*, may be made[59]). Second, the instruction refers to a suggestion or a request of actions given by the authorities. For example, the authorities can make official rules of conduct introduced by the verbs, such as *establish, fix*, and *grant* (*e.g., establishing a penalty* for that person[60]), or give official permission, suggestion, or request introduced by the verbs, such as *authorize, recommend*, and *order* (*e.g.*, the United Nations *is authorized* to effect registration[61]).

### 4.2.7 *Application* (APP)

APPLICATION as an event-type deals with the employment of legal provisions. It usually determines the material scope of the provisions by (1) positive specification or (2) negative specification (Table 4.8).[62] First, the positive specification demonstrates the general requirement provided for by a legal provision to a situation that meets the conditions thereof. For example, it can be introduced by the active verbs, such as *apply, provide*, and *cover*, to illustrate certain situations falling within the scope of the legal provisions (*e.g.*, the provisions of this Article shall *apply mutatis mutandis* ... to decisions under Article 10 to apply duties retroactively[63]), or by the passive verbs, such as *be invoked, be used*, or *be followed*, to indicate that the legal provisions should be properly employed (*e.g.*, Article XXXV of that Agreement had been invoked earlier[64]). Other common phrases, such as *become subject to, recourse to*, and *pursuant to*, can also signal the invocation of the legal provisions in relation to specific situations (*e.g.*, border measures ... shall *become subject to* the provisions of paragraph 2 of Article 4[65]). Second, the negative specification refers to a statement

59 ADP Art. 6.8: "In cases in which any interested party refuses access to, or otherwise does not provide, necessary information within a reasonable period or significantly impedes the investigation, *preliminary and final determinations, affirmative or negative*, may *be made* on the basis of the facts available."

60 TFA Art. 6.3.6: "... the Member is encouraged to, where appropriate, consider this fact as a potential mitigating factor when *establishing a penalty* for that person."

61 GATT Art. XXVI:7: "The United Nations *is authorized* to effect registration of this Agreement as soon as it enters into force."

62 Raftopoulos (n 24), 166.

63 ADP Art. 12.3: "The provisions of this Article shall *apply mutatis mutandis* to the initiation and completion of reviews pursuant to Article 11 and to decisions under Article 10 to apply duties retroactively."

64 MAR Art. XIII:2: "Paragraph 1 may *be invoked* between original Members of the WTO which were contracting parties to GATT 1947 only where Article XXXV of that Agreement *had been invoked* earlier. ..."

65 AG Annex 5, Para. 6 "Border measures other than ordinary customs duties maintained in respect of the designated products shall *become subject to* the provisions of paragraph 2 of

TABLE 4.8 The event-type of APPLICATION in WTO Law

| Criteria | Phrases | Examples |
|---|---|---|
| Positive Specification | – apply (*mutatis mutandis*) / provide/cover<br>– be invoked/be used /be reversed/be followed /be met/be bound /be determined under /be dealt with under<br>– become subject to /have recourse to/abide by /take into account (if relevant) / pursuant to | – the provisions of this Article shall apply *mutatis mutandis* to [decisions to apply duties] (ADP Art. 12.3); Articles 2 through 7 provide methods of [customs value determination] (Art. 1 of CV's Commentary)<br>– Article XXXV of that Agreement had been invoked earlier (MAR Art. XIII:2); [simplified consultation procedures] may also be used (Para. 8 of GATT's Understanding on BOP Provisions); the order of application of Articles 5 and 6 shall be reversed (CV Art. 4)<br>– border measures ... shall become subject to the provisions of paragraph 2 of Article 4 (AG Annex 5, Para. 6); [Members] shall have recourse to, and abide by, the rules and procedures of this Understanding (DSU Art. 23.1) |
| Negative Specification | – not apply to/not require / not give rise to obligations /not intended to prevent / not arise under /impose no obligation /no ... be bound / nothing in ... prevent / without prejudice to<br>– deviate from/depart from / release from/exempt from / postpone/suspend/delay/ reserve | – the provisions of Part II of GATT 1994 shall not apply to measures taken by a Member under specific mandatory legislation (Para. 3(a) of GATT 1994); the provisions of subparagraph (b) of this paragraph shall not require the elimination or substitution of procedures in force (GATT Art. X:3(c)); nothing in this Article shall prevent any contracting party from imposing at any time on the importation of any product (GATT Art. II:2) |

TABLE 4.8 The event-type of APPLICATION in WTO Law (*cont.*)

| Criteria | Phrases | Examples |
|---|---|---|
| | | – be free to deviate from the provisions (TRIMS Art. 4); be free to postpone the application of the provisions (GATT Art. III:3); a temporary suspension of a concession (GATT Annex I, Ad Art. XVIII, Paras. 18 and 22) |

that the legal provisions should not be employed (or not in the normal way) under certain conditions. For example, some situations can be carved out from the scope of the legal provisions introduced by the negative phrases, such as *not apply*, *not require*, and *not give rise to* (*e.g.*, the provisions of Part II of GATT 1994 shall *not apply* to measures taken by a Member under specific mandatory legislation[66]). The negative specification also can be expressed to allow the Members to bypass the normal employment of the legal provisions, such as *deviate*,[67] *postpone*,[68] and *suspend*.[69]

### 4.2.8 *Effect* (EFF)

EFFECT as an event-type illustrates (1) the existence or (2) the validity of legal provisions, measures, or entities (Table 4.9). First, the existence refers to the state of being known or recognized. For example, the legal provisions are usually introduced by the verb phrases, such as *entry into force* and *abandon*, to

Article 4 with effect from the beginning of the year in which the special treatment ceases to apply."

66 Para. 3(a) of GATT 1994: "The provisions of Part II of GATT 1994 shall *not apply to* measures taken by a Member under specific mandatory legislation, enacted by that Member before it became a contracting party to GATT 1947,…."

67 TRIMS Art. 4: "A developing country Member shall *be free to deviate* temporarily from the provisions of Article 2 to the extent and in such a manner as Article XVIII of GATT 1994…."

68 GATT Art. III:3: "… the contracting party imposing the tax shall *be free to postpone the application of* the provisions of paragraph 2 to such tax until such time as it can obtain release from the obligations of such trade agreement. …"

69 GATT Annex I, Ad Art. XVIII, Paras. 18 and 22: "Such contracting party would have the right to safeguard its interests through such a temporary *suspension of a concession*. …"

TABLE 4.9 The event-type of EFFECT in WTO Law

| Criteria | Phrases | Examples |
|---|---|---|
| Existence | – entry into force /(have or remain) in force /abandon<br>– [countries] come into existence /[a part of empire] detach from | – the provisions … have entered into force under the GATT 1947 (Para. 1(b) of GATT 1994); a Member has in force a system of equitable remuneration (TRIPS Art. 14.4); this Protocol was abandoned on 1 January 1968 (GATT Ad Art. XXXVI, Para. 1, Fn. 12)<br>– [the Dominions of India and Pakistan] had not come into existence (GATT Annex A, Para. 5); a part of the Ottoman Empire and detached from it on July 24, 1923 (GATT Art. I:3) |
| Validity | – (take, have, or enter) into effect /(become or make) effective /(be or remain) valid/validity<br>– expire (expiry) /terminate (termination) /elapse/ lapse/invalidate/revoke | – [withdrawal] shall take effect on the sixtieth day following the day (GATT Art. XVIII:12(e)); [a modification] shall become effective only where … (GPA Art. XIX:5); [assessments] shall remain valid for three years (RO Art. 2(h)); the period of licence validity shall be of reasonable duration (LIC Art. 3.5(g))<br>– this provision shall expire eight years from the date of … (SCM Art. 27.11); [any waiver] in effect on the date of entry into force of the WTO Agreement shall terminate (Para. 2 of GATT's Understanding on Waiver) |

represent their existence in the legal order (*e.g.*, *entry into force* of the WTO Agreement[70]). To describe the factual status of an entity, the verb phrases, such

70 Para. 1(b) of GATT 1994: "the provisions of the legal instruments set forth below that *have entered into force* under the GATT 1947 before the date of *entry into force* of the WTO Agreement;…."

as *come into existence* and *detach from*, can be found (*e.g.*, [The Dominions of India and Pakistan] *had not come into existence*[71]). Second, the validity refers to the fact of having (legal) force or being (legally) acceptable. For example, the wordings *effect* (*effective*) or *valid* (*validity*) are commonly employed to demonstrate the fact of being applicable (*e.g.*, such withdrawal shall *take effect*[72] or such assessment shall *remain valid*[73]). On the other hand, the verbs, such as *expire* or *terminate*, can be found to regulate the fact of coming to an end or not being in effect (*e.g.*, this provision shall *expire*[74] or any definitive countervailing duty shall *be terminated*[75]).

## 4.3 Eight Types of Procedural Events

In the general content of WTO Law, most of the procedural rules can be found in the DSU and the TPRM. However, as mentioned in the previous section, the purpose of this research is to establish the *event-types* for temporal rules in a syntactical sense, and therefore the concept of "procedural events" is used broadly to denote dynamic eventualities in legal process regardless of the legal nature of a specific agreement. Those procedural events usually can be broken down to smaller activities or stages which hold at short intervals or instants as part of the general legal process. In other words, these minimal activities or stages may be grouped together under a larger process of the similar kind. By close and careful reading of the twenty agreements of WTO Law, this section proposes eight types of procedural events, and provides criteria and examples in details as follows (Figure 4.2). The criteria and examples in the following subsections are representative not exhaustive.

71 GATT Annex A, Para. 5: "The Dominions of India and Pakistan have not been mentioned separately in the above list since they *had not come into existence* as such on the base date of April 10, 1947."

72 GATT Art. XVIII:12(e): "such withdrawal shall *take effect* on the sixtieth day following the day on which the notice is received by him."

73 RO Art. 2(h): "Such assessments shall *remain valid* for three years provided that the facts and conditions, including the rules of origin, under which they have been made remain comparable."

74 SCM Art. 27.11: "This provision shall *expire* eight years from the date of entry into force of the WTO Agreement."

75 SCM Art. 21.3: "... any definitive countervailing duty shall *be terminated* on a date not later than five years from its imposition. ..."

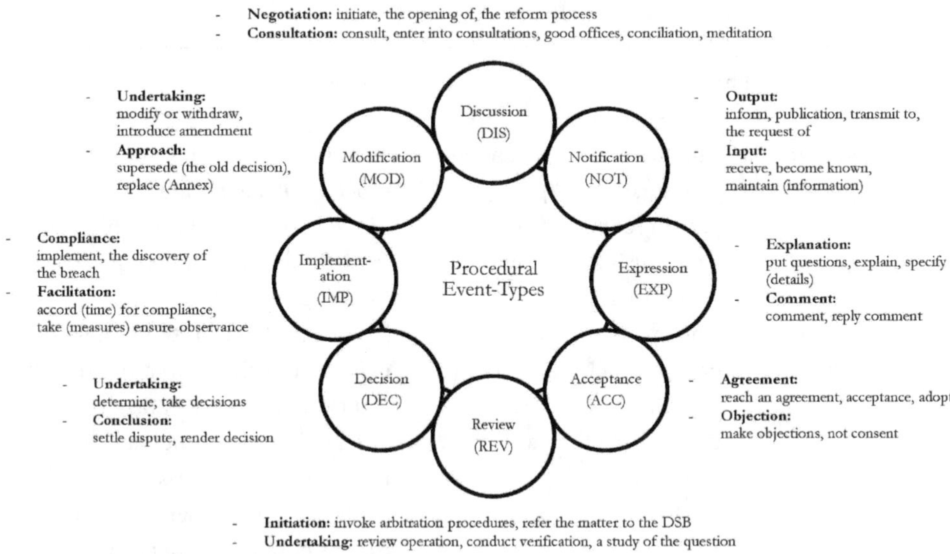


FIGURE 4.2 Eight types of procedural events in WTO Law

### 4.3.1 *Discussion (DIS)*

DISCUSSION as an event-type contains the general process of getting advice, exchanging opinions, or finding solutions. Based on the number of members involved, two criteria for DISCUSSION can be observed (Table 4.10). First, the negotiation emphasizes the process of formal discussion among the entire or broad membership with the attempt to reach an agreement or find solutions to the issue concerned. For example, the process of negotiation can be introduced by the verbs, such as *initiate*, *enter*, and *conclude*, to indicate the different stages of the overall process (*e.g.*, negotiations for continuing the process will be *initiated*[76]), or introduced by the noun phrases, such as *the opening of*, *rounds of*, and *the conclusion of*, to represent the progress in the activities (*e.g.*, *the opening of* negotiations on an agreement or arrangement[77]). The special term of *reform* can also signal the process of negotiation (*e.g.*, *the reform process* as determined under Article 20 of the Agreement on Agriculture[78]). Second, the consultation refers to the process of discussing an issue with a particular

---

76 AG Art. 20: "Members agree that *negotiations* for continuing the process will *be initiated* one year before the end of the implementation period,...."

77 GATS Art. VII:4(b): "Each Member shall ... promptly inform the Council for Trade in Services as far in advance as possible of *the opening of negotiations* on an agreement or arrangement of the type referred to in paragraph 1."

78 AG Art. 9: "The provisions of this Article shall remain in force for the duration of *the reform process* as determined under Article 20."

TABLE 4.10 The event-type of DISCUSSION in WTO Law

| Criteria | Phrases | Examples |
|---|---|---|
| Negotiation | – [initiate/enter into/undertake /take place/participate in /conclude/bring to a conclusion /complete] negotiation<br>– [the opening of/rounds of /the conclusion of] negotiation<br>– the reform process | – negotiations for continuing the process will be initiated (AG Art. 20); arranging for multilateral tariff negotiations to take place (GATT Annex I, Ad XXVIII, Para. 3); [any contracting party] shall participate in such negotiations (GATT Annex I, Ad XXVIII, Para. 1.3)<br>– as far in advance as possible of the opening of negotiations (GATS Art. VII:4(b)); through successive rounds of multilateral negotiations (the preamble of GATS)<br>– the duration of the reform process as determined under Article 20 (AG Art. 9) |
| Consultation | – consult/discuss<br>– [initiate/(invite to) enter into /(afford/grant/provide) opportunity for/ hold/occur/be invited for / participate in/complete] consultation/discussion<br>– [a forum for/procedures for] consultation<br>– [enter into/begin/continue /terminate] good offices, conciliation or mediation | – [the CONTRACTING PARTIES] may consult with any contracting party or parties (GATT Art. XXII:2); [the contracting party] shall ... discuss with the other contracting party or parties concerned (GATT Art. XVI:1)<br>– Members shall ... enter into consultations (SPS Art. 4.2); each contracting party shall afford ... opportunity for consultations (GATT Art. XXXVII:5)<br>– [a committee] is established to provide a regular forum for consultations (SPS Art. 15.1)<br>– [good offices, conciliation or mediation] may begin at any time and be terminated at any time (DSU Art. 5.3) |

member or a limited number of the membership in order to get their advice or opinions. For example, the wordings *consult* (*consultation*) and *discuss* (*discussion*) are commonly found to indicate the general obligation for conducting the process (*e.g.*, *consult* with any contracting party or parties[79]). By conjoining with the verbs, such as *enter*, *hold*, and *complete*, it highlights the different stages of consultation (*e.g.*, *enter* into consultations with the aim of achieving bilateral and multilateral agreements[80]). Other procedural mechanisms may be grouped together with consultation due to the fact that these processes also dealing with discussion between the particular members involved to end their disagreement, such as *good offices*, *conciliation*, and *mediation*.[81]

### 4.3.2 *Notification* (NOT)

NOTIFICATION as an event-type deals with the process of delivery or receipt of information. Based on the direction of the information flow, two criteria for NOTIFICATION can be observed (Table 4.11). First, the output information focuses on the action of telling officially about something that has happened or will happen. For example, the output can be introduced by the verbs, such as *inform*, *notify*, and *report*, to represent the act of giving information to someone (*e.g.*, *inform* the authorities of that Member[82]), or by the nouns, such as *information*, *notification*, and *publication* (*e.g.*, such *publication* shall take place[83]).[84] The verb phrases, such as *transmit to*, *send to*, and *forward to*, can

79 GATT Art. XXII:2: "The CONTRACTING PARTIES may, at the request of a contracting party, *consult* with any contracting party or parties in respect of any matter for which it has not been possible to find a satisfactory solution through consultation under paragraph 1."

80 SPS Art. 4.2: "Members shall, upon request, *enter into consultations* with the aim of achieving bilateral and multilateral agreements on recognition of the equivalence of specified sanitary or phytosanitary measures."

81 DSU Art. 5.3: "*Good offices, conciliation or mediation* may be requested at any time by any party to a dispute. They may *begin* at any time and *be terminated* at any time."

82 DSU Art. 13.1: "However, before a panel seeks such information or advice from any individual or body within the jurisdiction of a Member it shall *inform* the authorities of that Member."

83 LIC Art. 1.4(a): "*Such publication* shall *take place*, whenever practicable, 21 days prior to the effective date of the requirement but in all events not later than such effective date." Noting that the term "whenever practicable" is not denoted as a temporal rule due to the research focus on "events." *See supra*, Section 3.1.2.

84 *E.g.*, provide/submit/publish + [relevant information/necessary information/sufficient information/a list of all the information/a non-confidential summary of the information/the actual information/all pertinent information/documentation/documents/data/evidence/copies/brief reports/the full text of the written application/rules of origin, judicial decisions, and administrative rulings of general application relating to rules of origin/the modified or new rule/any modifications/brief reports].

TABLE 4.11 The event-type of NOTIFICATION in WTO Law

| Criteria | Phrases | Examples |
|---|---|---|
| Output | – inform/notify/publish/report/present /submit/deposit/share/exchange/disclose<br>– [supply/make available/provide/release] information /[serve/give/bring] notice /[make] notification /[take place] publication /[provide] documentation /[take place] disclosure<br>– transmit to/send to/forward to /circulate to/communicate to /convey to/furnish to/post on<br>– seek/request/apply/file (application) | – [the panel] shall inform the authorities of that Member (DSU Art. 13.1); [any changes] shall be notified to the Committee (TBT Art. 15.2); the deposit of its instrument of accession (GPA Art. XXII:2)<br>– if information is not supplied (ADP Annex II, Para. 1); such publication shall take place (LIC 1.4(a)); a procuring entity shall ... make available tender documentation (GPA Art. X:10(a))<br>– [the competent body] transmits ... the results of the procedure (SPS Annex C, Para. 1(b)); preshipment inspection entities send to exporters or to designated representatives of the exporters a Clean Report of Findings (PSI Art. 2.18)<br>– [a Member] shall make a request for information only after (TFA Art. 12.3); [waivers] be granted only on application by the contracting party (GATT Annex I, Ad Art. VI: 6(b)) |
| Input | – receive/obtain/access (remain accessible) / gather (information-gathering process)<br>– know (become known)/acquaint<br>– maintain/retain (retention)/record | – after the response to the questionnaire has been received (ADP Annex I, Para. 7); from the information obtained from other interested parties (ADP Annex II, Para. 7)<br>– after the adverse use of the protected indication has become generally known (TRIPS Art. 24.7)<br>– maintain the documentation and reports of tendering procedures and contract awards (GPA Art. XVI:3); the period of retention of such information (TFA Art. 12.10(d)) |

also represent the communication of information to others (*e.g.*, *transmit* the results of the procedure *to* the applicant[85]). In addition, the active verbs, such as *seek*, *request*, and *apply*, can also convey information regarding an intention or attempt to get something or to get someone to do something (*e.g.*, *the request of* the Chairman[86]). Second, the input information refers to the process of getting information from others and keeping it in a system or knowledge. This process can go through different stages, such as *receive* [information],[87] [information] *become known*,[88] and *maintain* [information].[89]

### 4.3.3 *Expression* (EXP)

EXPRESSION as an event-type involves the process of presenting the opinions or reasons in more detail. Two criteria for EXPRESSION can be observed (Table 4.12). First, the explanation emphasizes the details or reasons, that someone gives to make something clear or easy to understand. For example, the process can be invoked before someone provides the details or reasons introduced by the verbs, such as *put* [questions], *ask for* [explanations], and *invite* [views] (*e.g.*, *put* questions to the parties and *ask* them for explanations[90]). In terms of providing the details or reasons, the process can be introduced by the verbs, such as *answer* [enquiries], *explain* [justification], and *complete* [questionnaires] (*e.g.*, *explain* the justification for that technical regulation[91]). As for the

85 SPS Annex C, Para. 1(b): "the competent body *transmits* as soon as possible the results of the procedure in a precise and complete manner *to* the applicant so that corrective action may be taken if necessary. ..."

86 CV Annex II, Para. 9: "The date of the meeting may be varied either at *the request* of any member of the Technical Committee concurred in by a simple majority of the members of the Technical Committee or, in cases requiring urgent attention, at *the request* of the Chairman."

87 ADP Annex I, Para. 7: "[the on-the-spot investigation] should be carried out after the response to the questionnaire *has been received*. ..."

88 TRIPS Art. 24.7: "A Member may provide that any request made under this Section in connection with the use or registration of a trademark must be presented within five years after the adverse use of the protected indication *has become generally known* in that Member. ..."

89 GPA Art. XVI:3: "Each procuring entity shall, for a period of at least three years from the date it awards a contract, *maintain: a. the documentation and reports* of tendering procedures and contract awards. ..."

90 DSU Appendix 3, Para. 8: "The panel may at any time *put questions* to the parties and *ask them for explanations* either in the course of a meeting with the parties or in writing."

91 TBT Art. 2.5: "A Member preparing, adopting or applying a technical regulation which may have a significant effect on trade of other Members shall, upon the request of another Member, *explain the justification* for that technical regulation in terms of the provisions of paragraphs 2 to 4."

TABLE 4.12 The event-type of EXPRESSION in WTO Law

| Criteria | Phrases | Examples |
|---|---|---|
| Explanation | – put (questions)/ask for (explanations)/prepare (submissions) /invite (views)/raise (a point of order)/prepare and submit (a challenge)/communicate (claim)<br>– answer (enquiries)/explain (justification or reasons)/ complete (questionnaire)/ reply (questionnaire or the request)/response (questionnaire)/present (argumentation)/address (the issues raised)/provide or give (reasons) /defend (interests)/have the right to be heard/have the right to take the floor<br>– specify (the time-period) / indicate (the best mode) / describe (the measures) /state (the period of validity) /name (the contracting party which has requested the action) **[specific content]** | – put questions to the parties and ask them for explanations (DSU Appendix 3, Para. 8); provide sufficient time for the parties to the dispute to prepare their submissions (DSU Art. 12.4); be invited in writing to present their views (DSU Appendix 3, Para. 6)<br>– answer enquiries and provide the forms and documents (TFA Art. 1.3.4); explain the justification for that technical regulation (TBT Art. 2.5); undertake to complete the annual questionnaire on import licensing procedures (TFA Art. 7.3); the Appellate Body shall address each of the issues raised (DSU Art. 17.12)<br>– [the panel] shall specify in its recommendation the time-period (SCM Art. 4.7); indicate the best mode for carrying out the invention (TRIPS Art. 29.1); describe the measures which the Member proposes to take (Para. 1 of GATT's Understanding on Waivers) |
| Comment | – comment<br>– [make/submit/reply/ discuss/take into account] comment | – provide [a time period] to comment on the proposed introduction or amendment of laws and regulations (TFA Art. 2.1.1) |

TABLE 4.12 The event-type of EXPRESSION in WTO Law (*cont.*)

| Criteria | Phrases | Examples |
|---|---|---|
| | | – allow [time] for other Members to make comments in writing (SPS Annex B, Para. 5(d)); [comments] shall be replied to as promptly as possible (TBT Annex 3, Para. N); make comments in writing, discuss these comments ..., and take these written comments ... into account (SPS Annex B, Para. 5(d)) |

content of explanation, the verbs, such as *specify*, *indicate*, and *describe*, can be found to signal the specific details required (*e.g.*, *specify* in its recommendation the time period[92]). Second, the comment refers to the opinions or remarks that someone gives to something that was proposed and not completely certain. For example, the wording *comment* is employed to the act of expressing certain opinions on the proposals (*e.g.*, provide opportunities to *comment* on the proposed introduction or amendment of laws and regulations[93]). The act of comment can also process through different stages by conjoining with the verbs, such as *make*, *reply*, and *discuss* (*e.g.*, [c]omments received ... shall, if so requested, be *replied*[94]).

### 4.3.4 *Acceptance* (ACC)

ACCEPTANCE as an event-type contains the process of agreeing or objecting to an opinion or offering. Based on the outcome, two criteria for ACCEPTANCE can be observed (Table 4.13). First, the agreement describes the act of approving

92 SCM Art. 4.7: "In this regard, the panel shall *specify* in its recommendation the time-period within which the measure must be withdrawn."

93 TFA Art. 2.1.1: "Each Member shall ... provide opportunities and an appropriate time period to traders and other interested parties to *comment* on the proposed introduction or amendment of laws and regulations of general application related to the movement, release, and clearance of goods, including goods in transit."

94 TBT Annex 3, Para. N: "*Comments* received through standardizing bodies that have accepted this Code of Good Practice shall, if so requested, *be replied to* as promptly as possible."

TABLE 4.13 The event-type of ACCEPTANCE in WTO Law

| Criteria | Phrases | Examples |
|---|---|---|
| Agreement | – [reach/obtain] agreement /[be or remain open for] acceptance /[require/ obtain] approval /be considered for adoption / [reach/decide/be made or taken by] consensus /affirm adherence /require assurance /make commitment<br>– agreement/acceptance/ approval /adoption<br>– adopt/agree/accept/ approve/concur | – a Member has reached an agreement with any other country or countries (TBT Art. 10.7); [this Agreement] shall be open for acceptance (CA Art. 9.1.2); require approval by the Committee (TFA Art. 19.2(c))<br>– upon acceptance by two thirds of the Parties (GPA Art. XXII:11(i)); upon approval by the Ministerial Conference (MAR Art. X:8); the date of adoption of the panel's report or the Appellate Body's report (SCM Art. 4.10)<br>– the report shall be adopted by the DSB (SCM Art. 7.6); [the amendment] has been accepted by such Signatory (CA Art. 9.5.1); the Parties may agree to the delayed application of any specific obligation (GPA Art. V:4) |
| Objection | – object (objection)/refuse<br>– not consent /without the consent /not concur | – such objections shall be made within 45 days (GPA Art. XIX:2); The registration of a trademark for wines ... shall be refused (TRIPS Art. 23.2)<br>– either of the contracting parties ... does not consent to such application (GATT Art. XXXV:1(b)); without the consent of the patent owner (TRIPS Art. 34.1); the CONTRACTING PARTIES have not concurred in such measure (GATT Art. XVIII:17) |

or accepting an offering, or the fact of having the same opinion. For example, the process of agreement can go through different stages introduced by the verb phrases, such as *reach an agreement, obtain agreement,* and *be open for acceptance* (*e.g.*, a Member *has reached* an agreement with any other country or countries[95]), or simply by the nouns, such as *acceptance, approval,* and *adoption* (*e.g.*, upon *acceptance* by two thirds of the Parties[96]). In addition, various verbs can also represent the act of agreement, such as *adopt, agree,* and *accept* (*e.g.*, the report shall *be adopted* by the DSB[97]). Second, the objection concerns the act of expressing opposition or unwillingness to accept an opinion or offering. It is usually introduced by the (nominalized) verbs, such as *object* and *refuse* (*e.g.*, such *objections* shall be made[98]), or by the negative phrases, such as *not consent* and *not concur* (*e.g.*, either of the contracting parties ... does *not consent* to such application[99]).

### 4.3.5 *Review (REV)*

REVIEW as an event-type represents the process of examination to consider some issues or disputes carefully in order to discover or solve them. Based on the stages in the process, two criteria for REVIEW can be observed (Table 4.14). First, the initiation emphasizes the beginning point when the examination can be invoked or start. For example, it can be introduced by the verbs, such as *invoke* and *initiate*, to begin the process of examination (*e.g.*, a modifying or any objecting Party may *invoke* the arbitration procedures[100]). The verb phrases, such as *refer to, be submitted to,* and *be subject to,* are also found to direct the subject matter to the examination (*e.g.*, *refer* the matter to the

95 TBT Art. 10.7: "Whenever a Member *has reached an agreement* with any other country or countries on issues related to technical regulations, standards or conformity assessment procedures which may have a significant effect on trade, at least one Member party to the agreement shall notify other Members through the Secretariat. ..."

96 GPA Art. XXII:11(i): "An amendment shall enter into force: i. except as provided for in subparagraph (b), in respect of those Parties that accept it, upon *acceptance* by two thirds of the Parties and thereafter for each other Party upon *acceptance* by it;...."

97 SCM Art. 7.6: "Within 30 days of the issuance of the panel's report to all Members, the report shall *be adopted* by the DSB unless. ..."

98 GPA Art. XIX:2: "*Such objections* shall *be made* within 45 days from the date of the circulation to the Parties of the notification, and shall set out reasons for the objection."

99 GATT Art. XXXV:1(b): "either of the contracting parties, at the time either becomes a contracting party, *does not consent* to such application. ..."

100 GPA Art. XIX:7: "... a modifying or any objecting Party may *invoke the arbitration procedures* within 120 days of circulation of the notification of the proposed modification. ..."

TABLE 4.14 The event-type of REVIEW in WTO Law

| Criteria | Phrases | Examples |
|---|---|---|
| Initiation | – invoke (arbitration) / initiate (investigation or review)<br>– refer the matter to (the Dispute Settlement Body) /be submitted to (arbitration) /be subject to (review) /be lodged with (a court or tribunal) | – invoke the arbitration procedures (GPA Art. XIX:7); in any event before the initiation of any investigation (SCM Art. 13.1); the date of the initiation of the review (ADP Art. 9.5)<br>– refer the matter to the Dispute Settlement Body (SCM Art. 4.4); the determination ... shall be submitted to binding arbitration (SCM Art. 8.5); all restrictions ... shall be subject to periodic review (Para. 7 of GATT's Understanding on BOP Provisions) |
| Undertaking | – review/examine/investigate /assess/verify/appeal<br>– conduct (verification) / carry out (review) /undertake or complete (process or procedures) /terminate (investigation) /conclude (work on matters) /accelerate (proceedings)<br>– [make] a study of /[undertake] an overview of / [undertake] an appraisal of /[proceed] the panel process /[completion of] the appeal /the appellate proceeding /the consideration of rebuttal submissions and oral arguments | – review the operation of this Article (MAR Art. XIII:4); examine the request [for participation] (GPA Art. IX:11); investigate any matter so referred (GATT Art. XXIII:2)<br>– conducting price verification (PSI Art. 20(c)); the review process shall be undertaken (AG Art. 18.2); such [control, inspection and approval] procedures are undertaken and completed (SPS Annex C, Para. 1(a)<br>– a study of this question shall be made (CV Annex III, Para. 5); an annual overview of developments in the international trading environment (TPRM Para. G); undertake an appraisal of the operation (TPRM Para. F) |

Dispute Settlement Body[101]). Second, the undertaking focuses on the work or effort of examination. For example, the specific verbs, such as *review, examine,* and *investigate,* are commonly employed to represent the general act of examination (*e.g., review* the operation of this Article[102]). The working progress in the examination can be identified through other conjoined verbs, such as *conduct, accelerate,* and *complete* (*e.g., conducting* price verification[103]). The noun phrases, such as *a study of, an overview of,* and *an appraisal of,* are also found to represent the act of examination (*e.g., a study of* this question shall be made[104]).[105]

### 4.3.6 *Decision* (DEC)

DECISION as an event-type refers to the process of determination to make an official opinion or judgement about some issues or disputes. Based on the stages in the process, two criteria for DECISION can be observed (Table 4.15). First, the undertaking focuses on the work or effort of determination. For example, the act of determination can be introduced by the specific verbs, such as *determine* and *decide* (*e.g., determine* the rules and procedures to be followed[106]), or by the specific nouns, such as *decision, ruling,* and *recommendation* (*e.g.,* any *decision* to grant a waiver shall be taken[107]). Second, the conclusion emphasizes the ending point when the determination can be completed. For example, the (nominalized) verbs, such as *settle, render,* and *issue,*[108] are usually employed

101 SCM Art. 4.4: "... any Member party to such consultations may *refer the matter to the Dispute Settlement Body* ("DSB") for the immediate establishment of a panel, unless. ..."

102 MAR Art. XIII:4: "The Ministerial Conference may *review* the operation of this Article in particular cases at the request of any Member and make appropriate recommendations."

103 PSI Art. 20(c): "when *conducting price verification,* preshipment inspection entities shall make appropriate allowances for the terms of the sales contract and generally applicable adjusting factors pertaining to the transaction."

104 CV Annex III, Para. 5: "If such problems arise in practice in developing country Members applying the Agreement, *a study* of this question shall *be made,* at the request of such Members, with a view to finding appropriate solutions."

105 *E.g.,* appeal, assessment, review (process), examination, investigation, inspection, verification, (arbitration/control, inspection and approval) procedures, (dispute settlement) proceedings, or on-the-spot visit.

106 DSU Art. 1.2: "... the Chairman of the Dispute Settlement Body ... shall *determine* the rules and procedures to be followed within 10 days after a request by either Member."

107 MAR Art. IX:3(a): "If consensus is not reached during the time-period, *any decision* to grant a waiver shall *be taken* by three fourths of the Members."

108 *E.g.,* issue + [decision/administrative determinations/an advance ruling/an interim report/the descriptive (factual and argument) sections of its draft report/rulings or recommendations/assessments of the origin].

to signal the completion of determination or disputes (*e.g.*, an expeditious *settlement* of the dispute by the panel;[109] or the decision on the dispute shall *be rendered*[110]).

TABLE 4.15 The event-type of DECISION in WTO Law

| Criteria | Phrases | Examples |
|---|---|---|
| Undertaking | – determine/decide<br>– [take/make/take place/ carry out/lead to] decision/ruling/recommendation /determination | – determine the rules and procedures to be followed (DSU Art. 1.2); decide exclusively by consensus to add that agreement to Annex 4 (MAR Art. X:9)<br>– any decision to grant a waiver shall be taken by three fourths of the Members (MAR Art. IX:3(a)); make its decisions or recommendations in a timely fashion (GPA Art. XVIII:6(f)); the determination of the final liability for payment of anti-dumping duties shall take place (ADP Art. 9.3.1) |
| Conclusion | – settle/resolve (dispute/ situation/issue)<br>– render/issue/give/provide (decision/determination)<br>– provide/issue (report)<br>– present (conclusion)<br>– state/issue (ruling) | – an expeditious settlement of the dispute by the panel (PSI Art. 4(d))<br>– the decision … shall be rendered (PSI Art. 4(g))<br>– issue a Clean Report of Findings (PSI Art. 16)<br>– present its conclusions to the Members (SCM Art. 8.5)<br>– immediately state a ruling (CV Annex II, Para. 18) |

109 PSI Art. 4(d): "The independent trade expert shall take the necessary decisions to ensure an expeditious *settlement of the dispute* by the panel. …"

110 PSI Art. 4(g): "*The decision* on the dispute shall *be rendered* within eight working days of the request for independent review and be communicated to the parties to the dispute."

### 4.3.7 *Implementation* (*IMP*)

IMPLEMENTATION as an event-type refers to the process of putting legal rules, rulings, or commitments into action. Two criteria for IMPLEMENTATION can be observed (Table 4.16). First, the compliance concerns the act of obeying legal rules, rulings, or commitments. For example, the act of obeying can be introduced by the verbs, such as *implement, comply,* and *follow,* to require actions to be operated in line with the legal rules, rulings, or commitments (*e.g., implement* the provisions of paragraph 6[111]). To further ascertain the result of obeying, the verb phrases, such as *discover the breach, challenge the consistency,* and *raise the issue of implementation,* are employed to question if the actions obey the legal rules, rulings, or commitments (*e.g., the discovery of the breach* by the customs administration[112]). Second, the facilitation refers to the particular requirements to make the act of obeying possible or easier. For example, the obedience can be promoted through specific actions, such as *accord* (*time*) *for compliance, list* (*measures*) *which are inconsistent,* and *ensure* (*changes*) *not result in a lesser degree of consistency* (*e.g.,* longer time-frames *for compliance* should be accorded[113]). Besides, the general requests for taking actions to ensure obedience can also be found (*e.g.,* take such reasonable measures to *ensure its observance*[114]).

### 4.3.8 *Modification* (*MOD*)

MODIFICATION as an event-type relates to the process of changing legal rules, rulings, or commitments. Two criteria for MODIFICATION can be observed (Table 4.17). First, the undertaking focuses on the general act of changing legal rules, rulings, or commitments. For example, the verbs, such as *modify,*

---

111 AG Annex 5, Para. 5: "Where the special treatment is not to be continued at the end of the implementation period, the Member concerned shall *implement* the provisions of paragraph 6."

112 TFA Art. 6.3.6: "When a person voluntarily discloses to a Member's customs administration the circumstances of a breach of a customs law, regulation, or procedural requirement prior to *the discovery of the breach* by the customs administration, the Member is encouraged to, where appropriate, consider this fact as a potential mitigating factor when establishing a penalty for that person."

113 SPS Art. 10.2: "Where the appropriate level of sanitary or phytosanitary protection allows scope for the phased introduction of new sanitary or phytosanitary measures, longer time-frames *for compliance* should *be accorded* on products of interest to developing country Members so as to maintain opportunities for their exports."

114 DSU Art. 22.9: "When the DSB has ruled that a provision of a covered agreement has not been observed, the responsible Member shall *take such reasonable measures* as may be available to it *to ensure its observance*."

TABLE 4.16 The event-type of IMPLEMENTATION in WTO Law

| Criteria | Phrases | Examples |
|---|---|---|
| Compliance | – implement/comply/follow/ fulfil /(fail to) exercise<br>– discover the breach / challenge the consistency /[ensure/bring into] conformity /considered to be in compliance /delay implementation /raise the issue of implementation /the observance of ... be possible /deficiencies in performance of /concerning the enforcement of | – implement the provisions of paragraph 6 (AG Annex 5, Para. 5); comply with the essential requirements set out in the notices and tender documentation (GPA Art. XV:4); the recommendation of the DSB is not followed (SCM Art. 4.10)<br>– the discovery of the breach by the customs administration (TFA Art. 6.3.6); retain the right to challenge the consistency of any "other duty or charge" with such obligations (Para. 5 of GATT's Understanding on Art. II:1(b)); brought into conformity with the provisions of this Agreement (SCM Art. 28.1(b)) |
| Facilitation | – accord (time) for compliance /[list/discontinue/ eliminate] inconsistent (measures) /ensure consistent result (of changes) /acquire implementation (capacity) /provide (cooperation) to facilitate the implementation /make (adjustments) in conformity with the findings<br>– take (measure/step/action) to ensure [implementation/ observance /conformity] | – longer time-frames for compliance should be accorded (SPS Art. 10.2); list in that Annex measures ... which are inconsistent with [provisions] (Para. 1 of GATS's Second Annex on Financial Services); ensure that any changes ... do not result in a lesser degree of consistency with [provisions] (TRIPS Art. 65.5)<br>– take such reasonable measures as may be available to it to ensure its observance (DSU Art. 22.9); take appropriate action in implementation of [provisions] (GATT Art. XXXVII:4) |

TABLE 4.17 The event-type of MODIFICATION in WTO Law

| Criteria | Phrases | Examples |
|---|---|---|
| Undertaking | – modify/withdraw/extend/ shorten /amend/reissue/ alter/cancel /improve/ update/renew<br>– [introduce] amendment / [introduce] modification /[include] alteration / [communicate] change / [inform] development / [notify] withdrawal /[take] corrective action /[request for] extension /[avoid] curtailment /[give] departure | – modify or withdraw any commitment in its Schedule (GATS Art. XXI:1(a)); extend the scope of any such subsidization (GATT Art. XVI:4); the possibility of altering the periodicity of consultations (Para. 7 of GATT's Understanding on BOP Provisions)<br>– when amendments can still be introduced (SPS Annex B, Para. 5(b)); any substantial change in the plan or schedule (GATT Art. XXIV:7(c)); developments during the period covered by such reviews (ADP Art. 18.6) |
| Approach | – supersede (decision) / replace (annex) /add or delete (Agreement) /incorporate into (GATT) /reduce to (not less than 10 days) / shift from ... to ... (category) | – [the new decision] supersedes the [old] decision regarding the applicable date (Para. 8 of GATT's Understanding on Art. II:1(b)); [the Annex] replace the Annex to the Agreement as established heretofore (Art. 1 of CA's Protocol); delete that Agreement from Annex 4 (MAR Art. 9) |

*withdraw*, and *extend*, are introduced to indicate the act of changing the original settings (*e.g.*, *modify or withdraw* any commitment in its Schedule[115]). The nouns, such as *amendment*, *change*, and *development*, can also represent a change made to the original plan (*e.g.*, *amendments* can still be introduced[116]).

115 GATS Art. XXI:1(a): "A Member ... may *modify or withdraw* any commitment in its Schedule, at any time after three years have elapsed from the date on which that commitment entered into force force, in accordance with the provisions of this Article."

116 SPS Annex B, Para. 5(b): "Such notifications shall take place at an early stage, when *amendments* can still *be introduced* and comments taken into account;...."

Second, the approach refers to the specific ways of changing the content of legal rules, rulings, or commitments. For example, the verbs, such as *supersede*, *replace*, and *add*, can signal how the original rules, rulings, or commitments are modified in a particular way (*e.g.*, [the new decision] *supersedes* the [old] decision regarding the applicable date[117]).

## 4.4 The Distribution of Temporal Events Association in WTO Law

As shown in Section 3.2 of the previous chapter, the density of temporal rules identified in WTO Law is about 2 % (*i.e.*, 3,741 temporal rules/193,046 textual words including footnotes), which means that one temporal rule can be found within around 50 words of the legal texts, albeit this density ratio can vary due to the nature of the differing content in each agreement. To further explore legal content in relation to temporal rules, Section 4.1 in this Chapter takes a step toward establishing the 2-D "temporal events association" model, based on the assumption that it may serve as a valuable analytical tool for recognizing the role of time in diverse legal texts across different legal systems. Drawing on the sixteen *event-types* associated with temporal rules identified in Sections 4.2 and 4.3, this section continues to discover whether there is a statistical tendency of temporal rules associated with certain legal content within the 2-D model. In other words, this research proposes to unfold the nature of legal content through the identification of different *event-types* in general (*i.e.*, eight types of substantive events and eight types of procedural events), regardless of the character of the WTO agreements in particular. This section takes a further step to quantitively study on (1) whether one could expect (in the context of WTO Law) that temporal rules would be most frequently observed under specific *event-type*(s), and (2) whether a particular *event-type* would be typically found to be associated with other *event-type*(s) through the conjunction of temporal rules.

In the following subsections, the 2-D temporal events association will be presented in matrix form, which is a rectangular grid of numbers and ratios arranged in horizontal rows and vertical columns. In this research, the matrix is defined first by vertical columns (*i.e.*, the main *event-type* highlighted in yellow) and then by horizontal rows (*i.e.*, the supporting *event-type* highlighted in

117 Para. 8 of GATT's *Understanding on Art. II:1(b)*: "The decision in paragraph 2 regarding the date applicable to each concession for the purposes of paragraph 1(b) of Article II of GATT 1994 *supersedes* the decision regarding the applicable date taken on 26 March 1980 (BISD 27S/24)."

green). For example, reading the ratio of 22.3 % (73) at column 1(SUB) and row 1(SUB) in Table 4.18 below, it is referred to 22.3 % of the main events under the event-type of SUBSTANCE associated with the supporting events also under the event-type of SUBSTANCE through the conjunction of temporal rules. In other words, 73 out of 328 main events of SUBSTANCE are found to be associated with the supporting events of SUBSTANCE in a 2-D sense. It should be noted that not all temporal rules are necessarily associated with a supporting event (*e.g.*, the sentence ④ in Table 4.1 in Section 4.1 above). In this regard, this research also calculates the ratio of the 2-D temporal events association to the total number of temporal rules at the bottom of Tables 4.18 to 4.20 below. This ratio may demonstrate how importance temporal rules are to create the 2-D nexus of different events in legal content. The following subsections will proceed to present the statistical matrix of temporal events association for the eight types of substantive events (Section 4.4.1) and the eight types of procedural events (Section 4.4.2), respectively.

TABLE 4.18 The substantive temporal events association in WTO Law

| Ranking | 1. SUB | 2. DEF | 3. MET | 4. EFF | 5. APP | 6. INS | 7. ORD | 8. OBJ | Support Event |
|---|---|---|---|---|---|---|---|---|---|
| 1. SUB | 22.3 % (73) | 37.4 % (128) | 52.0 % (180) | 12.3 % (29) | 21.2 % (47) | 0.6 % (1) | 14.9 % (22) | 37.0 % (27) | 27.4 % (507) |
| 2. NOT | 8.2 % (27) | 11.1 % (38) | 8.4 % (29) | 27.7 % (65) | 7.7 % (17) | 28.4 % (44) | 20.3 % (30) | 1.4 % (1) | 13.6 % (251) |
| 3. EFF | 15.9 % (52) | 4.7 % (16) | 1.7 % (6) | 26.8 % (63) | 29.3 % (65) | 13.5 % (21) | 8.1 % (12) | 0.0 % (0) | 12.7 % (235) |
| 4. MET | 24.1 % (79) | 10.5 % (36) | 17.6 % (61) | 0.9 % (2) | 10.4 % (23) | 0.6 % (1) | 5.4 % (8) | 4.1 % (3) | 11.5 % (213) |
| 5. REV | 6.1 % (20) | 7.3 % (25) | 5.8 % (20) | 3.4 % (8) | 2.3 % (5) | 6.5 % (10) | 9.5 % (14) | 13.7 % (10) | 6.1 % (112) |
| 6. ACC | 3.0 % (10) | 0.0 % (0) | 0.9 % (3) | 15.3 % (36) | 2.7 % (6) | 7.1 % (11) | 5.4 % (8) | 5.5 % (4) | 4.2 % (78) |
| 7. INS | 1.2 % (4) | 5.0 % (17) | 0.9 % (3) | 3.8 % (9) | 5.4 % (12) | 15.5 % (24) | 4.1 % (6) | 4.1 % (3) | 4.2 % (78) |
| 8. IMP | 4.6 % (15) | 6.1 % (21) | 0.9 % (3) | 2.1 % (5) | 3.6 % (8) | 3.9 % (6) | 4.7 % (7) | 8.2 % (6) | 3.8 % (71) |
| 9. MOD | 0.0 % (0) | 4.4 % (15) | 2.9 % (10) | 2.1 % (5) | 8.1 % (18) | 0.6 % (1) | 10.8 % (16) | 2.7 % (2) | 3.6 % (67) |

TABLE 4.18 The substantive temporal events association in WTO Law (*cont.*)

| Ranking | 1. SUB | 2. DEF | 3. MET | 4. EFF | 5. APP | 6. INS | 7. ORD | 8. OBJ | Support Event |
|---|---|---|---|---|---|---|---|---|---|
| 10. APP | 5.2 % (17) | 5.8 % (20) | 1.7 % (6) | 1.3 % (3) | 4.5 % (10) | 1.3 % (2) | 3.4 % (5) | 1.4 % (1) | 3.5 % (64) |
| 11. ORD | 4.6 % (15) | 2.0 % (7) | 3.2 % (11) | 1.7 % (4) | 1.8 % (4) | 12.3 % (19) | 1.4 % (2) | 2.7 % (2) | 3.5 % (64) |
| 12. DEC | 2.4 % (8) | 3.5 % (12) | 0.3 % (1) | 2.1 % (5) | 0.5 % (1) | 1.9 % (3) | 4.1 % (6) | 11.0 % (8) | 2.4 % (44) |
| 13. DIS | 0.6 % (2) | 0.9 % (3) | 2.3 % (8) | 0.4 % (1) | 1.8 % (4) | 5.2 % (8) | 4.7 % (7) | 5.5 % (4) | 2.0 % (37) |
| 14. OBJ | 1.2 % (4) | 0.6 % (2) | 0.9 % (3) | 0.0 % (0) | 0.0 % (0) | 1.3 % (2) | 0.7 % (1) | 0.0 % (0) | 0.6 % (12) |
| 15. DEF | 0.6 % (2) | 0.3 % (1) | 0.3 % (1) | 0.0 % (0) | 0.9 % (2) | 0.6 % (1) | 0.7 % (1) | 2.7 % (2) | 0.5 % (10) |
| 16. EXP | 0.0 % (0) | 0.3 % (1) | 0.3 % (1) | 0.0 % (0) | 0.0 % (0) | 0.6 % (1) | 2.0 % (3) | 0.0 % (0) | 0.3 % (6) |
| 2-D | 328 | 342 | 346 | 235 | 222 | 155 | 148 | 73 | 1849 |
| Total | 394 | 389 | 363 | 254 | 247 | 203 | 158 | 76 | 2084 |
| 2-D/Total | 83.2 % | 87.9 % | 95.3 % | 92.5 % | 89.9 % | 76.4 % | 93.7 % | 96.1 % | 88.7 % |

### 4.4.1 *Substantive Temporal Events Association in WTO Law*

Table 4.18 above indicates that in a great majority of cases (88.7 %, 1849 out of 2084 temporal rules), a substantive event can be associated with a supporting event through the conjunction of temporal rules in the legal content. This high percentage of the 2-D temporal events association rate may suggest that temporal rules should be read in a broader context within the nexus of different events, and should avoid to read temporal rules to an isolated event. Generally speaking, the largest number of temporal rules is associated with the main event-type of SUBSTANCE (394 rules) among the eight types of substantive events, followed by DEFINITION (389 rules), METHOD (363 rules), EFFECT (254 rules), APPLICATION (247 rules), INSTITUTION (203 rules), ORDER (158 rules), and OBJECTIVE (76 rules). In cases of the 2-D temporal events association, the most frequent supporting events appear to fall under the event-type of SUBSTANCE (27.4 %), followed by NOTIFICATION (13.6 %), EFFECT (12.7 %), and METHOD (11.5 %). To be more specific, the statistical tendency of the 2-D temporal events association in each type of the main substantive events is demonstrated as follows. The illustrations are representative not exhaustive.

(1) SUBSTANCE: The highest ratio of the main events under SUBSTANCE is associated with METHOD (24.1 %), followed by SUBSTANCE (22.3 %) and EFFECT (15.9 %). To allow the Members to take certain measures, *point or period in time* can signal a particular METHOD as the precondition to take action, *e.g.*, the additional duty may be imposed "in any year" where the absolute volume of imports exceeds certain level "during the three preceding years."[118] In terms of SUBSTANCE, *period with sequence in time* can be found to coordinate more than one measures intended to be taken, *e.g.*, definitive duties may be levied not more than "90 days before" the application of the provisional measures.[119] With regard to EFFECT, *point in time* is found to be relevant to anchor the rights or obligations to take certain actions on the entry into force of the Agreement, *e.g.*, granting export subsidies as of "the date of entry into force of the WTO Agreement."[120]

(2) DEFINITION: The highest ratio of the main events under DEFINITION is associated with SUBSTANCE (37.4 %), followed by NOTIFICATION (11.1 %) and METHOD (10.5 %). In terms of SUBSTANCE, *timing* as a condition can be a decisive element to define the scope of a measure (the question of what), *e.g.*, the goods shall be deemed to be in transit "when" the passage is not a complete journey.[121] *Period in time* can further delineate the scope of a measure (the question of how long), *e.g.*, the term "four months" is employed to define the application of provisional measures.[122] In terms of NOTIFICATION, *point and period in time* are critical to regulate time to deliver information, *e.g.*, "the final date" for the submission of tenders

118 AG Art. 5.4: "In all cases *the additional duty* may *be imposed* in any year where *the absolute volume of* imports of the product ... *exceeds* the sum of (x) the base trigger level ... multiplied by the average quantity of imports during the three preceding years for which data are available. ..."

119 ADP Art. 8.6: "In such cases, *definitive duties* may *be levied* in accordance with this Agreement on products entered for consumption not more than 90 days before *the application of such provisional measures*, except that. ..."

120 SCM Art. 27.4, Fn. 55: "For a developing country Member not *granting export subsidies* as of the date of *entry into force* of the WTO Agreement, this paragraph shall apply. ..."

121 GATT Art. V:1: "Goods ... shall *be deemed to* be in transit across the territory of a contracting party when *the passage across such territory* ... is only a portion of a complete journey. ..."

122 ADP Art. 7.4: "*The application of provisional measures* shall *be limited to* as short a period as possible, *not exceeding* four months. ..."

is required to be more than "40 days" from the date of notice.[123] As for METHOD, *timing* can emphasize the relevant measurement to define a factual situation, *e.g.*, a system shall be presumed not to result in material injury "at times" in the sale at a price lower than the comparable price.[124] *Period in time* is also used to provide a benchmark for making a comparison, *e.g.*, the percentage of domestic consumption of imports "during the three preceding years" is employed to define market access opportunities.[125]

(3) METHOD: More than half of the main events under METHOD are associated with SUBSTANCE (52.0 %), followed by METHOD (17.6 %) and NOTIFICATION (8.4 %). To regulate a certain measurement, *period in time* can be desired as a base for conducting the calculation in related to SUBSTANCE, for example: (1) the *fixed period* of sales ("the most recent 12-month") to calculate the value of the product;[126] (2) the *prescribed period* of production ("the base period") to compare the amount of payments;[127] and (3) the *unspecified period* of realization of profit ("over a representative period of time") to estimate the adequate price.[128] In terms of METHOD, *period in time* is also relevant to make a comparison between different measurements, *e.g.*, the quantities of budgetary outlays at the end of "the implementation period" vis-à-vis the "1986–1990 base period" levels.[129] In terms of NOTIFICATION, *timing* and *point in*

123 GPA Art. XI:3: "… the final date for *the submission* of tenders shall *not be* less than 40 days from the date on which: a. in the case of open tendering, *the notice* of intended procurement *is published*;…."

124 GATT Art. VI:7: "A system for the stabilization of the domestic price …, which results at times in the sale of the commodity for export *at a price lower than* the comparable price …, shall *be presumed not to* result in material injury *within the meaning of* paragraph 6 if. …"

125 AG Art. 5.4: "… market access opportunities *defined as* imports as *a percentage of* the corresponding domestic consumption during the three preceding years for which data are available:…."

126 SCM Annex IV, Para. 3: "… the value of the product shall *be calculated* as the total value of the recipient firm's *sales of that product* in the most recent 12-month period,…."

127 AG Annex 2, Para. 6(c): "*The amount of such payments* in any given year shall not be related to, or based on, *the prices*, domestic or international, applying to *any production undertaken* in any year after the base period."

128 CV Note to Art. 1, Para. 2.3: "… the price *is adequate to* ensure recovery of all costs plus a profit which is representative of *the firm's overall profit realized* over a representative period of time. …"

129 AG Art. 9.2(b)(iv): "… the Member's budgetary outlays for export subsidies and *the quantities* benefiting from such subsidies, at the conclusion of the implementation period, *are no greater than 64 per cent and 79 per cent* of the 1986–1990 base period *levels*, respectively."

*time* can facilitate the act of measuring, especially for its initiation by the receipt of relevant information, *e.g.*, to count the time-limit for reply questionnaires "from the date of" receipt.[130]

(4) EFFECT: The highest ratio of the main events under EFFECT is associated with NOTIFICATION (27.7 %), followed by EFFECT (26.8 %), ACCEPTANCE (15.3 %), and SUBSTANCE (12.3 %). The effect of certain actions can be triggered by NOTIFICATION under a *point or period with sequence in time*, *e.g.*, the withdrawal takes effect "on the sixtieth day following the day on which" the notice is received;[131] or the modification elapses "130 days from the date of" circulation of the notification.[132] In addition, the effect of specific legal rules can be found to be anchored on another EFFECT by a *point in time*, namely, the date of entry into force of the Agreement, *e.g.*, the provision shall expire eight years from "the date of entry into force of the WTO Agreement."[133] As for ACCEPTANCE, *point in time* can be observed to prescribe the exact date of entry into force of the Agreement after its acceptance by the Members, *e.g.*, "on the thirtieth day" following the date of its acceptance.[134] In terms of SUBSTANCE, *period in time* may be expected to regulate the fact of coming to an end of certain measures, *e.g.*, the termination of the definitive countervailing duty on a date not later than "five years" from its imposition.[135]

(5) APPLICATION: The highest ratio of the main events under APPLICATION is associated with EFFECT (29.3 %), followed by SUBSTANCE (21.2 %). It is worth to note that the associations with EFFECT and SUBSTANCE appear to be in the context of negative specification to regulate the abnormal situation of applying certain legal provisions or commitments (*e.g.*, "not apply," "not require," and "suspend"). In terms of EFFECT, *point or period with sequence in time* can be found to mark the existence of a

130 ADP Art. 6.1.1, Fn. 15: "… the time-limit for exporters [to reply questionnaires used in an anti-dumping investigation] shall *be counted* from the date of *receipt* of the questionnaire,…."

131 GATT Art. XVIII:12(e): "… such withdrawal shall *take effect* on the sixtieth day following the day on which the notice *is received* by him."

132 GPA Art. XIX:7(a)(i): "… where 130 days from the date of *circulation* of the notification of the proposed modification under paragraph 1 *have elapsed*,…."

133 SCM Art. 27.11: "This provision shall *expire* eight years from the date of *entry into force* of the WTO Agreement."

134 CA Art. 9.3.1: "For each other government it shall *enter into force* on the thirtieth day following the date of *its acceptance* or accession to this Agreement."

135 SCM Art. 21.3: "… any definitive countervailing duty shall *be terminated* on a date not later than five years from *its imposition*. …"

particular entity or system in order to not apply certain legal provisions, *e.g.*, the provisions shall not apply to preferences between the countries "formerly" a part of the Ottoman Empire and detached from it "on July 24, 1923;"[136] or the provisions shall cease to apply "three years after" the date of entry into force of the WTO Agreement.[137] In terms of SUBSTANCE, *period with sequence in time* is found to allow the suspension of application due to the unusual measures taken by other Members, *e.g.*, the affected Members shall be free to suspend the application of concessions or obligations under GATT 1994 "not later than 90 days after" the safeguard measure taken.[138]

(6) INSTITUTION: The highest ratio of the main events under INSTITUTION is associated with NOTIFICATION (28.4 %), followed by INSTITUTION (15.5 %), EFFECT (13.5 %), and ORDER (12.3 %). In terms of NOTIFICATION, the *timing* of request is found to inform the demand for certain institutions to be established or to perform their functions, which can also be adjoined by a *period in time*, *e.g.*, a panel may establish a technical expert group "at the request" of a party;[139] or the Committee shall complete work "within one year and three months from" receipt of the request.[140] In terms of INSTITUTION, *period in time* is observed to facilitate the arrangement of the different stages of work, *e.g.*, the composition of the panel and its terms of reference shall be established "within 15 days" from the date when it is established.[141] In terms of EFFECT, the membership or function of the institution can be found to be anchored on the date of entry into force of the Agreement, *e.g.*, the contracting parties to GATT 1947 shall become original Members of the WTO "as of the date of entry into force of this Agreement;"[142] or the working party shall meet

136 GATT Art. I:3: "The provisions of paragraph 1 shall *not apply* to preferences between the countries formerly a part of the Ottoman Empire and *detached from* it on July 24, 1923,...."

137 GATS Art. X:3: "The provisions of paragraph 2 shall *cease to apply* three years after the date of *entry into force* of the WTO Agreement."

138 SG Art. 8.2: "... the affected exporting Members shall *be free*, not later than 90 days after *the measure is applied, to suspend ... the application of* substantially equivalent concessions or other obligations under GATT 1994,...."

139 TBT Art. 14.2: "At *the request* of a party to a dispute ..., a panel may *establish a technical expert group. ...*"

140 RO Art. 9.2(c)(ii): "The Technical Committee shall *complete the above work* within one year and three months from *receipt* of the request of the Committee."

141 SCM Art. 7.4: "*The composition of the panel and its terms of reference* shall *be established* within 15 days from the date when it *is established.*"

142 MAR Art. XI:1: "The contracting parties to GATT 1947 as of the date of *entry into force* of this Agreement ... shall *become original Members* of the WTO."

within a year of "the date of entry into force of the WTO Agreement."[143] As for ORDER, the *timing* of giving a particular job by authorities can also be emphasized in order to perform other duties or functions, *e.g.*, to exercise other responsibilities "as the Committee may assign to it."[144]

(7) ORDER: The highest ratio of the main events under ORDER is associated with NOTIFICATION (20.3 %), followed by SUBSTANCE (14.9 %) and MODIFICATION (10.8 %). The *timing* of request under NOTIFICATION is found to trigger the act of an authority to deliver an opinion or instruction, *e.g.*, to find, "upon request," whether the procedural requirements have been complied with;[145] or to grant, "upon request," specified, time-limited exceptions.[146] In addition, the authority can also provide instructions with regard to the events of SUBSTANCE by employing a *period in time*, *e.g.*, "the proposed time-frame" to form the customs union or free-trade area.[147] In terms of MODIFICATION, *degree modifier* can be observed to allow an authority to amend the original time period, *e.g.*, to "extend" the relevant period and, if so, for "how long."[148]

(8) OBJECTIVE: The highest ratio of the main events under OBJECTIVE is associated with SUBSTANCE (37.0 %), followed by REVIEW (13.7 %) and DECISION (11.0 %). Generally speaking, *speed modifier* is frequently found across all these supporting event-types to illustrate the goals of the agreements or rules. For instance, in terms of SUBSTANCE, the recognition of a need for a "rapid" expansion of the export earnings of the less-developed countries;[149] or the expectation for "expediting" the release of goods.[150] In terms of REVIEW, the "prompt" review is expected for maintaining

143 Para. 5 of GATT's *Understanding on Art. XVII*: "[The working party] shall *meet* within a year of the date of *entry into force* of the WTO Agreement and thereafter at least once a year."

144 CV Annex II, Para. 2(g): "The responsibilities of the Technical Committee shall include the following: ... to *exercise such other responsibilities* as the Committee may *assign* to it."

145 SG Art. 13.1(b): "... to *find*, upon *request* of an affected Member, *whether or not* the procedural requirements of this Agreement have been complied with in connection with a safeguard measure,...."

146 TBT Art. 12.8: "... the Committee on Technical Barriers to Trade ... *is enabled to grant*, upon *request*, specified, time-limited exceptions in whole or in part from obligations under this Agreement."

147 Para. 8 of GATT's *Understanding on Art. XXIV*: "... the working party may in its report *make appropriate recommendations on* the proposed time-frame ... to *complete the formation of the customs union or free-trade area.*"

148 DSU Art. 12.10: "... the Chairman of the DSB shall *decide, ..., whether* to *extend* the relevant period and, if so, for how long."

149 GATT Art. XXXVI:2: "There *is need for* a rapid and sustained *expansion of the export earnings* of the less-developed contracting parties."

150 TFA Art. 7.1.1: "Each Member shall adopt or maintain procedures allowing for the submission of import documentation and other required information, including manifests, in

judicial, arbitral or administrative tribunals or procedures.[151] In terms of DECISION, the "speedy" resolution of disputes is often recognized as a desire.[152]

TABLE 4.19 The procedural temporal events association in WTO Law

| Ranking | 1. NOT | 2. REV | 3. MOD | 4. DIS | 5. ACC | 6. EXP | 7. IMP | 8. DEC | Support Event |
|---|---|---|---|---|---|---|---|---|---|
| 1. NOT | 22.6 % (107) | 30.2 % (51) | 20.3 % (28) | 37.0 % (44) | 22.1 % (27) | 41.2 % (35) | 6.0 % (5) | 53.3 % (40) | 26.6 % (337) |
| 2. EFF | 21.7 % (103) | 39.6 % (67) | 19.6 % (27) | 25.2 % (30) | 13.1 % (16) | 3.5 % (3) | 55.4 % (46) | 1.3 % (1) | 23.2 % (293) |
| 3. SUB | 13.3 % (63) | 5.3 % (9) | 16.7 % (23) | 16.0 % (19) | 13.1 % (16) | 12.9 % (11) | 10.8 % (9) | 9.3 % (7) | 12.4 % (157) |
| 4. REV | 7.0 % (33) | 6.5 % (11) | 1.4 % (2) | 4.2 % (5) | 7.4 % (9) | 8.2 % (7) | 1.2 % (1) | 14.7 % (11) | 6.2 % (79) |
| 5. INS | 4.4 % (21) | 4.1 % (7) | 3.6 % (5) | 3.4 % (4) | 13.1 % (16) | 8.2 % (7) | 0.0 % (0) | 8.0 % (6) | 5.2 % (66) |
| 6. MOD | 8.2 % (39) | 0.0 % (0) | 8.0 % (11) | 2.5 % (3) | 6.6 % (8) | 1.2 % (1) | 1.2 % (1) | 0.0 % (0) | 5.0 % (63) |
| 7. IMP | 7.8 % (37) | 2.4 % (4) | 4.3 % (6) | 2.5 % (3) | 1.6 % (2) | 4.7 % (4) | 1.2 % (1) | 0.0 % (0) | 4.5 % (57) |
| 8. ORD | 3.0 % (14) | 5.9 % (10) | 4.3 % (6) | 0.8 % (1) | 3.3 % (4) | 2.4 % (2) | 3.6 % (3) | 1.3 % (1) | 3.2 % (41) |
| 9. ACC | 1.7 % (8) | 2.4 % (4) | 5.1 % (7) | 3.4 % (4) | 2.5 % (3) | 0.0 % (0) | 12.0 % (10) | 4.0 % (3) | 3.1 % (39) |
| 10. DEC | 2.1 % (10) | 2.4 % (4) | 5.8 % (8) | 0.8 % (1) | 5.7 % (7) | 5.9 % (5) | 0.0 % (0) | 1.3 % (1) | 2.8 % (36) |
| 11. DIS | 0.8 % (4) | 0.0 % (0) | 4.3 % (6) | 3.4 % (4) | 8.2 % (10) | 3.5 % (3) | 0.0 % (0) | 4.0 % (3) | 2.4 % (30) |

order to begin processing prior to the arrival of goods *with a view to* expediting *the release of goods* upon arrival."

151 ADP Art. 6.14: "Each Member ... shall maintain judicial, arbitral or administrative tribunals or procedures *for the purpose, inter alia, of* the prompt *review* of administrative actions. ..."

152 The Preamble of the PSI: "*Desiring to* provide for the speedy, effective and equitable *resolution of disputes* between exporters and preshipment inspection entities arising under this Agreement;...."

TABLE 4.19 The procedural temporal events association in WTO Law (*cont.*)

| Ranking | 1. NOT | 2. REV | 3. MOD | 4. DIS | 5. ACC | 6. EXP | 7. IMP | 8. DEC | Support Event |
|---|---|---|---|---|---|---|---|---|---|
| 12. MET | 2.5 % (12) | 0.6 % (1) | 0.0 % (0) | 0.8 % (1) | 0.0 % (0) | 4.7 % (4) | 2.4 % (2) | 2.7 % (2) | 1.7 % (22) |
| 13. APP | 1.9 % (9) | 0.6 % (1) | 2.9 % (4) | 0.0 % (0) | 2.5 % (3) | 1.2 % (1) | 4.8 % (4) | 0.0 % (0) | 1.7 % (22) |
| 14. EXP | 3.0 % (14) | 0.0 % (0) | 0.0 % (0) | 0.0 % (0) | 0.0 % (0) | 1.2 % (1) | 0.0 % (0) | 0.0 % (0) | 1.2 % (15) |
| 15. DEF | 0.0 % (0) | 0.0 % (0) | 2.2 % (3) | 0.0 % (0) | 0.8 % (1) | 0.0 % (0) | 0.0 % (0) | 0.0 % (0) | 0.3 % (4) |
| 16. OBJ | 0.0 % (0) | 0.0 % (0) | 1.4 % (2) | 0.0 % (0) | 0.0 % (0) | 1.2 % (1) | 1.2 % (1) | 0.0 % (0) | 0.3 % (4) |
| 2-D | 474 | 169 | 138 | 119 | 122 | 85 | 83 | 75 | 1265 |
| Total | 641 | 244 | 203 | 160 | 132 | 108 | 101 | 86 | 1675 |
| 2-D/Total | 73.9 % | 69.3% | 68.0 % | 74.4 % | 92.4 % | 78.7 % | 82.2 % | 87.2 % | 75.5 % |

### 4.4.2 *Procedural Temporal Events Association in WTO Law*

In comparison with the substantive temporal events association (88.7 %), Table 4.19 above indicates a slightly smaller percentage of cases (75.5 %, 1265 out of 1675 temporal rules) for a procedural event to have supporting events adjoined by temporal rules in the legal content. However, this percentage of the 2-D association is still significantly high and therefore cannot be neglected. Generally speaking, the largest number of temporal rules is associated with the main event-type of NOTIFICATION (641 rules) among the eight types of procedural events, followed by REVIEW (244 rules), MODIFICATION (203 rules), DISCUSSION (160 rules), ACCEPTANCE (132 rules), EXPRESSION (108 rules), IMPLEMENTATION (101 rules), and DECISION (86 rules). In cases of the 2-D temporal events association, the most frequent supporting events appear to fall under the event-type of NOTIFICATION (26.6 %), followed by EFFECT (23.2 %), and SUBSTANCE (12.4 %). To be more specific, the statistical tendency of the combination of the 2-D temporal events association in each type of the main procedural events is demonstrated as follows. The illustrations are representative not exhaustive.

(1) NOTIFICATION: The highest ratio of the main events under NOTIFICATION is associated with NOTIFICATION (22.6 %), followed by EFFECT (21.7 %) and SUBSTANCE (13.3 %). In terms of NOTIFICATION, the *timing*

of request is crucial for triggering the obligation to provide relevant information, which can also be fixed with a certain *period in time, e.g.*, to provide all relevant information "upon the request" of any contracting party having an interest;[153] or to submit the results of work "within three months" of receipt of the request.[154] In terms of EFFECT, the obligation of notification is found to be anchored on the date of entry into force of the Agreement, together with a *sequence and period in time, e.g.*, to notify "not later than 90 days after the date of entry into force of the WTO Agreement."[155] In addition, the notification can also be found to be anchored on the expiry of a *period in time, e.g.*, to notify "at the termination of the exemption period."[156] As for SUBSTANCE, *period in time* can be relevant to delineate information regarding the measures to be taken, *e.g.*, to give notice of the quantity or value of products to be imported "during a specified future period."[157]

(2) REVIEW: The highest ratio of the main events under REVIEW is associated with EFFECT (39.6 %), followed by NOTIFICATION (30.2 %). In terms of EFFECT, the obligation of review can be found to be anchored on the date of entry into force of the Agreement or the expiry of certain measures, together with a *period, sequence, or frequency in time, e.g.*, to review exemptions "not later than five years after the date of entry into force of the WTO Agreement" and "thereafter every two years;"[158] or to review any waivers annually "until the waiver terminates."[159] In terms of

153 GATT Art. XIII:3(a): "… the contracting party applying the restrictions shall *provide*, upon *the request* of any contracting party having an interest in the trade in the product concerned, *all relevant information* concerning. …"

154 RO Art. 9.2(c)(i): "The results of this work shall *be submitted* to the Committee within three months of *receipt* of the request from the Committee."

155 SCM Art. 28.1(a): "Subsidy programmes … shall *be*: (a) *notified* to the Committee not later than 90 days after the date of *entry into force* of the WTO Agreement for such Member; and. …"

156 GATS Annex on Article II Exemptions, Para. 7: "A Member shall *notify* the Council for Trade in Services at *the termination of* the exemption period that the inconsistent measure has been brought into conformity with paragraph 1 of Article II of the Agreement."

157 GATT Art. XIII:3(b): "… the contracting party applying the restrictions shall *give public notice* of the total quantity or value of the product or products which will be permitted to *be imported* during a specified future period. …"

158 Para. 3(b) of GATT 1994: "The Ministerial Conference shall *review* this exemption not later than five years after the date of *entry into force* of the WTO Agreement and thereafter every two years for as long as the exemption is *in force*. …"

159 MAR Art. IX:4: "Any waiver … shall *be reviewed* by the Ministerial Conference not later than one year after it is granted, and thereafter annually until the waiver *terminates*."

NOTIFICATION, the *timing* of request usually serves as a triggering point for the initiation of review, *e.g.*, to review the operation of this Article "at the request" of any contracting party.[160] Except for the initiation by the timing of request, the review can be invoked within a *period in time* after the notification of certain actions, *e.g.*, to invoke the arbitration procedures "within 120 days" of circulation of the notification of the proposed modification.[161]

(3) MODIFICATION: The highest ratio of the main events under MODIFICATION is associated with NOTIFICATION (20.3 %), followed by EFFECT (19.6 %) and SUBSTANCE (16.7 %). In terms of NOTIFICATION, the *timing* of request is found to be a trigger for conducting a modification, *e.g.*, to vary the date of the meeting "at the request" of any Member.[162] Besides, to reserve the right to modify, the notification is required to be conducted before a *point or period in time*, *e.g.*, to notify "before 1 January 1958 and before the end of any period envisaged" to reserve the right to modify the appropriate Schedule.[163] In terms of EFFECT, modification can be anchored on the date of entry into force of the Agreement or the expiry of certain measures, together with a *period and sequence in time*, *e.g.*, to improve, modify or withdraw the specific commitments "during a period of 60 days beginning four months after the date of entry into force of the WTO Agreement;"[164] or to renew the subsidy programme "upon its expiry."[165] In terms of SUBSTANCE, it usually regulates the extension of time for a measure, which can be adjoined by a *degree modifier* (*i.e.*, extend)

160 GATT Art. XXXV:2: "The CONTRACTING PARTIES may *review* the operation of this Article in particular cases at *the request* of any contracting party and make appropriate recommendations."

161 GPA Art. XIX:7: "... a modifying or any objecting Party may *invoke the arbitration procedures* within 120 days of *circulation of the notification* of the proposed modification:...."

162 CV Annex II, Para. 9: "The date of the meeting may *be varied* either at *the request* of any member of the Technical Committee concurred in by a simple majority of the members of the Technical Committee or,...."

163 GATT Art. XXVIII:5: "Before 1 January 1958 and before the end of any period envisaged in paragraph 1 a contracting party may elect by *notifying* the CONTRACTING PARTIES to *reserve the right*, for the duration of the next period, *to modify* the appropriate Schedule."

164 GATS Second Annex on Financial Services, Para. 2: "... a Member may, during a period of 60 days beginning four months after the date of *entry into force* of the WTO Agreement, *improve, modify or withdraw* all or part of the specific commitments on financial services inscribed in its Schedule."

165 SCM Art. 28.2: "No Member shall extend the scope of any such programme, nor shall such a programme *be renewed* upon *its expiry*."

and *period in time, e.g.*, to "extend the transition period" for the elimination of trade-related investment measures.[166]

(4) DISCUSSION: The highest ratio of the main events under DISCUSSION is associated with NOTIFICATION (37.0 %), followed by EFFECT (25.2 %) and SUBSTANCE (16.0 %). In terms of NOTIFICATION, the *timing* of request is found to be the initiating point for consultation, together with a *period and sequence in time* for its undertaking, *e.g.*, to enter, "upon request," into consultations with any other Member;[167] or to allow "a period of 60 days after" the date of receipt of the request for consultations.[168] In terms of EFFECT, it obliges the conduct of negotiation by anchoring on the date of entry into force of the Agreement, together with a *period, sequence, and frequency in time, e.g.*, to undertake further negotiations "not later than the end of three years from the date of entry into force of the Protocol" and "periodically thereafter."[169] In addition, the consultation can also be found to be anchored on the expiry of a *period in time, e.g.*, to enter into consultation not later than one year before the expiry of "the 8-year period."[170] As for SUBSTANCE, *speed modifier* and *sequence in time* can be employed to require consultations for the specific measures taken, *e.g.*, to initiate consultations "immediately after" the measure is taken.[171]

(5) ACCEPTANCE: The highest ratio of the main events under ACCEPTANCE is associated with NOTIFICATION (22.1 %), followed by EFFECT (13.1 %), SUBSTANCE (13.1 %) and INSTITUTION (13.1 %). In terms of NOTIFICATION, *period with sequence in time* is observed to regulate when the act of agreement or objection shall be made, *e.g.*, to reach agreement "within sixty days after" the notification.[172] In terms of EFFECT, it obliges the conduct of acceptance by anchoring on the date of entry into force of the Agreement or the expiry of *a period in time, e.g.*, to accept the Havana

166 TRIMS Art.5.3: "… the Council for Trade in Goods may *extend* the transition period for *the elimination of TRIMs* notified under paragraph 1 for a developing country Member,…."

167 TRIPS Art. 40.3: "Each Member shall *enter*, upon *request, into consultations* with any other Member. …"

168 DSU Art. 5.4: "… the complaining party must *allow* a period of 60 days after the date of *receipt* of the request *for consultations* before requesting the establishment of a panel."

169 GPA Art. XXII:7: "Not later than the end of three years from the date of *entry into force* of the Protocol Amending the Agreement on Government Procurement, adopted on 30 March 2012, and periodically thereafter, the Parties shall *undertake further negotiations*,…."

170 SCM Art. 27.4: "… [a developing country Member] shall not later than one year before *the expiry of* this period [i.e., 8 years] *enter into consultation* with the Committee,…."

171 SG Art. 12.4: "*Consultations* shall *be initiated* immediately after *the measure is taken*."

172 GATT Art. XVIII:7(b): "If *agreement is not reached* within sixty days after *the notification* provided for in subparagraph (a) above, the contracting party … shall promptly examine it."

Charter "by the date upon which it enters into force;"[173] or to agree on satisfactory compensation within 20 days after the date of expiry of "the reasonable period of time."[174] In terms of SUBSTANCE, *sequence in time* is utilized to display if the act of acceptance shall take place before or after the measures taken, *e.g.*, to accept the requests for assessments "before" trade in the good concerned begins or at any "later" point in time.[175] In terms of INSTITUTION, *sequence in time* can also be relevant, especially for the acceptance to a treaty and the accession as a Member, *e.g.*, whether the Government of Japan accept the present Agreement "prior to" its accession.[176] Besides, *period in time* can be found to allow the parties concerned to reach an agreement on the function of institution, *e.g.*, to agree a special terms of reference "within 20 days from" the establishment of the panel.[177]

(6) EXPRESSION: The highest ratio of the main events under EXPRESSION is associated with NOTIFICATION (41.2 %), followed by SUBSTANCE (12.9 %). In terms of NOTIFICATION, *timing* is found to be crucial for providing explanations, especially when relevant information is absent or without notice, *e.g.*, to provide justification and the reasons "whenever" a time-schedule is not publicly announced.[178] In addition, the date of receipt, together with a *period and sequence in time*, can be found for making a reply or comment, *e.g.*, to respond "within 10 days after the date of receipt of the request."[179] In terms of SUBSTANCE, an explanation may be requested at the time when a particular measure cannot

173 GATT Art. XXIX:5: "If any contracting party *has not accepted* the Havana Charter by the date upon which it *enters into force*, the CONTRACTING PARTIES shall confer to agree whether. …"

174 DSU Art. 22.2: "If no satisfactory compensation *has been agreed* within 20 days after the date of *expiry of* the reasonable period of time, any party having invoked the dispute settlement procedures may request authorization. …"

175 RO Art. 2(h): "Requests for such assessments shall *be accepted* before *trade in the good concerned begins* and may be accepted at any later point in time."

176 GATT Annex H: "If the present Agreement *has not been so accepted* prior to *the accession* of the Government of Japan, column II shall be applicable for the purposes of that paragraph."

177 DSU Art. 7.1: "Panels shall have the following terms of reference unless the parties to the dispute *agree* otherwise within 20 days from *the establishment of the panel*:…."

178 Para. 1 of GATT's *Understanding on BOP Provisions*: "Whenever a time-schedule *is not publicly announced* by a Member, that Member shall *provide justification as to the reasons therefor*."

179 DSU Art. 4.3: "If the Member *does not respond* within 10 days after the date of *receipt* of the request, or …, then the Member that requested the holding of consultations may proceed directly to request the establishment of a panel."

be conducted within a *period in time, e.g.*, where a refund is not made "within 90 days."[180] As for the content of explanation, *degree modifier* (*i.e.*, delay) or *period in time* is useful for regulating the measures taken, *e.g.*, to provide the reasons for "significant delay" in the release of perishable goods,[181] or to specify "the time-period" within which the measure must be withdrawn.[182]

(7) IMPLEMENTATION: More than half of the main events under IMPLEMENTATION is associated with EFFECT (55.4 %), followed by ACCEPTANCE (12.0 %) and SUBSTANCE (10.8 %). In terms of EFFECT, the date of the entry into force of the Agreement, together with a *period and sequence in time*, is an important anchor for considering the compliance of certain measures with the treaty, *e.g.*, to challenge the consistency of the level of concession "for a period of three years after the date of entry into force of the WTO Agreement."[183] In terms of ACCEPTANCE, *period in time* can be fixed for the conformity of the measures concerned after the adoption of the rulings, *e.g.*, to take appropriate steps to remove the adverse effects of the subsidy or withdraw the subsidy "within six months" from the adoption of the panel or Appellate Body report.[184] With regard to SUBSTANCE, *timing* and *period in time* can mark which legal provisions shall be implemented on the measures concerned, *e.g.*, where the special treatment is not to be continued "at the end of the implementation period," the Member concerned shall implement the provisions of paragraph 6.[185]

---

180 ADP Art. 9.3.1: "In any case, where *a refund is not made* within 90 days, the authorities shall *provide an explanation* if so requested."

181 TFA Art. 7.9.4: "In cases of significant delay in *the release of perishable goods*, and upon written request, the importing Member shall, to the extent practicable, *provide a communication on the reasons* for the delay."

182 SCM Art. 4.7: "In this regard, the panel shall *specify* in its recommendation the time-period within which *the measure must be withdrawn.*"

183 Para. 4 of GATT's *Understanding on Art. II:1(b)*: "It will be open to any Member to *challenge … the consistency of* the recorded level of any "other duty or charge" with the previously bound level, for a period of three years after the date of *entry into force* of the WTO Agreement…."

184 SCM Art. 7.9: "In the event the Member *has not taken appropriate steps to remove* the adverse effects of the subsidy or withdraw the subsidy within six months from the date when the DSB *adopts the panel report or the Appellate Body report,…."*

185 AG Annex 5, Para. 5: "Where *the special treatment is not to be continued* at the end of the implementation period, the Member concerned shall *implement* the provisions of paragraph 6."

(8) DECISION: The highest ratio of the main events under DECISION is associated with NOTIFICATION (53.3 %), followed by REVIEW (14.7 %). In terms of NOTIFICATION, the *timing* of request is crucial to undertake a decision, *e.g.*, to decide by consensus "upon the request" of the Members parties to a trade agreement.[186] For its completion, *period in time* can be employed to regulate the time of issuing a decision after notification, *e.g.*, to issue decision "within 60 days" from the date when the party notifies its intention to appeal.[187] In terms of REVIEW, the submission of the matter serves as a triggering event for the time to make a final decision, which can be adjoined by a *period in time*, *e.g.*, to make determination "within thirty days" of the submission of the matter to the CONTRACTING PARTIES.[188]

## 4.5 Summary

Following the study of quantitative distribution of temporal rules in Section 3.2, it is noticed that the research on temporal rules inevitably leads to the inquiry of their corresponding "events" in legal content due to their strong bonds with each other. To further understand their properties, this Chapter denotes the "events" in the twenty agreements of WTO Law, and categorizes them into sixteen *event-types* (Sections 4.2 and 4.3). The purpose of this categorization is to generalize the representation of legal content in order to establish the 2-D "temporal events association" between the temporal rules and events (Section 4.1). This 2-D model may serve as a valuable analytical tool to underpin the potential of "time" as an important internal element in law for a better understanding of the theoretical framework of legalization (Section 1.4). Lastly, this Chapter also statistically examines the temporal events association in WTO Law with the intention of providing empirical evidence on the relevance of "time" to arrange diverse content in the legal texts (Section 4.4).

186 MAR Art. X:9: "The Ministerial Conference, upon *the request* of the Members parties to a trade agreement, may *decide exclusively by consensus* to add that agreement to Annex 4."

187 SCM Art. 7.7: "Where a panel report is appealed, the Appellate Body shall *issue its decision* within 60 days from the date when the party to the dispute formally *notifies* its intention to appeal."

188 GATT Annex I, Ad Art. XXVIII, Para. 4.4: "*The determination* referred to in paragraph 4(d) shall *be made* by the CONTRACTING PARTIES within thirty days of *the submission of the matter* to them unless. …"

Section 4.1 first displays how the 2-D model can be established to evaluate the "temporal events association" between the temporal rules and relevant events. This model is distinct from the identification of "temporal relations" in natural language processing which extracts the specific *events* in a more practical (or absolute) sense. Instead, it is aiming to establish the "temporal association" of the general *event-types* in a more conceptual (or relative) sense. For the analytical approach, this research evaluates the temporal events association under "sentence structure" in legal texts. In other words, it denotes the relevant events in texts by capturing (1) *root verbs* at the sentence level and/or (2) certain *constituents* at the phrasal level that appear in close proximity to the corresponding temporal rules. To provide instructions on how to operate the 2-D model (Table 4.1), this book denotes temporal rules in legal texts (highlighted in grey) with (1) their *main events* to serve as the high-level or first dimensional contexts (highlighted in yellow), and (2) their *supporting events* to be the low-level or second dimensional anchors (highlighted in green). The interest of this 2-D model is to demonstrate what the relevant events for temporal rules could be, and how these temporal rules may be employed to establish certain nexus within legal content.

Sections 4.2 and 4.3 then proceed to classify the legal content of the twenty WTO agreements into eight substantive *event-types* and eight procedural *event-types*. The concept of "substantive *event-types*" is used broadly to denote stative eventualities in comparison with the concept of "procedural *event-types*" to denote dynamic eventualities which usually occur in a process. However, as mentioned above, these conceptual umbrellas for the event-types were used for the sake of convenience, and therefore they could also be abandoned by viewing the general content of WTO Law merely as sixteen event-types associated with temporal rules. Based on these sixteen event-types of WTO Law, Section 4.4 has established two 16 × 8 matrices for the substantive and procedural temporal events association, respectively (Tables 4.18 and 4.19). To merge the substantive and procedural umbrellas, Table 4.20 below represents the overall temporal events association in WTO Law as a 16 × 16 matrix, which is defined first by vertical columns (*i.e.*, the main event-type highlighted in yellow) and then by horizontal rows (*i.e.*, the supporting event-type highlighted in green).

TABLE 4.20 The overall temporal events association in WTO Law

| Ranking | 1. NOT | 2. SUB | 3. DEF | 4. MET | 5. EFF | 6. APP | 7. REV | 8. INS | 9. MOD | 10. DIS | 11. ORD | 12. ACC | 13. EXP | 14. IMP | 15. DEC | 16. OBJ | Support Event |
|---|---|---|---|---|---|---|---|---|---|---|---|---|---|---|---|---|---|
| 1. SUB | 13.3 % (63) | 22.3 % (73) | 37.4 % (128) | 52.0 % (180) | 12.3 % (29) | 21.2 % (47) | 5.3 % (9) | 0.6 % (1) | 16.7 % (23) | 16.0 % (19) | 14.9 % (22) | 13.1 % (16) | 12.9 % (11) | 10.8 % (9) | 9.3 % (7) | 37.0 % (27) | 21.3 % (664) |
| 2. NOT | 22.6 % (107) | 8.2 % (27) | 11.1 % (38) | 8.4 % (29) | 27.7 % (65) | 7.7 % (17) | 30.2 % (51) | 28.4 % (44) | 20.3 % (28) | 37.0 % (44) | 20.3 % (30) | 22.1 % (27) | 41.2 % (35) | 6.0 % (5) | 53.3 % (40) | 1.4 % (1) | 18.9 % (588) |
| 3. EFF | 21.7 % (103) | 15.9 % (52) | 4.7 % (16) | 1.7 % (6) | 26.8 % (63) | 29.3 % (65) | 39.6 % (67) | 13.5 % (21) | 19.6 % (27) | 25.2 % (30) | 8.1 % (12) | 13.1 % (16) | 3.5 % (3) | 55.4 % (46) | 1.3 % (1) | 0.0 % (0) | 17.0 % (528) |
| 4. MET | 2.5 % (12) | 24.1 % (79) | 10.5 % (36) | 17.6 % (61) | 0.9 % (2) | 10.4 % (23) | 0.6 % (1) | 0.6 % (1) | 0.0 % (0) | 0.8 % (1) | 5.4 % (8) | 0.0 % (0) | 4.7 % (4) | 2.4 % (2) | 2.7 % (2) | 4.1 % (3) | 7.5 % (235) |
| 5. REV | 7.0 % (33) | 6.1 % (20) | 7.3 % (25) | 5.8 % (20) | 3.4 % (8) | 2.3 % (5) | 6.5 % (11) | 6.5 % (10) | 1.4 % (2) | 4.2 % (5) | 9.5 % (14) | 7.4 % (9) | 8.2 % (7) | 1.2 % (1) | 14.7 % (11) | 13.7 % (10) | 6.1 % (191) |
| 6. INS | 4.4 % (21) | 1.2 % (4) | 5.0 % (17) | 0.9 % (3) | 3.8 % (9) | 5.4 % (12) | 4.1 % (7) | 15.5 % (24) | 3.6 % (5) | 3.4 % (4) | 4.1 % (6) | 13.1 % (16) | 8.2 % (7) | 0.0 % (0) | 8.0 % (6) | 4.1 % (3) | 4.6 % (144) |
| 7. MOD | 8.2 % (39) | 0.0 % (0) | 4.4 % (15) | 2.9 % (10) | 2.1 % (5) | 8.1 % (18) | 0.0 % (0) | 0.6 % (1) | 8.0 % (11) | 2.5 % (3) | 10.8 % (16) | 6.6 % (8) | 1.2 % (1) | 1.2 % (1) | 0.0 % (0) | 2.7 % (2) | 4.2 % (130) |
| 8. IMP | 7.8 % (37) | 4.6 % (15) | 6.1 % (21) | 0.9 % (3) | 2.1 % (5) | 3.6 % (8) | 2.4 % (4) | 3.9 % (6) | 4.3 % (6) | 2.5 % (3) | 4.7 % (7) | 1.6 % (2) | 4.7 % (4) | 1.2 % (1) | 0.0 % (0) | 8.2 % (6) | 4.1 % (128) |
| 9. ACC | 1.7 % (8) | 3.0 % (10) | 0.0 % (0) | 0.9 % (3) | 15.3 % (36) | 2.7 % (6) | 2.4 % (4) | 7.1 % (11) | 5.1 % (7) | 3.4 % (4) | 5.4 % (8) | 2.5 % (3) | 0.0 % (0) | 12.0 % (10) | 4.0 % (3) | 5.5 % (4) | 3.8 % (117) |
| 10. ORD | 3.0 % (14) | 4.6 % (15) | 2.0 % (7) | 3.2 % (11) | 1.7 % (4) | 1.8 % (4) | 5.9 % (10) | 12.3 % (19) | 4.3 % (6) | 0.8 % (1) | 1.4 % (2) | 3.3 % (4) | 2.4 % (2) | 3.6 % (3) | 1.3 % (1) | 2.7 % (2) | 3.4 % (105) |

TABLE 4.20 The overall temporal events association in WTO Law (*cont.*)

| Ranking | 1. NOT | 2. SUB | 3. DEF | 4. MET | 5. EFF | 6. APP | 7. REV | 8. INS | 9. MOD | 10. DIS | 11. ORD | 12. ACC | 13. EXP | 14. IMP | 15. DEC | 16. OBJ | Support Event |
|---|---|---|---|---|---|---|---|---|---|---|---|---|---|---|---|---|---|
| 11. APP | 1.9 % (9) | 5.2 % (17) | 5.8 % (20) | 1.7 % (6) | 1.3 % (3) | 4.5 % (10) | 0.6 % (1) | 1.3 % (2) | 2.9 % (4) | 0.0 % (0) | 3.4 % (5) | 2.5 % (3) | 1.2 % (1) | 4.8 % (4) | 0.0 % (0) | 1.4 % (1) | 2.8 % (86) |
| 12. DEC | 2.1 % (10) | 2.4 % (8) | 3.5 % (12) | 0.3 % (1) | 2.1 % (5) | 0.5 % (1) | 2.4 % (4) | 1.9 % (3) | 5.8 % (8) | 0.8 % (1) | 4.1 % (6) | 5.7 % (7) | 5.9 % (5) | 0.0 % (0) | 1.3 % (1) | 11.0 % (8) | 2.6 % (80) |
| 13. DIS | 0.8 % (4) | 0.6 % (2) | 0.9 % (3) | 2.3 % (8) | 0.4 % (1) | 1.8 % (4) | 0.0 % (0) | 5.2 % (8) | 4.3 % (6) | 3.4 % (4) | 4.7 % (7) | 8.2 % (10) | 3.5 % (3) | 0.0 % (0) | 4.0 % (3) | 5.5 % (4) | 2.2 % (67) |
| 14. EXP | 3.0 % (14) | 0.0 % (0) | 0.3 % (1) | 0.3 % (1) | 0.0 % (0) | 0.0 % (0) | 0.0 % (0) | 0.6 % (1) | 0.0 % (0) | 0.0 % (0) | 2.0 % (3) | 0.0 % (0) | 1.2 % (1) | 0.0 % (0) | 0.0 % (0) | 0.0 % (0) | 0.7 % (21) |
| 15. OBJ | 0.0 % (0) | 1.2 % (4) | 0.6 % (2) | 0.9 % (3) | 0.0 % (0) | 0.0 % (0) | 0.0 % (0) | 1.3 % (2) | 1.4 % (2) | 0.0 % (0) | 0.7 % (1) | 0.0 % (0) | 1.2 % (1) | 1.2 % (1) | 0.0 % (0) | 0.0 % (0) | 0.5 % (16) |
| 16. DEF | 0.0 % (0) | 0.6 % (2) | 0.3 % (1) | 0.3 % (1) | 0.0 % (0) | 0.9 % (2) | 0.0 % (0) | 0.6 % (1) | 2.2 % (3) | 0.0 % (0) | 0.7 % (1) | 0.8 % (1) | 0.0 % (0) | 0.0 % (0) | 0.0 % (0) | 2.7 % (2) | 0.4 % (14) |
| 2-D | 15.2 % (474) | 10.5 % (328) | 11.0 % (342) | 11.1 % (346) | 7.5 % (235) | 7.1 % (222) | 5.4 % (169) | 5.0 % (155) | 4.4 % (138) | 3.8 % (119) | 4.8 % (148) | 3.9 % (122) | 2.7 % (85) | 2.7 % (83) | 2.4 % (75) | 2.3 % (73) | 100 % (3114) |
| Total | 17.1 % (641) | 10.5 % (394) | 10.3 % (389) | 9.7 % (363) | 6.8 % (254) | 6.6 % (247) | 6.5 % (244) | 5.4 % (203) | 5.4 % (203) | 4.3 % (160) | 4.2 % (158) | 3.5 %) (132) | 2.9 % (108) | 2.7 % (101) | 2.3 % (86) | 2.0 % (76) | 100 % (3759) |
| 2-D/ Total | 73.9 % | 83.2 % | 87.9 % | 95.3 % | 92.5 % | 89.9 % | 69.3% | 76.4 % | 68.0 % | 74.4 % | 93.7 % | 92.4 % | 78.7 % | 82.2 % | 87.2 % | 96.1 % | 82.8 % |

In total, the 2-D temporal events association in WTO Law can be identified in 82.8 % of the cases (3114 out of 3759 temporal rules), which means temporal rules usually serve to adjoin different events in legal content and may create certain temporal events nexus worth to be found. Regardless of the existence of supporting events in a 2-D sense, the largest number of the total temporal rules, in the second-lowest row of Table 4.20, is associated with the event-type of NOTIFICATION (17.1 %), followed by SUBSTANCE (10.5 %), DEFINITION (10.3 %), METHOD (9.7 %), EFFECT (6.8 %), APPLICATION (6.6 %), and so on. These results may imply that temporal rules are immersed in different legal content and have diverse roles to play (explored in more detail in Section 6.1). In cases of the most frequent supporting events indicated in the last column of Table 4.20, the main events appear to be more regularly supported by the event-type of SUBSTANCE (21.3 %), followed by NOTIFICATION (18.9 %) and EFFECT (17.0 %). In other words, these three event-types usually serve as the most important anchors for the legal events.

First, the supporting events under SUBSTANCE, namely, (trade) measures taken by WTO Members, seem to be associated with the main event-types, such as: (1) METHOD: to establish a temporal benchmark for calculating the measures; (2) DEFINITION: to define the temporal scope of the measures; (3) OBJECTIVE: to stress the need to act quickly in implementing certain measures; (4) SUBSTANCE: to arrange the temporal order among different measures; and (5) APPLICATION: to regulate the temporal response to abnormal measures.

Second, the supporting events under NOTIFICATION are found to have relatively more associations with the main event-types, including: (1) DISCUSSION, REVIEW, INSTITUTION, NOTIFICATION, ORDER, and MODIFICATION: to use the timing of a request as the trigger for initiating certain actions; (2) EFFECT: to set the date of notice as the starting point for determining the validity period of certain actions; and (3) DECISION, EXPRESSION, DISCUSSION, REVIEW, and ACCEPTANCE: to set the duration counted from the request or notice as a temporal limit for completing certain actions.

Third, the supporting events under EFFECT appear to be associated with the main event-types, for example: (1) IMPLEMENTATION, REVIEW, EFFECT, DISCUSSION, NOTIFICATION, MODIFICATION, SUBSTANCE, INSTITUTION, and ACCEPTANCE: to anchor relevant actions on “the date of entry into force of the WTO Agreement;” (2) DISCUSSION, NOTIFICATION, and ACCEPTANCE: to emphasize “the expiry of a certain period of time” as the starting point for certain actions; (3) REVIEW and MODIFICATION: to rely on “the expiry of certain measures” as the ending point for certain actions; and (4) APPLICATION: to identify the temporal existence of a legal entity or system.

In sum, the relevant events associated with temporal rules could be highly complex and interconnected. Despite the preliminary attempt for the 2-D model to capture the embedded temporal events nexus, this research does not and cannot claim perfection. Instead, the purpose of this research is to put forward a new approach of framing the relevance of "time" in WTO Law to deal with diverse legal content. It builds a systemic way of identification on the omnipresent "temporal rules" in legal texts. With this 2-D temporal events association in mind, the following Chapter will go beyond the WTO legal texts and proceed to examine WTO practice in establishing, modifying, and elaborating temporal rules in WTO Law.

CHAPTER 5

# Establishment, Modification, and Elaboration of Temporal Rules in WTO Law

Following the implications of the 2-D temporal events association in the previous Section 4.5, temporal rules are omnipresent in legal texts, underpinning a wide range of events to form an internal structure of law, albeit they could be responsive to change in practice. As Abbott acknowledged, "change is the normal state of affairs" in a complex world, and "[w]e do not see a largely stable world that changes occasionally, but a continuously changing world that has macroscopic stabilities emerging throughout it."[1] Especially, law itself as a written document cannot always remain without alteration, as said by Aristotle, "certain laws will at certain times admit of alterations."[2] Luhmann also argued that, "[i]f one wants to rely on law, one can count on support against resistance and disappointments but one cannot expect that the law will not change."[3] In the field of IL, Pauwelyn et al. observed that, although not likely with sudden and deliberate change, traditional IL does "allow for organic change to reflect new social realities."[4] Uruena identified the driving force for the process of change for norms (*i.e.*, to adapt, evolve, and transform) in international settings, which relies on "the interactions among institutions and actors."[5] He urged for the vocabulary of IL (*i.e.*, its narrative of change) to consciously recognize the process of "incremental change" over time.[6] In sum, change in IL

1 Andrew Abbott, *Time Matters: On Theory and Method* (University of Chicago Press 2001), 296.

2 Aristotle, *Politics: A Treatise on Government* (CreateSpace Independent Publishing Platform 2015), chapter VIII. ("[I]t is impossible to express everything in writing with perfect exactness; for when we commit anything to writing we must use general terms, but in every action there is something particular to itself, which these may not comprehend; from whence it is evident, that certain laws will at certain times admit of alterations.")

3 Niklas Luhmann, *Law as a Social System* (Oxford University Press 2008), 471.

4 Joost Pauwelyn, Ramses A Wessel and Jan Wouters, 'When Structures Become Shackles: Stagnation and Dynamics in International Lawmaking' (2014) 25 European Journal of International Law 733, 744.

5 Rene Uruena, 'Temporariness and Change in Global Governance' (2014) 45 Netherlands Yearbook of International Law 19, 20.

6 *Ibid.*, 25. ("The problem is that international law *does* have a specific theory of change that, like is often the case with the deep grammar of law, remains unspoken. According to this theory, change is the sudden and complete replacement of the old by the new, which in turn implies the complete disappearance of the old. As a result of change, then, all looks as

 | DOI:10.1163/9789004745629_006

system appears to be inevitable and may be organic and incremental through the interactions among different institutions and actors.

In line with the recognition of organic and incremental change of IL, this Chapter is based on the assumption that examining temporal rules over time may provide a valuable indicator of change within a legal system. The temporal rule as a systematic promise in law is not only statically established in legal texts to regulate legal events, but also subject to change under dynamic interactions between the rules and its environment. In other words, comparing to the complete change of a legal system, temporal rules as internal elements in law may be relatively mutable to provide intrinsic flexibility to the legal events involved. However, the change of temporal rules seems to be a complex process under the interactions among different institutions and actors which has not yet attracted considerable attention. To fill this gap, this Chapter attempts to capture the diverse instances in which temporal rules in WTO Law have been established, modified, and elaborated in a dynamic manner.

In the WTO, several practices regarding the mechanisms for change have been gradually developed from the predecessor GATT to the current WTO. In the GATT era, the CONTRACTING PARTIES had followed different procedures for resolving issues or questions with regard to the treaty of GATT 1947, *e.g.*, Chairman's rulings, Council's decisions,[7] and Panel's or Working Parties' reports. To continue the GATT practices to the WTO, Article XVI:1 of the WTO Agreement provides that: "Except as otherwise provided under this Agreement or the Multilateral Trade Agreements, the WTO shall be guided by the decisions, procedures and customary practices followed by the CONTRACTING PARTIES to GATT 1947 and the bodies established in the framework of GATT 1947." To further affirm the continuing relevance of experience from the GATT acquis, the WTO adjudicators have stated that "incorporating the GATT 1994 into the [WTO Agreement] bring the legal history and experience under the GATT 1947 into

if nothing had ever changed: the norms and institutions that we have now look permanent, and completely unconnected to what came before them. Ultimately, international law's theory of change is one of a constant present.")

7 In the early days, issues of legal interpretation were often resolved by the Chairman of the CONTRACTING PARTIES giving a ruling, either at the request of a delegate (*e.g.*, GATT/CP.2/SR.11, p.7) or at his own initiative towards the end of a discussion (*e.g.*, GATT/CP.2/SR.11, p.4). The Council did not adopt reports of Panels or Working Parties before 1968, but merely noted them for later adoption by the CONTRACTING PARTIES at their next Session. In November 1968, the CONTRACTING PARTIES agreed that the Council should undertake a wider range of work, since then the Council has directly adopted such reports (*e.g.*, Council adoption of the four Panel Reports on tax legislation in L/5271 (28S/114)).

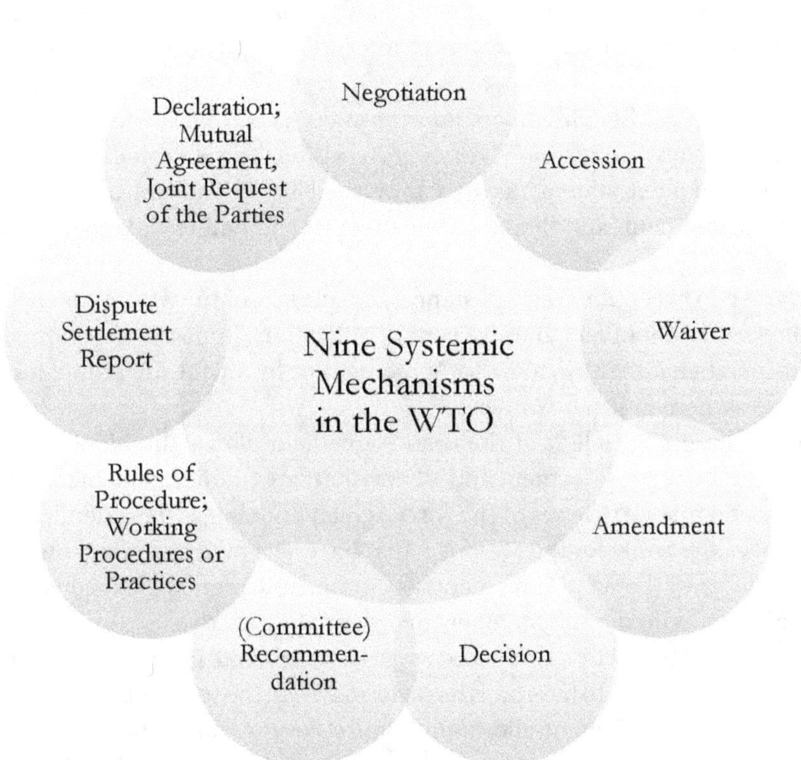


FIGURE 5.1 Nine systemic mechanisms for the establishment, modification, and elaboration of temporal rules in WTO Law

the new realm of the WTO in a way that ensures continuity and consistency in a smooth transition from the GATT 1947 system."[8] To this end, WTO Members and its predecessor GATT CONTRACTING PARTIES together have generated diverse mechanisms for resolving concerns of treaties, including their internal elements—temporal rules. There are nine potential systemic mechanisms to establish, modify, and elaborate temporal rules in WTO Law identified as follows (Figure 5.1):

(1) **Negotiation**: Pursuant to Article 32 of the *Vienna Convention on the Law of Treaties* (VCLT), the negotiating history of a treaty may serve as a supplementary means of interpretation. Although there is no officially

8 Appellate Body Report, *Japan—Alcoholic Beverages II*, p.14.

recorded WTO's negotiating history, the history of the GATT 1947 and the 1948 *Havana Charter for an International Trade Organization* has been referred by the WTO adjudicators to interpret the provisions of the GATT 1994.[9]

(2) **Accession:** All new Members join the WTO as a result of negotiations have their own terms in *Protocols of Accession*. These Protocols usually contain explicit statements that they shall be an integral part of the WTO Agreement, and therefore are effective and enforceable in dispute settlement.

(3) **Waiver:** In exceptional circumstances, Article IX:3 of the WTO Agreement allows WTO Members to waive certain obligations imposed on a particular Member, either by the WTO Agreement or by any of the multilateral trade agreements in its Annex 1.

(4) **Amendment:** Article X of the WTO Agreement allows the Members to amend the WTO Agreement and all the multilateral trade agreements. As a general rule, Article X:3 of the WTO Agreement obliges the amendment to take effect only for the Members that have accepted it. For exceptions, Article X:2 of the WTO Agreement lists some fundamental provisions that shall be accepted by all Members in order to be effective.

(5) **Decision:** The GATT's CONTRACTING PARTIES had in many instances adopted decisions to interpret the GATT 1947.[10] In the WTO era, Article IX:2 of the WTO Agreement allows the highest-level organ of the WTO (*i.e.*, the Ministerial Conference and General Council) to make decisions to adopt authoritative interpretations of the WTO Agreement and multilateral trade agreements. In addition, three specialized councils (*i.e.*, the Council for Trade in Goods (CTG), the Council for Trade in Services (CTS), and the Council for the TRIPS Agreement) might also take decisions from time to time, even though the power of decision-making is not explicitly included in their mandates.[11] Lastly, Article IV:7 of the WTO Agreement allows numerous committees to be established to facilitate

---

9 Peter Van den Bossche and Werner Zdouc, *The Law and Policy of the World Trade Organization: Text, Cases and Materials* (4th edition, Cambridge University Press 2017), 64.

10 *E.g.*, Decision of 9 August 1949 on Margins of Preference, II/11; Decisions of 18 November 1968 and 26 March 1980 on Rectification and Modification of Schedules, 16S/16 and 27S/25.

11 *E.g.*, the CTS has made five decisions to extend the three-year deadline for the entry into force of the result of negotiations on emergency safeguard measures in GATS Article X:1. Noting that Article IV:5 of the WTO Agreement provides for three "specialized councils" below the highest-level organ of the WTO. These councils operate under the general guidance of the General Council, and oversee the functioning of the multilateral trade agreements in goods, the GATS, and the TRIPS Agreement, respectively.

the operation of the Ministerial Conference and General Council, such as the Committee on Balance-of-Payments Restrictions and the Committee on Regional Trade Agreements. These committees sometimes carry out their functions independently due to the technical nature of their work, and might be authorized with a power of decision-making.[12]

(6) **Recommendation:** The GATT's CONTRACTING PARTIES had already had practices to adopt recommendations to provide guidance on the GATT 1947. In the WTO era, Article IX:2 of the WTO Agreement obliges that, for the interpretation of multilateral trade agreements in goods, the decisions to adopt authoritative interpretations as mentioned above shall be based on recommendations from the CTG overseeing the functioning of the multilateral trade agreements in goods. However, recommendations may also be remained at the committee level, which do not have binding effect in common practice.

(7) **Rules of Procedure, Working Procedures, or Working Practices:** Article IV:7 of the WTO Agreement allows the specialized councils to establish subsidiary bodies as required, such as working parties or working groups. These subsidiary bodies can establish their respective rules of procedure. It should be noted that if they are called upon to make a decision without mandates, they are usually required to refer the matter concerned to a high-level organ.

(8) **Dispute Settlement Report (DS Report):** In the GATT era, GATT Article XXIII:2 has given the CONTRACTING PARTIES the power to give a ruling on the nullification of a benefit or impairment of an objective under the GATT 1947 by adopting reports which include the interpretation of the treaty. In the WTO era, the DSU establishes "judicial-type institutions" (*i.e.*, the *ad hoc* dispute settlement panels and the standing Appellate Body) to adjudicate disputes among the Members.[13] Their reports are crucial for the clarification and interpretation of WTO Law.

(9) **Declaration, Mutual Agreement, or Joint Request of the Parties:** In some cases, a number of Members may reach agreements among themselves to certain issues related to the treaties. They might also request the bodies of the institution to interpret the treaties by taking into account their special needs or considerations.

It needs to be noted that the changes or outcomes through these nine mechanisms above may generate different or uncertain legal effects in terms of

12 *E.g.*, pursuant to SCM Art. 27.4, the SCM Committee can determine whether a request by a developing-country Member to extend the special transitional period for the maintenance of export subsidies is justified.

13 Van den Bossche and Zdouc (n 9), 209.

the enforcement as sources of law, which means whether they can derive specific and enforceable rights or obligations for the Members. For example, the Decision and Waiver might be considered as "a subsequent agreement" under VCLT Article 31(3)(a),[14] and need to be taken into account for the interpretation and application of legal provisions. In the case of the interpretative value of the *Doha Ministerial Decision on Implementation-related Issues and Concerns*, the adjudicators considered that, although this Decision was not *per se* an "authoritative interpretation" under Article IX:2 of the WTO Agreement,[15] it still constituted "a subsequent agreement between the parties, within the meaning of [VCLT] Article 31.3(a)."[16] The adjudicators nevertheless noted that the terms of the Decision do not "replace or override" the terms contained in the legal provisions; rather, they "constitute an interpretative clarification to be taken into account in the interpretation" of the relevant provisions.[17] The Recommendation, on the other hand, was understood to be "a useful guide" but as "a nonbinding document that sets out a common understanding of WTO Members, not of their legal obligations, but of best practices."[18] Lastly, the DS Report is generally only binding on the disputing parties involved. However, to ensure "security and predictability" referred in DSU Article 3.2, the adjudicators may still be required to "resolve the same legal question in the same way in a subsequent case."[19] Overall, the WTO is a member-driven institution, and the consensus principle preserves respect for national sovereignty and the

---

14 VCLT Art. 31.3(a): "There shall be taken into account, together with the context: (a) any subsequent agreement between the parties regarding the interpretation of the treaty or the application of its provisions." For the legal effect of Committee's Decision, *see* Appellate Body Report, *US—Tuna II (Mexico)*, para. 372. ("[T]he TBT Committee Decision can be considered as a 'subsequent agreement' within the meaning of [VCLT] Article 31(3)(a). The extent to which this Decision will inform the interpretation and application of a term or provision of the TBT Agreement in a specific case, however, will depend on the degree to which it 'bears specifically' on the interpretation and application of the respective term or provision.")

15 Appellate Body Report, *US—Clove Cigarettes*, paras. 254–255. ("We consider that the recommendation from the relevant Council is an essential element of Article IX:2 of the WTO Agreement, which constitutes the legal basis upon which the Ministerial Conference or the General Council exercise their authority to adopt interpretations of the WTO Agreement. ... [I]n the absence of evidence of the existence of a specific recommendation from the Council for Trade in Goods concerning the interpretation of Article 2.12 of the TBT Agreement, paragraph 5.2 of the Doha Ministerial Decision does not constitute a multilateral interpretation adopted pursuant to Article IX:2 of the WTO Agreement.")

16 *Ibid.*, para. 268.

17 *Ibid.*, para, 269.

18 Panel Report, *Russia—Commercial Vehicles*, para. 7.49.

19 Appellate Body Report, *US—Stainless Steel (Mexico)*, para. 160.

legal equality of the Members in the multilateral trading system.[20] The WTO Member's consent is an important source of legitimacy for the WTO.[21] While acknowledging this, this Chapter nevertheless aims to map the various modalities of incremental change through the establishment, modification, and elaboration of temporal rules in WTO Law. An in-depth discussion of the legal effects in each mechanism is beyond the scope of this research.

In sum, the ultimate goal of this Chapter is to demonstrate how mutable and dynamic the temporal rules could be in real cases, and to provide a systemic overview that enhances understanding of incremental change beyond static legal texts. The following sections will document how the six categories of temporal rules in WTO Law (Chapter 3) have been established, modified, and elaborated in WTO practice, which include: (1) point in time (Section 5.1); (2) timing (Section 5.2); (3) frequency in time (Section 5.3); (4) period in time (Section 5.4); (5) sequence in time (Section 5.5); and (6) conceptual expression in time (Section 5.6). Noting that the 33 cases provided in the following sections are representative not exhaustive.

## 5.1 Point in Time

As categorized in Section 3.1.1, this research defines "point in time" as *calendar time* which can be represented either with a numerical value (*i.e., fixed* point in time) or a non-numerical term (*i.e., prescribed* or *unspecified* point in time). These three types of point in time have been contemplated on several occasions in practice. The following subsections will provide a brief overview on the most significant of these occasions: (1) the establishment and modification of the *fixed* date (Section 5.1.1); (2) the establishment and modification of the *prescribed* date (Section 5.1.2); and (3) the modification and elaboration of the *unspecified* date (Section 5.1.3).

### 5.1.1 *Fixed Date: The Selected Date*

The establishment and modification of the fixed date were found in four cases (Table 5.1). First, a fixed date can be established through Negotiation. It was observed in the case of providing an exception to allow Members to take certain actions. The fixed dates were carefully chosen, built in gradually,

20 Mitsuo Matsushita and others, *The World Trade Organization: Law, Practice and Policy* (3rd edition, Oxford University Press 2015), 20.

21 Joshua Meltzer, 'State Sovereignty and the Legitimacy of the WTO' (2005) 26 University of Pennsylvania Journal of International Law 693, 693.

and open for selection to take into account political practicability and conflicts of interest (Case 1). Second, to adapt for new membership in Accession, the original fixed date of the Agreement can be diversified and replaced by the dates prescribed in the *Protocol of Accession* (Case 2). Third, to address exceptional circumstances, the original fixed date can be altered by a Waiver to grant alternative dates case-by-case in order to take into account the special need of the Member concerned. The new date may be subject to extension, if needed (Case 3). Lastly, to deal with unforeseen circumstances, the original fixed date may be postponed by a Decision, allowing a new date to be determined at a later stage (Case 4).

TABLE 5.1 Establishment and modification of the fixed date in WTO Law

| Modalities | Cases | Development |
|---|---|---|
| Establishment (Negotiation) **(Case 1)** | – Create exceptional fixed dates for maintenance of existing measures (GATT Art. III:6) | – No exception in general for maintenance of existing measures<br>– Choose base dates for permitting exception (I July 1939; 10 April 1947)<br>– Add an alternative base date for the exception (24 March 1948) |
| Modification (Accession) **(Case 2)** | – Diversify and replace the fixed date for acceding parities for the maintenance of existing measures in place on the date of the Agreement (GATT Art. XXVI:1) | – Original contracting parties (30 October 1947)<br>– Early acceding parties (24 March 1948)<br>– Subsequent acceding parties (the date of the *Protocol of Accession*) |
| Modification (Waiver) **(Case 3)** | – Change the base date under exceptional circumstances for the establishment of margins of preference (GATT Art. I:4(a)) | – Original base date (10 April 1947)<br>– Replace the base date case-by-case (*e.g.*, 1 August 1962)<br>– Renew and extend the base date |
| Modification (Decision) **(Case 4)** | – Change the date of meeting of the contracting parties due to unforeseen circumstances (GATT Art. XXIX:3) | – The original date of meeting (before 31 December 1949)<br>– Subsequent Decision by the CONTRACTING PARTIES |

*Case 1: Establishment of Optional Fixed Dates for Selection (Negotiation)*

To determine the scope of legal provisions, a fixed date can be helpful to facilitate the selection of the targeted measures. For example, GATT Article III:6 contains three fixed dates (*i.e.*, 1 July 1939, 10 April 1947, or 24 March 1948) for the contracting parties to select if their existing internal quantitative regulations would be subject to the national treatment obligation under GATT Article III:5.[22] According to the drafting history of the Havana Charter, these fixed dates were built in gradually in line with the purpose of the legal obligation. At the beginning, the complete elimination of existing internal quantitative regulations was considered to be desirable after a certain period from the entry into force of the Charter, albeit it might not be politically practicable due to the result of abnormal wartime condition.[23] In this regard, reconsidering the aim of the legal obligation, the exception permitting the continuance of existing measures was adopted and accompanied by the two fixed dates (*i.e.*, 1 July 1939 and 10 April 1947) so as to "take account of the departures from normal pre-war practices rendered necessary by war-time or post-war emergencies."[24] In a similar vein, the third fixed date was added during the Havana Conference, which was the date of the signing of the *Havana Final Act* (*i.e.*, 24 March 1948).[25] It is worth to note that this fixed date was chosen rather than the date of entry into force of the Charter in order "to avoid giving Members an opportunity to impose new regulations which would be contrary to [GATT Article III:5]."[26] In this sense, the selection of optional fixed dates was considered useful and necessary in negotiation of exceptions to cope with political practicability or conflicts of interest.

22 GATT Art. III:6: "The provisions of paragraph 5 shall not apply to any internal quantitative regulation in force in the territory of any contracting party on July 1, 1939, April 10, 1947, or March 24, 1948, at the option of that contracting party."

23 EPCT/174, p. 7–8. ("The [New York Draft provision] is aimed at preventing only those internal quantitative regulations which are clearly directed against imported products for the purposes of protecting domestic products. The new text removes the requirement that existing internal quantitative regulations not expressly approved by the Organization should be terminated at the expiration of one year after the entry into force of the Charter.")

24 *Ibid.* ("The revised draft would permit the continuation of regulations in force on 1 July 1939 or 10 April 1947, whichever date the Member selects, subject to the requirement that such requirements as are retained shall be negotiable and shall not be altered to the detriment of imports.") Noting that 10 April 1947 was the opening date of the Second Session of the Preparatory Committee at Geneva.

25 ICITO 1/8, p. 65, para. 60.

26 E/CONF.2/C.3/SR.40, p. 9.

*Case 2: Modification of the Original Fixed Date for New Membership (Accession)*

A fixed date may be diversified in line with new circumstances, especially in consideration of new acceding parties to the treaty. For example, there are several GATT provisions that permit the retention of the measures existing on "the date of this Agreement" (*i.e.*, 30 October 1947 referred in GATT Article XXVI:1), such as direct consignment requirements in GATT Article V:6,[27] currency conversion for customs valuation purposes in GATT Article VII:4(d),[28] and review of administrative action relating to customs matters in GATT Article X:3(c).[29] To adapt for new membership to the fixed date, its diversification was found as follows:

(1) Original contracting parties ("30 October 1947")
(2) Early acceding parties between 1948 and 1951 ("24 March 1948")
(3) Subsequent acceding parties ("the date of the *Protocol of Accession*")

First, the original date of 30 October 1947 applies in principle to the original parties to the GATT 1947. Second, when the modalities of accession to the GATT were first considered, the Working Party decided to draft the *Annecy Protocol of Terms of Accession* using the signing date of the *Havana Final Act* (*i.e.*, 24 March 1948) to replace the original date of 30 October 1947. This new date was adopted by the next group of accessions in the *Torquay Protocol of 1951*.[30] As such, for the party that early acceded between 1948 and 1951, the new date applied was 24 March 1948. Third, as for the accessions after 1951 (*i.e.*, started from the accession of Japan in 1955), the standard terms in accession protocols have provided that the original "date of this Agreement" shall be replaced by the date of the *Protocol of Accession*.[31] In the WTO era, these accession protocol

27 GATT Art. V:6: "Any contracting party shall, however, be free to maintain its requirements of direct consignment existing on *the date of this Agreement*, in respect of any goods in regard to which such direct consignment is a requisite condition of eligibility for entry of the goods at preferential rates of duty or has relation to the contracting party's prescribed method of valuation for duty purposes." (emphasis added)

28 GATT Art. VII:4(d): "Nothing in this paragraph shall be construed to require any contracting party to alter the method of converting currencies for customs purposes which is applicable in its territory on *the date of this Agreement*, if such alteration would have the effect of increasing generally the amounts of duty payable." (emphasis added)

29 GATT Art. X:3(c): "The provisions of subparagraph (b) of this paragraph shall not require the elimination or substitution of procedures in force in the territory of a contracting party on *the date of this Agreement* which in fact provide for an objective and impartial review of administrative action even though such procedures are not fully or formally independent of the agencies entrusted with administrative enforcement." (emphasis added)

30 Annecy Protocol, dated 10 October 1949, I/79, 81, para. 5(b); Torquay Protocol, dated 21 April 1951, I/86, 88, para. 5(b).

31 *E.g.*, Protocol for the Accession of Bolivia, L/6562, 37S/5.

provisions are incorporated in the GATT 1994 by virtue of Paragraph 1(b)(ii) of the GATT 1994 incorporation text. All in all, to adapt for acceding parties, the original fixed date of the Agreement can be diversified and replaced by the dates prescribed in the *Protocol of Accession*.

*Case 3: Modification of the Original Fixed Date under Exceptional Circumstances (Waiver)*

Once fixed dates are incorporated into the legal provisions, there remains the possibility that they can be altered by a Waiver under exceptional circumstances. For example, with respect to the base date (*i.e.*, 10 April 1947) for establishing maximum margins of preference in GATT Article I:4(a),[32] the GATT's Panel Report on *Jamaica—Margins of Preference* suggested to change the base date for Jamaica from the original date of "10 April 1947" to the new date of "1 August 1962."[33] This Panel Report highlighted the need to find a solution to "the uniqueness of the Jamaican case" for increases in margins of preference after 10 April 1947, and therefore permitted Jamaica to "apply in a legally correct manner margins of preference as they were in effect on 1 August 1962, the date the [GATT] was first applied to the territory of Jamaica."[34] Based on this panel's suggestion, the GATT's CONTRACTING PARTIES subsequently granted a waiver to Jamaica to change the base date to 1 August 1962 by stating that "these circumstances are sufficiently exceptional."[35] Moreover, the new date granted by a Waiver can be subject to extension, if needed. For example, the WTO's General Council approved the renewals of the waivers in respect of the base date applicable to South Africa and Zimbabwe from 19 November 1960 to 31 December 1997.[36] In sum, the original fixed date can

32 GATT Art. I:4(a): "… if no preferential rate is provided for, the preferential rate shall for the purposes of this paragraph be taken to be that in force *on* April 10, 1947,…."

33 L/3485–18S/183, para. 15. ("[I]n the light of the exceptional circumstances the CONTRACTING PARTIES consider taking a decision in accordance with the provisions of [GATT Article XXV:5] to change with respect to Jamaica the base date referred to in [GATT Article I:4] from 10 April 1947, to 1 August 1962.")

34 *Ibid.*, para. 14. Noting that Jamaica achieved independence on 6 August 1962 and was deemed a contracting party under the provisions of GATT Article XXVI:5(c) by Certification of 31 December 1963, its rights and obligations dating from the date of independence. The rights and obligations assumed by Jamaica are the rights and obligations resulting from the application to it of the GATT by the United Kingdom as from 1 August 1962, including the provision of GATT Article I:4 establishing 10 April 1947 as the base date for permissible margins of preference.

35 L/3503.

36 WT/L/189. ("[W]ith respect to dates applicable to Members for purposes of paragraph 4 and Annex G to GATT 1994, which waiver was originally granted by the CONTRACTING

be altered and extended by a Waiver in the light of exceptional circumstances invoked by Members.

*Case 4: Modification of the Original Fixed Date under Unforeseen Circumstances (Decision)*

A fixed date may also be changed by a Decision in the event of unforeseen circumstances. For example, GATT Article XXIX:3 is linked to the entry into force of the Havana Charter, which provides that if the Charter has not entered into force by 30 September 1949, the contracting parties shall meet "before 31 December 1949" to determine whether they desire to bring the GATT into force.[37] However, due to the unforeseen circumstance of the Charter's pending status of entry into force (thereafter, indefinitely postponed[38]), the CONTRACTING PARTIES decided on 21 March 1950 that the meeting referred to hold "before 31 December 1949" shall be held "at such time as may subsequently be decided by the CONTRACTING PARTIES."[39] In this unforeseen case, the original fixed date became contingent upon a subsequent Decision.

### 5.1.2 *Prescribed Date: The Date to Be Determined*

The establishment and modification of the prescribed date (*i.e.*, the date to be determined by an authority) were found in three cases (Table 5.2). First, to ascertain the expiry date of a waiver, the prescribed date was introduced during Negotiation as a solution, mandating that any decision granting a waiver shall explicitly state its termination date (Case 5). Second, to establish the date for review, the prescribed date was also inserted during Negotiation, which allows the Members to make determinations in accordance with the conditions that arise (Case 6). Third, once a date is officially prescribed, corresponding arrangements may be necessary to ensure stability and support an orderly transition. For this reason, in the case of the date of entry into force of the WTO Agreement, several Decisions were adoped to provide transitional arrangements, including the transational period from the GATT 1947 to the WTO and

PARTIES to GATT 1947 ... on 19 November 1960 ... the provisions of [GATT Article I:4] shall be modified with respect to the Government of Zimbabwe until 31 December 1997.")

37 GATT Art. XXIX:3 "If by September 30, 1949, the Havana Charter has not entered into force, the contracting parties shall meet before December 31, 1949, to agree whether this Agreement shall be amended, supplemented or maintained."

38 GATT/CP/86. Noting that the United States issued a statement on 6 December 1950 indicating that the Havana Charter would not be submitted again to the United States Congress, and therefore it subsequently became evident that the entry into force of the Charter would be indefinitely postponed.

39 Decision at GATT/CP.4/29, GATT/CP/61 p. 8; adoption at GATT/CP.4/SR.17 p. 7.

TABLE 5.2 Establishment and modification of the prescribed date in WTO Law

| Modalities | Cases | Development |
|---|---|---|
| Establishment (Negotiation) **(Case 5)** | – Create an obligation to state the expiration date for a waiver (MAR Art. IX:4) | – Provide no legal rule for the termination of the waiver without an expiry date<br>– Oblige to state the expiry date for the termination of a waiver |
| Establishment (Negotiation) **(Case 6)** | – Prescribe the date for review of the BOP measures (GATT Art. XII:4(b)) | – Oblige an original deadline (not later than 1 January 1951)<br>– Consider an alternative date (on a date to be determined) |
| Modification (Decision) **(Case 7)** | – Transitional arrangements for entry into force of the WTO Agreement (MAR Art. XIV:1) | – Prescribe the date of entry into force (1 January 1995)<br>– Provide a transitional period (one-year period in principle)<br>– Confirm the deadline for acceptance (1 January 1997)<br>– Extend the deadline for acceptance retroactively (25 February 1997) |

the confirmation of the general deadline for acceptance of the Agreement (Case 7).

*Case 5: Establishment of the Prescribed Date for the Expiration of Waivers (Negotiation)*

A prescribed date may be required to ensure that events come to a definitive end. For example, in the early GATT era, there was no rule in the GATT governing the waiver without an expiry date. Concerning whether the waiver could be modified or terminated, the GATT Panel has relied on the implied power of the CONTRACTING PARTIES by stating that "[t]he power of the CONTRACTING PARTIES to grant waivers under [GATT] Article XXV:5 implies the power to withdraw or modify the waivers granted."[40] To solve this concern more explicitly, Article IX:4 of the WTO Agreement was further negotiated to

40 L/6631, 37S/228, 259, para. 5.16.

oblige a decision by the Ministerial Conference granting a waiver to prescribe "the date on which the waiver shall terminate."[41] The WTO adjudicators also acknowledged that waivers should be inherently limited in duration by stating that: "Article IX:4 requires that the decision granting the waiver state the date on which the waiver shall terminate, thus ensuring that waivers are granted for limited periods of time."[42] In this regard, the mandate to state an expiry date for waivers is regarded as desirable to guarantee their termination within a limited duration.

*Case 6: Establishment of the Prescribed Date for Review (Negotiation)*

A prescribed date can also be incorporated into the law to regulate specific procedures. For example, GATT Article XII was negotiated to allow a contracting party to restrict imports in order to safeguard its balance-of-payments (BOP) difficulty, although the BOP restrictions must be reviewed at some time by the CONTRACTING PARTIES. To this end, the dates for the review of the BOP restrictions were established as follows. First, when GATT Article XII:4(b) was first drawn up in 1947, it required that a review to be conducted not later than a fixed date on "1 January 1951."[43] This fixed date as the original deadline was inserted into the Article due to the belief of the negotiators that "within a few years the world economy would recover from the post-war financial disequilibrium sufficiently to allow the restoration of currency convertibility and the removal of most [BOP] restrictions."[44] Second, this deadline was nevertheless re-examined and revised to call for an alternative date to complement the periodic consultations to apply BOP restrictions.[45] According to the revised

41 MAR Art. IX:4: "A decision by the Ministerial Conference granting a waiver shall state the exceptional circumstances justifying the decision, the terms and conditions governing the application of the waiver, and the date on which the waiver shall terminate."

42 Appellate Body Reports, *EC—Bananas III (Article 21.5—Ecuador II) / EC—Bananas III (Article 21.5—US)*, para. 380.

43 GATT Art. XII:4(b) (first draft): "Not later than 1 January 1951, the CONTRACTING PARTIES shall review all restrictions existing on that day and still applied under this Article at the time of the review." *See Final Act Adopted at the Conclusion of the Second Session of the Preparatory Committee of the United Nations Conference on Trade and Employment* [hereinafter "GATT Final Act"], https://worldtradelaw.net/document.php?id=misc/Final%20Act.pdf (last visited 15 June 2025).

44 GATT/CP.6/12/Rev.2, p. 3.

45 L/1005, p. 2. ("While the rules and criteria governing the use of import restrictions for [BOP] reasons were not substantially changed it was considered appropriate to provide for periodic consultations to be held with the countries applying restrictions. It was also decided that before such consultations were started, there should be an opportunity for the CONTRACTING PATTES to take stock of all the restrictions maintained for [BOP] reasons.")

Article, all BOP restrictions shall be reviewed "on a date to be determined" by the CONTRACTING PARTIES.[46] This prescribed date is subject to an interpretative note in GATT Annex 1 which further defines the date in principle as "within ninety days after the entry into force of the amendments of this Article." However, the CONTRACTING PARTIES still preserves its right to "determine a later date" provided that it finds that "conditions were not suitable for the application of the provisions of this subparagraph at the time envisaged." In this sense, the CONTRACTING PARTIES maintains the final authority to set the date for the BOP review in line with prevailing conditions.[47]

*Case 7: Transitional Arrangements for Entry into Force of the Agreement* (*Decision*)

Once the date is prescribed, corresponding arrangements may be made through a subsequent Decision. For example, according to Article XIV:1 of the WTO Agreement, the date of entry into force of the WTO Agreement shall be determined by Ministers.[48] Since the GATT 1947 would also be an integral part of the WTO Agreement on the same date, corresponding arrangements for smooth transition from the GATT to the WTO would be demanded after the confirmation of the exact date of entry into force of the WTO Agreement, which include:

(1) Prescribe a date for entry into force of the WTO Agreement ("1 January 1995")

(2) Allow a transitional co-existence of the GATT 1947 (one-year period in principle)

(3) Confirm the deadline for acceptance of the WTO Agreement ("1 January 1997")

(4) Extend the deadline for acceptance retroactively ("25 February 1997")

First, on 8 December 1994, the presribed date (*i.e.*, "the date determined by Ministers") for entry into force of the WTO Agreement was confirmed to be "1 January 1995."[49] This confirmed date triggered the subsequent transitional arrangements from the GATT 1947 to the WTO. Second, the Preparatory Committee thereafter adopted the *Decision on the Transitional Co-existence of*

---

46 GATT Art. XII:4(b) (revised): "On a date to be determined by them, the CONTRACTING PARTIES shall review all restrictions still applied under this Article on that date."

47 In practice, when the revised Article came into force in October 1957, the CONTRACTING PARTIES decided that this review should be effected in 1958 and was carried out by the CONTRACTING PARTIES in 1958–59.

48 MAR Art. XIV:1: "This Agreement and the Multilateral Trade Agreements annexed hereto shall enter into force on the date determined by Ministers in accordance with paragraph 3 of the Final Act Embodying the Results of the Uruguay Round of Multilateral Trade Negotiations. ..."

49 PC/M/10, para. 4.

*the GATT 1947 and the WTO Agreement* by acknowledging that "the stability of multilateral trade relations would therefore be furthered if the [GATT 1947] and the WTO Agreement were to co-exist for a limited period of time." This Decision further clarified the "limited period of time" for the termination of the GATT 1947 as one year after 1 January 1995 in principle, however, with the possibility of a one-year extension in the light of unforeseen circumstances.[50] Third, the prescribed date "1 January 1995" also gave rise to the confirmation of the general deadline (*i.e.*, 1 January 1997) for acceptance of the WTO Agreement.[51] In practice, all contracting parties to GATT 1947 that were eligible to become original Members of the WTO before 1 January 1997 became original Members, except the Republic of the Congo. Fourth, considering the Republic of the Congo was the only remaining contracting party to the GATT 1947 which was not yet a WTO Member, another Decision was thereafter adopted retroactively to extend the deadline for the Republic of the Congo from 1 January 1997 to 25 February 1997 (*i.e.*, the date when the Director-General (DG) received notice of its ratification of the WTO Agreement).[52] In sum, the confirmation of the date of entry into force of the WTO Agreement on "1 January 1995" was followed by a number of Decisions to provide corresponding arrangements, such as the transational period from the GATT 1947 to the WTO and the general deadline for acceptance of the WTO Agreement. These arrangements were made to ensure stability and support an orderly transition of the legal system.

### 5.1.3 *Unspecified Date: The Date of an Event*

The modification and elaboration of the unspecified date (*i.e.*, the date of an event) were found in three cases (Table 5.3). First, the anchored event for an unspecified date can be replaced by a Decision. In the case of the date of

50 PC/15, L/7586. ("The [GATT 1947] is herewith terminated one year after the date of entry into force of the WTO Agreement. In the light of unforeseen circumstances, the signatories may decide to postpone the date of termination by no more than one year.")

51 MAR Art. XIV:1: "This Agreement and the Multilateral Trade Agreements annexed hereto … shall remain open for acceptance for a period of two years following that date [of entry into force of this Agreement] unless the Ministers decide otherwise." Noting that the date of entry into force of the WTO Agreement was confirmed to be 1 January 1995, and therefore, the general deadline for acceptance, *i.e.*, for a period of two years following the date of entry into force, is 1 January 1997.

52 WT/L/208. ("The General Council … [d]ecides to extend, retroactively, the time-limit for acceptance by the Republic of the Congo of [the WTO Agreement] to 25 February 1997, the date of receipt by the [DG] of the notification of ratification of the Agreement by the Republic of the Congo, whence the Republic of the Congo would be deemed a Member of the Organization as of 27 March 1997, thirty days after receipt of the notification.")

TABLE 5.3 Modification and elaboration of the unspecified date in WTO Law

| **Modalities** | **Cases** | **Development** |
|---|---|---|
| Modification (Decision) **(Case 8)** | – Replace the anchored event of the date for notification of TRIMS (TRIMS Art. 5.1) | – Start on the date of entry into force of the WTO Agreement<br>– Replaced by the date of acceptance of the WTO Agreement |
| Elaboration (Declaration) **(Case 9)** | – Agree on the date to implement the provisions of the Article (GATT Art. XVI:4) | – Implement on "the earliest practicable date" after 1 January 1958<br>– Agree to give effect on "the date of entry into force of the Declaration" for the parties accepted |
| Elaboration (Working Practices) **(Case 10)** | – Clarify the date of circulation of a panel report (DSU Art. 16.4)<br>– Clarify the date of expiration of time-periods on a *non-working day* under the DSU | – Use the date printed on the WTO document on a trial basis<br>– Use the first working day of the WTO Secretariat following the day on which such time-period would normally expire (Working Practices Concerning Dispute Settlement Procedure) |

notification, the unspecified date was altered from the date of "entry into force" of the WTO Agreement to the date of "acceptance" of the WTO Agreement to address a practical difficulty (Case 8). Second, the unspecified date may be elaborated and agreed on by a Declaration of Members. In the case of "the earliest practicable date" for implementing a legal provision, a number of Members had agreed among themselves to subscribe a concrete date for implementation (Case 9). Third, the unspecified date can also be elaborated by the Working Practices of the institution. The Working Practices were found to clarify both the date of circulation of a document and the treatment of an expiration date that falls on a non-working day (Case 10).

*Case 8: Replacement of the Anchored Event for Notification (Decision)*

An event anchored to an unspecified date may be substituted by a Decision. For example, Article 5.1 of the TRIMS Agreement requires a notification of trade-related investment measures (TRIMS) within 90 days of "the date of *entry into force* of the WTO Agreement."[53] However, the TRIMs Committee noted the practical difficulty arising from the fact that a period which could have expired at the time of acceptance of the WTO Agreement by states or separate customs territories that were eligible to become original Members but that accepted the WTO Agreement after the date of its entry into force. Therefore, a draft recommendation was prepared and provided that the governments in question that accepted the WTO Agreement after its entry into force would have a period of 90 days from "the date of their *acceptance* of the WTO Agreement" to make notifications.[54] In line with this Recommendation, the General Council thereafter adopted a Decision and permitted states and separate customs territories to submit these notifications within 90 days from "the date of *acceptance* of the WTO Agreement."[55] As such, the anchored event of the unspecified date for notification of TRIMs was altered from the date of "entry into force" to the date of "acceptance" of the WTO Agreement by a Decision.

*Case 9: Elaboration on the Earliest Practicable Date for Implementation (Declaration)*

The unspecified date may be subject to further elaboration and agreement by Members through a formal Declaration. For example, GATT Article XVI:4 obliges that, "as from 1 January 1958" or "the earliest practicable date thereafter," contracting parties shall cease to grant export subsidies on non-primary products. However, in practice, the base date of 1 January 1958 had elapsed and no agreement on "the earliest practicable date" for this Article reached. The GATT Working Party therefore contemplated on what steps should be taken to implement the provisions of the Article in order to become effective on "the earliest practicable date" after 1 January 1958. The Working Party first noted that "a number of contracting parties [had] agreed to extend [the base date of 1 January 1958] beyond that date by means of a declaration."[56] Following this practice, it drafted the *Declaration Giving Effect to the Provisions of Article XVI:4*, which provided that the governments subscribing to it "agree that the date on which the aforementioned provisions of [GATT Article XVI:4] come into force shall be, for each party to this Declaration, the date on which this Declaration

53 TRIMS Art. 5.1: "Members, within 90 days of the date of *entry into force* of the WTO Agreement, shall notify the Council for Trade in Goods of all TRIMs they are applying that are not in conformity with the provisions of this Agreement." (emphasis added)

54 WT/GC/M/3, section 5. (emphasis added)

55 WT/L/64. (emphasis added)

56 L/1381, para. 2.

enters into force for that party."[57] Accordingly, the earliest practicable date for implementing GATT Article XVI:4 was defined and agreed to be the date of entry into force of the Declaration. In practice, the Declaration entered into force on 14 November 1962 and was in force for the seventeen contracting parties of which had accepted the Declaration.

*Case 10: Elaboration on the Date of Circulation and the Expiry on a Non-Working Day (Working Practices)*

The unspecified date can also be elaborated by the Working Practices of the WTO. For example, DSU Article 16.4 provides that, as a general rule, the panel report shall be adopted by the Dispute Settlement Body (DSB) within 60 days after "the date of [its] *circulation*" to the Members.[58] To clarify this unspecified date, the DSB has relied on the Working Practices and suggested to use "the date printed on the WTO document" with the assurance of the Secretariat on a trial basis.[59] In addition, the DSB has also agreed to the Working Practices concerning the date of expiration of time-periods on a "non-working day" by stating that "any such communication or action will be deemed to have been made or taken on the WTO non-working day if lodged on the first working day of the WTO Secretariat following the day on which such time-period would normally expire."[60] In these cases, the unspecified dates of circulation and expiration were clarified in accordance with the Working Practices of the WTO.

## 5.2 Timing

As categorized in Section 3.1.2, this research defines "timing" as establishing a temporal focus on a particular event without being referred to *calendar time*,

57 9S/32, 33, para. 1.

58 DSU Art. 16.4: "Within 60 days after *the date of circulation* of a panel report to the Members, the report shall be adopted at a DSB meeting [original footnote omitted] unless a party to the dispute formally notifies the DSB of its decision to appeal or the DSB decides by consensus not to adopt the report." (emphasis added)

59 WT/DSB/6, p. 2. ("When there is a reference to the terms 'date of circulation' or 'issuance to all Members' or 'issuance to the Members' in the DSU and its additional and special rules, the date to be used is the date printed on the WTO document to be circulated with the assurance of the Secretariat that the date printed on the document is the date on which this document is effectively put in the pigeon holes of delegations in all three working languages. This practice will be used on a trial basis and be subject to revision when necessary.")

60 *Ibid.*

such as the lexical realization by prepositional phrases (*e.g.*, "in time of" and "at any time") and temporal clauses (*e.g.*, "when" and "whenever"). In practice, the establishment, modification, and elaboration of timing were found in three cases (Table 5.4). First, timing can be progressively established and modified during Negotiation. In the case of the timing for notification (*i.e.*, whenever any significant changes are made), several types of temporal rules were developed in progress and consolidated into clearer and more precise formulations, such as from the requirement to notify "promptly" to the requirement to notify "prior to or not later than 30 days after" the announcement of the changes (Case 11). Second, additional timing may be provided as guidance through a Recommendation. In another case of the timing for notification (*i.e.*, when amendments can still be introduced and taken into account), additional timing (*i.e.*, when a draft … is available) was built in to guide the consideration of whether the notification occurs "at an early appropriate stage" (Case 12). Third, timing can be elaborated by a DS Report. In the case of the timing for security exception (*i.e.*, taken in time of war or other emergency), the adjudicators clarified the timing by emphasizing the chronological concurrence and the temporal link between the action and its surrounding circumstances (Case 13).

TABLE 5.4 Establishment, modification and elaboration of timing in WTO Law

| Modalities | Cases | Development |
|---|---|---|
| Establishment & Modification (Negotiation) **(Case 11)** | – Create the timing for an obligation to notify new BOP measures (GATT Art. XII:4(a) & Para. 9 of Understanding on BOP Provisions) | – Establish the notification obligation ("promptly")<br>– Add the timing for notification (whenever any significant changes are made)<br>– Clarify the timing of notification for significant changes made ("in advance of implementation" or "promptly *ex post facto*")<br>– Consolidate the timing of notification ("prior to or not later than 30 days after their announcement") |

TABLE 5.4 Establishment, modification and elaboration of timing in WTO Law (*cont.*)

| Modalities | Cases | Development |
|---|---|---|
| Elaboration (Recommendation) **(Case 12)** | – Add an additional timing for the notification at an early appropriate stage for the coverage of the proposed technical regulation (TBT Arts. 2.9.2 & 5.6.2) | – Original: *when* amendments can still be introduced and taken into account<br>– Additional: *when* a draft with the complete text of a proposed technical regulation or procedures for assessment of conformity is available |
| Elaboration (DS Report) **(Case 13)** | – Clarify the phrase "taken in time of" war or other emergency in international relations (GATT Art. XXI:(b)(iii)) | – Connote a chronological concurrence (taken "during" the war or other emergency)<br>– Create a temporal link between the action and its circumstances |

*Case 11: Establishment and Modification of the Timing for Notification (Negotiation)*

Timing can be progressively established during the course of Negotiation. For example, GATT Article XII:4(a) obliged the contracting party modifying its BOP restrictions to consult immediately with the CONTRACTING PARTIES. However, except for consultation, this Article did not explicitly set out any obligation with regard to the notification of the BOP measures at issue.[61] Instead, the obligation to notify was developed over time with several temporal rules incorporated as follows:

(1) Establish the notification obligation ("promptly" furnish detailed information)
(2) Add the timing for notification ("whenever any significant changes are made")

61 GATT Art. XII:4(a), "any contracting party applying new restrictions or raising the general level of its existing restrictions by a substantial intensification of the measures applied under this Article shall immediately after instituting or intensifying such restrictions (or, in circumstances in which prior consultation is practicable, before doing so) consult with the CONTRACTING PARTIES…."

(3) Clarify the timing of notification for significant changes made ("in advance of implementation" or "promptly *ex post facto*")
(4) Consolidate the timing for notification ("prior to or not later than 30 days after their announcement")

First, the GATT's Working Party agreed to revise GATT Article XII:4(a) in 1952 so as to require a contracting party modifying its BOP restrictions to furnish detailed information "promptly" to the Executive Secretary for immediate circulation to other contracting parties. The purpose of this new notification obligation was to make sure that governments would not delay to submit full information of new BOP restrictions to the Executive Secretary.[62] Second, the *Procedures for Dealing with New Import Restrictions Applied for Balance-of-Payments Reasons* was adopted in 1960 to further clarify and strengthen the timing for the obligation to notify. It required contracting parties to furnish information "whenever any significant changes are made in their restrictive systems."[63] Third, the 1979 *Understanding regarding Notification, Consultation, Dispute Settlement and Surveillance* reaffirmed the timing for notification, and went further to expect new BOP restrictions to be notified "in advance," or if not possible, "promptly *ex post facto*" of implementation of the BOP restrictions.[64] Fourth, to consolidate all the temporal rules developed over time in the GATT era, the *Understanding on BOP Provisions* ultimately laid down a more concrete period which requires the notification to be made "prior to or not later than 30 days after" the announcement of the new BOP measures.[65] In sum, several temporal rules had been established and developed progressively for the notification of BOP measures in the GATT era, and finally formalized into a more precise provision to include a concrete duration in the WTO era.

*Case 12: Elaboration on the Additional Timing for Notification (Recommendation)*

Guidance on timing may be offered through a Recommendation. For example, Articles 2.9.2 and 5.6.2 of the TBT Agreement require Members to notify other Members of the products to be covered by the proposed technical

62 L/55, paras. 10 and 11.

63 BISD 9S/18. ("[C]ontracting parties should furnish such information not only when they wish to initiate a consultation pursuant to [GATT] Articles XII:4(a) or XVIII:12(a) but whenever any significant changes are made in their restrictive systems. …")

64 L/4907, para. 3. ("Contracting parties should endeavour to notify such measures in advance of implementation. In other cases, where prior notification has not been possible, such measures should be notified promptly *ex post facto*.")

65 Para. 9 of the *Understanding on BOP Provisions*: "Significant changes shall be notified to the General Council prior to or not later than 30 days after their announcement."

regulation at a given time, namely, "at an early appropriate stage, when amendments can still be introduced and comments taken into account."[66] This timing of notification (*i.e.*, "at an early appropriate stage, when ...") was further discussed within the TBT Committee. In 1995, the Committee held discussions on procedures for notification and information exchange under the TBT Agreement, and thereafter adopted a Recommendation which added an additional timing to the original one (*i.e.*, "when amendments can still be introduced and comments taken into account") to be considered for the notification to take place "at an early appropriate stage." This additional timing requires that a notification should also be made "when a draft with the complete text of a proposed technical regulation or procedures for assessment of conformity is available."[67] In this regard, the additional timing was provided by a Recommendation to guide the determination of whether the notification occurs "at an early appropriate stage."

*Case 13: Elaboration on the Timing for Security Exception (DS Report)*

Timing can also be elaborated by a DS Report. For example, GATT Article XXI:(b)(iii) allows any contracting party to take necessary action to protect its essential security interests "taken in time of" war or other emergency in international relations.[68] The WTO adjudicators have examined this temporal linking phrase (*i.e.*, "taken in time of") in this Article, and stated that this phrase connotes a chronological concurrence which means the action must be taken "during" the war or other emergency in international relations.[69] Moreover,

66 TBT Art. 2.9.2 (or Art. 5.6.2): "Members shall ... notify other Members through the Secretariat of the products to be covered by the proposed technical regulation, together with a brief indication of its objective and rationale. Such notifications shall take place at an early appropriate stage, when amendments can still be introduced and comments taken into account;...."

67 G/TBT/W/2/Rev.1, p. 7. ("When implementing the provisions of Articles 2.9.2, 3.2 of the TBT Agreement (in relation to Article 2.9.2), 5.6.2 and 7.2 (in relation to Article 5.6.2), a notification should be made when a draft with the complete text of a proposed technical regulation or procedures for assessment of conformity is available and when amendments can still be introduced and taken into account.")

68 GATT Art. XXI:(b)(iii): "Nothing in this Agreement shall be construed ... to prevent any contracting party from taking any action which it considers necessary for the protection of its essential security interests ... taken in time of war or other emergency in international relations. ..."

69 Panel Report, *Russia—Traffic in Transit*, para. 7.70. ("The phrase 'taken in time of' in subparagraph (iii) describes the connection between the action and the events of war or other emergency in international relations in that subparagraph. The Panel understands this phrase to require that the action be taken during the war or other emergency in

the adjudicators also emphasized the temporal linkage of this phrase to create a link between the action and the relevant circumstances.[70] In this case, the adjudicators clarified the timing for security exception (*i.e.*, taken in time of war or other emergency) by emphasizing the chronological concurrence and the temporal link between the action and its surrounding circumstances.

## 5.3 Frequency in Time

As categorized in Section 3.1.3, this research defines "frequency in time" to convey the *fixed* number of occurrences an event happens within a given period (*e.g.*, "once every six months"), or the *unspecified* indication of repetition of an event (*e.g.*, "regular"). In practice, the establishment, modification, and elaboration of frequency in time were found in three cases (Table 5.5). First, frequency in time can be established over time by Decisions and Recommendations. In the case of state trading notifications, the three-year period for conducting a notification was first established by a Decision (*i.e.*, every three years with update), and then replaced by the two-year period (*i.e.*, every two years without update) set forth in Recommendations which implemented on a trial basis (Case 14). Second, frequency in time can be modified by an Amendment and the Rules of Procedure. To solve the practical difficulty, the frequency for conducting trade policy review was amended for longer periods (*i.e.*, from "every two/four/six years" to "every three/five/seven years"), together with a degree of flexibility provided in the Rules of Procedure (Case 15). Third, frequency in time may also be elaborated by the Rules of Procedure. To clarify the obligation of the "regular" report, the Rules of Procedure provide more precise timelines for Members to submit their report (Case 16).

---

international relations. This chronological concurrence is also an objective fact, amenable to objective determination.")

70 Panel Report, *US—Steel and Aluminium Products (Turkey)*, para. 7.155. ("[A]ction for the protection of essential security interests must be 'taken in time of' an emergency in international relations. … [T]he Panel understands these opening terms of subparagraph (iii) to qualify and describe the 'action' referred to in [GATT] Article XXI(b). The phrase 'taken in time of' in subparagraph (iii) describes the temporal link between the action taken by a Member under [GATT] Article XXI(b) and the 'war or other emergency in international relations' in subparagraph (iii) of that Article.")

TABLE 5.5 Establishment, modification, and elaboration of frequency in time in WTO Law

| Modalities | Cases | Development |
|---|---|---|
| Establishment (Decision & Recommendation) **(Case 14)** | – Create the frequency of state trading notifications (GATT Art. XVII:4(a)) | – Establish the frequency (every three years with update)<br>– Decide the appropriate deadlines by the Working Party<br>– Replace the frequency (trial) (every two years without update)<br>– Finalize the frequency (every two years without update) |
| Modification (Amendment & Rules of Procedure) **(Case 15)** | – Replace the frequency of the review cycles (TPRM Para. C(ii)) | – The original review cycles (2, 4, or 6 years)<br>– The amended review cycles (3, 5, or 7 years)<br>– Provide flexibility for the review cycles under the *Rules of Procedure* (up to 6 months) |
| Elaboration (Rules of Procedure) **(Case 16)** | – Clarify the regularity of report from Members ("regularly") (TPRM Para. D) | – Submit reports under the current timelines (at least 5 weeks before the meeting of review)<br>– Submit reports under the alternative timelines (at least 8 weeks before the meeting of review) |

*Case 14: Establishment of the Frequency for Notification (Decision and Recommendation)*

Frequency in time can be established over time by a series of Decisions and Recommendations. For example, to ensure the transparency of the activities of state trading enterprises, GATT Article XVII:4(a) obliges Members to notify the products which are imported into or exported from their territories by state trading enterprises, albeit without temporal rules to further indicate when the notification shall take place.[71] In practice, this general notification obligation had been developed over time to incorporate "frequency in time" as follows:

(1) Establish the frequency for notification (every three years with update)
(2) Decide the appropriate deadlines for notification by the Working Party
(3) Replace the frequency of notification on a trial basis (every two years without update)
(4) Finalize the frequency of notification (every two years without update)

First, the CONTRACTING PARTIES adopted a Decision in 1962 to establish a frequency for state trading notifications (*i.e.*, every three years). This 1962 Decision provides that contracting parties are invited to submit every third year beginning from January 1963 new and full notifications with updating notifications to be submitted in the intervening years.[72] Second, in the WTO era, the CTG adopted another Decision in 1995 to continue the three-year period for state trading notifications in the 1962 Decision. In addition, it proposed a deadline for the submission of notifications (*i.e.*, 30 June 1995). It also stated that the appropriate deadlines for future notifications would be established by the Working Party on State Trading Enterprises.[73] Third, due to an effort to reduce the burden of notifications on Members and help them to improve compliance with their notification obligations, the Working Party adopted a Recommendation in 2003 to eliminate the requirement of updating notifications in the intervening years. Besides, it also modified the frequency of state trading notifications so that notifications would be due "every two years" instead of "every three years." The Working Party recommended a trial period of four years for implementing this revised frequency commencing on 30 June 2004 which was further extended to 30 June 2012.[74] Lastly, the CTG adopted a final Decision

---

71 GATT Art. XVII:4(a): "Contracting parties shall notify the CONTRACTING PARTIES of the products which are imported into or exported from their territories by enterprises of the kind described in [GATT Article XVII:1(a)]."

72 BISD 11S/58.

73 G/C/M/1, para. 5.5. ("[I]n order to give delegations sufficient time to prepare their notifications, and to ensure that the necessary material was before the Working Party as soon as possible, the deadline of 30 June 1995 had been proposed for the current year's notification obligation. With respect to all future notifications, the Working Party itself would decide what deadlines were appropriate.") Noting that the Working Party accordingly set forth the following deadlines: (1) 30 June 1995 for the 1995 notifications (G/STR/N/1); (2) 30 September 1998 for the 1998 new and full notifications (G/STR/N/4); and (3) 29 June 2001 for the 2001 new and full notifications (G/STR/N/7).

74 G/STR/5, paras. 3–4. ("After the four-year trial period, the Working Party shall review the situation, with regard to compliance with the notification obligation and the frequency of

in 2012 to approve a Recommendation by the Working Party, and to definitively set the frequency of new and full notifications to "two years" and eliminate the need for updating notifications in the intervening years.[75] In sum, the three-year period for conducting state trading notifications was first established by a Decision (*i.e.*, every three years with update), and then replaced by a Recommendation (*i.e.*, every two years without update) which was undergone a trial phrase to finalization by another Decision.

*Case 15: Modification of the Frequency for Review (Amendment and Rules of Procedure)*

Frequency in time can be modified by an Amendment and the Rules of Procedure. For example, TPRM Paragraph C obliges the Trade Policy Review Body (TPRB) to undertake trade policy reviews for all Members. In terms of the review cycles, the original version of TPRM Paragraph C(ii) had already prescribed varying review frequencies for individual Members based on their impact on the functioning of the multilateral trading system (*i.e.*, "every two years" for the first four trading entities, "every four years" for the next sixteen, and "every six years" for the others).[76] However, in 2017, WTO Members were informed by the Secretariat with regard to the challenges and burden of workload of review due to the increasing number of membership, and thereafter agreed to discuss ways to address this challenges.[77] As a result, WTO Members decided to amend the frequencies for undergoing a trade policy review

notifications, with a view to determining whether to extend the application of this recommendation, either as presently drafted or in a modified form for a further period.") Noting that this revised frequency of notifications was implemented until 30 June 2008. In 2008, the Working Party adopted two recommendations to subsequently extend the trial phase for two years two times to 30 June 2010 in G/STR/6, and thereafter to 30 June 2012 in G/STR/7.

75 G/C/M/111, item III. The text of the recommendation can be found in G/STR/8.

76 TPRM Para. C(ii) (original): "The first four trading entities so identified (counting the European Communities as one) shall be subject to review every two years. The next 16 shall be reviewed every four years. Other Members shall be reviewed every six years, except that a longer period may be fixed for least-developed country Members."

77 WT/MIN(17)/9, para. 2.3. ("Given the increasing number of WTO Members, the current review cycles (2, 4 or 6 years) meant that some 24 reviews had to be completed each year. This was already stretching the resources of both Members and the Secretariat to the limit, and building up backlogs. The Secretariat anticipated that, once all the countries currently in the accession proceedings had become WTO Members, the number of [Trade Policy Reviews] required would increase to 30 per year, which would not be sustainable in the long run. Members therefore discussed ways to address this challenge. Members noted that, notwithstanding the revised review cycles ..., the general flexibility of up to six months provided for in the Rules of Procedure for Meetings of the TPRB would remain unchanged.")

from "every two/four/six years" to "every three/five/seven years."[78] Besides, Paragraph 3 of the *Rules of Procedure for Meetings of the* TPRB provides a possibility to flexibly conduct the assigned review cycles up to six months with the conditions to establish schedules for subsequent reviews in advance and to adhere strictly to the timetables.[79] In this case, the frequency for conducting trade policy reviews was amended for longer periods in time, together with a degree of flexibility permitted under the Rules of Procedure.

*Case 16: Elaboration on the Regularity for Reporting* (*Rules of Procedure*)

Frequency in time may also be elaborated by the Rules of Procedure. For example, TPRM Paragraph D obliges each Member to report "regularly" to the TPRB for the enhancement of transparency.[80] This "regular" report obligation has been developed by the *Rules of Procedure for Meetings of the* TPRB, which requires the Members to submit review documents in line with the specific time of review. It requests the Members to submit their government reports to the WTO "not less than five weeks in advance of the TPRB meeting" for their review if they choose the current timelines shown in Annex 1 of the Rules of Procedure, and "at least eight weeks in advance" if they choose the alternative timelines.[81] In this regard, the Rules of Procedure establish clearer temporal guidelines to ensure Members submit their trade policy reports "regularly," as mandated in TPRM Paragraph D.

## 5.4 Period in Time

As categorized in Section 3.1.4, this research defines "period in time" as a length of time when an event occurs, which can be represented either with a numerical

78 *Ibid.*, para. 2.4(1).

79 WT/TPR/6/Rev.4. ("The cycle of reviews provided for in [TPRM] Paragraph C(ii) shall be applied with a general flexibility of up to six months, if and as may be necessary. Schedules of subsequent reviews shall be established counting from the date of the previous review meeting. Members should adhere strictly to the timetables for the preparation of reviews, once agreed.")

80 TPRM Para. D: "In order to achieve the fullest possible degree of transparency, each Member shall report regularly to the TPRB."

81 WT/TPR/6/Rev.4. ("Documentation relating to each review meeting shall be circulated in all working languages not less than five weeks in advance of the relevant meetings under the current timelines, or eight weeks in advance in the case of Members under review having volunteered to apply the alternative timelines.") Noting that the current timelines and the alternative timelines shown in Annex 1 of the Rules of Procedure are as options for the submission of written questions and answers. The choice will be made by the Member under review at the time of agreeing on the date of review.

value (*i.e.*, *fixed* period in time) or a non-numerical term (*i.e.*, *prescribed* or *unspecified* period in time). Similar to the "point in time" in Section 5.1 above, these three types of period in time have been contemplated on several occasions in practice. The following subsections will provide a brief overview on the most significant of these occasions: (1) the establishment and modification of the *fixed* period in time (Section 5.4.1); (2) the establishment and modification of the *prescribed* period in time (Section 5.4.2); and (3) the elaboration of the *unspecified* period in time (Section 5.4.3).

### 5.4.1 *Fixed Period: The Selected Period*

The establishment and modification of a fixed period were found in six cases (Table 5.6). The first three cases are related to the "establishment" of a fixed period. First, a fixed period can be established during the course of Negotiation. For example, to ensure the firm validity of the concessions, a three-year period was established for Members to modify their concessions in the right of renegotiation, subject to extension on a case-by-case basis through a subsequent decision (Case 17). Second, a fixed period can be established by a Decision. For example, to strengthen the dispute settlement proceedings, a Decision was adopted to establish several procedures regarding consultation with a number of fixed periods applied on a trial basis (Case 18). Third, a fixed period can also be established by a Recommendation. For example, to establish reference periods in determining negligible imports, a Recommendation was adopted to set three optional time-frames (including fixed periods) as guidance for making the determination of negligible imports (Case 19).

The other three cases are related to the "modification" of a fixed period, namely, the extension of a given period. First, a fixed period can be extended by a Decision. For example, to extend fixed periods for multilateral negotiations and application of legal provisions, several decisions were adopted in a row to postpone the completion of the negotiations and the application of the provisions to "a later date," either fixed or open-ended. Especially, due to practical and political difficulties, the final deadline for the negotiations was no longer considered to be predictable, and therefore was left open-ended (Case 20). Second, a fixed period can be extended by a Joint Request of the Parties. For example, to extend a fixed period for adopting Panel Reports, the Joint Request of the Parties was presented to the DSB for making a decision to postpone the adoption of the Reports to "a later date" under the consideration of practical difficulties (Case 21). Third, a fixed period can also be extended by a Mutual Agreement. For example, in the context of suspension of concessions between the parties concerned, mutual agreements for extension were developed as a regular practice without much difficulty in the light of the sovereign right of the parties (Case 22).

TABLE 5.6 Establishment and modification of the fixed period in WTO Law

| Modalities | Cases | Development |
|---|---|---|
| Establishment (Negotiation) **(Case 17)** | – Create a time-frame for modification of the concessions to ensure their validity (GATT Art. XXVIII:1) | – Establish the firm validity by a time-frame (three-year period)<br>– Extend the time-frame by a *Decision* (case-by-case) |
| Establishment (Decision) **(Case 18)** | – Create time-frames for consultation of GATT dispute settlement on a trial basis (GATT Art. XXII:1) | – Reply to the request for consultation (10 days after receipt)<br>– Enter into consultation (30 days from request)<br>– Request the establishment of a panel or a working party (60 days from the request for consultation)<br>– Exceptional for urgency (shortened time-frames) |
| Establishment (Recommendation) **(Case 19)** | – Create three optional time-frames as guidance for determination of negligible imports to terminate anti-dumping investigation (ADP Art. 5.8) | – The period of data collection for the dumping investigation<br>– The most recent 12 consecutive months prior to initiation of the investigation<br>– The most recent 12 consecutive months prior to the date on which the application was filed, provided that the lapse of time between the filing and the initiation of the investigation is no longer than 90 days |
| Modification (Decision) **(Case 20)** | – Extend the three-year period for negotiations of non-preferential rules of origin (RO Art. 9.2(a)), and for negotiations on the question of emergency safeguard measures (GATS Art. X:1) | – Extend the three-year period to later dates to complete the negotiations, and ultimately without a concrete deadline (open-ended) |

TABLE 5.6 Establishment and modification of the fixed period in WTO Law (*cont.*)

| Modalities | Cases | Development |
|---|---|---|
| | – Extend the ten-year transition period for application of provisions in the TRIPS Agreement (TRIPS Art. 66.1) | – Extend the ten-year period to later dates to apply the legal provision (*e.g.*, 1 July 2034) |
| Modification (Joint request of the parties) **(Case 21)** | – Extend the 60-day period for adoption of a panel report (DSU Art. 16.4) | – Extend the 60-day deadline to a later date |
| Modification (Mutual Agreement) **(Case 22)** | – Extend the time-frames for suspension of concessions or other obligations on a case-by-case basis (GATT Art. XIX:3(a) & SG Art. 8.2) | – Extend the thirty-day period for notification of any proposed suspension of concessions or obligations to a later date<br>– Extend the ninety-day period for suspension of concessions or obligations to a later date |

*Case 17: Establishment of the Fixed Period for Modification of Concessions (Negotiation)*

A fixed period can be established during the course of Negotiation. For example, GATT Article XXVIII:1 prescribes exact timing for contracting parties to modify or withdraw a concession to ensure its firm validity, which is "on the first day of each three-year period" or "any other period that may be specified by the CONTRACTING PARTIES."[82] These time-frames make sure that the concessions would be valid during the given periods. In other words, the modification or withdrawal of the concessions should not be undertaken during these given periods. However, this Article as originally agreed in 1947 did not contain the time-frames, and only stated that the concessions would be modifiable on

82 GATT Art. XXVIII:1: "On the first day of each three-year period, the first period beginning on 1 January 1958 (or on the first day of any other period that may be specified by the CONTRACTING PARTIES by two-thirds of the votes cast) a contracting party ... may, ... , modify or withdraw a concession included in the appropriate schedule annexed to this Agreement."

or after 1 January 1951 to ensure that they would have firm validity before that date.[83] There was no further rule regarding the validity of the concessions after 1 January 1951 which renegotiation could occur.

To reflect the view for the possibility of renegotiation and modification of the concessions after 1 January 1951, the revised Article was drafted by the Working Party, whose Report "provided for the extension of the firm validity of the concessions by three-year periods, but with greater flexibility in the right of renegotiation and in the procedures for negotiation."[84] In this regard, except for the fixed three-year period established, the CONTRACTING PARTIES was able to make a decision to accord "sympathetic consideration" to the requests for renegotiation of the concessions beyond the fixed duration of three years on a case-by-case basis. In practice, the deadline of renegotiation was on occasion extended by the Council for all or for specific contracting parties.[85] In sum, a three-year period was established for Members to conduct renegotiation and modification of the concessions, along with the flexibility to extend the period through a subsequent decision on a case-by-case basis.

*Case 18: Establishment of the Fixed Period for Dispute Settlement Consultation (Decision)*

A fixed period can be established by a Decision. For example, GATT Article XXII:1 provides a general obligation of consultation for the dispute settlement in the GATT era. However, this plain Article does not have relevant procedures in detail or provide any temporal rules for its conduction.[86] To further ensure prompt and effective resolution of disputes to the benefit of all contracting parties, the procedures for consultation evolved to include several time-frames designed to regulate the related proceedings. Especially, the *1989 Decision*

83 GATT Final Act (n. 43), Art. XXVIII:1. ("On or after January 1, 1951, any contracting party may, by negotiation and agreement with any other contracting party with which such treatment was initially negotiated, and subject to consultation with such other contracting parties as the CONTRACTING PARTIES determine to have a substantial interest in such treatment, modify, or cease to apply, the treatment which it has agreed to accord under Article II to any product described in the appropriate Schedule annexed to this Agreement.")

84 L/329, adopted on 26 February 1955, 3S/205, 217, para. 27(iii).

85 *E.g.*, C/W/165, C/M/63 p. 5 (agreement to extend the deadline from 1 January 1970 to 31 December 1970); C/W/315, C/M/131 (agreement to extend the deadline from 1 January 1979 to 30 June 1979 for Czechoslovakia and to 31 March 1979 for the United States).

86 GATT Art. XXII:1: "Each contracting party shall accord sympathetic consideration to, and shall afford adequate opportunity for consultation regarding, such representations as may be made by another contracting party with respect to any matter affecting the operation of this Agreement."

*on Improvements to the GATT Dispute Settlement Rules and Procedures* was adopted, prescribing several procedures and time-frames with regard to GATT Article XXII consultations on a trial basis as follows:

(1) Reply to the request for consultation (10 days after receipt)
Enter into consultation (30 days from request)

(2) Request the establishment of a panel or a working party
(60 days from the request for consultation)

(3) Exceptional and shortened time-frames for urgency
- Enter into consultation (10 days from request)
- Request the establishment of a panel or a working party
(30 days from the request for consultation)

First, the 1989 Decision established time-frames for replying a request of consultation (*i.e.*, 10 days after receipt) and entering into such consultation (*i.e.*, 30 days from request).[87] Second, with regard to the request for establishment of a panel or a working party for the dispute, it allowed the disputing party to proceed after 60 days from the request of consultation if it fails to settle a dispute.[88] Third, in cases of urgency, it provided the shortened time-frames for entry into consultation (*i.e.*, 10 days from request) and request the establishment of a panel or a working party (*i.e.*, 30 days from request).[89] This 1989 Decision nevertheless agreed that the above improvements would be applied on a trial basis, and the CONTRACTING PARTIES would "continue negotiations with the aim of further improving and strengthening the GATT dispute settlement system taking into account the experience gained in the application of these improvements."[90] Finally, on 1 January 1995, the WTO Agreement

87 L/6489, para. C.1. ("If a request is made under [GATT] Article XXII:1 or XXIII:1, the contracting party to which the request is made shall, unless otherwise mutually agreed, reply to the request within ten days after its receipt and shall enter into consultations in good faith within a period of no more than thirty days from the date of the request, with a view to reaching a mutually satisfactory solution.")

88 *Ibid.*, para. C.2. ("If the consultations under [GATT] Article XXII:1 or XXIII:1 fail to settle a dispute within sixty days after the request for consultations, the complaining party may request the establishment of a panel or a working party under Article XXIII:2. The complaining party may request a panel or a working party during the sixty-day period if the parties jointly consider that consultations have failed to settle the dispute.")

89 *Ibid.*, para. C.4. ("In cases of urgency, including those which concern perishable goods en route, parties shall enter into consultations within a period of no more than ten days from the date of the request. If the consultations have failed to settle the dispute within a period of thirty days after the request, the complaining party may request the establishment of a panel or a working party.")

90 *Ibid.*, para. A.3. ("[The improvements] shall be applied on a trial basis from 1 May 1989 to the end of the Uruguay Round in respect of complaints brought during that period under [GATT] Article XXII and XXIII; it is also agreed to keep the application of these

entered into force with the DSU for the dispute settlement mechanism, and the 1989 Decision lapsed accordingly. In sum, a Decision was adopted to establish several procedures regarding the dispute settlement consultation in the GATT era, which contained a number of fixed periods to be applied on a trial basis until the entry into force of the DSU in the WTO era.

*Case 19: Establishment of Optional Reference Periods for Determination of Negligible Imports (Recommendation)*

A fixed period can also be established by a Recommendation. For example, Article 5.8 of the Anti-Dumping Agreement provides a general obligation for Members to terminate anti-dumping investigation in cases of negligible imports, albeit it does not establish a period in time over which the imports are to be counted in determining whether the volume of imports is negligible.[91] The Committee on Anti-Dumping Practices therefore adopted a Recommendation considering that guidance regarding an appropriate time-frame for the determination of negligible imports would be useful. Accordingly, three optional reference periods were provided as follows:[92]

> (a) the period of data collection for the dumping investigation; or (b) the most recent 12 consecutive months prior to initiation for which data are available; or (c) the most recent 12 consecutive months prior to the date on which the application was filed, for which data are available, provided that the lapse of time between the filing of the application and the initiation of the investigation is no longer than 90 days.

All in all, this Recommendation set three optional time-frames, including fixed periods "12 months" and "90 days," as guidance for making the determination of negligible imports.

*Case 20: Extension of the Fixed Period for Negotiation and Application of Legal Provisions (Decision)*

A fixed period can be extended by a Decision. For example, Article 9.2(a) of the Agreement on Rules of Origin and GATS Article X:1 oblige Members to conduct multilateral negotiations in relation to the harmonization of

---

improvements under review during the remainder of the Round and to decide on their adoption before the end of the Round. …")

91 ADP Art. 5.8: "There shall be immediate termination [of investigation] in cases where the authorities determine that … the volume of dumped imports, actual or potential, is negligible."

92 G/ADP/10.

non-preferential rules of origin and emergency safeguard measures, respectively. Both of the Articles contain a three-year period for the negotiations to be completed.[93] However, in practice, this three-year duration for the negotiations could not be fulfilled due to practical and political difficulties, and was extended several times by the Council's Decision.

In the case of Article 9.2(a) of the Agreement on Rules of Origin, the negotiation of Harmonization Work Programme (HWP) was formally launched on 20 July 1995 and originally scheduled for its completion by 20 July 1998.[94] Due to the complexity of issues, the work could not be completed while considerable progress had been made. In this regard, the CTG adopted a Decision to approve the Committee on Rules of Origin to continue its work and set a deadline to complete the work by November 1999.[95] Thereafter, the Committee still considered that the remaining work could not be completed on a best-endeavour basis by the deadline,[96] and came to a virtual halt in 2007 due to divergences on a number of core policy issues. Finally, due to the difference in Members' views, it is difficult for the Committee to draw a future roadmap or to put forward any concrete deadline of work on the HWP.[97] In a similar vein, GATS Article X:1 requires the negotiations on the question of emergency safeguard measures to complete within a three-year period due on 1 January 1998.[98] Due to practical and political difficulties, the CTS subsequently adopted Decisions to extend the said period by concrete deadlines on four instances;[99] nevertheless, the fifth Decision, adopted in 2004, set no further end-date for the negotiations.[100]

---

93 RO Art. 9.2(a): "The work programme shall be initiated as soon after the entry into force of the WTO Agreement as possible and will be completed within three years of initiation."; GATS Art. X:1: "There shall be multilateral negotiations on the question of emergency safeguard measures based on the principle of non-discrimination. The results of such negotiations shall enter into effect on a date not later than three years from the date of entry into force of the WTO Agreement."

94 G/RO/M/1.

95 G/RO/25.

96 G/RO/42.

97 G/L/1047. Noting that, until 2025, the HWP has not yet been finalized due to the complexity of certain topics.

98 Noting that the date of entry into force of the WTO Agreement was confirmed to be 1 January 1995, and therefore, the general deadline for entry into effect of the results of the negotiations, *i.e.*, not later than three years from the date of entry into force, is 1 January 1998.

99 The first decision adopted in S/L/43. ("[T]he first sentence of [GATS Articles X:1 and 2] shall continue to apply until 30 June 1999.") For the subsequent extensions of the deadline: 15 December 2000 (S/L/73), 15 March 2002 (S/L/90), and 15 March 2004 (S/L/102).

100 S/L/159. ("Subject to the outcome of the mandate in paragraph 1, the results of such negotiations shall enter into effect on a date not later than the date of entry into force of the results of the current round of services negotiations.")

Aside from the extension of the three-year negotiation period, another example can be found in the application of legal provisions. For example, the extension for the 10-year transition period in Article 66.1 of the TRIPS Agreement was frequently observed.[101] The Council for the TRIPS Agreement had adopted a number of Decisions to extend the 10-year transition period for the least-developed country Members (LDCs) to apply legal rules to future dates.[102] As of this writing, the most recent Decision in 2021 has extended the transition period to 1 July 2034 in line with the long-term social and economic impacts of the COVID-19 pandemic on LDCs.[103] Similar instances can also be found for the extended transition period with respect to the protection and enforcement of rights related to patents and undisclosed information in the pharmaceutical sector under Sections 5 and 7 of the TRIPS Agreement. In the *2001 Doha Declaration on the TRIPS Agreement and Public Health,* Ministers agreed that the LDCs would not be obliged to implement or apply Sections 5 and 7 of the TRIPS Agreement until 1 January 2016.[104] In 2015, the Council for the TRIPS Agreement adopted a Decision providing for a further extension of the transition period until 1 January 2033.[105] In sum, the fixed periods (*i.e.*, the three-year negotiation period and the ten-year transition period) were extended to future dates by a number of Decisions, although the final deadline may not be clearly predictable and could remain open due to practical and political challenges.

*Case 21: Extension of the Fixed Period for Adoption of Panel Reports (Joint Request of the Parties)*

A fixed period can be extended by a Joint Request of the Parties. For example, DSU Article 16.4 obliges the DSB to adopt a panel report within a 60-day period unless a party to the dispute decides to appeal or the DSB decides not to

101 TRIPS Art. 66.1: "In view of the special needs and requirements of least-developed country Members, their economic, financial and administrative constraints, and their need for flexibility to create a viable technological base, such Members shall not be required to apply the provisions of this Agreement, other than Articles 3, 4 and 5, for a period of 10 years from the date of application as defined under [Article 65.1]."

102 *E.g.*, IP/C/40, para. 1. ("... until 1 July 2013, or until such a date on which they cease to be a least-developed country Member, whichever date is earlier.")

103 IP/C/88, para. 1.

104 WT/MIN(01)/DEC/2, para. 7.

105 IP/C/73, para. 1. *See also* IP/C/M/80. At the meeting of 6 November 2015, the Council for the TRIPS Agreement approved a recommendation regarding a decision to waive the obligations under Articles 70.8 and 70.9 of the TRIPS Agreement (IP/C/74) which was subsequently adopted by the General Council on 30 November 2015 (WT/L/971).

adopt the report.[106] However, in fact, the DSB has agreed in several disputes to extend this 60-day deadline to a later date by the Joint Request of the Parties to the dispute.[107] In other words, by the Joint Request, the DSB agreed to extend the deadline for the adoption or appeal of the panel report between both parties to a later date.[108] In a number of cases, this 60-day period has been extended on account of the workload of the Appellate Body, *e.g.*, the parties considered that the extension would "provide greater flexibility in scheduling any possible appeal."[109] Generally speaking, the Joint Request of the Parties may be presented to the DSB for making a decision to postpone its work for adoption of panel reports to a later date under the consideration of practical difficulties.

*Case 22: Extension of the Fixed Period for Suspension of Concessions (Mutual Agreement)*

A fixed period can be extended by a Mutual Agreement. For example, according to GATT Article XIX:3(a) and Article 8.2 of the Agreement on Safeguards, the Member to whose exports the safeguard measure is being applied has the right, no later than "ninety days" after the safeguard is applied, to suspend substantially equivalent concessions or other obligations; provided that "thirty days" have lapsed since the WTO received the notification of the

106 DSU Art. 16.4: "Within 60 days after the date of circulation of a panel report to the Members, the report shall be adopted at a DSB meeting unless a party to the dispute formally notifies the DSB of its decision to appeal or the DSB decides by consensus not to adopt the report."

107 *E.g.*, *Brazil—Retreaded Tyres*, WT/DS332/8; *Thailand—Cigarettes (Philippines)*, WT/DSB/M/290, paras. 53–58; *EU—Footwear (China)*, WT/DSB/M/308, paras. 100–101; *US—COOL*, WT/DSB/M/310, paras. 9–12; *India—Agricultural Products*, WT/DSB/M/352, paras. 6.5–6.6; *Peru—Agricultural Products*, WT/DSB/M/353, paras. 6.6–6.7; *China—HP-SSST (Japan)*, WT/DSB/M/359, paras. 8.6–8.7.

108 *E.g.*, Appellate Body Report, *US—Tuna II (Mexico)*, para. 4. ("In a communication dated 31 October 2011, Mexico and the United States jointly requested the [DSB] to agree to an extension of the 60-day period provided for in [DSU] Article 16.4 for the adoption or appeal of the Panel Report until 20 January 2012. At a meeting held on 11 November 2011, the DSB agreed that, upon a request by Mexico or the United States, it would adopt the Panel Report no later than 20 January 2012, unless the DSB decided by consensus not to do so, or either party to the dispute notified the DSB of its decision to appeal.")

109 WT/DS381/9. ("Taking into account the current workload of the Appellate Body, Mexico and the United States of America would like to request that the [DSB] adopt the draft decision attached to this letter with respect to the dispute [*US—Tuna II (Mexico)*] (WT/DS381). We consider that the draft DSB decision, if adopted, would provide greater flexibility in scheduling any possible appeal.")

such suspension.[110] These Articles provide two time-frames (*i.e.*, the thirty-day and ninety-day periods) for governing the right to suspend concessions or obligations in order to counter the safeguard measures taken by other Members.

First, in the early days, the thirty-day period for notification of any proposed suspension of concessions or obligations was extended on several occasions by the decisions of the CONTRACTING PARTIES.[111] However, following the evolution of practice, the thirty-day period had been extended to a later date through a mutual agreement between the contracting parties concerned by submitting a joint communication for the extension to the other contracting parties.[112] Second, with regard to the ninety-day period for suspension of concessions or obligations, there were also precedents for extensions by mutaul agreements between the parties.[113] Despite the practice of mutual agreements,

---

110 GATT Art. XIX:3(a): "… if such action is taken or continued, the affected contracting parties shall then be free, not later than ninety days after such action is taken, to suspend, upon the expiration of thirty days from the day on which written notice of such suspension is received by the CONTRACTING PARTIES, the application to the trade of the contracting party taking such action,…."; SG Art. 8.2: "If no agreement is reached within 30 days in the consultations under [Art. 12.3], then the affected exporting Members shall be free, not later than 90 days after the measure is applied, to suspend, upon the expiration of 30 days from the day on which written notice of such suspension is received by the [CTG], the application of substantially equivalent concessions or other obligations under GATT 1994, to the trade of the Member applying the safeguard measure, the suspension of which the [CTG] does not disapprove."

111 *E.g.*, SR.7/11, p. 1, L/44/Add.1. A request by the Turkish Government, with the consent of the United States, was agreed by the CONTRACTING PARTIES for an extesion of the notification period by another ninety days. For the reasons of the extension, the Turkish delegation said that "consultations were now taking place between the delegations of Turkey and the United States on the subject of the United States increase in the duty on dried figs. His Government wished to await the result of these consultations before deciding to have recourse to measures envisaged under [GATT] Article XIX:3. A time limit was, however, specified in that paragraph for notification which would expire in this case on 29 October. He requested the CONTRACTING PARTIES to extend the time limit by another ninety days."

112 *E.g.*, L/7219/Add.7. A joint communication from Australia and Canada agreed to extend the notification period to suspend substantially equivalent concessions to a later date by stating that: "The Permanent Missions of Australia and Canada have agreed that their reciprocal rights and obligations under the General Agreement will be maintained for this purpose. The two delegations have further agreed that the time period set forth in [GATT] Article XIX:3(a) within which Australia must notify any intention to suspend substantially equivalent concessions has been extended to 12 March 1994."

113 *E.g.*, L/4099/Add.1. The European Communities had asked for several extensions by mutual agreements of the period of ninety days for the safeguard measure on imports of certain footwear taken by Australia. The relevant statement is as follows: "Consultations between Australia and the European Economic Community were entered into on 7 March 1975, in

at the 1975 Council meeting, a question was raised to concern whether the prolongation of the period of ninety days by nature would have to be taken by the CONTRACTING PARTIES. By that time, the responses at the meeting indicated that "they had never encountered any difficulty in reaching agreement with the other party for an extension of the period referred to in [GATT] Article XIX:3(a) in order to continue consultations rather than having recourse to retaliation."[114] The DG also appeared to respond to the similar question by emphasizing the "sovereign right" of the parties.[115] In the WTO era, the practice of parties mutually agreeing to extensions remains common in several cases.[116] In sum, Mutual Agreements to extend the suspension of concessions or obligations appear to have developed into a regular and largely uncontroversial practice, as they respect the sovereign rights of the parties.

### 5.4.2 *Prescribed Period: The Period to Be Determined*

The establishment and modification of the prescribed period (*i.e.*, the period to be determined by an authority) were found in two cases (Table 5.7). First, a prescribed period can be established through a Recommendation. To build the

Geneva, under [GATT] Article XIX, These consultations, however, could not be concluded within the period provided for in Article XIX. Therefore the Australian Government and the European Economic Community have agreed that their reciprocal rights and obligations under the General Agreement will be maintained as though the ninety-day period set forth in Article XIX:3 began to run as from 25 January 1976." For subsequent extensions from 1976 to 1982, *see* L/4099/Add.2 to Add. 23.

114 C/M/103, p. 20.

115 C/M/174, p. 11. ("[I]f the Community agreed to the US request for an extension of the date of entry into force of the retaliatory measures, this could be done. If the Community did not agree, its retaliatory measures could be put into place on 1 March unless the Council were to disapprove of them; but, in the absence of disapproval, the Council could not postpone the entry into force of the measures, because this was the Community's sovereign right.")

116 *E.g.*, G/SG/202. The Members have notified the CTG of mutual agreements to extend the ninety-day period in Article 8.2 of the Agreement on Safeguards to a later date, or for as long as the safeguard measure remains in force. The relevant statement is as follows: "On 8 January 2019, Thailand and the United States conducted consultations with a view to discuss the information ... related to the safeguard measure on solar products, exchange views on the safeguard measure, and reach an understanding on ways to achieve the objective set out in [Article 8.1 of the Agreement on Safeguards]. ... They have agreed to continue these discussions and that their reciprocal rights and obligations under the Safeguards Agreement and the [GATT] 1994 will be maintained. For this purpose, and without prejudice to their positions under Article 8.3 of the Agreement on Safeguards, they have further agreed that the 90-day period set forth in Article 8.2 of the Agreement on Safeguards and Article XIX:3(a) of the [GATT] 1994 shall be considered to expire as between them on 7 May 2021."

TABLE 5.7 Establishment and modification of the prescribed period in WTO Law

| Modalities | Cases | Development |
| --- | --- | --- |
| Establishment (Recommendation) **(Case 23)** | – Create a period for the concept of *de facto* application of the GATT beyond legal texts (GATT Art. XXVI:5(c)) | – Prescribe a reasonable period<br>– Establish a general time-frame (a two-year period)<br>– Eliminate the application period (replaced by review or report) |
| Modification (Decision) **(Case 24)** | – Extend the prescribed period for acceptance of the amendment, *i.e., the Protocol Amending the TRIPS Agreement* (MAR Art. X:3) | – Specify an end-date for acceptance the Protocol (until 1 December 2007)<br>– Extend the deadline to a later date (*e.g.*, 31 December 2025) |

concept of *de facto* application of the GATT beyond legal provisions, several Recommendations were adopted to allow newly-independent territories to *de facto* apply the GATT. They established the application period first by prescribing a reasonable period on a case-by-case basis, and then by setting a general fixed period of two years for all the cases. However, due to the repeated requests of prolongation, the period for *de facto* application was abandoned and replaced by review and report mechanisms (Case 23). Second, a prescribed period can be modified by a Decision. To extend the prescribed period for acceptance of the amendment of the TRIPS Agreement, nine Decisions have been adopted in a row, and as of this writing, the latest extension sets the deadline at 31 December 2025 (Case 24).

*Case 23: Establishment of the Prescribed Period for de facto Application (Recommendation)*

A prescribed period can be established through a Recommendation. For example, the concept of *de facto* application of the GATT arose beyond GATT Article XXVI:5(c) as a means to provide some time for governments of newly-independent territories to consider their future commercial policy and the question of their relations with the GATT, while continuing the pre-existing arrangements governing the trade relations between the newly-independent country and the contracting parties to the GATT.[117] In practice, although the CONTRACTING PARTIES never defined the meaning of *de facto* application, the time-frame for *de facto* application has been contemplated through several Recommendations. These Recommendations provide periods during which the contracting parties would continue to apply the GATT in their relations with newly-independent territories. The development of the relevant periods for *de facto* application is as follows:

(1) Prescribe a reasonable period for *de facto* application (case-by-case)
(2) Establish a general time-limit for *de facto* application (two-year period)
(3) Extend the time-limit for *de facto* application (case-by-case)
(4) Eliminate the time-limit for *de facto* application
(replaced by review and report)

First, in the early days, a reasonable period of *de facto* application was prescribed in each case by a Recommendation to the newly-independent country.[118] Second, considering the reasonable period normally being required, the Recommendation of 18 November 1960 set a general period of *de facto* application at two years from the acquisition of autonomy for all the following cases.[119] Accordingly, various Recommendations established and permitted a period of up to two years of *de facto* application. Third, taking into account that prolongations of *de facto* application had repeatedly been requested and that they had always been granted,[120] the CONTRACTING PARTIES thereafter

117 GATT Art. XXVI:5(c): "If any of the customs territories, in respect of which a contracting party has accepted this Agreement, possesses or acquires full autonomy in the conduct of its external commercial relations and of the other matters provided for in this Agreement, such territory shall, upon sponsorship through a declaration by the responsible contracting party establishing the above-mentioned fact, be deemed to be a contracting party."

118 *E.g.*, 6S/10. The Recommendation of 22 November 1957 on *Application of the General Agreement to Laos, Cambodia and Tunisia* provided that the reasonable period should end in the case of Laos and Cambodia two weeks after the commencement of the Thirteenth Session and in the case of Tunisia two weeks after the commencement of the Fourteenth Session. *See also* the Recommendation of 19 November 1959 on *Application of the General Agreement to Guinea*, 8S/8. It set the end of the "reasonable period" in the case of Guinea at two weeks after commencement of last session of the CONTRACTING PARTIES in 1961.

119 9S/16, 17. ("[C]ontracting parties should continue to apply de facto the [GATT] in their relations with any territory which has acquired full autonomy in the conduct of its external commercial relations and of other matters provided for in the General Agreement, for a period of two years from the date on which such autonomy was acquired.")

120 *E.g.*, 10S/17 (extending time-limit for one year for any State to which the previous Recommendation was applicable and which requested an extension), approval at SR.19/12, p. 199, Secretariat draft at W.19/19. *See also* Decision on "Newly independent African States" of 14 November 1962, 11S/53 (extension until close of last Session in 1963, for Cameroon,

adopted the Recommendation on 11 November 1967 in which no time-frame was laid down for *de facto* application of the GATT. Instead, the CONTRACTING PARTIES decided that they would, on the request of any contracting party, review their Recommendation in respect of any territory. It further required the DG to submit a report on its application every three years.[121] In sum, Recommendations were adopted by the CONTRACTING PARTIES to allow newly-independent territories to *de facto* apply the GATT. They established the application period first by prescribing a particular period on a case-by-case basis, and then by setting a general fixed period of two years for all the cases. Finally, this application period was replaced by review and report mechanisms.

*Case 24: Extension of the Prescribed Period for Acceptance (Decision)*

Following the prescription of the period, it may be further extended by a Decision. For example, Article X:3 of the WTO Agreement provides that the Ministerial Conference may specify a period for the Members to accept the amendment of the WTO Agreements.[122] In the case of the *Protocol Amending the TRIPS Agreement* adopted on 6 December 2005, the General Council has conducted the functions of the Ministerial Conference to adopt a Decision to prescribe a period by setting an end-date for the Members to accept the Protocol. This Decision stated that "[t]he Protocol shall be open for acceptance by Members until 1 December 2007 or such later date as may be decided by the Ministerial Conference."[123] As such, this Decision not only specified a fixed acceptance period ending on 1 December 2007, but also allowed for a possible extension through a future decision. In practice, the acceptance of the Protocol

---

Central African Republic, Chad, Congo, Côte d'Ivoire, Dahomey, Gabon, Madagascar, Mali, Mauritania, Niger, Senegal, Togo, Upper Volta and Zaïre); Decision of 2 March 1964, 12S/34 (extension until end of Twenty-second Session for Zaïre and Mali), Decision of 22 March 1965, 13S/12 (extension until end of Twenty-third Session for Algeria, Mali, Rwanda and Zaïre) Decision of 6 April 1966, 14S/12 (extension until end of Twenty-fourth Session for Algeria, Mali and Zaïre; determination that 1960 Recommendation applied in respect of Singapore and Zambia until 24 October 1966).

121 L/2910. ("[C]ontracting parties should continue to apply de facto the [GATT] in their relations with each territory which acquires full autonomy in the conduct of its external commercial relations and in respect of which a contracting party had accepted the Agreement, provided such territory continues to apply de facto the Agreement to its trade with the contracting parties.")

122 MAR Art. X:3: "The Ministerial Conference may decide by a three-fourths majority of the Members that any amendment made effective under this paragraph is of such a nature that any Member which has not accepted it within a period specified by the Ministerial Conference in each case shall be free to withdraw from the WTO or to remain a Member with the consent of the Ministerial Conference."

123 WT/L/641, para. 2.

takes longer than initially foreseen, and therefore, as of this writing, the deadline for acceptance has been extended for nine instances (each with an additional two-year period).[124] Most recently, the General Council has extended the period for acceptance of the Protocol until 31 December 2025 with a possibility for future extension.[125] In sum, a series of successive Decisions have been adopted to extend the prescribed period for acceptance of the Protocol by establishing later deadlines.

### 5.4.3 *Unspecified Period: The Period of an Event*

The elaboration of the unspecified period (*i.e.*, the period of an event) were found in four cases (Table 5.8). First, an unspecified period can be clarified by normal conditions established during Negotiation. For example, the negotiators had reached agreements to set an additional time-frame (*i.e.*, the three-year or ten-year period) as a reference to interpret the unspecified period, such as the "representative" or "reasonable" period applied in normal cases (Case 25). Second, an unspecified period can be defined by a Decision which reflects the normal understanding among the Members. To clarify the terms "a reasonable interval" and "longer time-frames," a Decision was thereafter adopted to state the normal understanding of the periods to be not less than six months (Case 26). Third, an unspecified period can be elaborated by a Recommendation which provides useful guidelines. In practice, there were a number of Recommendations adopted to propose fixed or extended time-frames for data collection and the submission of comments (Case 27). Fourth, an unspecified period can be elaborated by a DS Report which emphasizes normal practices. To elaborate on "a previous representative period," a three-year period was kept by the adjudicators, albeit subject to modification when special factors are taken into account on a case-by-case basis (Case 28).

---

124 *See* WT/L/711 (the 2007 extension), WT/L/785 (the 2009 extension), WT/L/829 (the 2011 extension), WT/L/899 (the 2013 extension), WT/L/965 (the 2015 extension), WT/L/1024 (the 2017 extension), WT/L/1081 (the 2019 extension), WT/L/1122 (the 2021 extension). Noting that the Protocol has entered into force on 23 January 2017 in respect of those Members that accepted it on or before such date. As for each other Member that accepts the Protocol after its entry into force, the Protocol will take effect upon acceptance by such Member, in accordance with Article X:3 of the WTO Agreement. *See* WT/Let/1236.

125 WT/L/1180. ("The period for acceptances by Members of the Protocol Amending the TRIPS Agreement referred to in paragraph 2 of the TRIPS Amendment Decision and paragraph 3 of the Protocol, and extended by the 2021 Extension Decision, shall be further extended until 31 December 2025 or such later date as may be decided by the Ministerial Conference.")

TABLE 5.8 Elaboration of the unspecified period in WTO Law

| Modalities | Cases | Development |
|---|---|---|
| Elaboration (Negotiation) **(Case 25)** | – Set a time-frame for interpretation of "a previous representative period" for application of export subsidies (GATT Art. XVI:3)<br>– Set a time-frame for interpretation of "a reasonable length of time" for formation of regional arrangements (GATT Art. XXIV:5(c)) | – *A previous representative period*: the three most recent calendar years in which normal market conditions existed<br>– *A reasonable length of time*: exceed 10 years only in exceptional cases |
| Elaboration (Decision) **(Case 26)** | – Clarify the "reasonable interval" for publication of SPS/TBT regulations (SPS Annex B(2) & TBT Art. 2.12)<br>– Clarify the "longer time-frames" for compliance with the SPS measure (SPS Art. 10.2) | – Normally a period of not less than 6 months |
| Elaboration (Recommendation) **(Case 27)** | – Provide guidelines for the time-frame of data collection for anti-dumping investigations (ADP Art. 2)<br>– Provide guidelines of the reasonable time for the submission of comments (TBT Arts. 2.9.4 & 5.6.4) | – *Data collection*: 12 months and no less than 6 months for dumping and sales below cost investigation; at least 3 years for injury investigation<br>– *Submission of Comments*: normally 60 days; encourage to extend by indicating the final date |
| Elaboration (DS Report) **(Case 28)** | – Clarify "a previous representative period" for quota allocation (GATT Arts. XI:2 & XIII: 2(d)) | – Keep with the normal practice in principle (three-year period)<br>– Change reference period by taking special factors into account (sufficient reasons) |

*Case 25: Elaboration on the Unspecified Period: Normal Conditions for Interpretation (Negotiation)*

During the course of Negotiation, the negotiators may establish a normal condition for the unspecified period by reaching a separate agreement that provides a reference timeframe for its interpretation. For example, GATT Article XVI:3 obliges Members to apply export subsidies on certain primary products by taking into account the shares of the affected Members during "a previous representative period."[126] This unspecified representative period was further discussed and elaborated by Article 10:2(c) of *the 1979 Agreement on Interpretation and Application of Articles VI, XVI and XXIII of the General Agreement.* It provides a three-year period as a reference for interpretation under normal conditions by stating that "'a previous representative period' shall normally be the three most recent calendar years in which normal market conditions existed."[127] Besides, in the case of the interim agreements of regional arrangements, GATT Article XXIV:5(c) anticipates Members to form a customs union or free-trade area within "a reasonable length of time."[128] This unspecified reasonable period has likewise been agreed upon in the course of WTO negotiations. According to the agreement laid in Paragraph 3 of the *Understanding on Art. XXIV*, a reasonable length of time should not exceed 10 years in normal cases.[129] In sum, the fixed periods (*i.e.*, the three-year and ten-year periods) were established as benchmarks for the interpretation of the unspecified "representative" and "reasonable" periods.

*Case 26: Elaboration on the Unspecified Period: Normal Understanding among the Members (Decision)*

A Decision may be taken to clarify the unspecified period in line with its normal understanding among the Members. For example, Annex B(2) of the SPS

126 GATT Art. XVI:3: "... such subsidy shall not be applied in a manner which results in that contracting party having more than an equitable share of world export trade in that product, account being taken of the shares of the contracting parties in such trade in the product during a previous representative period, and any special factors which may have affected or may be affecting such trade in the product."

127 26S/69.

128 GATT Art. XXIV:5(c): "[A]ny interim agreement referred to in subparagraphs (a) and (b) shall include a plan and schedule for the formation of such a customs union or of such a free-trade area within a reasonable length of time."

129 Para. 3 of the *Understanding on Art. XXIV*: "The 'reasonable length of time' referred to in [GATT Article XXIV:5(c)] should exceed 10 years only in exceptional cases. In cases where Members parties to an interim agreement believe that 10 years would be insufficient they shall provide a full explanation to the Council for Trade in Goods of the need for a longer period."

Agreement (similar in Article 2.12 of the TBT Agreement) regulates the publication of a sanitary or phytosanitary regulation (or a technical regulation). It requires Members to allow "a reasonable interval" between the publication and the entry into force of such regulation.[130] To further clarify the meaning of the "reasonable interval," the *Doha Ministerial Decision on Implementation-Related Issues and Concerns* was adopted in 2001 and agreed that this unspecified period "shall be understood to mean normally a period of not less than 6 months."[131] In addition, this Decision also clarified the meaning for the term "longer time-frame for compliance" to developing country Members under Article 10.2 of the SPS Agreement[132] to be "normally as a period of not less than 6 months."[133] As such, the Doha Ministerial Decision affirmed the normal understanding of the unspecified periods (*i.e.*, "a reasonable interval" and "longer time-frames") to be not less than six months.

130 SPS Annex B(2): "Except in urgent circumstances, Members shall allow a reasonable interval between the publication of a sanitary or phytosanitary regulation and its entry into force in order to allow time for producers in exporting Members, and particularly in developing country Members, to adapt their products and methods of production to the requirements of the importing Member."; TBT Art. 2.12: "Except in those urgent circumstances referred to in paragraph 10, Members shall allow a reasonable interval between the publication of technical regulations and their entry into force in order to allow time for producers in exporting Members, and particularly in developing country Members, to adapt their products or methods of production to the requirements of the importing Member."

131 WT/MIN(01)/17, para. 3.2 for the SPS Agreement and para. 5.2 for the TBT Agreement. ("Subject to the conditions specified in [SPS Annex B(2)], the phrase 'reasonable interval' shall be understood to mean normally a period of not less than 6 months. It is understood that time-frames for specific measures have to be considered in the context of the particular circumstances of the measure and actions necessary to implement it. The entry into force of measures which contribute to the liberalization of trade should not be unnecessarily delayed."; "Subject to the conditions specified in [Article 2.12 of the TBT Agreement], the phrase 'reasonable interval' shall be understood to mean normally a period of not less than 6 months, except when this would be ineffective in fulfilling the legitimate objectives pursued.")

132 SPS Art. 10.2: "Where the appropriate level of sanitary or phytosanitary protection allows scope for the phased introduction of new sanitary or phytosanitary measures, longer time-frames for compliance should be accorded on products of interest to developing country Members so as to maintain opportunities for their exports."

133 WT/MIN(01)/17, para. 3.1. ("Where the appropriate level of sanitary and phytosanitary protection allows scope for the phased introduction of new sanitary and phytosanitary measures, the phrase 'longer time-frame for compliance' referred to in Article 10.2 of the SPS Agreement, shall be understood to mean normally a period of not less than 6 months.")

*Case 27: Elaboration on the Unspecified Period: Useful Guidelines on Procedures (Recommendation)*

A Recommendation offering useful guidelines may serve to elaborate an unspecified period. For example, the Committee on Anti-Dumping Practices adopted a Recommendation concerning the period of data collection for anti-dumping investigations in order to determine the existence of dumping and consequent injury.[134] At its beginning, this Recommendation noted that there was no temporal guidance regarding the data collection for investigations, and considered that it would be useful to provide guidelines for determining what period or periods of data collection may be appropriate. In this sense, it set out a general rule for the period of data collection under three different types of investigations (*i.e.*, for dumping, for sales below cost, and for injury). In principle, the period of data collection for dumping and sales below cost should be twelve months and no less than six months. For injury investigations, the period should be normally at least three years.[135]

In addition, useful guidelines through Recommendations can also be observed in the context of the submission of comments in Articles 2.9.4 and 5.6.4 of the TBT Agreement. These Articles provide that Members applying the technical regulations shall allow "reasonable time" for other Members to make comments.[136] With respect to this unspecified "reasonable time" for comments, a Recommendation in 2000 agreed a normal time-frame of 60 days and encouraged Members to extend this time limit, if capable, by indicating the final date for comments in the notification.[137] In terms of the extension, a Recommendation in 2003 especially encouraged developed country

134 G/ADP/6.

135 *Ibid.*, para. 1. ("(a) the period of data collection for dumping investigations normally should be twelve months, and in any case no less than six months, ending as close to the date of initiation as is practicable; (b) the period of data collection for investigating sales below cost, and the period of data collection for dumping investigations, normally should coincide in a particular investigation; (c) the period of data collection for injury investigations normally should be at least three years, unless a party from whom data is being gathered has existed for a lesser period, and should include the entirety of the period of data collection for the dumping investigation.")

136 TBT Arts. 2.9.4 and 5.6.4: "Members shall without discrimination, allow reasonable time for other Members, whose trade may be significantly affected, to make comments in writing, discuss these comments upon request, and take these written comments and the results of these discussions into account."

137 G/TBT/9, p. 22. ("The normal time limit for comments on notifications should be 60 days. Any Member which is able to provide a time limit beyond 60 days, such as 90 days, is encouraged to do so, and should indicate this in the notification.")

Members to provide more than a 60-day comment period to developing country Members.[138] To reiterate the importance of the comment period, another Recommendation in 2009 explained that "an insufficient period of time for presentation of comments on proposed technical regulations and conformity assessment may prevent Members from adequately exercising their right to submit comments."[139] In sum, several Recommendations were adopted in practice to provide specific time-frames as useful guidelines on the unspecified period for data collection and the submission of comments.

*Case 28: Elaboration on the Unspecified Period: Normal Practices of the Members (DS Report)*

An unspecified period may be further elaborated by highlighting normal practices in a *DS Report*. For example, GATT Articles XI:2 and XIII: 2(d) oblige Members to pay due regard to the proportion prevailing "during a previous representative period" in determining their quota allocation.[140] To clarify the term "a representative period," the GATT's Panel on *EEC Restrictions on Imports of Apples from Chile* first decided to keep with normal practice of the representative period, which was "a three-year period" prior the year in which the measures were in effect (*i.e.*, the years 1976 to 1978). Then, it proceeded to consider whether the year of 1976 as representative.[141] Aside from normal practice of the three-year reference period, the GATT's Panel on *EEC—Restrictions on Imports of Dessert Apples—Complaint by Chile* emphasized the possibility of

138 G/TBT/13, para. 26. ("To improve the ability of developing country Members to comment on notifications, and consistent with the principle of special and differential treatment, developed country Members are encouraged to provide more than a 60-day comment period.")

139 G/TBT/26, para. 40(c). *See also* G/TBT/19, para. 57.

140 GATT Arts. XI:2 and XIII:2(d): "In determining this proportion, the contracting party shall pay due regard to the proportion prevailing during a previous representative period and to any special factors which may have affected or may be affecting the trade in the product concerned."; "... the contracting party concerned shall allot to contracting parties having a substantial interest in supplying the product shares based upon the proportions, supplied by such contracting parties during a previous representative period, of the total quantity or value of imports of the product, due account being taken of any special factors which may have affected or may be affecting the trade in the product."

141 L/5047-27S/98, para.4.8. ("In keeping with normal GATT practice, the Panel considered it appropriate to use as a 'representative period' a three-year period previous to 1979, the year in which the EEC measures were in effect. Due to the existence of restrictions in 1976, the Panel held that that year could not be considered as representative, and that the year immediately preceding 1976 should be used instead. The Panel thus chose the years 1975, 1977 and 1978 as a 'representative period'.")

relevant special factors to be taken into account as sufficient reason to modify the three-year reference period.[142]

Furthermore, in WTO's Panel Report on *EU—Poultry Meat (China)*, the adjudicators took a different approach to interpret the indefinite article "a" embedded in the term "during a previous representative period," and considered its clear implication that "there is no general rule that applies in all cases regarding the selection of the reference period."[143] In WTO's Panel Report on *EU—Safeguard Measures on Steel (Turkey)*, the adjudicators reaffirmed that the use of the indefinite article "a" instead of the definite article "the" to imply a margin of discretion in selecting a previous period that it considers to be representative.[144] In sum, normal practice of the three-year reference period may be initially maintained for considering "a previous representative period" for quota allocation, albeit subject to modification when special factors are taken into account on a case-by-case basis.

## 5.5 Sequence in Time

As categorized in Section 3.1.5, this research defines "sequence in time" as a series of temporal events, either in a *consecutive* order (*e.g.*, "before" and "after"), or in a *simultaneous* order (*e.g.*, "at the same time"). In practice, the modification and elaboration of sequence in time were found in two cases (Table 5.9). First, sequence in time can be modified by a Decision. In the case

142 L/6491-36S/93, para. 12.22. ("It observed that the previous three years were normally considered to be the appropriate reference period, with due account taken of relevant special factors. The Panel did not construe 'special factors' applicable to only one, or some, exporters as sufficient reason to change the base period which applied to all—though these special factors should be taken into account in considering individual quota allocations.")

143 Panel Report, *EU—Poultry Meat (China)*, para. 7.349. ("The reference to 'a' previous representative period in [GATT] Article XIII:2(d) implies that there is no general rule that applies in all cases regarding the selection of the reference period. Furthermore, [GATT] Article XIII:4 envisages the 'the selection of a representative period' being made 'initially' by the importing Member, subject to reappraisal. The clear implication is that there is no general rule, applicable to all cases, regarding the reference period that must be used for the purpose of [GATT] Article XIII:2(d).")

144 *Ibid.*, para. 7.288. ("[T]he use of the indefinite article 'a' instead of the definite article 'the' in reference to the notion of '[a] previous representative period' shows that the Member applying the [Tariff Rate Quota] has a margin of discretion in selecting a previous period that it considers to be representative for the purpose of allocating country-specific shares in the [Tariff Rate Quota] at issue.")

TABLE 5.9 Modification and elaboration of sequence in time in WTO Law

| Modalities | Cases | Development |
|---|---|---|
| Modification (Decision) **(Case 29)** | – Replace the sequence in time to launch a new negotiating round on agriculture (AG Art. 20) | – Original time for initiation of negotiations: one year "before" the end of the implementation period (1 January 2000)<br>– Propose to launch the negotiations afterward in the Special Session of the Committee (23–24 March 2000) |
| Elaboration (Recommendation) **(Case 30)** | – Clarify the sequence in time by adding speed modifiers to the time of notification for anti-dumping investigation (ADP Art. 5.5) | – [ + *as soon as possible*] **after** the receipt by the investigating authorities of a properly documented application<br>– [ + *as early as possible*] **before** the decision is taken regarding initiation of an investigation on the basis of that properly documented application |

of superseding the original agreement that required negotiations to commence "before" a specified date, a Decision was adopted retrospectively to recognize the lapse of time without initiation of the mandated negotiation, and to propose new dates for subsequent negotiation rounds (Case 29). Second, sequence in time can be elaborated by a Recommendation. To provide general guidelines, a Recommendation was adopted to clarify the time to notify the intention to undertake an anti-dumping investigation by adding *speed modifiers* to the original expressions of sequence in time (*i.e.*, "*as soon as possible* after" and "*as early as possible* before") (Case 30).

*Case 29: Modification of the Sequence for Launching New Negotiations (Decision)*

Sequence in time can be modified by a Decision. For example, pursuant to Article 20 of the Agreement on Agriculture, negotiations for continuing the reform process on agriculture would be initiated one year "before" the end of the implementation period (*i.e.*, 1 January 2000).[145] In practice, the implementation period elapsed and no negotiation had been officially initiated. The General Council thereafter adopted a Decision by acknowledging that "a number of procedural matters remained to be settled before the work could start in practice." It proposed an alternative solution "after" the implementation period by launching a new negotiating round on agriculture in the Committee on Agriculture's meeting in Special Sessions which would be held on 23–24 March 2000.[146] In this sense, a Decision was adopted retrospectively to recognize that the time had elapsed without initiation of the mandated negotiation "before" the end of the implementation period, and therefore it proposed to conduct new rounds of negotiation to later dates "after" the original time.

*Case 30: Elaboration on the Sequence for Notification (Recommendation)*

Sequence in time may be elaborated by a Recommendation. For example, Article 5.5 of the Anti-Dumping Agreement obliges the authorities of Members intending to undertake an anti-dumping investigation to notify other Members "*after* receipt of a properly documented application" for investigation and "*before* proceeding to initiate an investigation."[147] In other words, it calls for a notification to be provided at the time between receipt of application and initiation of investigation. However, this Article does not establish any guidelines to determine more precisely when that notification must be made. Instead of establishing a specific date for the notification obligation, the Committee on Anti-Dumping Practices considered to establish more general guidelines due to the fact that "different Members have different

145 AG Art. 20: "Members agree that negotiations for continuing the process will be initiated one year before the end of the implementation period,…." Noting that according to Article 1(f) of the Agreement on Agriculture, the implementation period would end in the year of 2000, *i.e.*, "the six-year period commencing in the year 1995."

146 WT/GC/M/53, para. 12. ("In this regard, and in the light of wide and intensive consultations with and among Members on the structure of the negotiations, [the Chairman] proposed that the negotiations be conducted in the Committee on Agriculture meeting in Special Sessions. Progress in the negotiations would be reported directly to the General Council on a regular basis. The first Special Session of the Committee on Agriculture would be scheduled back-to-back with the next regular meeting of the Committee, to be held on 23–24 March 2000.")

147 ADP Art. 5.5: "The authorities shall avoid, unless a decision has been made to initiate an investigation, any publicizing of the application for the initiation of an investigation. However, *after* receipt of a properly documented application and *before* proceeding to initiate an investigation, the authorities shall notify the government of the exporting Member concerned." (emphasis added)

processes and deadlines for the examination of applications and the initiation of investigations."[148] Accordingly, the Committee adopted a Recommendation concerning the temporal requirements for notification, incorporating *speed modifiers* (*i.e.*, "as soon as possible" and "as early as possible") prior to the original expressions of sequence in time (*i.e.*, "after" and "before") in Article 5.5 of the Anti-Dumping Agreement, which were stated as follows: "*as soon as possible after* the receipt … a properly documented application," and "*as early as possible before* the decision is taken regarding initiation of an investigation."[149] As such, a Recommendation may be adopted to elaborate sequence in time by adding *speed modifiers* on its original expressions (*i.e.*, "*as soon as possible* after" and "*as early as possible* before").

## 5.6 Conceptual Expression in Time

As categorized in Section 3.1.6, this research defines "conceptual expression in time" as adding special temporal meaning to events via the use of modifiers, either related to the *speed* representing "how fast" an event should happen (*e.g.*, "immediate" and "prompt"), or related to the *degree* representing "how long" an event should last (*e.g.*, "provisional" and "temporary"). In practice, the modification and elaboration of the conceptual expression in time were found in three cases (Table 5.10). First, the speed modifier may be adjusted by adding a timeline in the course of Negotiation or by means of the Rules of Procedure, such as providing a standard period (*e.g.*, "within four years"), a standard date (*e.g.*, "by 30 September"), or a list of optional timelines from which Members may select (Case 31). Second, the speed modifier may be revised by introducing new regulations through a Decision. To strengthen the obligation of "prompt" notification of regional trade agreements (RTAs), a Decision was adopted to establish new regulations with multiple temporal rules, such as to provide information regarding "the date of signature" as well as to notify "no later than ratification" of the RTAs (Case 32). Third, the speed and degree modifiers may be elaborated in accordance with their ordinary meanings through interpretation in a DS Report. To elaborate on the speed modifier "prompt" and the

148 G/ADP/5. ("Thus, a specific guideline, establishing a date certain by which the notification should be made, might be unworkable. Nonetheless, the Committee considers that more general guidelines can be established.")

149 *Ibid.* ("[T]he notification required by the second sentence of Article 5.5 of [the Anti-Dumping Agreement] should be made *as soon as possible after* the receipt by the investigating authorities of a properly documented application, and *as early as possible before* the decision is taken regarding initiation of an investigation on the basis of that properly documented application.") (emphasis added)

degree modifier "temporary," the adjudicators have interpreted their ordinary meanings with due regard to the specific context and particular circumstances (Case 33).

TABLE 5.10 Modification and elaboration of conceptual expression in time in WTO Law

| Modalities | Cases | Development |
|---|---|---|
| Modification (Negotiation & Rules of Procedure) **(Case 31)** | – Set a timeline for the "immediate" consultations (GATT Arts. XII:4(a) & XVIII:12(a))<br>– Set a timeline for the "prompt" completion of the questionnaires (LIC Art. 7.3)<br>– Set optional timelines for "timely" distribution and receipt of documents (TPRM & MAR Art. IV:4) | – Set a standard period for *immediate* consultations ("within four years")<br>– Set a standard date for *prompt* completion the questionnaire each year ("by 30 September")<br>– Set a list of standard and alternative timelines for *timely* submission of written questions and answers |
| Modification (Decision) **(Case 32)** | – Add new regulations with multiple temporal rules for "prompt" notification of RTAS (GATT Art. XXIV: 7(a) & Transparency Mechanism for Regional Trade Agreements) | – Provide information regarding the "date of signature" or "any foreseen timetable for its entry into force or provisional application"<br>– Notify "no later than ratification of the RTA" or "before the application of preferential treatment"<br>– Subsequently notify "as soon as possible after the changes occur"<br>– Report "at the end of the RTA's implementation period" |
| Elaboration (DS report) **(Case 33)** | – Clarify the meaning of "prompt" for publication of the trade regulations (GATT Art. X:1)<br>– Clarify the meaning of "prompt" for review and correction of administrative action (GATT Art. X:3(b)) | – *Prompt* publication: "quickly;" "without undue delay;" "not an absolute concept, *i.e.*, a pre-set period of time applicable in all cases"<br>– *Prompt* review and correction: "a quick and effective manner and without delay;" depend "on the context and particular circumstances" |

TABLE 5.10 Modification and elaboration of conceptual expression in time (*cont.*)

| Modalities | Cases | Development |
|---|---|---|
| | – Clarify the meaning of "temporarily" applied in terms of export prohibitions or restrictions (GATT Art. XI:2(a))<br>– Clarify the meaning of "temporary" for the suspension of concessions or other obligations (DSU Art. 22.8) | – *Temporary* application of measures: "lasting or meant to last for a limited time only; not permanent; made or arranged to supply a passing need"<br>– *Temporary* suspension: "not meant to remain indefinitely" |

*Case 31: Modification of the Speed Modifier by Adding (Optional) Timelines (Negotiation & Rules of Procedure)*

Speed modifiers may be adjusted by incorporating a timeline either during the course of Negotiation or through the application of the Rules of Procedure. For example, pursuant to GATT Articles XII:4(a) and XVIII:12(a), any Member applied BOP restrictions shall consult with the WTO "immediately" after the adoption or intensification of their BOP restrictions.[150] This obligation of "immediate" consultation was further negotiated and replaced by a standard period in time under Paragraph 6 of the *Understanding on BOP Provisions*. This new Understanding obliges Members to enter into consultations with the WTO "within four months" of the adoption or intensification of their BOP restrictions.[151]

As for the modification of speed modifiers by means of the Rules of Procedure, Article 7.3 of the Agreement on Import Licensing requires Members to "promptly" complete the annual questionnaire on import licensing

150 GATT Arts. XII:4(a) and XVIII:12(a): "Any contracting party applying new restrictions or raising the general level of its existing restrictions by a substantial intensification of the measures applied under this Article shall immediately after instituting or intensifying such restrictions ... consult with the CONTRACTING PARTIES as to the nature of its balance of payments difficulties, alternative corrective measures which may be available, and the possible effect of the restrictions on the economies of other contracting parties."

151 Para. 6 of the *Understanding on BOP Provisions*: "A Member applying new restrictions or raising the general level of its existing restrictions by a substantial intensification of the measures shall enter into consultations with the Committee within four months of the adoption of such measures."

procedures.[152] To add a timeline to this "prompt" completion, the Committee on Import Licensing has agreed on the Rules of Procedure for this Article, which requires all Members to complete the annual questionnaire by a standard date of "30 September" each year.[153] In addition, the timelines set out in the Rules of Procedure may also remain optional for Members to choose from. In the case of the TPRM, Annex 1 of the *Rules of Procedure for Meetings of the TPRB* establishes both standard and alternative timelines to ensure "timely" submission of written answers during the TPRB meetings (*i.e.*, how many weeks (working days) before the meetings).[154] Although the "timely" question-and-answer process was demanded, the Members could not reach a consensus on the timelines and decided to maintain the standard one while allowing volunteers to apply the alternative timelines on a pilot basis.[155] The alternative timeline as an option provides longer time for Members under review to prepare and review written answers. The choice will be made by Members under review at the time of agreeing on the date of review.[156] In sum, speed modifiers may be modified by introducing standard or optional timelines, such as a standard period for immediate consultation "within four years," a standard date for prompt completion of annual questionnaires "by 30 September," or a list of optional timelines from which Members may choose for the timely submission of written answers.

*Case 32: Modification of the Speed Modifier by Adding New Regulations (Decision)*

Speed modifiers may be revised through the introduction of new regulations by means of a *Decision*. For example, GATT Article XXIV:7(a) provides only a general obligation for Members to "promptly" notify their decisions to form RTAs.[157] In practice, this "prompt" notification obligation was progressively evolved to give rise to more concrete regulations due to the consideration that RTAs had greatly increased in number and become an important component in Members' trade policies and developmental strategies. To be more specific, the General Council adopted a *Decision on the Transparency Mechanism for*

152 LIC Art. 7.3: "Members undertake to complete the annual questionnaire on import licensing procedures promptly and in full."

153 G/LIC/3, para. 3.

154 WT/MIN(11)/6, para. 26. ("Currently, these written answers are distributed on the day of the meeting, which allows little time for them to be fully considered and understood by Members. They considered that more timely distribution of written answers could be achieved by allowing more time for Members under review to prepare written answers.")

155 *Ibid.*, para. 27.

156 WT/TPR/6/Rev.4, para. 13.

157 GATT Art. XXIV: 7(a): "Any contracting party deciding to enter into a customs union or free-trade area, or an interim agreement leading to the formation of such a union or area, shall promptly notify the CONTRACTING PARTIE."

*Regional Trade Agreements* in 2006, and agreed on the procedural mechanisms governing the notification which contain multiple temporal rules as follows:[158]

(1) Early announcement: to provide information on the RTAS, including its "date of signature" and "any foreseen timetable for its entry into force or provisional application"
(2) Notification: to take place "no later than directly following the parties' ratification of the RTA or any party's decision on application of the relevant parts of an agreement, and before the application of preferential treatment between the parties"
(3) Subsequent notification: to notify "as soon as possible after the changes occur"
(4) Reporting: to submit a short written report at "the end of the RTA's implementation period"

All in all, the Decision was adopted to establish new regulations accompanied by various temporal rules in order to strengthen the obligation of "prompt" notification of the RTAS.

*Case 33: Elaboration on the Speed/Degree Modifier for its Ordinary Meaning (DS Report)*

The elaboration of speed and degree modifiers is addressed in multiple *DS Reports*. For example, in terms of the speed modifier, GATT Article X:1 imposes requirements relating to the "prompt" publication of trade regulations.[159] The adjudicators have clarified the meaning of "prompt," and considered that it was not "an absolute concept, *i.e.* a pre-set period of time applicable in all cases." Rather, it requires a case-by-case assessment to decide whether a measure had been published "quickly" and "without undue delay."[160] In addition, GATT Article X:3(b) also utilizes a speed modifier to govern the "prompt" review and correction of administrative action relating to customs matters.[161] The adjudicators interpreted the "promptness" of review and correction as the action to be performed "in a quick and effective manner and without delay," depending on the context and particular circumstances.[162]

158 WT/L/671, paras. 1(b), 3, 14, and 15.

159 GATT Art. X:1: "Laws, regulations, judicial decisions and administrative rulings of general application … shall be published promptly in such a manner as to enable governments and traders to become acquainted with them."

160 Panel Reports, *EC—IT Products*, para. 7.1074.

161 GATT Art. X:3(b): "Each contracting party shall maintain, or institute as soon as practicable, judicial, arbitral or administrative tribunals or procedures for the purpose, inter alia, of the prompt review and correction of administrative action relating to customs matters."

162 Appellate Body Report, *Thailand—Cigarettes (Philippines)*, para. 203. ("[T]he due process objective reflected in [GATT] Article X:3 suggests that 'prompt review and correction' is to be understood as review and correction of administrative action that is performed in a

With regard to the degree modifier, GATT Article XI:2(a) exempts export prohibitions or restrictions "temporarily" applied to prevent or relieve critical shortages of certain products from the application of GATT Article XI:1.[163] For greater clarity, the adjudicators defined the word "temporarily" as "[l]asting or meant to last for a limited time only; not permanent; made or arranged to supply a passing need."[164] In addition, DSU Article 22.8 also uses the degree modifier "temporary" to regulate the suspension of concessions or other obligations.[165] For its meaning, the adjudicators found the suspension of concessions or obligations to be "an abnormal state of affairs that is not meant to remain indefinitely."[166] In sum, the adjudicators have interpreted and clarified the ordinary meanings of the speed modifier ("prompt") and the degree modifier ("temporary") in several occasions by considering their specific context and particular circumstances.

## 5.7 Summary

Following the study of the 2-D temporal events association in Chapter 4, temporal rules are important elements in WTO Law to underpin diverse legal events, although they are not static within the legal texts and are subject to dynamic change in practice. To underpin their "organic" and "incremental" change within the WTO system, this Chapter closely studies temporal rules over time, and notices that they have undergone changes through nine potential systemic mechanisms (Figure 5.1 above), displaying dynamic interactions between the rules and its practical environment. For this reason, this Chapter argues that temporal rules as internal elements in law can be relatively mutable to provide intrinsic flexibility to the legal system.

To be more specific, this Chapter maps the modalities of the organic or incremental changes of temporal rules through their establishment, modification, and elaboration in practice (Figure 5.2 below). Especially, it provides

---

quick and effective manner and without delay. What is quick or performed without delay depends on the context and particular circumstances, including the nature of the specific type of action to be reviewed and corrected. Whether a system does or does not ensure prompt review thus cannot be determined in the abstract.")

163 GATT Art. XI:2(a): "The provisions of paragraph 1 of this Article shall not extend to ... [e]xport prohibitions or restrictions temporarily applied to prevent or relieve critical shortages of foodstuffs or other products essential to the exporting contracting party;...."

164 Appellate Body Reports, *China—Raw Materials*, para. 323..

165 DSU Art. 22.8: "The suspension of concessions or other obligations shall be temporary. ..."

166 Appellate Body Report, *Canada—Continued Suspension*, para. 310.

a systemic overview on the development of the six categories of temporal rules established in Chapter 3, including (1) point in time (Section 5.1); (2) timing (Section 5.2); (3) frequency in time (Section 5.3); (4) period in time (Section 5.4); (5) sequence in time (Section 5.5); and (6) conceptual expression in time (Section 5.6). To the best effort of this research, thirty-three representative cases were identified in the GATT/WTO practice with the intention of demonstrating the fluid character of temporal rules in WTO Law.

Section 5.1 addresses "point in time" represented by three types under ten cases (Cases 1~10): the fixed date, the prescribed date, and the uspecified date. First, *the fixed date* appears to be one of the most precise temporal rules in the legal texts. To insert a fixed date into legal provisions in the first place, negotiators might choose an exact date carefully, add extra dates gradually, and provide optional dates openly in consideration of political practicability and potential conflicts of interest (Case 1). After the fixed date is in place, it might still be subject to change under special occasions, especially (1) to adapt the date for the new membership by means of the *Protocol of Accession* (Case 2); (2) to grant an alternative date on a case-by-case basis by means of Waivers under exceptional circumstances (Case 3); and (3) to postpone to a later date by means of Decisions under unforeseen circumstances (Case 4).

Second, *the prescribed date* is a date to be determined by an authority. To further ascertain a date, negotiators might oblige the authority to explicitly state the prescribed date (Case 5), or allow the authority to subsequently determine the date in line with suitable conditions (Case 6). After the date is officially prescribed, some corresponding arrangements might be demanded by means of Decisions to facilitate an orderly transition or to provide confirmation for the relevant deadlines involved (Case 7).

Third, *the unspecified date* is the date of an event. To address practical difficulties, the anchored event for the date might be substituted by means of Decisions, such as the replacement from the date of "entry into force" of the WTO Agreement to the date of "acceptance" of the WTO Agreement (Case 8). To determine the date of an event, Members might agree on a date amongst themselves by means of Declarations (Case 9), or the authority might play its role on suggesting a date on a trial basis and rely on its experience gained from the Working Practices of the institution (Case 10).

Section 5.2 identifies "timing" as a temporal focus of an event without being referred to the specific "date" of an event, which can be represented by prepositional phrases (*e.g.*, "in time of") or temporal clauses (*e.g*, "when" and "whenever") under three cases (Cases 11~13). To establish and modify the timing for an event, negotiators might consider to deploy multiple temporal rules in progress of Negotiation and consolidate them toward a more precise temporal expression at the final stage (Case 11). To clarify the timing for an event, Recommendations might be adopted to introduce an additional timing as guidance. For example, the additional timing (*i.e.*, when a draft ... is available) was provided to guide the consideration of whether the notification occurs "at an early appropriate stage, when amendments can still be introduced and taken into account" (Case 12). Furthermore, the timing for an event might also be clarified by means of DS Reports in which the adjudicators might emphasize the temporal link between the action and its surrounding circumstances (Case 13).

Section 5.3 presents "frequency in time" under three cases (Cases 14~16), which refers to either the set number of times an event occurs within a given time-frame (*e.g.*, "every ... years"), or the unspecified indication of repetition of an event (*e.g.*, "regular"). To establish the fixed frequency for an event, the selection of its particular time-frame might be discussed and implemented on a trial basis through a series of Decisions and Recommendations (Case 14). To address practical difficulties after its establishment, the selected time-frame might be amended to a longer duration in tandem with a degree of flexibility provided by the Rules of Procedure (Case 15). In addition, the Rules of Procedure might also be deployed to provide additional regulations and to clarify the unspecified frequency (*e.g.*, "regular" report) by establishing more precise temporal rules (Case 16).

Section 5.4 addresses "period in time" represented by three types under twelve cases (Cases 17~28): the fixed period, the prescribed period, and the uspecified perod. First, *the fixed period* contains a numerical expression, which could be established (1) by negotiators who might select a fixed number with the consideration of the possiblity of extension (Case 17); (2) by means of Decisions to adopt new procedures beyond the original legal provisions with a number of fixed periods applied on a trial basis (Case 18); and (3) by means of Recommendations to provide optional reference periods as guidance for making a determination (Case 19). In terms of the modification of the fixed period due to practical or political difficulties, it might be extended to a later date (1) by means of Decisions for multilateral events among the entire membership, such as the issue of negotiations or the application of legal provisions (Case 20); (2) by means of the Joint Request of the Parties for institutional events related to the bodies of the WTO, such as the adoption of panel reports (Case 21); and (3) by means of Mutual Agreements for bilateral events between the parties involved, such as the suspension of concessions (Case 22).

Second, *the prescribed period* is a period to be determined by an authority. To derive a new concept beyond legal provisions, Recommendations might be adopted in a row (1) to establish the prescribed period for the new concept on a case-by-case basis; then (2) to consider setting a general fixed period for all the cases; and finally (3) to abolish the fixed period due to the repeated requests of prolongation (Case 23). The prescribed period might also be continuously extended to a later date by means of Decisions, such as the ninth extension of the period for acceptance of the TRIPS amendment as until 31 December 2025 (Case 24).

Third, *the unspecified period* is the period of an event, which can be elaborated upon by incorporating a fixed reference period through four distinct approaches: (1) in the course of Negotiation, negotiators might reach an agreement on setting a normal condition for its interpretation (Case 25); (2) Decisions might be adopted to state the normal understanding among the Members (Case 26); (3) Recommendations might be deployed to provide useful guidelines on the event to be applied (Case 27); and (4) in DS Reports, adjudicators might intend to maintain normal practices, albeit still taking special factors into account on a case-by-case basis (Case 28).

Section 5.5 identifies "sequence in time" under two cases (Cases 29~30), referring to a series of temporal events in a consecutive order (*e.g.*, "before" and "after"). To modify the sequence of events, Decisions might be adopted "retrospectively" to acknowledge the lapse of time and propose a new beginning for the event thereafter (Case 29). To elaborate the sequence of events, Recommendations might propose the addition of a speed modifier to the original expression (*e.g.*, "*as soon as possible* after") (Case 30).

Section 5.6 deals with "conceptual expression in time" under three cases (Cases 31~33), which adds special temporal meanings to an event by modifiers, either related to the *speed* (*e.g.*, "immediate") or the *degree* (*e.g.*, "temporary"). In practice, speed modifiers might be amended (1) by adding a standard or optional timeline, either a date or a period, during the course of Negotiation or by means of the Rules of Procedure (Case 31); and (2) by introducing new regulations along with multiple temporal rules by means of Decisions (Case 32). To elaborate on the speed/degree modifiers, DS Reports might rely on their ordinary meanings and take into account their particular context and circumstances (Case 33).

Taken together, the modalities of the establishment, modification, and elaboration of temporal rules in WTO Law appear to be considerably diverse and mutable. In terms of the establishment, the selection for a numerical expression (for point, frequency, or period in time) could be under discussion during the course of Negotiation concerning whether it should be optional, extendable, or on trial. As for a non-numerical expression, the concerns might rest on whether it should be subsequently determined (under what conditions), whether it should be explicitly stated after determination, and whether it

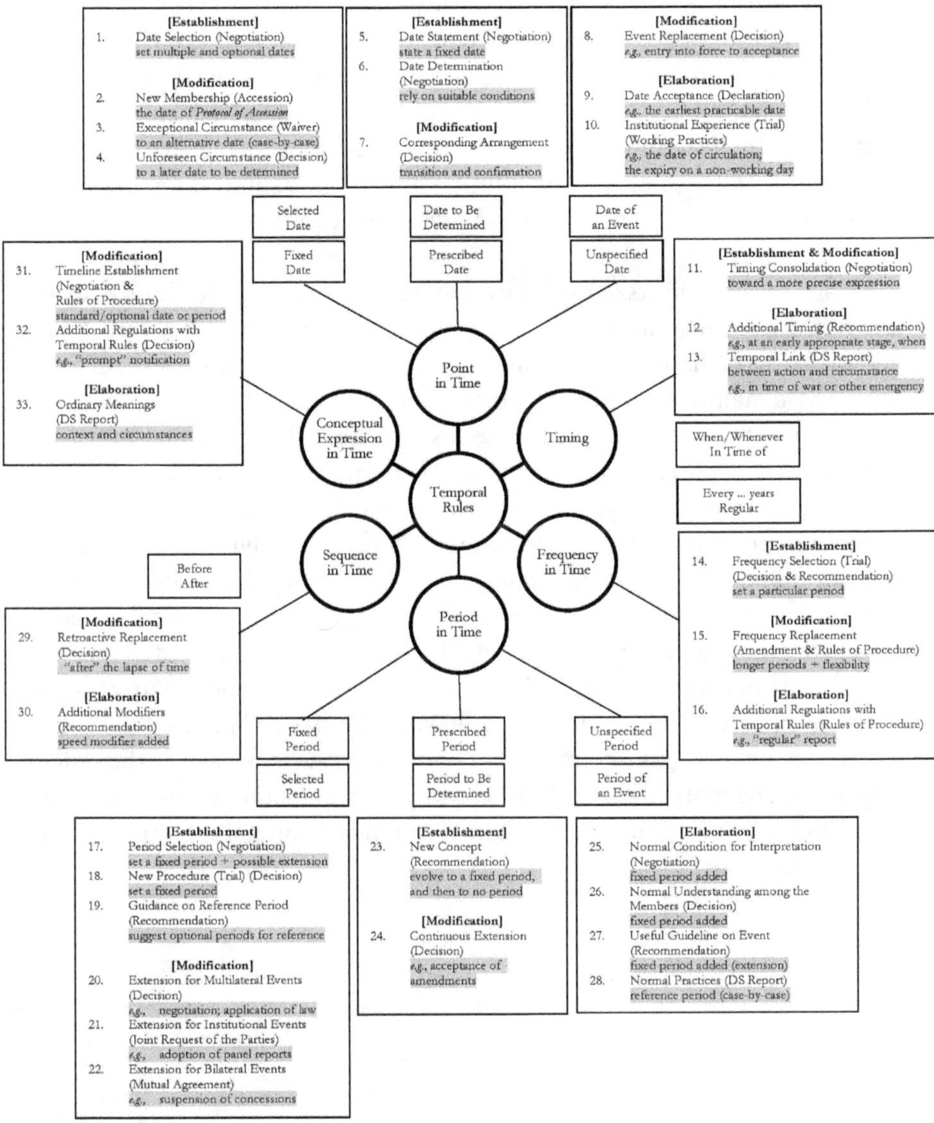


FIGURE 5.2 The establishment, modification, and elaboration of temporal rules in WTO Law

should be consolidated into a more precise expression or replaced by other non-temporal regulations or procedures. In terms of the modification, the following inquiries might be relevant: (1) what are the *reasons* for making a modification? (*e.g.*, new membership, exceptional or unforeseen circumstances, practical or political difficulties); (2) what are the *forms* of modification? (*e.g.*, the replacement of the numerical term or the anchored event of original temporal rules, the incorporation of new temporal rules, or the corresponding arrangement following the effect of temporal rules); and (3) who are the *actors* involved in modification? (*e.g.*, multilateral, institutional, or bilateral). In terms of the elaboration, it can rely on the Members concerned to make Decisions or Declarations, the institution to issue guidelines through Recommendations, or the adjudicators to provide an interpretation or clarification in their DS Reports.

Finally, despite efforts to map the establishment, modification, and elaboration of the six categories of temporal rules in WTO Law, the thirty-three cases provided in this Chapter should only be seen as the tip of the iceberg to demonstrate the dynamic or fluid character of temporal rules in use. Nevertheless, the aim of this Chapter is to take the insights from the 2-D temporal events association (Chapter 4) a step further, and to posit that the 2-D model between the temporal rules and legal events may also be extended and perceived under a three-dimensional (3-D) infrastructure to consider its dynamic interactions through different *systemic mechanisms* in practice. In other words, the temporal rule as a systematic promise in law is not only statically established in legal texts to regulate legal events, but also subject to change under dynamic interactions between the rules and its systemic environment. With this 3-D systemic infrastructure in mind, the following Chapter will proceed to explore the overall implications of temporal rules in WTO Law in respect of the rationality of making temporal rules in legal texts, the application of temporal rules in practice, as well as the potential contribution of temporal rules to the theoretical framework of legalization.

CHAPTER 6

# Implications of Temporal Rules in WTO Law

Following the 3-D systemic approach of temporal rules in the previous Section 5.7, it is noticed that temporal rules not only statically underpin diverse events in WTO Law, but also dynamically respond to change through several systemic mechanisms in WTO practice. However, the appearance or functioning of temporal rules in law is not always well-established or without problem. Temporal rules have the potential to both influence and be influenced by legal practice, and perhaps even the process of legalization. For example, Article 30.3 of the *Vienna Convention on the Law of Treaties* (VCLT) underlines the principle of *lex posterior* (*derogat legi priori*) in favor of the later treaty relating to the same subject matter.[1] In practice, although states and tribunals have rarely mentioned the possibility that two treaties might conflict in time (or have simply addressed this issue by political means), academics and other observers do pay attention to the problem of a treaty conflict.[2] To address the outcome of a treaty conflict, Borgen argued that:[3]

> The answer lies not in a place, such as a court to hear more and more of these conflicts, nor in a rule, such as a rewritten Article 30 of VCLT. Rather, the answer lies in a process. What is required to address this problem is a series of standard procedures ranging from drafting tools to interpretive techniques, as well as a new understanding of what makes effective conflict rules.

1 *E.g.*, VCLT Art. 30.3: "When[Timing] all the parties to the earlier treaty are *parties*[INS] also to the later treaty but the earlier treaty is not terminated or suspended in operation under article 59, the earlier treaty *applies*[APP] only to the extent that its provisions are compatible with those of the later treaty." Noting that, based on the purpose of denotation in this research, the sequential expressions (the "earlier" and "later" treaty) would not be highlighted as temporal rules due to the fact that they refer to documentation. *See supra*, Section 3.2.

2 Christopher J Borgen, 'Resolving Treaty Conflicts' (2005) 37 George Washington International Law Review 573, 605. (*See also* at 578. The author argued that "the VCLT's treaty conflict provisions are neither an accurate description of current state practice, nor are they adequate prescriptions for how states should act.")

3 *Ibid.*, 620. (*See also* at 647. The author concluded that "[t]here are two basic requirements for an effective response to treaty conflicts: (1) default rules that give better predictability as to which treaty would be enforceable in the case of conflict; and (2) standard procedures for treaty negotiators and drafters to maximize the probability of avoiding conflicts.")

 | DOI:10.1163/9789004745629_007

Accordingly, temporal rules in practice may create specific legal problems or concerns, leading us to reflect on the implications within *a broader process* from (1) drafting, (2) interpretation, to (3) a theoretical understanding.

In this regard, the following sections will discuss the implications of temporal rules in WTO Law in *a process*. Section 6.1 will address the rationality for *making* temporal rules in WTO Law in line with the presumption of rational design and the theory of secondary rules of law. Section 6.2 will document how temporal rules have been *applied* in WTO practice to establish shared understandings for the consideration of their dynamic legitimacy through interpretation. Lastly, Section 6.3 will demonstrate how temporal rules may contribute to *the theoretical framework of legalization*.

## 6.1 Implications for Making Temporal Rules

The academic interest in international rulemaking is hardly a novelty. The rational design of international institutions (including laws) has stood as an important school in literature. It is based on the presumption of rational-choice analysis that "states use international institutions to further their own goals, and they design institutions accordingly."[4] In other words, states flight over institutional design since it affects outcomes, and the outcomes cannot be altered promptly and easily alongside states' growing power. For this reason, the institutional design is not random and should be the result of "rational, purposive interactions among states and other international actors to solve specific problems."[5] To be more specific, states and international actors must reckon with key elements of the institutional design of laws. For example, five key elements of international law (IL) have been identified as dependent variables to solve cooperation problems in international settings, which are: (1) whether membership rules are restrictive or all-inclusive; (2) whether the scope of agreements covers single or multiple issue areas; (3) whether the tasks in agreements are centralized and delegated to authority; (4) how the institution controls its collective decision-making; and (5) how the institution provides flexibility of arrangements to accommodate to changing circumstances.[6]

With these five key elements of IL in mind, this research is based on the assumption that temporal rules embedded in IL may also be singled out as an

4 Barbara Koremenos, Charles Lipson and Duncan Snidal, 'The Rational Design of International Institutions' (2001) 55 International Organization 761, 762.

5 *Ibid.*

6 Barbara Koremenos, Charles Lipson and Duncan Snidal, 'Rational Design: Looking Back to Move Forward' (2001) 55 International Organization 1051, 1056–1062.

important element for considering the institutional design of IL, and can be designed rationally and purposively to solve cooperation problems. For example, to deal with the perception of risks in a treaty, the drafters may seek to design specific temporal rules as "risk-management techniques" through the deliberate establishment of a limited duration or trial period for the treaty's application.[7] This choice for the duration of a treaty, either an indefinite or a finite period, has been considered to be one of the most important strategies to balance the costs and effects or to distribute the gains of a treaty. In addition, as shown in an empirical study, the choice of the duration is affected by the degree of uncertainty, renegotiation costs, and relative risk aversion.[8] In other words, the option of a finite duration allows "adjustment in the face of international uncertainty without dismantling cooperation," and in fact, two-thirds of treaties are not intended to be permanent.[9]

Another example of the institutional design of temporal rules can be found in the case of withdrawal provisions in a treaty. For example, the length of the notice and waiting periods to regulate the act of withdrawal from a treaty has been considered as an outcome of rational design intended to facilitate cooperation. This means that the longer notice period levels the playing field by "reducing fear that the remaining states would be taken advantage of and eliminating one of the advantages to withdrawing." Therefore, the longer waiting period before giving notice of the intention to withdraw helps the state to solve domestic commitment problem and to ensure its partner states for the credibility of cooperation.[10] In addition, it was observed that the notice periods as procedural constraints are in line with the principle of good faith, and enable "all treaty Members to plan their behavior in advance of any particular instance of exit."[11] To sum up, the design of some temporal rules in treaties (*e.g.*, the finite period for applying a treaty or the notice and waiting period for

7 Richard B Bilder, *Managing the Risks of International Agreement* (University of Wisconsin Press 1981), 20.

8 Barbara Koremenos, 'Contracting around International Uncertainty' (2005) 99 The American Political Science Review 549, 562.

9 *Ibid.*, 561–562.

10 Barbara Koremenos and Allison Nau, 'Exit, No Exit' (2010) 21 Duke Journal of Comparative & International Law 81, 82–83. (*See also* at 95, 97, and 98. The authors defined (1) a notice period as "the amount of time between the point at which a member gives notice of its withdrawal and the point at which a member gives notice of its withdrawal and the point at which its withdrawal becomes effective;" and (2) a withdrawal waiting period as "the designated period of time before a member that wants to withdraw from the agreement is fully freed from its commitments under the agreement," *i.e.*, "the total amount of time between the entry into force of the agreement and the full release of member obligation.")

11 Laurence R Helfer, 'Exiting Custom: Analogies to Treaty Withdrawals' (2010) 21 Duke Journal of Comparative & International Law 65, 69.

treaty withdrawal) has been identified as a crucial element to solve cooperation problems in international settings. In the particular context of WTO Law, this research will go a step further to identify more temporal rules that may be relevant to the consideration of the institutional design of IL. To this end, it aims to outline the potential rationale behind temporal rules to support future in-depth studies.

Prior to the identification of the potential rationale for temporal rules in WTO Law, the general logic for making temporal rules in law may also be viewed through the theory of "secondary rules of law." At the theoretical level, temporal rules in the legal system may themselves be considered as secondary rules of law. According to Hart's theory, the primary rules are concerned with the *actions or behaviors* that must or must not be taken. On the other hand, the secondary rules focus on the *ways* in which the primary rules may *be ascertained, introduced*, or *changed*.[12] In particular, the secondary rules as "the rules of recognition" provide certain *ways* or authoritative *criteria* for the identification of actions or behaviors governed by the primary rules. These secondary rules *per se* can "neither be valid nor invalid but is simply accepted as *appropriate*" for their usage or application under the general operation of the system.[13] Moreover, the "appropriateness" of the secondary rules can also be referred to the concept of "legal efficacy" which is concerned with the intentional design of rules to be regarded more as pragmatic necessities than moral imperatives. In other words, "a rule may exist because it is *convenient* or *necessary* to have some clear fixed rule about the subject [*e.g.*, arbitrary distinctions, formalities, and highly specific detail] with which it is concerned, but not because any *moral* importance is attached to the particular rule."[14] As such, this research posits that temporal rules can also be considered as important functional elements in law in line with the theory of "secondary rules of law" by focusing on whether they provide *appropriate* (*e.g.*, convenient or necessary) *ways* or *criteria* to ascertain the primary rules of law.

In WTO practice, the "appropriateness" of temporal rules has been addressed in actual cases. For example, one of the earliest cases concerns whether the backdating of the effectivity of a transitional safeguard measure was permitted by ATC Article 6.10. The adjudicators at that time noted that ATC Article 6.10 contains temporal rules, allowing a safeguard measure to be taken prospectively (*i.e.*, within 30 days following the 60-day period for consultations). They argued that this intentional design of temporal rules is "appropriate" due to the

12 HLA Hart, *The Concept of Law* (Oxford University Press 1972), 92.
13 *Ibid.*, 105. (emphasis added)
14 *Ibid.*, 223–224. (emphasis added)

nature of the safeguard measure concerned. To be more specific, the adjudicators stated that "a presumption arises from the very text of Article 6.10 that such a measure may be applied only prospectively," and this prospective presumption appeared "entirely *appropriate* in respect of measures which are limitative or deprivational in character or tenor and impact upon Member countries and their rights or privileges and upon private persons and their acts."[15] The adjudicators further concluded their believe by stating that "[t]his is the commonplace inference that is properly drawn from such disappearance [of the express provision for backdating the operative effect of a restraint measure]. [They] are not entitled to assume that that disappearance was merely accidental or an inadvertent oversight on the part of either harassed negotiators or inattentive draftsmen."[16] Accordingly, the design of prospective temporal rules in ATC Article 6.10 appears to be *rational* rather than negligent, and was considered as an *appropriate* way to regulate the effectivity of a safeguard restraint measure.

Drawing on the presumption of rational design and the appropriateness of secondary rules of law, the following subsections will examine the underlying rationale for making temporal rules in WTO Law, especially as an appropriate way to ascertain the primary rules of WTO Law. It should be noted that there are countless ways in which temporal rules can be rationally and appropriately integrated into law to determine legal events. The aim of this section is only indicative by highlighting seven general strategic assumptions underpinned by the relevant temporal rules found in the context of WTO Law. The list below does not and cannot claim completeness. Appendix 1 offers a summation of the relevant cases in WTO Jurisprudence.

(1) As a benchmark for calculation or evaluation
(2) As a means of regulating the proceedings
(3) As a means of balancing the interests of the measures
(4) As a facilitator of transparency and notification
(5) As a tactic of special and differential treatment
(6) As a facilitator of implementation
(7) As a response to change in law

15 Appellate Body Report, *US—Underwear*, p. 14. (emphasis added) ("Under the express terms of [ATC] Article 6.10, the importing Member which 'propose[s] to take safeguard action' may, 'after the expiry of the period of 60 days' from the date of receipt of the request for consultations without agreement having been reached, 'apply the restraint (measure)' 'within 30 days following the 60-day period for consultations ….'")

16 *Ibid.*, p. 17.

### 6.1.1 *As a Benchmark for Calculation or Evaluation*

The temporal rule can set a benchmark for calculating the amount of measures (*e.g.*, subsidies, tariffs, and compensations). First, to establish a specific benchmark for calculation, a *fixed point or period in time* can be explicitly stipulated in legal texts. For example, the adjudicators have construed the meaning of the temporal rule "during the 1992 marketing year" in Article 13(b)(ii) of the Agreement on Agriculture, and opined that this fixed point in the marketing year of 1992 is "a very specific limitation on the establishment of the benchmark" for calculating the amount of subsidies.[17] Second, to set a general benchmark for calculation, the term "most recent" and the "representative" *period in time* are found to be most relevant. For example, in the case of the price gap calculation for tariff equivalents in Annex 5 of the Agreement on Agriculture, the arbitrators expressed the view that the calculation should be based on "the most recent representative reference period," and stated the reason behind for using this general benchmark as to "minimize the need for ad hoc adjustments to be made to the data and correspond as closely as possible to the trade regime as applied."[18] The temporal rules concerning "the most recent three-year period" and "the most recent year" are also deployed as the basis for calculating future trade prospects in Paragraph 6 of the *Understanding on Article XXVIII*. Third, the general benchmark can be further interpreted in consideration of its static character. As the adjudicators clarified, the general benchmark for the calculation of future trade prospects should be the most recent period or year preceding "the initiation of the negotiations" rather than "the conclusion of the negotiations." In the course of their analysis, the adjudicators stated the reasons that "the benchmark is meant to serve as the basis for negotiations and the calculation of compensation," and "[the] use of a continually moving benchmark as the basis for negotiations could perpetuate negotiations indefinitely."[19] Accordingly, the temporal rule can set a benchmark for

17 Panel Report, *US—Upland Cotton*, para. 7.438.

18 Award of the Arbitrator, *EC—The ACP-EC Partnership Agreement*, paras. 82–83.

19 Panel Report, *EU—Poultry Meat (China)*, para. 7.272. ("[I]n order to achieve the purpose of facilitating the negotiations under [GATT] Article XXVIII:2 by providing a benchmark that the negotiating Members can use as a basis for the calculation of compensation, it cannot be the case that the Members engaged in the negotiations would be legally obliged to change the benchmark defined in that provision from year to year until the negotiations have been concluded. We note that to adjust the benchmark year-to-year would not be complicated as such, insofar as it would be the result of a simple mathematical formula applied to import statistics. The difficulty that would arise is that the benchmark is meant to serve as the basis for negotiations and the calculation of compensation. To require the negotiating Members to use of a continually moving benchmark as the basis for negotiations could perpetuate negotiations indefinitely.")

calculation not only by a specific expression through a fixed point or period in time, but also by a general expression such as the "most recent" and/or "representative" period in the light of its static character.

In addition, the temporal rule can also establish a benchmark for conducting evaluations to make factual determinations (*e.g.*, the existence of dumping, the *de facto* specificity of subsidies, and the spread of diseases). In other words, one may derive opinions on the issue concerned based on the evaluation of certain situations occurred within *a given period in time*. This given period ensures an objective and unbiased factual determination of the issues. Three examples are provided as follows: First, to evaluate the existence of dumping under the Anti-Dumping Agreement, the proper use of the "period of investigation" as a given period was emphasized by the adjudicators to allow the determination to "be less likely to be subject to market fluctuations or other vagaries that may distort a proper evaluation." The adjudicators opined that "the standardized reliance on a [period of investigation], although not fixed in duration by the [Anti-Dumping Agreement], assures the investigating authority and exporters of a consistent and reasonable methodology for determining present dumping."[20] Second, a given period can be found in the evaluation of the *de facto* specificity of subsidies in Article 2.1(c) of the SCM Agreement. This Article states a given period to determine whether a subsidy is *de facto* specific as "the length of time during which the subsidy programme has been in operation." As the adjudicators pointed out, this given period functions as a safeguard that keeps in check the flexibility for investigating authorities to consider specificity in a number of factual scenarios that may arise when making a determination.[21] Third and lastly, to evaluate the likelihood of an area remaining free of a disease under Article 6.3 of the SPS Agreement, the adjudicators also highlighted a given period to be useful to determine the spread of a disease by stating that "[o]ne useful element for the assessment of the effectiveness of these control measures, to the extent it is available, is data regarding the actual spread of a disease *within a given time frame*."[22] Taken together, a *given period in time* may be considered as an important benchmark for evaluation to make

20 Appellate Body Report, *EC—Tube or Pipe Fittings*, para. 80.

21 Panel Report, *US—Countervailing Measures (China) (Article 21.5—China)*, para. 7.272.

22 Panel Report, *Russia—Pigs (EU)*, para. 7.411. (emphasis added) Noting that the aim of Article 6.3 of the SPS Agreement is to assess whether the evidence is of "a nature, quantity, and quality sufficient" to enable the authorities ultimately to make a determination, and therefore does not itself contemplate "a certain period of time for the importing Member to evaluate and verify the evidence provided by the exporting Member." *See also* Appellate Body Report, *Russia—Pigs (EU)*, paras. 5.83 and 5.86.

a factual determination, although without specifying a fixed duration (*e.g.*, the period of investigation, operation, and spread).

### 6.1.2 *As a Means of Regulating the Proceedings*

At a general level, *a speed modifier* (*e.g.*, "prompt") can be deployed to govern the proceedings and ensure their effective functioning. For example, as stated in DSU Article 3.3, the "prompt" settlement of disputes "is essential to the effective functioning of the WTO and the maintenance of a proper balance between the rights and obligations of Members."[23] At a practical level, the temporal rule can be used to regulate the stages of the proceedings in two ways: (1) by setting a *fixed period* as a time-limit to ensure the predictability and control of the undertakings, and (2) by allowing a *reasonable period* to balance the special needs of the parties involved.

First, a *fixed period in time* can be imposed as a time-limit to preserve the predictability of the procedures and take control of the proceedings. For example, Article 5.10 of the Anti-Dumping Agreement prescribes a general one-year period for conducting an anti-dumping investigation, and "in no case more than 18 months," in order to preserve predictability and reduce uncertainty about the outcome of the investigation. The adjudicators noted that this Article "preserves predictability for the interested parties in an investigation by ensuring that when an investigation is initiated, interested parties are not left in the uncertainty about the outcome of the investigation for more than one year 'and in no case more than 18 months'."[24] Besides, the adjudicators also emphasized that "in the absence of time-limits, authorities would effectively cede control of investigations to the interested parties, and could find themselves unable to complete their investigations within the time-limits mandated under the [Anti-Dumping Agreement]." For these reasons, they reaffirmed that "in the interest of orderly administration[,] investigating authorities do, and indeed must establish such deadlines."[25]

---

23 *E.g.*, Appellate Body Report, *US—Upland Cotton* (*Article 21.5—Brazil*), para. 246. ("Requiring a WTO Member to initiate new proceedings to challenge the same type of recurrent subsidies that were found to result in adverse effects, simply because the subsidies were provided subsequent to the original proceedings, does not promote 'prompt settlement' nor 'prompt compliance'.")

24 Panel Report, *Pakistan—BOPP Film* (*UAE*), para. 7.471.

25 Appellate Body Report, *US—Hot-Rolled Steel*, para. 73. ("We note, in that respect, that Article 5.10 of [the Anti-Dumping Agreement] stipulates that anti-dumping investigations shall normally be completed within one year, and in any event in no longer than 18 months, after initiation. Furthermore, Article 6.14 provides generally that the procedures set out in Article 6 'are not intended to prevent the authorities of a Member from proceeding expeditiously'.")

Second, a *reasonable period in time* can be utilized to balance the special needs of the parties involved against a fixed time-limit for the proceedings established above. For example, Annex II(6) of the Anti-Dumping Agreement allows the parties to submit explanations "within a reasonable period" during anti-dumping investigation. The adjudicators emphasized that the aim of setting a reasonable period is to "balance the need to provide an adequate period for the provision of the explanations referred to against the time constraints applicable to the various phases of the investigation and to the investigation as a whole."[26] In addition, Article 6.8 of the Anti-Dumping Agreement also deploys the temporal rule "within a reasonable period" to regulate the submission of necessary information by any interested party. The adjudicators further explained that "if information is, in fact, supplied 'within a reasonable period', the investigating authorities cannot use facts available, but must use the information submitted by the interested party."[27] In sum, a *reasonable period in time* seems to provide a degree of flexibility in consideration of the needs of the parties during the proceedings; however, at the same time, the overarching functioning of the time-limits is still acknowledged to ensure the predictability and control in a broader procedural sense.

It is worth to note that the adoption of these two strategies (*i.e.*, a fixed period and a reasonable period) might sometimes overlap with each other. For example, Article 12.1.1 of the SCM Agreement envisages that investigating authorities can impose fixed time-limits for questionnaire responses. However, the adjudicators opined that "the mere fact that information is provided after the expiry of such time-limits does not, without more, establish that the information was not provided within a 'reasonable period' under Article 12.7 of the SCM Agreement." By differentiating the usage of the different terms "time-limit" and "reasonable period" in the legal texts, the adjudicators understood that a fixed time-limit imposed does not *ipso facto* constitute a reasonable period in all circumstances.[28] A reasonable period appears to be an independent temporal element to be taken into account in each different circumstance.

---

26 Panel Report, *Egypt—Steel Rebar*, para. 7.282.

27 Appellate Body Report, *US—Hot-Rolled Steel*, para. 77. ("Article 6.8 of [the Anti-Dumping Agreement] identifies the circumstances in which investigating authorities may overcome a lack of information, in the responses of the interested parties, by using 'facts' which are otherwise 'available' to the investigating authorities. According to Article 6.8, where the interested parties do not 'significantly impede' the investigation, recourse may be had to facts available only if an interested party fails to submit necessary information 'within a reasonable period'.")

28 Panel Report, *US—Anti-Dumping and Countervailing Duties (Korea)*, para. 7.351. ("[T]he drafters' careful choice of words also implies that they carry different meanings. This supports our understanding that a time-limit imposed by an investigating authority does

### 6.1.3 *As a Means of Balancing the Interests of the Measures*

The temporal rule can be incorporated into legal texts alongside the establishment of different rights and obligations in a process. It balances the interests of the measures imposed by Members which might have (negative) effects on others. The process contains (1) consultation, (2) publication to entry into force, (3) imposition, (4) review for continuity, and (5) termination.

First, before a measure is considered to be imposed, *sufficient time* for consultation is demanded for Members to exchange views in order to arrive at a mutual understanding. For example, Article 12.3 of the Agreement on Safeguards obliges Members applying or extending a safeguard measure to provide adequate opportuanity for prior consultations with Members affected by the measure. As explained by the adjudicators, Members taking the measure should provide "sufficient information and time to allow for the possibility, through consultations, for a meaningful exchange on the issues identified."[29]

Second, before a measure becomes valid, a *reasonable interval* between its publication and entry into force is found to be cruical for balancing the interests of the actor and those affected. For example, Article 2.12 of the TBT Agreement obliges Members to to provide a "reasonable interval" between the publication and the entry into force of their technical regulations. As stated by the adjudicators, this interval "carefully balances the interests of, on the one hand, the exporting Member whose producers might be affected by a technical regulation and, on the other hand, the importing Member that wishes to pursue a legitimate objective through a technical regulation."[30]

Third, after a measure is officially imposed, a *necessary (or fixed) period* for its imposition is established to regulate the duration for applying the measure. For example, Article 7.1 of the Agreement on Safeguards provides a general statement that "[a] Member shall apply safeguard measures only *for such period of time as may be necessary* to prevent or remedy serious injury and to facilitate adjustment."[31] To be more specific, according to Article 7.2 of the Agreement on Safeguards, the initial period must not exceed "four years," and the extension is possible only under certain conditions. Article 7.3 further states the overall time-limit that the total period of application of a safeguard measure

---

not ipso facto constitute a 'reasonable period' in all circumstances. While it is proper for an investigating authority to attach importance to time-limits fixed for questionnaire responses, in determining whether information is submitted within a reasonable period of time, an investigating authority is required to do more than merely establish that a deadline was exceeded.")

29 Appellate Body Report, *US—Wheat Gluten*, para. 136.

30 Appellate Body Report, *US—Clove Cigarettes*, para. 274.

31 Emphasis added.

shall not exceed "eight years." These time-limits prevent safeguard measures (*i.e.*, temporary by nature) to be circumvented by their repeated application on the imports. In the context of the TRIPS Agreement, the measure to protect intellectual property rights is not extended indefinitely either, but is limited to a particular term of protection. For example, the duration for the patent protection in Article 33 of the TRIPS Agreement is "a period of twenty years counted from the filing date." In addition, the adjudicators clarified that "[t]he opportunity to obtain a twenty-year term must be a readily discernible and specific right, and it must be clearly seen as such by the patent applicant when a patent application is filed."[32]

Fourth, after the imposition of a measure, a *reasonable period* after imposition and *the timing of request* can be relevant to initiate a review to assess whether the measure should be continued. For example, Article 11.2 of the Anti-Dumping Agreement requires investigating authorities under certain circumstances, such as at the request of an interested party after a reasonable period of time, to review the need for the continued imposition of the anti-dumping duty. The adjudicators explained that Article 11.2 conditions the obligation of review on (1) "the passage of a reasonable period of time since imposition of the definitive duty;" and (2) "the submission by the interested party of 'positive information' substantiating the need for a review."[33]

Fifth and lastly, in terms of the termination of a measure, the legal provisions may require its termination *on a date not later than a fixed period* counting from its imposition or its sunset review. For example, Article 11.3 of the Anti-Dumping Agreement provides a sunset clause for termination of definitive anti-dumping duties "on a date not later than five years from its imposition (or from the date of the most recent review ...)." As such, the adjudicators acknowledged that this Article provides not only a fixed five-year sunset period, but allows an implicit opportunity to *effectively extend* the period in a situation where a review has taken place during the five-year period.[34]

To sum up, when adopting a measure, various temporal rules may be designed as a means for Members to balance the interests of the actor and those affected within a given process, including: (1) *sufficient time* for prior consultation; (2) a *reasonable interval* between its publication and entry into force;

32 Appellate Body Report, *Canada—Patent Term*, para. 92.

33 Appellate Body Report, *Mexico—Anti-Dumping Measures on Rice*, para. 314.

34 *Ibid.*, fn. 494. ("Article 11.3 of [the Anti-Dumping Agreement] provides also for another situation whereby this five-year period can be otherwise effectively extended, viz in a situation where a review ... covering both dumping and injury has taken place. If, for instance, such a review took place at the four-year point, it could effectively extend the sunset review until 9 years from the original determination.")

(3) a *necessary* or *fixed period* for its imposition; (4) a review *after a reasonable period* and *at request* of the parties involved; and (5) termination *on a date not later than a fixed period* with an opportunity for effective extension.

### 6.1.4 *As a Facilitator of Transparency and Notification*

The concept of transparency and the obligation of notification are interconnected and usually employed to increase awareness of the new or modified measures so as to enable appropriate adjustments. In the WTO, the concept of transparency has been highlighted "to achieve a greater degree of clarity, predictability and information about trade policies, rules and regulations of Members," and "[i]n implementing this concept, Members use notifications."[35] In the specific context of the SPS Agreement, it was further noted that "notifications are used to inform other Members about new or changed regulations that may significantly affect their trading partners."[36] To strengthen the notification obligation, a number of temporal rules can be integrated into legal texts. Three examples can be found as follows.

First, a *speed modifier* (*e.g., prompt*) can be built in as a temporal requirement to strengthen the notification obligation by ensuring adequate time for adaptation. For example, GATT Articles X:1 and X:2 require Members to publish "promptly" certain measures of their general application. The adjudicators interpreted this prompt publication for its purpose to ensure that "traders are made aware of measures that may have an impact on them, so that they have time to become acquainted with, and to adapt to, the new measures."[37] To be more specific, the essential implication of the promptness appears to ensure that traders "have a reasonable opportunity to acquire authentic information about [the new] measures and accordingly to protect and adjust their activities or alternatively to seek modification of such measures."[38]

Second, a *sequence in time* (*e.g., in advance before the measures applied*) for notification to occur may also be considered relevant to prevent the potential desire of delay. For example, GATT Article XIX:2 obliges Members to notify their safeguard measures "as far in advance as may be practicable." In practice, the desirability of delaying has been pointed out by the adjudicators due to the fact that a premature disclosure of safeguard measures to the public would

35 G/SPS/7/Rev.4.

36 G/SPS/7/Rev.4, paras. 1–2.

37 Appellate Body Report, *US—Countervailing and Anti-Dumping Measures* (*China*), para. 4.65. (They "create expectations among traders that they will not have to face measures that they could not be aware of because such measures were published late or because they were not yet published.")

38 Appellate Body Report, *US—Underwear*, p. 21.

cause some difficulties in the course of consultations with other Members.[39] To solve this potential delay, the adjudicators have read GATT Article XIX:2 in conjunction with Article 12.1(c) of the Agreement on Safeguards to further clarify the notification obligation to be undertaken "before the measure is applied" but not necessarily "before the measure is adopted."[40]

Third, a *fixed frequency in time* can be helpful for the recurring notification which requires the measures concerned to be notified repeatedly. For example, Article 25.1 of the SCM Agreement requires Members to notify all specific subsidies every year (*i.e.*, by "30 June of each year").[41] Annex 3 (J) of the TBT Agreement requires standardizing bodies to publish, "at least every six months," their work programme and report on the progress regarding the preparation and adoption of new standards.[42] In sum, temporal rules as a facilitator of transparency and notification are dedicated to ensuring adequate time for Members to be aware of any new or modified measures taken in order to make a corresponding adjustment, including: (1) a prompt notification; (2) a notification as far in advance as practicable before the measures applied; and (3) a recurring notification with a fixed frequency in time.

### 6.1.5 *As a Tactic of Special and Differential Treatment*

As recognized in the preamble of the WTO Agreement, one of the crucial objectives for the WTO is that "there is need for *positive efforts* designed to ensure that developing countries, and especially the least developed among them, secure a share in the growth in international trade commensurate with the needs of their economic development."[43] In line with this requirement of "positive efforts," a number of provisions in WTO Law have established the so-called "special and differential treatment" for developing countries, including the incorporation of temporal rules to regulate the application or implementation of certain legal provisions.

39 GATT/CP/106, para. 46. ("[T]he release of any public announcement on any proposed action under [GATT] Article XIX, as a premature disclosure to the public would make it difficult for the government proposing to take action to take fully into consideration the representations made by other contracting parties in the course of consultations.")

40 Panel Report, *Dominican Republic—Safeguard Measures*, para. 7.433.

41 SCM Art. 25.1: "Members agree that, without prejudice to the provisions of [GATT Art. XVI:1], their notifications of subsidies shall be submitted not later than 30 June of each year and shall conform to the provisions of paragraphs 2 through 6."

42 TBT Annex 3 (J): "At least once every six months, the standardizing body shall publish a work programme containing its name and address, the standards it is currently preparing and the standards which it has adopted in the preceding period."

43 Emphasis added.

First, one of the common tactics in favor of developing countries is to provide them with a *fixed transitional period* to apply legal provisions. For example, Article 66.1 of the TRIPS Agreement prescribes "a period of 10 years" for least-developed countries (LDCs) to exempt from applying certain provisions of the TRIPS Agreement in consideration of their "economic, financial and administrative constraints" and "their need for flexibility to create a viable technological base."[44] In the context of Article 14 of the SPS Agreement, it allows LDCs and other developing countries to delay application of the provisions of the SPS Agreement for "a period of five and two years," respectively. The adjudicators have emphasized that the right to defer application of the provisions is to tackle the special circumstance "where such application is prevented by lack of technical expertise, technical infrastructure or resources."[45]

Second, a *prescribed date* (*i.e., self-designated implementation date*) is considered as an innovation in recent days for allowing developing countries to take the initiative themselves to flexibly decide when to implement legal provisions. For example, due to potential difficulties related to the capacity to implement the trade facilitation measures, TFA Article 14.1 enables developing countries to self-designate, through unilateral notifications, the implementation dates of their commitments under three approaches: Category A ("upon entry into force" of the TFA for developing countries or "within one year after entry into force" for LDCs), Category B ("on a date after a transitional period of time following the entry into force" of the TFA), or Category C ("on a date after a transitional period of time … and requiring the acquisition of implementation capacity"). This Article allows each developing countries to prescribe their dates of implementation, and is different to the conventional strategies for setting a fixed transitional period that applies to all developing countries at the same time.

Third, the possibility of an *extension* has also been taken into account following the innovation in the self-designated implementation date. For example, TFA Article 17.2 allows the automatic grant for a *short extension* upon early warning (*i.e.*, less than 18 months for developing countries or 3 years for LDCs). As for a *long extension*, TFA Article 17.4 obliges the Committee on Trade Facilitation to "give sympathetic consideration" to the request for the

44 TRIPS Art. 66.1: "In view of the special needs and requirements of least-developed country Members, their economic, financial and administrative constraints, and their need for flexibility to create a viable technological base, such Members shall not be required to apply the provisions of this Agreement, other than Articles 3, 4 and 5, for a period of 10 years from the date of application as defined under [Article 65.1]."

45 Appellate Body Report, *EC—Hormones*, fn. 99.

extensions. In practice, it has been argued that the flexibility for the countries to unilaterally alter their commitments may have provided more comfort for signing the TFA and encouraged more ambitious self-designated implementation dates. However, it needs to be mindful that a series of different notification documents submitted at varying times may cause some inconvenience for interested parties to retrieve and compare the information of the commitments.[46] To sum up, temporal rules as a tactic of special and differential treatment can be deployed to allow more (flexible) time for developing countries to apply or implement certain legal provisions, including: (1) a fixed transitional period; (2) a self-designated date of implementation; and (3) the possibility for a short or long extension.

### 6.1.6 *As a Facilitator of Implementation*

The temporal rule can facilitate the implementation of the commitments, agreements, or rulings to ensure their practical value or use. First, a *prescribed period in time* is expected of implementation of a commitment or agreement to ensure its practical value. For example, GATS Article XX:1(d) obliges each Member to specify in its Schedule of Specific Commitments "the time-frame for implementation of such commitments."[47] The adjudicators considered that the objective of the "time-frame" for implementation is to ensure clarity and precision, and therefore does not "allow a window of discretion with regard to temporal aspects of these commitments that could erode the practical value of a commitment."[48] In the context of the consistency of the BOP restrictions, GATT Article XVIII:12(c)(ii) provides a mechanism for the WTO Committee to address possible violations and make appropriate recommendations for securing conformity with the legal provisions "within a

---

46 Ben Czapnik, 'The Unique Features of the Trade Facilitation Agreement: A Revolutionary New Approach to Multilateral Negotiations or the Exception Which Proves the Rule?' (2015) 18 Journal of International Economic Law 773, 780–782. (*See also* at 794. With regard to the potential of this "Member-specific approach" for other WTO's issue areas or Agreements, the author concluded that: "WTO Members should consider whether they are prepared to allow some variation in rules for different Members in order to find an overall balance which is acceptable to all. This type of approach would certainly create additional technical work for negotiators. However, it would provide more tools for achieving political balance which is often the biggest obstacle in multilateral trade negotiations.")

47 GATS Art. XX:1(d): "Each Member shall set out in a schedule the specific commitments it undertakes under Part III of this Agreement. With respect to sectors where such commitments are undertaken, each Schedule shall specify: ... where appropriate the time-frame for implementation of such commitments;...."

48 Panel Report, *Mexico—Telecoms*, para. 7.368.

specified period." The adjudicators noted that the purpose of this Article is to provide "for a period of time to be granted to the Member in order to implement the requirement to remove or modify the inconsistent measures."[49]

Second, a *fixed frequency in time* for a periodic review can be established to ascertain the actual implementation of an agreement in order to recommend an adjustment. For example, Article 15.3 of the TBT Agreement obliges the TBT Committee to undertake an "annual" review of the implementation and operation of the TBT Agreement. Moreover, Article 15.4 of the TBT Agreement requires the Committee to have in-depth review every three years by stating that the review should be conducted "[n]ot later than the end of the third year from the date of entry into force of the [WTO Agreement] and at the end of each three-year period thereafter."

Third, a *fixed period in time* can be established as a reference time to initiate a review and keep under surveillance the implementation of the adopted ruling until the issue resolved. For example, DSU Article 21.6 requires the issue of implementation of the recommendations or rulings to be placed on the agenda of the DSB meeting "after six months" following the date of establishment of the reasonable period of time for implementation, and to remain on the agenda until the issue is resolved. In sum, temporal rules as a facilitator of implementation can be designed to ensure the pracitical value or use of commitments, agreements, or rulings, including: (1) a prescribed period for implementation; (2) a fixed frequecy for periodic review of implementation; and (3) keeping under surveillance for implementation after a fixed period in time.

### 6.1.7 *As a Response to Change in Law*

The temporal rule can be responsive to change in law, which means it may be helpful to facilitate a smooth transition or to establish exceptaional conditions when a change in law occurs or will occur, such as (1) the establishment of a *transition* for new institutional frameworks, and (2) the establishment of *an exception or exemption* for new legal rules.

First, to establish new institutional frameworks, a *prescribed period in time* for allowing the co-existence with the old and a *prescribed date* for termination are relevant to ensure an orderly transition of the system. For example, a *Decision on Transitional Co-existence of the GATT 1947 and the WTO Agreement* was adopted in 1994 to prescribe a general one-year period for the co-existence

49 Panel Report, *India—Quantitative Restrictions*, para. 5.227.

of the two institutional frameworks.[50] In addition to this prescribed period for co-existence, the Preparatory Committee for the WTO also stated the desire for establishing a prescribed date (*i.e.*, "on a date agreed in advance") to end the period of co-existence "so as to provide predictability for policy makers and facilitate an orderly termination of the institutional framework of the Agreement."[51] In a similar vein, to terminate an old institutional framework such as the *1979 Agreement on Import Licensing Procedures*, the parties to the Agreement also adopted a Decision in 1995 to agree on its termination date as of 1 January 1996 "so as to provide predictability for policy makers and facilitate an orderly termination of the institutional framework of the [1979] Agreement."[52]

Second, to establish new legal rules, *the date of the Agreement* can be considered as an important temporal reference for drafting an exception for the newly-established legal rules under consideration of special difficulties already known or existed at the time of negotiation. For example, in principle, GATT Article V:6 requires Members to accord treatments no less favourable to all goods that have been in international transit.[53] However, its proviso allows Members to maintain direct consignment requirements existing "on the date of this Agreement" (*i.e.*, 30 October 1947)[54] in order to tackle the special difficulties of certain countries which required that goods benefiting from historical preferences accorded by them be shipped directly to them from the country of origin.[55] The adjudicators further analyzed the scope of this Article, and confirmed that "a Member is nevertheless permitted to maintain any direct consignment requirements that existed in 1947 (when commitments

50 PC/12, L/7583. ("The legal instruments through which the contracting parties apply the GATT 1947 are herewith terminated one year after the date of entry into force of the WTO Agreement. In the light of unforeseen circumstances, the CONTRACTING PARTIES may decide to postpone the date of termination by no more than one year.")

51 PC/15, L/7586.

52 LIC/25; BISD 42S/198.

53 GATT Art. V:6: "Each contracting party shall accord to products which have been in transit through the territory of any other contracting party treatment no less favourable than that which would have been accorded to such products had they been transported from their place of origin to their destination without going through the territory of such other contracting party."

54 GATT Art. V:6: "... Any contracting party shall, however, be free to maintain its requirements of direct consignment existing on the date of this Agreement, in respect of any goods in regard to which such direct consignment is a requisite condition of eligibility for entry of the goods at preferential rates of duty or has relation to the contracting party's prescribed method of valuation for duty purposes."

55 EPCT/C.II/42 p. 5–6; EPCT/C.II/54/Rev.1 p. 11.

among Members were negotiated) without violating the obligation in the first sentence."[56]

In addition, to establish new legal rules, a *sequence in time* (*i.e.*, "prior to entry into force" of the Agreement) can also be a crucial temporal reference for the enactment of an exemption to a new obligation due to special considerations. For example, the TRIPS Agreement introduces a most-favoured-nation treatment obligation which did not exist in other international agreements related to the protection of intellectual property. For this reason, Article 4(d) of the TRIPS Agreement provides one of the most important exemptions for advantages deriving from the predated international agreements "prior to the entry into force" of the WTO Agreement.[57] Such advantages need not be granted to all WTO Members on a most-favoured-nation basis if certain conditions are met. In sum, temporal rules as a response to change in law can be helpful (1) to ensure the orderly transition to a new institutional framework by setting a *prescribed period* for co-existence and a *prescribed date* for termination of the old; or (2) to establish an exception or exemption for a new institutional rule by permitting historical preferences *on the date of the Agreement* or predated advantages *prior to entry into force of the Agreement.*

## 6.2 Implications for Applying Temporal Rules

Apart from the implications for making temporal rules in WTO Law in the previous Section 6.1, applying temporal rules to a concrete case in WTO practice can also shed light on the relevance of their appearance. As Hart argued, "[t]he range of application of a law is always a question of its interpretation." Generally speaking, the task of interpretation can be delegated and centralized to certain institutions (such as an administration and courts), and their "authentic opinion" instituted by the legal order can further establish legal relevance.[58] In the WTO legal order, WTO Law comprises a number of multilateral or plurilateral agreements which can be applied and interpreted as a whole in a defined institutional context, namely, the dispute settlement system of

56 Panel Report, *Colombia—Ports of Entry*, para. 7.466.

57 TRIPS Art. 4(d): "Exempted from this obligation are any advantage, favour, privilege or immunity accorded by a Member: … deriving from international agreements related to the protection of intellectual property which entered into force prior to the entry into force of the WTO Agreement, provided that such agreements are notified to the Council for TRIPS and do not constitute an arbitrary or unjustifiable discrimination against nationals of other Members."

58 Hart (n 12), 42 and 94.

the WTO. In other words, as Van Damme explained, "the legal standard under a provision of one agreement evolves in tandem with the case law regarding the meaning of a provision's legal standard in another agreement."[59] In WTO practice, the adjudicators also pointed out that: "While the application of a provision may be regarded as confined to the context in which it takes place, the relevance of clarification contained in adopted Appellate Body reports is not limited to the application of a particular provision in a specific case."[60] In keeping with this distinctive nature of the application or interpretation of WTO Law, this research operates on the assumption that temporal rules in WTO Law should be evaluated not only based on their rational design in legal texts, but also on how they are applied or interpreted in practice to establish their legal relevance.

Besides, in the real-world situations, "temporal information [conveyed by nature language] is often imprecise about the temporal location of events (*indeterminacy*) and comes at different granularities."[61] In cases where explicit and definite time adverbials are absent, temporal information may be inferred implicitly, relying on "semantic content, knowledge of causation and knowledge of language use, as well as sentential syntax and compositional semantics."[62] For this reason, to establish legal relevance for temporal rules in the context of WTO Law, their application or interpretation can sometimes transcend a plain reading of legal texts, placing greater emphasis on "shared understandings" in legal practice. These "shared understandings" are crucial for the consideration of the "dynamic legitimacy" of temporal rules, and can be established through the standardized means of interpretation in the WTO dispute settlement system.[63]

---

59 Isabelle Van Damme, 'Understanding the Choice for Evolutionary Interpretation' in Georges Abi-Saab and others (eds), *Evolutionary Interpretation and International Law* (Hart Publishing 2019), 175–176.

60 Appellate Body Report, *US—Stainless Steel (Mexico)*, para. 161.

61 Luca Chittaro and Carlo Combi, 'Extending the Event Calculus with Temporal Granularity and Indeterminacy' (2000) AAAI Technical Report WS-00-08, 53.

62 Alex Lascarides and Nicholas Asher, 'Temporal Interpretation, Discourse Relations and Commonsense Entailment' (1993) 16 Linguistics and Philosophy 437, 438.

63 Noting that, although the WTO dispute settlement system has proven to be a more legalized mechanism to clarify the existing WTO Law, shared understandings of temporal rules in practice may still be influenced by international legal discourse, politics, and constitutional structure. *See* Richard H Steinberg, 'Judicial Lawmaking at the WTO: Discursive, Constitutional, and Political Constraints' (2004) 98 The American Journal of International Law 247, 248. In addition, as Howse and Nicolaidis argued, "the legitimacy of the multilateral trading order requires greater democratic contestability and a more inclusive view of those who are entitled to influence the shape of the system." Robert Howse and Kalypso

According to the earlier scholarship on "legal legitimacy," it attempts to identify how the IL *per se* influences international actors with its four distinctive traits: (1) determinacy (or clarity); (2) symbolic validation (the communication of authority through ritual or stable practice); (3) coherence (or consistency with other rules); and (4) adherence (vertical nexus of a rule to a pyramid of secondary rules).[64] In furtherance of this concept of "legal legitimacy," the later scholarship has added on the dynamic effect of legal rules to establish "dynamic legitimacy" through legal interactions to consider the broader capacity of law to generate "fidelity" by (1) building up shared understandings of rules; (2) fulfilling the specific criteria of legality; and (3) reinforcing through a continuing practice of legality.[65] In other words, as Brunnée and Toope argued:[66]

> For law to exist and to endure, a community of practice needs to maintain or expand underlying shared understandings, and to embed those understandings in a legal practice that assures day-to-day application in concrete settings of the criteria of legality.

As such, legal legitimacy appears to be cultivated not only *internally*, through the distinctive traits of legal rules, but also *externally*, through dynamic interactions that foster shared understandings in practice.

In WTO practice, shared understandings of temporal rules can be established through the standardized means of interpretation in the WTO dispute settlement system. Pursuant to DSU Article 3.2, the WTO dispute settlement system

---

Nicolaidis, 'Enhancing WTO Legitimacy: Constitutionalization or Global Subsidiarity?' (2003) 16 Governance 73, 74. In this sense, the exploration of the broader influence of relevant actors to shape the application of temporal rules could also be an important issue to shed light on the "dynamic legitimacy" of temporal rules, but it is beyond the scope of this research.

64 *See* Thomas M Franck, *Fairness in International Law and Institutions* (Oxford University Press 1998), 30–46.

65 *See generally* Jutta Brunnée and Stephen John Toope, *Legitimacy and Legality in International Law: An Interactional Account* (Cambridge University Press 2010), 142–204.

66 *Ibid.*, 352. *See also* Lon L. Fuller, *The Morality of Law* (14th edition, Yale University Press 1977), 46–91. According to Fuller, the concept of "fidelity" to law is established on the potential to the fulfillment of eight criteria of legality, *i.e.*, the inner morality of law, to attract the adherence of law: (1) *generality*: to act impersonally and apply to general classes; (2) *promulgation*: to be published for identification; (3) *retroactivity*: the problem of due process; (4) *clarity*: to be understandable; (5) *contradiction*: to violate the law of identity, *e.g.*, not correspond to any sensible legislative purpose; (6) *impossibility*: to require conduct beyond capacity; (7) *constancy*: not to be changed too frequently; and (8) *congruence*: the problem of interpretation.

"serves to preserve the rights and obligations of Members under the covered agreements" and "to clarify the existing provisions of those agreements."[67] In addition, in order to clarify the existing legal rules, its adjudicators are mandated to follow "customary rules of interpretation of public international law," namely, the general rule of interpretation set out in VCLT Article 31[68] and supplementary means of interpretation in VCLT Article 32.[69] According to these Articles of the VCLT, the adjudicators shall firstly interpret legal rules by virtue of the *ordinary meaning* of the words in their *context* and in light of the *object and purpose* of the treaty. If the meaning is still "ambiguous or obscure" or leads to a "manifestly absurd or unreasonable" result, they may recourse to *supplementary* means of interpretation which are "the preparatory work of the treaty and the circumstances of its conclusion." As such, the VCLT allows both persistence and flexibility for treaty interpretation. As argued by Mortenson, "[t]he VCLT text is certainly capable of supporting different interpretive approaches. That was, after all, the point."[70]

Drawing on the dynamic legitimacy of temporal rules in practice and the standardized means of interpretation in the WTO dispute settlement system, the following subsections will outline three interpretative approaches identified as relevant to the formation of shared understandings regarding temporal rules in WTO practice: (1) explicit temporal rules (Section 6.2.1); (2) implicit temporal rules (Section 6.2.2); and (3) no temporal rule by default (Section 6.2.3). Appendix 1 offers a summation of the cases in WTO Jurisprudence.

---

67 DSU Art. 3.2: "The Members recognize that it serves to preserve the rights and obligations of Members under the covered agreements, and to clarify the existing provisions of those agreements in accordance with customary rules of interpretation of public international law."

68 VCLT Art. 31.1: "A treaty shall be interpreted in good faith in accordance with the ordinary meaning to be given to the terms of the treaty in their context and in the light of its object and purpose." *See also* Appellate Body Report, *US—Gasoline*, paras. 15–16.

69 VCLT Art. 32: "Recourse may be had to supplementary means of interpretation, including the preparatory work of the treaty and the circumstances of its conclusion, in order to confirm the meaning resulting from the application of [VCLT Article 31], or to determine the meaning when the interpretation according to [VCLT Article 31]: (a) leaves the meaning ambiguous or obscure; or (b) leads to a result which is manifestly absurd or unreasonable." *See also* Appellate Body Report, *Japan—Alcoholic Beverages II*, para. 104.

70 Julian Davis Mortenson, 'The Travaux of Travaux: Is the Vienna Convention Hostile to Drafting History?' (2013) 107 American Journal of International Law 780, 822. (*See also* at 820–821. "The doctrinal mechanics of [VCLT Articles] 31 and 32 do require interpreters to start by focusing on text as the presumptive object of interpretation;" however, "in addition to tools like dictionaries, context, and subsequent practice, interpreters should rely on drafting history in every plausibly contestable case to shed light on the meaning that text—and in some cases even to override what had initially seemed like its clear import.")

### 6.2.1 *Explicit Temporal Rules*

Explicit temporal rules in WTO Law are those rules clearly established in legal texts, which can be identified and read without much difficulty and ambiguity in light of their relevant legal context, object, and purpose. The interpretation of explicit temporal rules can often rely on the ordinary meaning of the words, and simply reaffirm the scope or intention for their application to specific cases. In WTO practice, this research identified three instances in which explicit temporal rules are subject to interpretation by virtue of their ordinary meanings, namely: (1) temporal application of legal rules; (2) temporal scope of measures; and (3) temporal requirement of procedures.

#### 6.2.1.1 *Temporal Application of Legal Rules*

The temporal application of legal rules is one of the most crucial issues in treaty law. Pursuant to the default VCLT Article 28, a treaty shall not be applied retroactively unless a different intention appears from the treaty or is otherwise established.[71] Absent a contrary intention, a treaty cannot apply to acts or facts that took place, or situations that no longer existed, prior to the date of its entry into force. In other words, a treaty in general is only relevant once it has entered into force and only in exceptional circumstances extends the application of its provisions retroactively.[72] Accordingly, it is widely acknowledged that the temporal application of treaties generally follows the principle of non-retroactivity. Some examples in the context of WTO Law are provided as follows.

Article 18.3 of the Anti-Dumping Agreement provides an explicit temporal rule for the application of the provisions of the Agreement following the principle of non-retroactivity. It states that "the provisions of this Agreement shall apply to investigations, and reviews of existing measures, initiated pursuant to applications which *have been made on or after the date of entry into force* for a Member of the WTO Agreement," namely, the post-WTO reviews.[73] By virtue of the ordinary meaning of this explicit temporal rule in its context, the adjudicators ruled that "pre-WTO measures do not become subject to [the

---

71 VCLT Art. 28: "Unless a different intention appears from the treaty or is otherwise established, its provisions do not bind a party in relation to any act or fact which took place or any situation which ceased to exist before the date of the entry into force of the treaty with respect to that party."

72 *See generally* Christina Binder and Jane Hofbauer, 'The Temporal Scope of Application of Investment Treaties and the Effects on General International Law' in Christian Tams, Stephan Schill and Rainer Hofmann (eds), *International Investment Law and General International Law* (Edward Elgar Publishing 2023).

73 Emphasis added.

Anti-Dumping Agreement] simply because they continue to be applied on or after the date of entry into force."[74] The same statement for temporal application (*i.e.*, "on or after the date of entry into force") can also be found for countervailing duty investigations or reviews in Article 32.3 of the SCM Agreement. The adjudicators highlighted the explicit intention of the negotiators to "draw the line of application of the new WTO Agreement to countervailing duty investigations and reviews at a different point in time from that for other general measures."[75] In this sense, the adjudicators appear to interpret the ordinary meaning of the explicit temporal rule by pointing out its intentional design to draw the line of temporal application of the legal provisions by the drafters of the treaty.

In addition to the principle of non-retroactivity to apply legal rules "on or after the date of entry into force" of the Agreement, the explicit transitional period for developing countries to apply legal rules can also be found. For example, Article 27.2(b) of the SCM Agreement provides for a transition period of "eight years from the date of entry into force of the WTO Agreement," during which the prohibition in Article 3.1(a) of the SCM Agreement shall not apply. In practice, the adjudicators have relied on the ordinary meaning of this explicit temporal rule, and confirmed the exact transitional period as "running from 1 January 1995 to 1 January 2003." They also acknowledged the explicitness of the temporal rule by stating that "[t]he text of Article 27.2(b) does not leave

---

74 Panel Report, *US—DRAMS*, para. 6.14.

75 Appellate Body Report, *Brazil—Desiccated Coconut*, p.18. ("Because a countervailing duty is imposed only as a result of a sequence of acts, a link had to be drawn, and drawn sharply, to avoid uncertainty, unpredictability and unfairness concerning the rights of states and private parties under the domestic laws in force when the WTO Agreement came into effect.") Noting that TRIPS Article 70.1 also specifies an explicit temporal rule for application of the TRIPS Agreement by stating that the Agreement "does not give rise to obligations in respect of acts which occurred *before the date of application* of the [TRIPS Agreement] for the Member in question." (emphasis added) However, in WTO practice, instead of interpreting the temporal rule (*i.e.*, "before the date of application of the [TRIPS Agreement]"), the adjudicators drew attention on the term "acts which occurred" and confirmed that this Article "cannot be interpreted to exclude existing rights, such as patent rights, even if such rights arose through acts which occurred before the date of application of the [TRIPS Agreement] for a Member." *See* Appellate Body Report, *Canada—Patent Term*, para. 60. (For further explanation, *see* para. 59: "If the phrase 'acts which occurred' were interpreted to cover all continuing situations involving patents which were granted before the date of application of the [TRIPS Agreement] for a Member ... then Article 70.1 would preclude the application of virtually the whole of the [TRIPS Agreement] to rights conferred by the patents arising from such 'acts'. This is not consistent with the object and purpose of the [TRIPS Agreement], as reflected in the preamble of the Agreement.")

scope for ambiguity in respect of the end date of that transition period."[76] In a similar vein, the adjudicators have confirmed the end date of the transitional periods in Article 65.4 of the TRIPS Agreement (*i.e.*, "five years from the entry into force of the WTO Agreement") as to "1 January 2000," and an additional five years to provide for product patents in areas of technology not so patentable as to "1 January 2005."[77] Taken together, the interpretation of the temporal application of legal rules may rely on the ordinary meaning of explicit temporal rules (1) to emphasize the drafters' intention of explicitness (*e.g.*, to draw the line of application of the new WTO Agreement), or (2) to confirm the precise date (*e.g.*, the end date of the transition period).

#### 6.2.1.2 *Temporal Scope of Measures*

The temporal scope of measures can also be explicitly defined within the treaty to regulate Members' actions. By relying on the ordinary meaning of the text, the adjudicators may clarify explicit temporal rules in a legal context through various ways. The following are examples provided for illustration. First, with regard to the explicit temporal rule (*i.e.*, the 20-year period) for the term of patent protection in Article 33 of the TRIPS Agreement,[78] the adjudicators have opined that "the words used in Article 33 present very little interpretative difficulty," and then viewed that "the obligation in Article 33 is *straightforward* and *mandatory*: to provide, as a specific right, a term of protection that does not end before the expiry of a period of twenty years counted from the filing date."[79] Second, in terms of the temporal scope for applying provisional measures, Articles 17.3 and 17.4 of the SCM Agreement are also unambiguous in that they clearly specify that these measures shall not be applied "sooner than 60 days from the date of initiation of the investigation," and their application shall be limited "as short a period as possible, not exceeding four months." The adjudicators noted that Article 20 of the SCM Agreement contains *no exception*

---

76 Panel Report, *India—Export Related Measures*, para. 7.39.

77 Panel Report, *India—Patents (US)*, para. 7.27. ("[F]or transitional periods for developing countries: in general five years from the entry into force of the WTO Agreement, i.e. 1 January 2000, and an additional five years to provide for product patents in areas of technology not so patentable as of 1 January 2000. Thus, in such areas of technology, developing countries are not required to provide product patent protection until 1 January 2005.")

78 TRIPS Art. 33: "The term of protection available shall not end before the expiration of a period of twenty years counted from the filing date."

79 Appellate Body Report, *Canada—Patent Term*, paras. 85 and 95. (emphasis added) ("The text of Article 33 gives no support to the notion of an 'effective' term of protection as distinguished from a 'nominal' term of protection.")

to the rules relating to the periods as provided for in the Articles.[80] Third and finally, Article 20.6 of the SCM Agreement expressly indicates the temporal scope for applying definitive countervailing duties, which allows for the retroactive application of the duties at a time when no provisional measures were in place and thus no provisional duties were collected (*i.e.*, "prior to the date of application of provisional measures").[81] Drawing on the principle of effective treaty interpretation—which holds that interpretation must give meaning and effect to all the terms of a treaty—the adjudicators emphasized the explicit temporal scope of applying definitive duties established in Article 20.6, and rejected the opposite argument that another Article (*i.e.*, Article 20.3 of the SCM Agreement) "would preclude a Member from collecting definitive duties for the period prior to the date of application of provisional measures."[82] Based on the three examples provided above, the ways to clarify the explicit temporal scope of measures in a legal context may entail (1) whether the rules are straightforward and mandatory; (2) whether the rules provide any exception; and (3) how the rules give meaning and effect to other terms of the treaty (*i.e.*, effective treaty interpretation).

In addition to the clarification of explicit temporal rules in a legal context, the adjudicators may also rely on the ordinary meaning of temporal rules to establish the (in-)consistency of legal provisions. For example, in the context of the non-discriminatory application of quantitative restrictions, GATT Article XIII:3(b) requires that both the total quota and shares allocated shall be publicly notified for "a specified future period."[83] In accordance with this

80 Panel Report, *US—Softwood Lumber III*, para. 7.100. ("Nothing in Article 20 of the SCM Agreement provides an exception to the rules relating to the minimum period between initiation and application of provisional measures or the maximum period of application of such measures as provided for in Articles 17.3 and 17.4 of the SCM Agreement.")

81 SCM Art. 20.6: "In critical circumstances where for the subsidized product in question the authorities find that injury which is difficult to repair is caused by massive imports in a relatively short period of a product benefiting from subsidies paid or bestowed inconsistently with the provisions of GATT 1994 and of this Agreement and where it is deemed necessary, in order to preclude the recurrence of such injury, to assess countervailing duties retroactively on those imports, the definitive countervailing duties may be assessed on imports which were entered for consumption not more than 90 days prior to the date of application of provisional measures."

82 Panel Report, *US—Softwood Lumber III*, para 7.97. ("We consider that the principle of effective treaty interpretation requires the treaty interpreter to 'read all applicable provisions of a treaty in a way that gives meaning to all of them, harmoniously.")

83 GATT Art. XIII:3(b): "In the case of import restrictions involving the fixing of quotas, the contracting party applying the restrictions shall give public notice of the total quantity or value of the product or products which will be permitted to be imported during a specified future period and of any change in such quantity or value."

explicit temporal scope of a specified "future" period for quota and shares, the adjudicators considered that the allocation of "back-dated" quotas did not conform to the requirements of Article XIII:3(b).[84] Moreover, Annex B(2) of the SPS Agreement obliges Members to allow a "reasonable interval" between the publication and the entry into force of the SPS regulations except in urgent circumstances.[85] The adjudicators found the violation of Annex B(2) of the SPS Agreement by stating that "[i]t is undisputed by the parties that [the SPS measure at issue] was published … and came into effect on that same date," and clearly "did not allow any interval at all between publication and entry into force."[86] It is worth to note that the adjudicators also found that there were inconsistencies of certain temporal requirements in Annex B(5)(a), (b), and (d) of the SPS Agreement since the party failed (1) to publish a notice "at an early stage;" (2) to notify other Members through the WTO Secretariat "at an early stage;" and (3) to allow "reasonable time" for other Members to make comments.[87] In sum, the interpretation of the explicit temporal scope of measures may rely on its ordinary meaning not only (1) to clarify its usage in a legal context (*e.g.*, straightforward and mandatory, no exception, and effective interpretation), but also (2) to establish the (in-)consistency of legal provisions.

#### 6.2.1.3 *Temporal Requirement of Procedures*

The explicit temporal requirement of procedures can be interpreted according to their ordinary meaning, in light of various objects and purposes. The following are illustrative examples. First, Article 5.10 of the Anti-Dumping Agreement and Article 11.11 of the SCM Agreement contain explicit temporal rules (*i.e.*, "in no case more than 18 months") for conducting investigations.[88] To interpret this explicit requirement, the adjudicators considered that the purpose of Article 5.10 of the Anti-Dumping Agreement is to prevent interested parties to

---

84 L/6491-36S/93, para. 12.26. ("It found that EEC Commission Regulation 1040/88 constituted a back-dated quota in respect of Chile, since although it published a quota share for Chile it simultaneously declared that share to be filled and, in fact, continued the suspension of imports from Chile enacted eight days before quotas were published. The EEC had therefore not observed the notification requirements of Article XIII:3(b) and (c).")

85 SPS Annex B(2): "Except in urgent circumstances, Members shall allow a reasonable interval between the publication of a sanitary or phytosanitary regulation and its entry into force in order to allow time for producers in exporting Members, and particularly in developing country Members, to adapt their products and methods of production to the requirements of the importing Member."

86 Panel Report, *India—Agricultural Products*, para. 7.758.

87 *Ibid.*, paras. 7.784, 7.790, and 7.796.

88 ADP Art. 5.10 and SCM Art. 11.11: "Investigations shall, except in special circumstances, be concluded within one year, and in no case more than 18 months, after their initiation."

be "left in the *uncertainty* about the outcome of the investigation."[89] The adjudicators saw "no basis in [Article 11.11 of the SCM Agreement] (nor authority in any other part of [the SCM Agreement]) to prolong an investigation beyond 18 months for any reason, including requests from interested parties."[90] Second, to ascertain Member's procedural right to request the establishment of a panel in DSU Article 4.7, the adjudicators drew on the explicit temporal requirement for consultations (*i.e.*, within 60 days after the date of receipt of the request for consultations")[91] to consider their duty to examine whether the 60-day period has lapsed before the request to establish a panel.[92] Third, to prevent effective circumvention of the proceedings, the adjudicators have referred to the explicit temporal requirement (*i.e.*, "[w]ithin 60 days after the date of circulation of a panel report") for adoption of the report or filing appeal to disallow the conditional withdrawal of appeal or the filing of a replacement notice in DSU Article 16.4.[93] In order to secure this explicit deadline, they ruled that "if the conditional withdrawal or the filing of a new notice were to take place after the 60-day deadline in [DSU] Article 16.4 for adoption of panel reports, this would effectively circumvent the requirement to file appeals within 60 days of circulation of panel reports."[94] Fourth and finally, explicit temporal requirements may sometimes only be read as indicative only. As the adjudicators opined in the context of the DSU, "as a matter of law, since most of the time-limits in the DSU are either minimum time-limits without ceilings or maximum

---

89 Panel Report, *Pakistan—BOPP Film (UAE)*, para. 7.471. (emphasis added) ("[Article 5.10 of the Anti-Dumping Agreement] preserves predictability for the interested parties in an investigation by ensuring that when an investigation is initiated, interested parties are not left in the uncertainty about the outcome of the investigation for more than one year 'and in no case more than 18 months'.")

90 Panel Report, *Mexico—Olive Oil*, para. 7.121.

91 DSU Art. 4.7: "If the consultations fail to settle a dispute within 60 days after the date of receipt of the request for consultations, the complaining party may request the establishment of a panel."

92 Panel Report, *Turkey—Textiles*, para. 9.24. ("[T]he only function [they] have as a panel ... is to ascertain whether consultations were properly requested, in terms of the DSU, that the complainant was ready to consult with the defendant and that the 60-day period has lapsed before the establishment of a panel was requested by the complainant.")

93 DSU Art. 16.4: "Within 60 days after the date of circulation of a panel report to the Members, the report shall be adopted at a DSB meeting unless a party to the dispute formally notifies the DSB of its decision to appeal or the DSB decides by consensus not to adopt the report. If a party has notified its decision to appeal, the report by the panel shall not be considered for adoption by the DSB until after completion of the appeal. This adoption procedure is without prejudice to the right of Members to express their views on a panel report."

94 Appellate Body Report, *EC—Sardines*, para. 147.

time-limits that are, nonetheless, *indicative* only, DSU proceedings—from the request for consultations to the adoption of findings by the DSB—may take longer than 18 months and have in practice often led to time-frames beyond 18 months."[95] To sum up, the interpretation of explicit temporal requirements in procedures may be guided by different objects and purposes, such as (1) to provide certainty regarding the outcome; (2) to ascertain the rights of Members; (3) to prevent circumvention of the proceedings; and (4) to be read as indicative only.

### 6.2.2 *Implicit Temporal Rules*

Implicit temporal rules in WTO Law are those rules which themselves are not stated expressly in legal texts, and may be derived from the interpretation of law by inference of the relevant context, the object and purpose, or general principles of law. As has been mentioned above, the adjudicators shall interpret legal provisions in accordance with the ordinary meaning of the words in their context and in light of the object and purpose of the treaty. According to VCLT Article 31.2, the relevant context includes the rest of the text of the treaty, the preamble, and annexes, *etc.*[96] In addition, pursuant to VCLT Article 31.3, the adjudicators must also consider any subsequent agreement, subsequent practice, and relevant rules of international law.[97] Especially, with regard to "relevant rules of international law," the adjudicators noted that their coverage seems to be "sufficiently broad to encompass all generally accepted sources of public international law," and one of them can be "the recognized general principles of law." [98] As Klabbers further explained, general principles of law (*e.g.*, the principles of due process and good faith) do not directly specify a particular legal outcome but may be useful for filling possible gaps in the law.[99] In WTO practice, this research identifies four instances which may give rise to

95 Panel Report, *US—Section 301 Trade Act*, para. 7.31.

96 VCLT Art. 31.2: "The context for the purpose of the interpretation of a treaty shall comprise, in addition to the text, including its preamble and annexes: (a) any agreement relating to the treaty which was made between all the parties in connection with the conclusion of the treaty; (b) any instrument which was made by one or more parties in connection with the conclusion of the treaty and accepted by the other parties as an instrument related to the treaty."

97 VCLT Art. 31.3: "There shall be taken into account, together with the context: (a) any subsequent agreement between the parties regarding the interpretation of the treaty or the application of its provisions; (b) any subsequent practice in the application of the treaty which establishes the agreement of the parties regarding its interpretation; (c) any relevant rules of international law applicable in the relations between the parties."

98 Panel Report, EC—*Approval and Marketing of Biotech Products*, para. 7.67.

99 Jan Klabbers, *International Law* (2nd edition, Cambridge University Press 2017), 37.

implicit temporal rules in the course of interpretation of legal provisions by inference of the relevant context, the object and purpose, or general principles of law, namely: (1) intrinsic temporal meaning by definition; (2) implied temporal limitation in the nature of procedures; (3) temporal discretion for procedures under the due process principle; and (4) temporal expectation for procedures under the good faith principle.

#### 6.2.2.1 *Intrinsic Temporal Meaning by Definition*

Implicit temporal rules can be derived from the interpretation of certain legal terms that inherently convey temporal meanings. Some examples are provided as follows. First, the adjudicators have considered the temporal scope for imposing anti-dumping duties in Article 11.2 of the Anti-Dumping Agreement under the term "continued imposition." They read the word "continued" to have an intrinsic temporal meaning to cover "a temporal relationship between past and future."[100] Second, the word "emergency" related to safeguard actions in GATT Article XIX may also generate several implicit temporal rules, such as "temporary," "short-term," "limited duration," *etc.* Referring to the negotiating history of the 1946 London Preparatory Conference, the temporal aspect of this Article regarding "emergency actions" was discussed and agreed to provide "only for a *temporary* relaxation of commitments, not for a permanent revision."[101] It was further noted that "in general you would expect that it would be *short-term*."[102] The GATT Report also concluded that "action under Article XIX is essentially of an emergency character and should be of *limited duration*."[103] The 1984 Report on Safeguards by the Chairman of the Council finally summarized the opinions and confirmed that safeguard actions are not intended to last for "an unlimited period of time," and should be "temporary by definition."[104]

Third, GATT Article XIX:1(a) prescribes that the increase in imports must occur as a result of "unforeseen development." The adjudicators interpreted

100 Panel Report, *US—DRAMS*, para. 6.27. ("[T]he word 'continued' would be redundant if the investigating authority were restricted to considering only whether the duty was necessary to offset present dumping.")

101 EPCT/C.II/38, p.5. (emphasis added)

102 EPCT/C.II/QR/PV/5, p.77. (emphasis added)

103 GATT/CP/106, para. 50. (emphasis added)

104 MDF/4, 31S/136, 137, para. 7. ("There is a convergence of views that safeguard actions are not intended to protect domestic producers for an unlimited period of time. Safeguard actions are emergency measures which should therefore be temporary by definition and progressively liberalized during the period of their application, unless they are maintained for such a short time as to make this impractical.")

the term "unforeseen development" and inferred an implicit temporal rule by asserting that development must have been unforeseen "at the time when the concession was negotiated."[105] Fourth, Article 21.1 of the SCM Agreement concerns the duration of countervailing duties, ensuring that they "remain in force" only as long as and to the extent necessary. The adjudicators emphasized "the amount of time that a duty may *remain* in force," and reaffirmed the general analysis of this Article "as imposing disciplines regarding the 'continued application' of countervailing duties, which apply 'after the imposition' thereof."[106] Fifth and finally, to interpret the relevant temporal meaning for the "insufficiency" of relevant scientific evidence in Article 5.7 of the SPS Agreement, the adjudicators opined that it "is *not a perennial state*, but rather *a transitory one*, which lasts only until such time as the imposing Member procures the additional scientific evidence which allows the performance of a more objective assessment of risk."[107] In sum, implicit temporal rules can be derived from the interpretation of certain semantic terms in legal texts that convey intrinsic temporal meanings by definition, such as *continued* imposition, *emergency* actions, *unforeseen* development, *remain* in force, and *insufficient* evidence.

#### 6.2.2.2 *Implied Temporal Limitation in the Nature of Procedures*

Implicit temporal rules can be derived from the nature of certain procedural obligations. As the adjudicators have observed, "it is clear that certain provisions of the covered agreements that establish procedural obligations may, depending on *the nature of the procedural obligation* contained therein, necessarily carry an *implied limitation on when* the required action must be performed."[108] As such, a few examples are provided below. First, Article 15.1

105 Appellate Body Report, *Argentina—Footwear* (EC), para. 96.

106 Panel Report, *Japan—DRAMS* (*Korea*), para. 7.350. (emphasis added) ("The focus, therefore, is on the amount of time that a duty may remain in force, rather than the circumstances under which that duty initially entered into force.")

107 Appellate Body Report, *Canada—Continued Suspension*, para. 679. (emphasis added)

108 Panel Report, *Thailand—Cigarettes* (*Philippines*) (*Article 21.5—Philippines*), para. 7.432. (emphasis added) (*See also* fn. 943. "For example, in *US—Offset Act* (*Byrd Amendment*), the Appellate Body acknowledged that the text of [DSU] Article 9.2 'contains no requirement for the request for a separate panel report to be made by a certain time'. However, the Appellate Body considered that the provision had to be read in the light of the object and purpose of the DSU, and upheld the panel's decision to deny the US request for separate reports on the grounds that the request came too late. We further recall the un-appealed findings of the original panel that the Thai Customs Department had acted inconsistently with [GATT] Articles X:3(a) and (b) due to the 'overall delays shown throughout the course of the review process' and the 'excessive delays that have been caused in the ... appeals before the BoA', respectively.")

of the SCM Agreement does not set forth an explicit limitation regarding the selection of "the period of investigation" for the purpose of conducting an injury analysis. The adjudicators, however, did not interpret the Article to mean that "an investigating authority's discretion in this respect is unlimited." In their view, the selection of the period should fulfill the purpose to "ensure the *comprehensiveness* and *reliability* of the data used as the basis for an injury determination."[109] To be more specific, the adjudicators addressed the implicit period of data collection for an injury determination in Article 15.2 of the SCM Agreement by stating that "the data on which the injury analysis is based should be *sufficiently recent* in order for this data to be *relevant* and *probative* such as to constitute positive evidence of injury caused by subsidized imports."[110]

Second, in the case of the timing to request for a separate panel report in DSU Article 9.2, the Article also contains no explicit limitation for the request to be made by a certain deadline. The adjudicators again considered the timing of request should not be unlimited due to the reason that "the overall object and purpose of the DSU to ensure the 'prompt settlement' of disputes."[111] Third, in the case of the notification of countervailing duties (or anti-dumping legislations) in Article 32.6 of the SCM Agreement (or Article 18.5 of the Anti-Dumping Agreement), the adjudicators inferred implicit temporal limitation in consideration of the object of effectiveness by stating that "[d]espite the absence of a specific deadline, in our view, in order for any notification to be *effective*, it must be made within a reasonable time."[112]

Fourth, in the case of the review of continued imposition of countervailing duties in Article 21.2 of the SCM Agreement, the adjudicators identified an implied temporal requirement for the review, indicating that it should

109 Panel Report, *Mexico—Olive Oil*, para. 7.267. (emphasis added) ("In our view, the requirements in Article 15.1 of the SCM Agreement to base a determination of injury on positive evidence and pursuant to an objective examination impose certain constraints on an investigating authority's discretion in selecting the period of investigation necessary to ensure the comprehensiveness and reliability of the data used as the basis for an injury determination.")

110 Panel Report, *EC—Countervailing Measures on DRAM Chips*, para. 7.341. (emphasis added)

111 Appellate Body Report, *US—Offset Act (Byrd Amendment)*, paras. 315–316. ("If the right to a separate panel report under Article 9.2 were 'unqualified', this would mean that a panel would have the obligation to submit a separate panel report, pursuant to the request of a party to the dispute, at any time during the panel proceedings. Moreover, a request for such a report could be made for whatever reason—or indeed, without any reason—even on the day that immediately precedes the day the panel report is due to be circulated to WTO Members at large. Such an interpretation would clearly undermine the overall object and purpose of the DSU to ensure the 'prompt settlement' of disputes.")

112 Panel Report, *US—Customs Bond Directive*, para. 7.283. (emphasis added)

encompass not only a "present and retrospective" analysis but also a "prospective" one in line with the purpose to determine "whether the injury would be likely to continue or recur."[113] Fifth, in the case of the risk assessment in Article 5.1 of the SPS Agreement, the adjudicators highlighted the purpose of risk assessment and considered "both a risk assessment carried out before the adoption of a particular safeguard measure and a risk assessment carried out after its adoption could 'sufficiently warrant', or 'reasonably support', the maintenance of that measure."[114]

Sixth, in the case of the control, inspection and approval procedures in Annex C(1) of the SPS Agreement, the adjudicators referred to the purpose of the procedures to "check and ensure fulfilment of SPS measures," and suggested an implicit temporal requirement by stating that the SPS measures subject to the procedures should "exist *prior to* the operation, undertaking or completion of, the relevant procedures."[115] Seventh and finally, to determine a threat of serious injury in Article 4.2(a) of the Agreement on Safeguards, the adjudicators considered that "in principle, within the period of investigation as a whole, evidence from the most recent past will provide *the strongest indication* of the likely future state of the domestic industry."[116] In sum, implicit temporal rules may be derived from the nature of procedures that carry implied temporal limitations in line with the purpose of relevant conducts, such as to ensure the comprehensiveness and reliability of the data, the prompt settlement of disputes, the effective notification of countervailing duties or anti-dumping legislations, and so on.

#### 6.2.2.3 *Temporal Discretion for Procedures under the Due Process Principle*

Implicit temporal rules can be derived from considerations of procedural due process, which may grant adjudicators a certain degree of discretion over temporal issues by requiring a balance of interests under varying circumstances throughout the proceedings. In principle, the adjudicators have acknowledged the concept of due process in the context of the DSU to require "a balancing of various interests, including systemic interests as well as those of the parties,

113 Appellate Body Report, *US—Carbon Steel (India)*, para. 4.530. ("[A] present and retrospective analysis as it relates to the necessity and impact of the duty prior to and during the administrative review, as well as a prospective analysis focusing on the likely future consequences of the maintenance, changing, or removal of the duty.")

114 Panel Reports, *EC—Approval and Marketing of Biotech Products*, para. 7.3030.

115 Appellate Body Report, *Australia—Apples*, para. 436. (emphasis added)

116 Appellate Body Report, *US—Lamb*, para. 137. (emphasis added)

and both general and case-specific considerations."[117] To be more specific, the adjudicators stated that "the DSU leaves panels a margin of discretion to deal, always in accordance with due process, with specific situations that may arise in a particular case and that are not explicitly regulated."[118] Drawing on the concept of due process, the adjudicators may exercise a certain degree of discretion in formulating implicit temporal rules for specific procedures, in particular, by means of (1) placing time constraints or (2) granting permission for time during the proceedings.

First, the adjudicators may exercise their discretion to establish implicit temporal rules as "constraints" in accordance with due process to consider various interests involved during the proceedings. For example, to address the timing of objections to the panel's jurisdiction, which is not explicitly regulated in DSU Article 7, the adjudicators opined that "[a]n objection to jurisdiction should be raised *as early as possible* and panels must ensure that the requirements of due process are met."[119] In terms of the submission of evidence, the adjudicators also reiterated that "due process will best be served by working procedures that provide 'for appropriate factual discovery *at an early stage* in panel proceedings', and that '[d]ue process may be of particular concern in cases where a party raises new facts *at a late stage* of the panel proceedings'."[120] Accordingly, to reject evidence submitted by the complainants after the second substantive meeting, the adjudicators stated that the evidence "could have been submitted *earlier* and in a manner consistent with due process."[121] As for the time-limit to file *amicus curiae* briefs in DSU Article 13, the adjudicators deemed a brief inadmissible due to its late filing to secure due process by ensuring that "participants and third participants are given an adequate opportunity fully to consider any written submission filed with the Appellate Body."[122]

117 Appellate Body Report, *Thailand—Cigarettes (Philippines)*, para. 150. ("In our view, panels are best situated to determine how this balance should be struck in any given proceeding, provided that they are vigilant in the protection of due process and remain within the bounds of their duties under [DSU] Article 11.")

118 Panel Report, *EC—Export Subsidies on Sugar (Australia)*, para. 2.2.

119 Appellate Body Report, *US—1916 Act*, para. 54. (emphasis added) ("[T]he interim review was not an appropriate stage in the Panel's proceedings to raise objections to the Panel's jurisdiction for the first time.")

120 Appellate Body Report, *Thailand—Cigarettes (Philippines)*, para. 149. (emphasis added)

121 Panel Reports, *China—Rare Earths*, para. 7.27. (*See also* para. 7.23. "[T]he submission by any party of a large bundle of evidence *at a very late stage* in the proceedings, especially when such evidence could have been provided earlier, raises due process issues for the opposing party ..., whose opportunity to make its defence could be undermined, and complicates a panel;' task of resolving disputes in a timely manner.") (emphasis added)

122 Appellate Body Reports, *EC—Seal Products*, para. 1.15.

Apart from the context of the DSU, in the case of the extension of the 30-day response deadline for the questionnaire in Article 6.1.1 of the Anti-Dumping Agreement and Article 12.1.1 of the SCM Agreement, the adjudicators emphasized the need to preserve the due process right in the Articles, and stated that the 30-day deadline "'cannot *extend indefinitely*' but, instead, are limited by the investigating authority's need to 'control the conduct' of its inquiry and to 'carry out the multiple steps' required to reach a timely completion of the proceeding."[123] In a similar vein, Article 16 of the Customs Valuation Agreement does not impose a time-limit during which an explanation must be provided. However, the adjudicators opined that a time-limit serves "an important transparency and due process objective" and provides "a window through which domestic tribunals and WTO panels review and understand a customs authority's valuation determination."[124] For this reason, they deemed a late explanation provided three and a half years after it was requested to be inconsistent with Article 16 of the Customs Valuation Agreement.[125] In these cases above, the adjudicators appear to exercise their discretion in accordance with due process to derive "time constraints" (*e.g.*, as early as possible, not indefinite) for specific procedures, and render a decision on whether the time constraints were satisfied in the case at hand (*e.g.*, inadmissibility due to late filing, inconsistency due to late explanation).

Second, the adjudicators may also exercise their discretion to establish implicit temporal rules as a form of "permission," based on special considerations of systemic interests or the specific interests of the parties in particular circumstances. For example, DSU Article 6.2 does not set out an explicit temporal condition or limitation on the measures that can be identified in a panel request. The adjudicators acknowledged, on the one hand that, "as a general rule, the measures included in a panel's terms of reference must be measures that are *in existence at the time of* the establishment of the panel." However, on the other hand, they might still exercise discretion to permit "the measures enacted *subsequent to* the establishment of the panel," and those measures "may, in certain limited circumstances, fall within a panel's terms of

123 Appellate Body Report, *Mexico—Anti-Dumping Measures on Rice*, para. 282. (emphasis added)

124 Panel Report, *Thailand—Cigarettes (Philippines) (Article 21.5—Philippines)*, para. 7.432.

125 *Ibid.*, para. 7.433. ("[A]n explanation provided three and a half years after it was requested, and, in the specific context of this dispute, several years after the conclusion of the appeal of the customs valuation determination before the Thai Tax Court, does not satisfy the requirements of Article 16.")

reference."[126] Another example of permission is to accommodate the parties' concerns in relation to the deadlines set out in the timetable for the panel proceedings in DSU Article 12.3. The adjudicators noted that the timetable was likely to "impose a heavy burden on parties in terms of their obligations to make submissions," and therefore ruled that "the calendar may be changed during the panel process."[127] Furthermore, in the case of the time-limit for comments on the descriptive sections of panel's draft report in DSU Article 15.1, the adjudicators first noted that the disputing party did not take advantage of the period provided to comment, although they still decided to accept some requests for changes "in order to ensure the accuracy of the description of the facts in [the] Report."[128]

In addition, the adjudicators may exercise their discretion to permit the submission of evidence by the parties at different times. For example, in the context of evidence underlying the dumping determination in Article 2.1 of the Anti-Dumping Agreement, the adjudicators were of the view that "temporal scope [of evidence] is not, alone, dispositive, and that therefore [they] must assess the authority's choice of the [period of investigation] for dumping in light of all the relevant circumstances surrounding the authority's decision at the time."[129] To be more specific, in the context of Article 7.10 of the SCM Agreement, the adjudicators took into account post-reference period evidence and provided the reason for their permission "to place as accurate a value as reasonably possible on the adverse effects identified in the compliance proceedings, and not to alter adverse effects already found to exist in the compliance proceedings or to establish any additional adverse effects."[130] In the case of accepting new evidence or allegations in Article 4 of the SCM Agreement, the adjudicators evaluated whether the circumstances continued to respect the defense's due process rights, and saw "no reason why any such new allegation should necessarily be rejected by the panel as a matter of course, simply

126 Appellate Body Report, *US—Zeroing (Japan) (Article 21.5—Japan)*, para. 121. (emphasis added) ("Indeed, in *US—Upland Cotton*, where the issue was raised in the context of measures that had expired prior to the panel proceedings, the Appellate Body explained that 'nothing inherent in the term 'at issue' sheds light on whether measures at issue must be currently in force, or whether they may be measures whose legislative basis has expired'.")

127 Appellate Body Report, *US—Steel Safeguards*, para. 5.3.

128 Panel Report, *US—Clove Cigarettes*, para. 6.3.

129 Panel Report, *Pakistan—BOPP Film (UAE)*, para. 7.59.

130 Decision by the Arbitrator, *US—Large Civil Aircraft (2nd complaint) (Article 22.6—US)*, para. 6.65.

because it is submitted after the first substantive meeting with the parties."[131] In these cases above, the adjudicators seem to exercise discretionary authority to grant "permission for time" (*e.g.*, accepting the measures enacted subsequent to the panel establishment, allowing the change of calendar, or taking into account new evidence). Their exercise of discretion is consistent with due process principles aimed at balancing interests under specific circumstances (*e.g.*, to avoid a heavy burden on parties, to ensure the accuracy of the factual description in the panel report, or to respect the rights of defense).

#### 6.2.2.4 *Temporal Expectation for Procedures under the Good Faith Principle*

Implicit temporal rules can also be derived as legitimate expectations grounded in the principle of good faith, which may enable adjudicators to assess potential procedural abuse. As explained by the adjudicators in the context of GATT Article XX, the principle of good faith is to avoid "[a]n abusive exercise by a Member of its own treaty right thus results in a breach of the treaty rights of the other Members and, as well, a violation of the treaty obligation of the Member so acting."[132] The following are examples of implicit temporal rules consistent with the good faith principle. First, DSU Article 3.10 provides that all Members must engage in dispute settlement in good faith. The adjudicators relied on this obligation of good faith to derive a temporal expectation for the timely raising of arguments by stating that the disputing parties "should not withhold *until* the interim review stage arguments that they could be legitimately expected to have raised *at a much earlier stage* of the proceedings."[133] Second, in the case of DSU Article 3.7 for Members' obligation to exercise judgement as to whether action under dispute settlement procedures would be fruitful, the adjudicators read this obligation alongside the good faith principle articulated in DSU Article 3.10, and expected that the obligation of exercising judgement covers the time of "the entire spectrum of dispute settlement, *from* the point of initiation of a case *through* implementation."[134] Third and finally, in the case of undertaking and completing approval procedures "without undue delay" in Annex C(1)(a) of the SPS Agreement, the adjudicators acknowledged this provision "essentially as a good faith obligation," and therefore expected that "Members to proceed with their approval procedures *as promptly as possible*."[135]

---

131 Panel Report, *Canada—Aircraft*, para. 9.74.
132 Appellate Body Report, *US—Shrimp*, para. 158.
133 Panel Report, *US—1916 Act* (EC), para. 5.18. (emphasis added)
134 Appellate Body Report, EC—*Export Subsidies on Sugar*, para. 312. (emphasis added)
135 Panel Reports, EC—*Approval and Marketing of Biotech Products*, para. 7.1498. (emphasis added)

In sum, implicit temporal rules may be derived from the principle of good faith, establishing temporal expectations for certain procedures so as to prevent abusive conduct by a Member during the relevant proceedings.

### 6.2.3 *No Temporal Rule by Default*

In some cases, temporal rules are deliberately omitted from legal texts not because they are unhelpful, but to maintain the flexibility that comes from avoiding the formalization of explicit rules. When there is no explicit temporal rule in law, adjudicators may distinguish between situations for which temporal rules should be implicitly derived during the course of interpretation (Section 6.2.2 above), and those for which there should be no temporal rule by default (this Section). In WTO practice, this research identified four instances in which the absence of a default temporal rule may be considered either intentional or left open to interpretation, including: (1) no temporal default for the application of legal rules; (2) no temporal default for the scope of measures; (3) no temporal default for the requirement of procedures; and (4) no temporal reference for factual determination.

#### 6.2.3.1 *No Temporal Default for the Application of Legal Rules*

As discussed in Section 6.2.1, the principle of non-retroactivity for the application of legal rules provides that treaties have no retroactive effect unless explicitly stated otherwise. However, this principle of non-retroactivity may not apply uniformly across all treaties or in every situation. International tribunals still require to strike a balance between this prospective principle and the regulatory rights of states seeking to achieve legitimate policy goals.[136] In WTO practice, the adjudicators have also exercised caution in cases where no specific provision defines temporal application of legal rules. For example, the SPS Agreement does not contain any article limiting its temporal application, or of any provision thereof, to SPS measures adopted before its entry into force on 1 January 1995. As a result, the adjudicators rejected the non-retroactive assumption that the central provisions of the SPS Agreement "do not apply to measures which were enacted before 1995 but which continue to be in force thereafter." To be more specific, they opined that "Articles 5.1 and 5.5 of the SPS Agreement do not distinguish between SPS measures adopted before

136 Yarik Kryvoi and Shaun Matos, 'Non-Retroactivity as a General Principle of Law' (2021) 17 Utrect Law Review 46, 48. ("[I]n the context of criminal law, non-retroactivity has become a binding general principle of international law. Outside the criminal law context, however, states can conclude treaties and adopt administrative regulations with retroactive effect to pursue legitimate public policy objectives.")

1 January 1995 and measures adopted since, the relevant implication is that they are intended to be applicable to both."[137] The adjudicators also referred to Article 14 of the SPS Agreement which authorizes delays in the application of some or all of the SPS provisions in the context of finding that the SPS Agreement applies to SPS measures that were enacted before 1 January 1995 but were maintained thereafter.[138]

Similarly, in the context of the TBT Agreement, the adjudicators concluded that the Agreement applied to technical regulations which were already in force prior to the entry into force of the TBT Agreement. They stated the reason that it would not "allow Members to avoid using international standards as a basis for their technical regulations simply by enacting preemptive measures and thereby undermine the object and purpose of developing international standards."[139] Furthermore, in the context of the adverse effects addressed in Article 5 of the SCM Agreement, the adjudicators rejected the argument of non-retroactivity that "no obligation arising out of Article 5 of the SCM Agreement is to be imposed on a Member in respect of subsidies granted or brought into existence prior to the entry into force of the SCM Agreement." They considered that a subsidy granted prior to the entry into force of the treaty may still fall within the scope of the Article due to "its possible nexus to the continuing situation of causing, through the use of this subsidy, adverse effects."[140] In

137 Appellate Body Report, *EC—Hormones*, para. 128. ("If the negotiators had wanted to exempt the very large group of SPS measures in existence on 1 January 1995 from the disciplines of provisions as important as Articles 5.1 and 5.5 of the SPS Agreement, it appears reasonable to us to expect that they would have said so explicitly.")

138 Panel Report, *EC—Hormones (US)*, para. 8.26. ("Except for Article 14 of the SPS Agreement which authorizes delays in the application of some or all of the provisions of the SPS Agreement for least-developed and other developing countries, no transition periods are provided for. The fact that Article 14 explicitly provides for a two-year transition period for developing countries with respect to some of their existing [SPS] measures, confirms that the SPS Agreement generally applies to measures enacted before the entry into force of the SPS Agreement but which are maintained in force after that date.")

139 Panel Report, *EC—Sardines*, para. 7.76. *See also* Appellate Body Report, *EC—Sardines*, para. 2.11.

140 Appellate Body Report, *EC and certain member States—Large Civil Aircraft*, para. 686. ("The relevant question for purposes of determining the temporal scope of Article 5 of the SCM Agreement is whether the causing of adverse effects has 'ceased to exist' or continues as a 'situation'. We consequently disagree with the European Union that, by virtue of Article 28 of the Vienna Convention, no obligation arising out of Article 5 of the SCM Agreement is to be imposed on a Member in respect of subsidies granted or brought into existence prior to the entry into force of the SCM Agreement. This may mean that a subsidy granted prior to 1 January 1995 falls within the scope of Article 5 of the SCM Agreement, but this is only because of its possible nexus to the continuing situation of causing, through the use of this subsidy, adverse effects to which Article 5 applies.")

sum, no temporal rule by default can be found for the application of certain legal provisions, leaving the matter open to interpretation, particularly in relation to the principle of non-retroactivity and its potential application to existing measures enacted prior to the entry into force of the Agreement.

#### 6.2.3.2 *No Temporal Default for the Scope of Measures*

Temporal rules may be considered irrelevant in determining the scope of certain measures. For example, in the case of the temporal scope of market access measures in the Services Schedule under GATS Article XVI:2, the adjudicators noted that "none of the six categories [of measures in the Article] relate to temporal limitations," and therefore "temporal elements are *not part of the substantive elements* that can be market access limitations under [the Article]."[141] In addition, regarding the temporal scope of the "internal charge" in GATT Article III:2, the adjudicators also noted that "the time at which a charge is collected or paid is *not decisive*."[142] Finally, with respect to the temporal scope of quota reallocation, GATT Article XIII:4 only imposes an obligation on the Member receiving a request from a substantial supplier to enter into consultations and not to reallocate quota shares. In interpreting this Article, the adjudicators found no temporal indication or specific guidance within the wording of the Article of "*any time frame as to when or how often* such reallocation would have to take place, or based on the occurrence of which events."[143] Overall, the absence of a default temporal rule for the scope of certain measures may be interpreted as signifying (1) no limitation, (2) a lack of decisiveness, and (3) no indication or guidance.

141 Panel Report, *Mexico—Telecoms*, paras. 7.358 and 7.361. (emphasis added) ("The six categories of measures in [GATS] Article XVI:2 refer to the types of market access limitations that can be imposed on the supply of a service.")

142 Appellate Body Reports, *China—Auto Parts*, para. 162. (emphasis added) ("[W]hen an internal charge is 'collected or enforced in the case of the imported product at the time or point of importation', such a charge 'is nevertheless to be regarded' as an internal charge. What is important, however, is that the obligation to pay a charge must accrue due to an internal event, such as the distribution, sale, use or transportation of the imported product.")

143 Panel Report, *EU—Poultry Meat (China)*, para. 7.478. (emphasis added) ("There is no specific guidance in the text of [GATT] Article XIII:4 on whether, for example, the reallocation would have to be done yearly or instead at some other regular interval, or whether it would have to be done when any Member that did not receive a country-specific share experiences a surge in its import shares of the relevant product, or even when a Member that has already received a country-specific share significantly increases its share of imports beyond that which it has been allocated.")

### 6.2.3.3 *No Temporal Default for the Requirement of Procedures*

The absence of temporal rules in procedural provisions should sometimes be interpreted cautiously to avoid imposing additional limitations or requirements on the rights and obligations of Members. Some illustrative examples follow. First, in the context of the timing of disclosure for written submissions under DSU Article 18.2, the adjudicators have found that this Article "sets no temporal limits on Members' rights and obligations" and saw "nothing in this provision which would impose any limits on rights accruing to Members."[144] Second, in the case of the publication of an investigation report, Article 3.1 of the Agreement on Safeguards merely requires that "[t]he competent authorities shall publish a report setting forth their findings and reasoned conclusions reached on all pertinent issues of fact and law." The procedure for publication under this legal provision is not subject to any temporal rule, and therefore the adjudicators opined that it was "improper to read a word—'promptly'—into the text of Article 3.1 of the Agreement on Safeguards that would add to, and amplify, the basic publication requirement that is imposed in Article 3.1."[145] Third and finally, with respect to the submission of evidence to a panel under the dispute settlement system, the adjudicators noted that no temporal rule for the submission of evidence is established in DSU Article 11 or the Working Procedures in Appendix 3 of the DSU.[146] By virtue of DSU Article 11, the adjudicators acknowledged the temporal scope of evidence in general by stating that: "A panel is not precluded from assessing a piece of evidence for the mere reason that it *pre-dates* or *post-dates* its establishment."[147] In particular, the adjudicators further stressed in the context of Article 2.1 of the TBT Agreement that "[n]othing in Article 2.1 enjoins panels from taking into account evidence *pre-dating* the establishment of a panel to the extent that such evidence informs the panel's assessment of the consistency of the measure at that point in time."[148] In sum, no temporal rule by default for certain procedures should

144 Panel Report, *Argentina—Poultry Anti-Dumping Duties*, para. 7.15.

145 Panel Report, *Ukraine—Passenger Cars*, para. 7.440.

146 Appellate Body Report, *Argentina—Textiles and Apparel*, para. 79. ("[DSU] Article 11 does not establish time limits for the submission of evidence to a panel. [DSU] Article 12.1 directs a panel to follow the Working Procedures set out in Appendix 3 of the DSU, but at the same time authorizes a panel to do otherwise after consulting the parties to the dispute. The Working Procedures in Appendix 3 also do not establish precise deadlines for the presentation of evidence by a party to the dispute.")

147 Appellate Body Report, *EC—Selected Customs Matters*, para. 188. (emphasis added) *See also* Panel Report, *US—Animals*, para. 7.447; Panel Reports, *US—COOL*, para. 6.13 and fn. 20.

148 Appellate Body Report, *US—Clove Cigarettes*, para. 206. (emphasis added)

be approached with caution, as it may be interpreted as imposing (1) no limitation on rights (*e.g.*, the timing for disclosure of written submissions), (2) no additional or amplified requirement on obligations (*e.g.*, the timing for publication of reports), or (3) no preclusion (*e.g.*, the timing for submission of evidence).

#### 6.2.3.4 *No Temporal Reference for Factual Determination*

As mentioned in Section 6.1.1, a specified reference period can be instrumental in securing an objective and unbiased factual determination of issues. However, it is not always explicitly prescribed. For example, in the case of no reference period for determination of injury under Article 3 of the Anti-Dumping Agreement, the adjudicators observed that "neither [Articles 3.1 and 3.5 of the Anti-Dumping Agreement], nor any other provision of [the Anti-Dumping Agreement], contains any specific rule as to the time periods to be covered by the injury or dumping investigations, or any overlap of those time periods."[149] Similarly, Article 11.3 of the Anti-Dumping Agreement does not require the investigating authority to specify the time-frame on which it bases its injury determination. As a result, the adjudicators considered that an explicit reference period might not be decisive to make a factual determination regarding injury by stating that "determination of injury can be properly reasoned and rest on a sufficient factual basis even though the time-frame for the injury determination is not explicitly mentioned."[150]

Beyond highlighting the possibility of reasoning without explicit temporal rules, adjudicators may show reluctance to adopt a fixed reference period. For example, in the case of no reference period for determination of adverse effects of subsidies under Article 5 of the SCM Agreement, the adjudicators were cautious to establish a given period themselves by noting that "in the absence of any specific guidance on this issue, [they] should avoid making an *a priori* choice of reference period."[151] In addition, Article 6.3(c) of the SCM Agreement also does not contain any temporal reference for determining the significant price suppression effect of subsidies. The adjudicators opined that the examination of the effect is not limited to "the short-term perspective," but "can also be assessed on the basis of *a long-term perspective* that focuses on how the subsidy affects decisions of producers to enter or exit a given industry."[152]

149 Panel Report, *Egypt—Steel Rebar*, para. 7.130.
150 Appellate Body Report, *US—Oil Country Tubular Goods Sunset Reviews*, para. 364.
151 Panel Report, *EC and certain member States—Large Civil Aircraft*, para. 7.1694.
152 Appellate Body Report, *US—Upland Cotton (Article 21.5—Brazil)*, para. 392. (emphasis added) ("[N]othing in Article 6.3(c) of the SCM Agreement suggests that the examination

In the case of no reference period for calibrating level of safeguard measures necessary to prevent or remedy serious injury in Article 5.1 of the Agreement on Safeguards, the adjudicators made a comparison with Article 4 of the same Agreement for determination of serious injury, and avoided finding a correlation of the reference period for determination of the necessary level of safeguard measures. They illustrated that the Agreement on Safeguards "does not require that the time periods that are used for setting the level of the safeguard be the same as the period that is used for the injury analysis."[153] In sum, the absence of a default temporal reference for factual determination may be understood as (1) not decisive in a certain situation which can be solved by proper reasoning on a sufficient factual basis, or (2) not appropriate to make an *a priori* choice or to find a correlation of the reference periods.

## 6.3 Temporal Rules as the Foundations of Legalization

As suggested in the foregoing Section 1.4, this research on temporal rules in WTO Law may offer a meaningful contribution to the theoretical framework of "legalization" in the disciplines of IL/IR. The framework of legalization studies on the causes and consequences of IL as a particular form of institutionalization characterized by three dimensions (*i.e.*, precision, obligation, and delegation). These three dimensions as a whole represent the *strength* of IL, namely, "hard" or "soft" law. In particular, WTO Law was considered as "hard law" in all the dimensions of legalization. Besides, IL is dynamic and continuously serves as a crucial institutional backdrop through which diverse actors may pursue their interests and values in practice. As a result, the fourth dimension of the theoretical framework, namely, "implementation," has been considered to be incorporated so as to address "legalization over time" which acknowledges the dynamic nature of IL shaped by politics. This additional dimension draws our attention to the *effect* of IL (*i.e.*, whether the IL leads positively or negatively to compliance). It differs from the original three-dimensional framework concerning the *strength* of IL from a merely legal perspective (*i.e.*, whether the IL is deemed as hard or soft law).

---

of the effect of a subsidy must focus exclusively on the short-term perspective. Whether production of a particular product is higher than it would have been in the absence of the subsidy is often a critical issue in establishing whether the effect of the subsidy is significant price suppression.")

153 Panel Report, *EU—Safeguard Measures on Steel (Turkey)*, paras. 7.257.

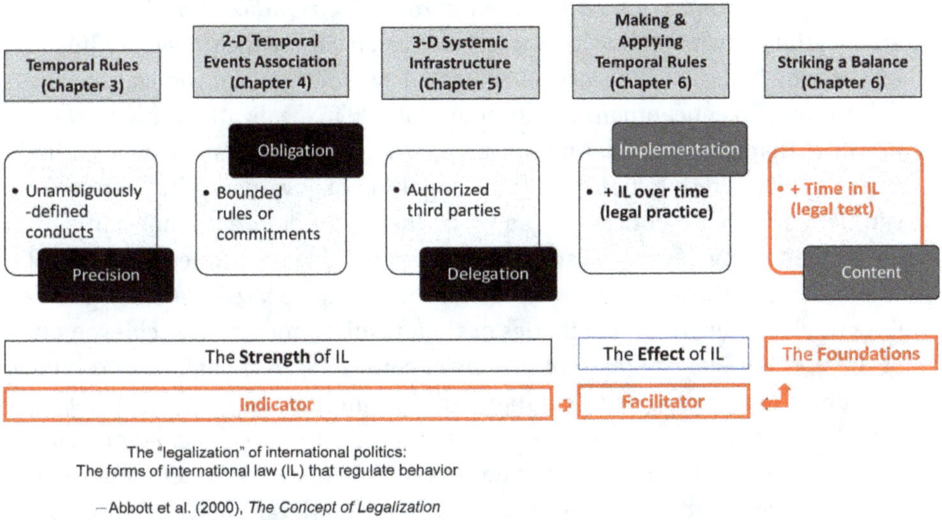


FIGURE 6.1 The contribution of temporal rules to the theoretical framework of legalization

With this four-dimensional framework of legalization in mind, this research takes a step further to argue that "temporal rules" in IL may lay the foundations of legalization (either for the *strength* or for the *effect*), and one should pay attention to their potential design and political influences. The main contributions of this research can be summarized as follows. The omnipresent temporal rules in WTO Law (Chapter 3) appear to establish the sophisticated 2-D temporal events association in legal texts (Chapter 4). These temporal rules demonstrate mutability and operate within a 3-D infrastructure, facilitating dynamic engagement through various systemic mechanisms in practice (Chapter 5). In this regard, temporal rules may be regarded as crucial elements in WTO Law, which inform the broader understanding of legalization, either the *strength* or the *effect* of WTO Law. Especially, the reasoning here is based on the findings that temporal rules are not only subject to strategical design to manage diverse legal events in WTO Law (Section 6.1), but also subject to application or interpretation to establish their shared understandings in WTO practice (Section 6.2). More specifically, the following subsections will draw a closer connection between the temporal rules and the *strength*/*effect* of WTO Law, and demonstrate how temporal rules may be relevant to the theoretical framework of legalization (Figure 6.1 above).

### 6.3.1 *The Strength of WTO Law: Temporal Rules as Indicators*

This section focuses on how temporal rules can facilitate the understanding of legalization in terms of the *strength* of WTO Law (*i.e.*, precision, obligation, and delegation). To conceptualize their potential role in legalization, this research proposes that temporal rules may be understood as a sort of "standards" within WTO Law. It is worth to note that the recognition of governance by "standards" can be found in the context of the WTO. Taking the "international standard" under the TBT Agreement as an example, the adjudicators defined the concept of standards as those that "provide for common and repeated use, rules, guidelines or characteristics for activities or their results aimed at the achievement of the optimum degree of order in a given context."[154] Although this example appears to recognize an *external* standard (*i.e.*, international standard) beyond WTO Law to deal with a specific issue area (namely, technical regulations), it is my contention that one may consider the possibility to frame temporal rules as *internal* standards in WTO Law, serving to govern legal events in an orderly and coherent manner.

Methodologically, the challenge lies in how to establish temporal rules as internal standards in WTO Law. This research proposes to employ temporal rules as "indicators" to shape or regulate legal events. Drawing inspiration from the literature on *Global Governance by Indicators*, the use of indicators can serve as a useful technique for exercising global governance. The indicator is defined as "distinctive in the ways in which it represents and conveys compiled numerical data, and it has particular attractions as a means of representation for use in comparing or evaluating particular units of analysis."[155] To be more specific, there are four crucial characteristics of indicators as standard-setting instruments, which are: (1) *name or naming*—to produce knowledge and to define or shape the way the phenomenon is understood; (2) *simplification or reductionism*—to be convenient and easy to understand and use; (3) *ordinal structure*—to enable comparison and to contain some elements of ranking; and (4) *evaluative tool*—to be capable of being used for evaluation against certain standards or ideologies.[156] As Davis et al. argued, indicators have regulatory effects mainly due to the acceptance "as guides to appropriate conduct" by actors, which may "play significant roles in global governance in helping to constitute actors and shape identities."[157]

---

154 Panel Report, *US—Tuna II (Mexico)*, para. 7.672.

155 Kevin E Davis, Benedict Kingsbury and Sally Engle Merry, 'Introduction: Global Governance by Indicators' in Kevin Davis and others (eds), *Governance by Indicators: Global Power through Quantification and Rankings* (Oxford University Press 2012), 7.

156 *Ibid.*, 7–10.

157 *Ibid.*, 14 and 16.

Furthermore, to enhance the design of "indicators" as standard-setting instruments, there are five crucial elements needed to be taken into account, which are: (1) *efficiency*—the use of "easily-produced or already-available indicators" to reduce the burden of processing information; (2) *consistency*—the use of "unequivocal ordinal data" (*e.g.*, in a numerical or mathematical form) to increase the legal or moral authority of decision-making; (3) *transparency*—the "simplicity of indicators" to make relatively easy to communicate them to third parties; (4) *scientific authority*—the "credibility of decisions based on indicators" to be endorsed by various scientific communities and the amount of authority commanded by those communities; and (5) *impartiality*—the use of "publicly disseminated indicators" to exclude subjective considerations or private data known only to the particular decision-maker.[158] With this technique of "indicators" as strategies for global governance in mind, the following will demonstrate how temporal rules may be considered as temporal "indicators" embedded internally in law, serving to enhance our understanding of the *strength* of IL under it three dimensions (*i.e.*, precision, obligation, and delegation).

#### 6.3.1.1 *The Dimension of Precision: Naming and Simplification*

The dimension of precision in legalization is characterized by "rules [that] unambiguously define the conduct they require, authorize, or proscribe" (Section 1.4). To "define the conduct" under this dimension, this research contends that legal rules may sometimes inevitably incorporate temporal rules to shed light on *when, how long*, or *how often* the conduct (*i.e.*, legal events) should take place. These temporal rules could be seen as temporal "indicators" in law to convey diverse data, as categorized in Chapter 3, either in numerical terms (*e.g.*, 1994, annual, or 90 days) or non-numerical terms (*e.g.*, upon acceptance, regular, or before/after). These temporal "indicators" can be used in analyzing particular temporal units or facts for relevant legal events in legal provisions, which means: (1) when a legal event should happen (*i.e.*, point in time, timing, sequence in time, and speed modifier); (2) how long a legal event should last (*i.e.*, period in time and degree modifier); or (3) how often a legal event should occur (*i.e.*, frequency in time). For example, as the design of temporal rules discussed in Section 6.1, a fixed or representative period is commonly used as a standard indicator for conducting calculations. A reasonable period can serve as an indicator for balancing competing needs during proceedings. The timing of a request can help determine whether to extend the implementation date of a treaty. Section 6.1 provides primary resources of knowledge for consideration of temporal rules as "indicators" in WTO Law.

---

158 *Ibid.*, 16–18.

As mentioned earlier, the key characteristics of indicators as a useful technique for exercising global governance are not only (1) to be "named" for the purpose of producing knowledge and shaping the way the phenomenon is understood, but also (2) to be "simplified" or "reduced" for greater convenience, comprehensibility, and usability. In this regard, apart from the six categories of temporal rules established in Chapter 3 as a taxonomic system to define their names and contours, their simplification and reductionism may be accentuated by framing them as "default rules of guidance" in both design and function. Drawing inspiration from the establishment of the "choice architecture" as an instrument of governance, as Sunstein noted, default rules of guidance with *clear*, *simple*, and *explicit* information have large impact on nudging our choices and behavior.[159] He provided three contributing factors to explain why defaults work: (1) the power of inertia and the tendency to procrastination; (2) implicit endorsement; and (3) the reference point for decisions.[160] He also acknowledged that "[d]efault rules are pervasive, even when we do not notice them, and they have major effects on outcomes."[161] In WTO practice, the nudging effect of temporal rules seems to be found in the context of the DSU. For example, around half of the dispute settlement cases circulated its appellate body report by almost the exact date (*i.e.*, 90 or 91 days) expired on the mandatory 90-day deadline set in DSU Article 17.5.[162]

In this sense, if temporal rules would be established as "default rules of guidance," one might pay attention to their clarity, simplicity, and explicitness. For example, to ensure the functioning and effectiveness of the WTO dispute settlement system, the DSU provides for several overlapping legal provisions that set forth temporal rules to guide each stage of the dispute settlement process (Table 6.1 below).[163] These temporal provisions advise or oblige a

159 Cass R Sunstein, *Simpler: The Future of Government* (Simon and Schuster 2013), 58–60. (*See also* at 37. The definition of the "choice architecture" is as follows: "[T]he design of the social environment in a way that influences people's choices—for example, by affecting ease or accessibility, by providing information, or by making certain features of the situation salient and clear or instead invisible.")

160 *Ibid.*, 111.

161 *Ibid.*, 212.

162 *See* WorldTradeLaw.net statistics, Timing of Appeal, Circulation and Adoption of Appellate Body Reports, https://www.worldtradelaw.net/databases/abtiming.php (last visited 31 July 2023): 42 cases out of 123 cases (34%) by the 90th day and 20 cases out of 123 cases (16%) by the 91st day. Noting that 25 out of 148 cases in the database from compliance DSU Article 21.5 appellate review proceedings were deleted manually.

163 *See* Appellate Body Report, *US—FSC*, para. 166. ("The procedural rules of WTO dispute settlement are designed to promote, not the development of litigation techniques, but simply the fair, prompt and effective resolution of trade disputes.")

TABLE 6.1 The overview of the temporal provisions in the DSU

| | Consultations | | | | Panel proceedings | | | | | Standard appellate review proceedings | | |
|---|---|---|---|---|---|---|---|---|---|---|---|---|
| DSU | Request | Reply | Enter | Panel request | Establish | Compose | Issue | Circulate | Adopt | Appeal | Circulate | Adopt |
| Art. 4.3 | * | 10 days | 30 days | | | | | | | | | |
| Art. 4.7 | * | | | 60 days | | | | | | | | |
| Art. 4.8 | * | | 10 days | 20 days | | | | | | | | |
| Art. 6.1 | | | | * | 2nd DSB meeting | | | | | | | |
| Art. 8.7 | | | | | * | 20–30 days | | | | | | |
| Art. 12.8 | | | | | | * | 6/3 months | | | | | |
| Art. 12.9 | | | | | * | | | 9 months | | | | |
| Art. 16.4 | | | | | | | | * | 60 days | 60 days | | |
| Art. 17.5 | | | | | | | | | | * | 60/90 days | |
| Art. 17.14 | | | | | | | | | | | * | 30 days |
| Art. 20 | | | | | * | | | | 9 months | | | 12 months |

number of actors (*e.g.*, Members, the panel, the Appellate Body, or the DSB) to undertake a range of actions within a fixed period triggered by specified events (as indicated by * in Table 6.1). These provisions set out several interrelated time-frames for various steps, though they are not necessarily distinct or clearly delineated. To use temporal rules as "default rules of guidance," one might consider whether or how to harmonize these legal provisions towards the direction to be more clear, simple, and explicit.

#### 6.3.1.2 *The Dimension of Obligation: Ordinal Structure and Evaluation Tool*

The dimension of obligation in legalization is defined as the extent to which "states or other actors are bound by a rule or commitment or by a set of rules or commitments … in the sense that their behavior thereunder is subject to scrutiny under the general rules, procedures, and discourse of [IL]" (Section 1.4). To shed additional light on "a (set of) rule(s) or commitment(s)" under this obligation dimension, this research posits that temporal rules function as key indicators in identifying the nexus between rules or commitments (*i.e.*, temporal events association in Chapter 4). Especially, they can guide us to the identification of relevant *event-types* and be used to examine the dimension of obligation within legal texts. As mentioned above, the remaining two key characteristics that make indicators a useful technique are (1) to be "ordinal" for the purpose of making a comparison or ranking in a specific order, and (2) to be "evaluative" against certain standards or ideologies. To unfold the rules or commitments in legal texts, the 2-D model of temporal events association established in this research demonstrates how WTO Members are bound by sixteen *event-types* through the adjacency of temporal rules in WTO Law. This 2-D temporal events association can display, in numbers and percentages, the pattern of its frequency distribution within a 16 × 16 matrix organized in an ordinal structure (Table 4.20). It may be developed as a means of representation to facilitate the comparison and evaluation of rules or commitments, both within and across various legal regimes.

In other words, this research may be of interest not only due to (1) the qualitative naming of temporal rules (Section 3.2) and the relevant *event-types* (Sections 4.2 and 4.3) to be utilized as "already-available (temporal) indicators" in law, but also (2) the quantitative representation of their distribution in WTO legal texts (Sections 3.3 and 4.4) to serve as "unequivocal ordinal data" for future comparison and evaluation. In particular, as Kaplow argued, "if the cases are anticipated to arise frequently and have important recurring characteristics, rules will not only be preferable, but might be expected to be more precise."[164] In the context of the temporal events association in WTO Law, as shown in Table 4.20, the largest proportion of temporal rules (17.1 %) are found to be associated with the main event-type of NOTIFICATION, which most commonly occur in conjunction with the supporting event of NOTIFICATION (22.6 %). This association is chiefly formed by temporal rules, including *timing* (*e.g.*, upon the request) and a *fixed period in time* (*e.g.*, within three months of receipt of the request) (Section 4.4.2). Given this ordinal data, NOTIFICATION may be regarded as one of the most significant recurring event-types related to time in WTO Law. Accordingly, future negotiators might consider whether or how to establish temporal rules under the event-type of NOTIFICATION as "default rules of guidance," to ensure greater precision in their design, elaboration, implementation, and beyond.

#### 6.3.1.3 *The Dimension of Delegation: Credibility and Impartiality*

The delegation dimension of legalization is typically described as "third parties [who] have been granted authority to implement, interpret, and apply the rules; to resolve disputes; and (possibly) to make further rules" (Section 1.4). In line with the possibility of granting "third parties" the authority to engage with rules under the delegation dimension, the examination of the establishment, modification, and elaboration of temporal rules in Chapter 5 offers insight into how "third parties" interact within the legal system (*i.e.*, the 3-D systemic infrastructure). In other words, once temporal rules and their events association are established as indicators in legal texts, they generally do not remain static. They are often subject to "incremental or organic change" under varying circumstances through a number of systemic mechanisms, enabling relevant parties to engage with the original rules in practice. As a result, following the proposal of this research to view temporal rules as internal "indicators" in law, it is important not to overlook the relevant parties involved in establishing, modifying, and elaborating these temporal rules dynamically, which aligns with the delegation dimension of legalization. It leads us further to an inquiry about the two important elements of "indicators," namely, their credibility (*i.e.*, to be endorsed by reliable authorities) and impartiality (*i.e.*, to avoid subjective considerations).

In addition, the engagement of relevant parties with temporal rules can be confined to a Member itself or contingent upon the collaborative behavior of

164 Louis Kaplow, 'Rules versus Standards: An Economic Analysis' (1992) 42 Duke Law Journal 557, 622.

multiple authorities (*e.g.*, another Member, a group of Members, the Members as a whole, or a body of the WTO) (Figure 5.2). For this reason, the questioning of credibility and impartiality in relation to temporal rules seems unavoidable in a landscape filled with diversity and uncertainty. For example, in the current WTO dispute settlement environment, the mandatory 90-day deadline stipulated in DSU Article 17.5 for appellate review increasingly appears unrealistic, with no clear instructions on addressing potential delays. As part of a package of reforms to improve institutional balance, the deadline was proposed be removed, extended, or deemed to be met when certain objective conditions are met. Nevertheless, it could also be argued that the mandatory 90-day deadline would still remain its relevance if it could be governed by a clear systemic mechanism that allows it to adapt to new conditions.

To unfold the potential systemic mechanisms for the adaption of temporal rules in WTO Law, Chapter 5 provides a preliminary overview of the establishment, modification, and elaboration of temporal rules in WTO practice (Figure 5.2). Generally speaking, it identifies nine potential systemic mechanisms through which authority is exercised to establish, modify, and elaborate temporal rules under specific conditions or circumstances (Figure 5.1). According to Raftopoulos, the institutional life of the conventional regime can generate "internal context of reference" from which "the parties may draw and properly articulate their amendment proposals, evaluating their overall weight for the possible improvement of the conventional regime, as well as the desired scope of the revisionary renegotiation."[165] As such, the general examination of how temporal rules are established, modified, and elaborated may offer a foundational reference for future reflections on confronting or adjusting such rules from a systemic standpoint.

It should be noted that, although Chapter 5 has examined the general modalities of temporal rules in WTO Law to be established, modified, or elaborated amid dynamic interactions between the rules and the WTO's systemic environment, future in-depth research on temporal rules could also explore the "contextual variation" of the institution. This suggests that existing institutional arrangements are shaped not only by current conditions but also by the historical development of the institution. In other words, institutional design often involves addressing problems that arose from the failure and breakdown of earlier institutions. When pursuing common interests in new areas, actors may prefer, wherever possible, to make use of pre-existing institutions rather than build entirely new ones from the ground up. As Duffield believed,

165 Evangelos Raftopoulos, *International Negotiation: A Process of Relational Governance for International Common Interest* (Cambridge University Press 2019), 227–228.

the focus shifts from determining which new institutional design is most rational to asking "when and to what degree the actors will avail themselves of pre-existing institutional arrangements."[166] To be more specific, in the case of the design of a finite duration for a treaty, Copelovitch and Putnam highlighted "the need to pay closer attention to the importance of prior institutional and legal commitments in shaping states' choices about the design features of new agreement."[167] In this sense, the in-depth exploration of how temporal rules become incorporated in WTO Law in consideration of "contextual variation" of the institution, and how prior institutional arrangements beyond the GATT/WTO influence the choices of actors or drafters would be helpful.

In particular, the concept of "experiential learning" may play an important role on explaining the influence of prior agreements on later cooperation and choices. As argued by Elsig and Eckhardt, "experiential learning" as an important contextual variable of the negotiations has been overlooked by the existing literature.[168] Based on the assumptions that a key element in negotiations is uncertainty and that actors look for information to address uncertainty, they argued that negotiators rely on actual behavior as a proxy for forming their expectations about a future system. In other words, expectations are shaped through a process referred to as "learning" from the outputs of the current system.[169] Past experience can prompt not only the refinement of negotiation strategies, but also shifts in preferences and a pursuit of mutually agreeable solutions.[170] For example, in the context of the WTO dispute settlement system, Elsig defined "experiential learning" as experience with existing dispute settlement system that "leads to an updating of information and in turn to changes in preferences."[171] Accordingly, in furtherance of how prior institutional arrangements influence the design of temporal rules, future research might compare the current system with past experience of the institutions, and explore how "experiential learning" might support the formation of expectations for the current and future design of temporal rules.

166 John S Duffield, 'The Limits of "Rational Design"' (2003) 57 International Organization 411, 418.

167 Mark S Copelovitch and Tonya L Putnam, 'Design in Context: Existing International Agreements and New Cooperation' (2014) 68 International Organization 471, 488.

168 Manfred Elsig and Jappe Eckhardt, 'The Creation of the Multilateral Trade Court: Design and Experiential Learning' (2015) 14 World Trade Review 13, 13.

169 *Ibid.*, 16.

170 *Ibid.*, 17.

171 Manfred Elsig, 'Legalization in Context: The Design of the WTO's Dispute Settlement System' (2017) 19 The British Journal of Politics and International Relations 304, 305.

### 6.3.2 *The Effect of WTO Law: Temporal Rules as Compliance Facilitators*

In addition to the positioning of temporal rules as "indicators" to underpin the legalization framework regarding the *strength* of WTO Law (*i.e.*, precision, obligation, and delegation) in the previous Section 6.3.1, this section focuses on how temporal rules facilitate legalization in terms of the *effect* of WTO Law (*i.e.*, implementation). This implementation dimension concerns whether IL leads positively or negatively to "compliance," which means "the impact of implementation as a positive outcome if the rule leads to compliance and negative if it permits and/or facilitates non-compliant or illiberal, rule by law" (Section 1.4). At the practical level, assessing the actual outcomes of implementation or the degree of compliance with WTO Law, facilitated by temporal rules, would require additional empirical research, which lies beyond the scope of this study. Nevertheless, at the theoretical level, it is my contention that temporal rules may serve as "compliance facilitator." In other words, (1) temporal rules may "improve compliance" with WTO Law in theory, and (2) temporal rules may enhance the "effectiveness" of WTO Law in practice.

#### 6.3.2.1 *The Dimension of Implementation: Improving Compliance by Temporal Rules*

As WTO Law has become relatively complete and is considered as a "hard law" in accordance with the legalization framework concerning the *strength* of IL, it is natural that attention then turns to the actual compliance with the adopted legal rules in legal practice. When the legal rules are not complied with, as stated by Kessler, "the first question lawyers ask is what norm is to be applied, how that norm relates to other norms, and what legal consequences in terms of responsibility, accountability, or compensation arise."[172] In the context of IL, Meyer also argued that "much legal practice focuses on compliance because judges and arbitrators are forced to make determinations about whether a state's conduct satisfies a legal standard."[173] In general, as Shelton observed, the rule of law requires compliance to ensure the effectiveness of legal norms, which makes compliance a central concern in IL.[174]

However, the concern with "compliance" in determining legal consequences can also be understood broadly. As Dunoff and Pollack acknowledged,

172 Oliver Kessler, 'The Same as It Never Was? Uncertainty and the Changing Contours of International Law' (2011) 37 Review of International Studies 2163, 2180.

173 Timothy Meyer, 'How Compliance Understates Effectiveness' (2014) 108 AJIL Unbound 93, 93.

174 Dinah Shelton, 'Law, Non-Law and the Problem of "Soft Law"' in Dinah Shelton (ed), *Commitment and Compliance: The Role of Non-binding Norms in the International Legal System* (Oxford University Press 2003), 9.

"[a]n emphasis on compliance tends to reinforce the traditional view of law as commands backed by sanctions, while overlooking law's aspirational, expressive, constitutive, and learning element."[175] Bilder also pointed out that "[a]n emphasis on compliance may point towards a backwards-looking and essentially legalistic approach focusing on state 'misbehavior', rather than towards a productive enquiry into devising and deploying better normative techniques and arrangements that facilitate more effective international dealings and cooperation."[176] To broaden the conception of "compliance," Guzman suggested that it might speak of whether compliance is "encouraged" or "improved."[177] He further provided an explanation that the design of legal rules *per se*, by providing greater transparency, can "improve compliance" due to the fact that it enables the classification of behavior as compliant or violative, enhancing the likelihood of compliance by clearly distinguishing violators from non-violators.[178] Except for the design of legal rules *per se*, as Haas demonstrated, the improvement of compliance may also be achieved through other institutional mechanisms, such as monitoring, verification, and capacity building.[179]

With this broader understanding of the concept of "compliance" in mind, this research posits that temporal rules may also function as crucial elements in law to "improve compliance" by signaling *when*, *how long*, or *how often* the relevant legal events should exist or take place. As demonstrated in Section 6.1, temporal rules can generally be understood as "secondary rules of law" that support legal efficacy by helping to ascertain primary legal rules, such as serving as a benchmark for calculation (Section 6.1.1), as a means of balancing the

175 Jeffrey L Dunoff and Mark A Pollack (eds), *Interdisciplinary Perspectives on International Law and International Relations: The State of the Art* (Cambridge University Press 2013), 47.

176 Richard B Bilder, 'Beyond Compliance: Helping Nations Cooperate' in Dinah Shelton (ed), *Commitment and Compliance: The Role of Non-binding Norms in the International Legal System* (Oxford University Press 2003), 72.

177 Andrew T Guzman, *How International Law Works: A Rational Choice Theory* (Oxford University Press 2008), 22–23.

178 *Ibid.*, 96.

179 *See generally* Peter M Haas, 'Choosing to Comply: Theorizing from International Relations and Comparative Politics' in Dinah Shelton (ed), *Commitment and Compliance: The Role of Non-binding Norms in the International Legal System* (Oxford University Press 2003), 53–58. *See also* Anne-Marie Slaughter, *A New World Order* (4th edition, Princeton University Press 2005), 4. (The author provided an explanation of capacity building to improve compliance with IL by stating that "[i]n a world in which a major set of obstacles to effective global regulation is a simple inability on the part of many developing countries to translate paper rules into changes in actual behavior, governments must be able not only to negotiate treaties but also to create the capacity to comply with them.")

interests for adopting a measure (Section 6.1.3), as a response to change in law (Section 6.1.7), and so forth. In WTO practice, Section 6.2 draws attention on the application or interpretation of temporal rules, and finds that, rather than establishing specific legal consequences for temporal rules, adjudicators appear to focus on their functional roles within legal provisions, for example: the use of explicit temporal rules to establish a clear line for legal application (Section 6.2.1), the use of implicit temporal rules to infer the intrinsic meaning or limitation of legal terms (Section 6.2.2), as well as the use of no temporal rule by default to preserve openness of legal interpretation (Section 6.2.3). To this end, I propose the potential role of temporal rules in "improving compliance" with WTO Law in theory. The following discussion will explore how they might enhance the "effectiveness" of WTO Law in practice.

#### 6.3.2.2 *The Effectiveness of WTO Law: Striking a Balance by Temporal Rules*

In support of the notion of "improving compliance," the modern principle of the "effectiveness" of IL has evolved over time, offering a new perspective on the original concept of "compliance." It widens the conventional concern with compliance by directing the attention to the need to cover broader discussions on improving compliance, enforcement, and moral consideration in practice.[180] As Zappalà observed, the ancient roots of the principle of effectiveness in compliance form the foundation of the legal system, based on the presumption that its rules can be applied concretely. However, this early conception of effectiveness has gradually been eroded and replaced by more specific rules concerning "the notions of legitimacy, lawfulness, and legality, which place the legal dimension above any factual element."[181] In other words, the attention to the effectiveness of IL shifts from the *factual* dimension concerning actual effects (*i.e.*, effectiveness as compliance) to the *legal* dimension concerning the fundamental structure of IL and "its ability to display effects in the

180 Liam Murphy, 'Varieties of Effectiveness: What Matters?' (2014) 108 AJIL Unbound 99, 99–102. (There are four senses of effectiveness regarding IL: (1) *effectiveness as compliance*: unless IL is by and large complied with and applied, it is not a legal system that is actually in effect; (2) *effectiveness as improving compliance*: since compliance is not perfect and so, assuming that greater compliance would make the world better, we have reason to investigate ways of increasing it; (3) *effectiveness as enforcement*: given that we do not have perfect compliance, it matters whether the legal system can be reformed so that it enforces the law more effectively and thus increases compliance; and (4) *effectiveness as providing moral reason for compliance*: IL can and does induce compliance by providing moral reasons for compliance that states (rightly) accept.)

181 Salvatore Zappalà, 'Can Legality Trump Effectiveness in Today's International Law?' in Antoni Cassese (ed), *Realizing Utopia: The Future of International Law* (Oxford University Press 2012), 106.

world of facts and vice versa" (*i.e.*, effectiveness as improving compliance).[182] It directs the focus of inquiries into the effectiveness of IL from the factual outcome of "compliance" to the legal capacity to "improve compliance."

To address the capacity for "effectiveness," the key issue is "how to strike a balance" in managing the effectiveness of modern social system (including the legal one) to display effects in the real world. In the modern society, the difficulty of preserving balance has increasingly intensified, which corresponds to the notion of "dynamic stabilization" in the context of social acceleration. As Rosa defined, the "dynamic stabilization" as a mode of modern society is the inherent logic that the society "systematically requires growth, innovation, and acceleration for its structural reproduction and [...] maintain[s] its socioeconomic and institutional status quo."[183] In fact, the drive of the logic of dynamic stabilization is due to "the institutional fabric of a capitalist modernity that can only operate in a mode of dynamic stabilization, and that can only meet the temporal requirements of dynamic stabilization through acceleratory technologies."[184] Especially, the phenomenon of acceleration appears to align with neoliberal globalization. As stated by Hassan, "a fast-paced, instrumentally oriented economic neoliberalism ... is focused far more on the short-term horizon, and on doing things ever more quickly to satisfy profit-driven expectations," and this phenomenon of acceleration has reached "into every realm of the social, economic and cultural, into our very consciousness."[185]

Accordingly, the phenomenon of acceleration and the very idea of "dynamic stabilization" have been devoted to the consideration of the "effectiveness" of the legal system which requires law itself to be improved and adjusted incessantly.[186] The tension between law and social acceleration gives rise to the urges for law to "speed up" and to become more adaptive to changes in the environment. To be more specific, Rosa and Trejo-Mathys noted that the problem of social acceleration or "speed up" is not so much that society is changing, but rather "the growing instability of time horizons and bases of selection produced by the ongoing revision of expectations and reconstructed

---

182 *Ibid.*, 107.

183 Hartmut Rosa, 'De-Synchronization, Dynamic Stabilization, Dispositional Squeeze: The Problem of Temporal Mismatch' in Judy Wajcman and Nigel Dodd (eds), *The Sociology of Speed: Digital, Organizational, and Social Temporalities* (Oxford University Press 2016), 31–32.

184 *Ibid.*, 41.

185 Robert Hassan, *Empires of Speed: Time and the Acceleration of Politics and Society* (Brill Nijhoff 2009), 6–8.

186 Rosa (n 183), 33.

experiences."[187] In response to this growing instability due to constant revision and reconstruction, two general approaches to strike a balance in the legal system were developed in tandem, referred to Fuller's general conception[188] and Werner's explanations:[189] (1) *supporting structure*: perceiving law as "inherently conservative and inflexible," which seeks to "stabilize expectations throughout society" and "create stickiness on social relations;" and (2) *adaptive fluidity*: perceiving law as "inherently dynamic," which allows for much greater flexibility and adaptability by adopting new laws. Based on these two general approaches to the legal system, this research addresses the effectiveness of WTO Law by emphasizing not only (1) the potentiality of temporal rules to facilitate *supporting structure* in law, but also (2) the potentiality of temporal rules to facilitate *adaptive fluidity* in law.

In terms of *supporting structure* in law, although temporal rules are by no means the only possible means of what can be achieved for effective arrangement of legal events, they may be a necessary precondition in law to facilitate the effectiveness of the legal system. In other words, temporal rules may stabilize expectations or create stickiness on legal events due to the potential effect of time. As Gordon indicated in the production of globally standardized time, "material units of temporal order play a constitutive role in the production of governmental rationalities, even as governmental rationalities condition and instrumentalize material units of temporal order."[190] In addition, based on the general notion of "temporal structuring" in organizational practice, Orlikowski and Yates explained that "people in organizations experience time through the shared temporal structures they enact recurrently in their every-day practices." This means "when taking action in the world, people routinely draw on common temporal structures that they (and others) have previously enacted to organize their ongoing practices."[191] To be more specific, Dyson found the

187 Hartmut Rosa and Jonathan Trejo-Mathys, *Social Acceleration: A New Theory of Modernity* (Columbia University Press 2013), 77.

188 Fuller (n 66), 29. (As Fuller argued, a pervasive problem of social design for the morality of law is that of "maintaining a balance between supporting structure and adaptive fluidity.")

189 Wouter G Werner, 'Regulating Speed: Social Acceleration, and International Law' in Moshe Hirsch and Andrew Lang (eds), *Research Handbook on the Sociology of International Law* (Edward Elgar Publishing 2018), 92–93. (The author pointed out that "[e]mphasizing the need to adhere to pre-given rules and legal logic comes with the risk that law is simply outdated in the face of rapidly changing environments.")

190 Geoff Gordon, 'Engaging an Infrastructure of Time Production with International Law' (2021) 9 London Review of International Law 319, 345.

191 Wanda J Orlikowski and JoAnne Yates, 'It's about Time: Temporal Structuring in Organizations' (2002) 13 Organization Science 684, 686.

effect of time in the study of the "timescapes" (*i.e.*, the time-boundaries) in European economic governance that "time-rules have been seen as central to mobilizing political and market action, gaining commitment and securing compliance, and synchronizing action."[192] In this sense, the potential effect of time appears capable of establishing a certain "temporal order" or "temporal structure" that generates rationalities, sets routines, and mobilizes actions in the real world. Therefore, this research argues that building temporal rules into WTO Law may have the potential to enhance the effectiveness of the legal system by providing a *supporting structure* that helps stabilize expectations (*e.g.*, produce rationalities and routines) and create stickiness (*e.g.*, mobilize actions).

On the other hand, in terms of *adaptive fluidity* in law, temporal rules can evolve over time and may be regarded as one of the most inherently dynamic elements of law. In other words, once temporal rules are built into law to provide a *supporting structure*, systemic mechanisms that allow for fluid adaptation to new conditions should not be neglected when considering the role of temporal rules in facilitating the effectiveness of the legal system. The demand of being shaped by temporal structures (*i.e.*, temporal rules) and (re)shaping temporal structures (*i.e.*, systemic mechanisms) usually exist hand in hand with each other. As Orlikowski and Yates underlined, "people are purposive, knowledgeable, adaptive, and inventive actors who, while they are shaped by established temporal structures, can also choose (whether explicitly or implicitly) to (re)shape those temporal structures to accomplish their situated and dynamic end."[193] Soave also noticed that "[t]ime boundaries are never purely objective or purely technical; rather, they are the site of a fierce power struggle between the actors involved."[194] In particular, in the context of treaty negotiations, Raftopoulos found that the possibility of extending and maximizing the "time horizon" (*i.e.*, artificially created time-frame) of negotiation ensures "the possibility of a continuing flow of negotiations and the assurance of its periodicity considerably facilitates the approximation of the rival parties and reinforces their desire for a joint management of the conflict."[195] In this regard,

192 Kenneth Dyson, 'The Evolving Timescapes of European Economic Governance: Contesting and Using Time' (2009) 16 Journal of European Public Policy 286, 289.

193 Orlikowski and Yates (n 191), 688.

194 Tommaso Soave, 'The Politics of Time in Domestic and International Lawmaking' in Klara Polackova Van der Ploeg, Luca Pasquet and León Castellanos-Jankiewicz (eds), *International Law and Time: Narratives and Techniques* (Springer International Publishing 2022), 158.

195 Raftopoulos (n 165), 37. (The time horizon of negotiations can be mutually controlled both (1) procedurally by "the appropriate institutionalization of the negotiating process

this research posits that the dynamic character of temporal rules, and the systemic mechanisms that support it, should also be considered in assessing their potential to ensure the effectiveness of WTO Law, as they contribute to *adaptive fluidity* within the legal system.

In sum, this research concludes that the key feature of temporal rules in striking a balance and enhancing the effectiveness of WTO Law lies in their ability, on the one hand, to establish a complex temporal structure for legal events as a *supporting structure* in law (Chapter 4), and on the other hand, to remain dynamic and adaptive in practice through various systemic mechanisms that facilitate *adaptive fluidity* in law (Chapter 5).

## 6.4 Summary

Following the 3-D systemic infrastructure for temporal rules identified in the previous Chapter 5, temporal rules appear to be crucial elements in WTO Law, not only underpinning diverse legal events in law but also evolving through various systemic mechanisms in practice. To further reflect on the systemic implications of temporal rules within a process, this Chapter is dedicated to exploring (1) the rationality for *making* temporal rules in WTO legal texts (Section 6.1); (2) shared understandings for *applying* temporal rules in WTO practice (Section 6.2); and (3) the contribution of temporal rules to *the theoretical framework of legalization* (Section 6.3). In particular, Section 6.1 identifies seven strategic assumptions underlying temporal rules in consideration of their rational design in WTO Law, and Section 6.2 provides three interpretative approaches for temporal rules in consideration of their dynamic legitimacy in WTO practice (Table 6.2 below). Section 6.3 draws a connection between the temporal rules and the *strength/effect* of WTO Law.

Section 6.1 discusses the rationl design of temporal rules in WTO Law, which rests on the perception that certain temporal rules have been addressed across various treaties, demonstrating their empirical influence in solving cooperation problems in IR (*e.g.*, the period for treaty application as well as the notice and waiting period for treaty withdrawal). This research takes a focused approach to studying the WTO legal regime, aiming to identify additional temporal rules that may be of interest for future research on their institutional design. Generally speaking, the functioning of temporal rules can be

at various levels," and (2) substantively by "giving priority to the negotiation of issues or measures involving long-term commitments by the parties.")

considered as "secondary rules of law" which provide certain temporal criteria as one of the appropriate ways to ascertain the primary rules of actions or behaviors. Particularly, the "appropriateness" of temporal rules in light of their rational design in WTO Law may be understood through seven strategic assumptions: (1) temporal rule as a benchmark for calculation or evaluation; (2) temporal rule as a means of regulating the proceedings; (3) temporal rule as a means of balancing the interests of the measures; (4) temporal rule as a facilitator of transparency and notification; (5) temporal rule as a tactic of special and differential treatment; (6) temporal rule as a facilitator of implementation; and (7) temporal rule as a response to change in law.

To be more specific, the *numerical* expression of temporal rules may be considered as appropriate for providing a specific benchmark for calculation, ensuring predictability and control of the proceedings, setting the ending point for the measures, as well as regulating the frequency of recurring events. As for the *non-numerical* expression of temporal rules, *unspecified periods* can be found in several instances, for example, a representative period as a general benchmark, a reasonable period for balancing the needs of the parties involved in the proceedings, sufficient time for consultation on the measures about to be taken, and so forth. *Timing*, *sequence*, and *conceptual expression in time* are also relevant, for instance, in cases of allowing the implementation date to be extended "upon request," establishing an exception for advantages granted "prior to" the treaty's entry into force with respect to new legal obligations, and aiming for "prompt" undertakings during the proceedings. Overall, from the perspective of secondary rules of law, it does not appear necessary to prescribe a specific legal consequence solely for the breach of temporal rules. It is only necessary that these temporal rules should be considered as "appropriate" guidance to arrange relevant legal events in law.

Section 6.2 demonstrates the application of temporal rules in WTO practice, which refers to the interpretation of temporal rules to establish legal relevance that may, or may not, extend beyond the literal wording of WTO legal texts. Through the process of interpretation, shared understandings of temporal rules are cultivated in practice, which in turn illuminate the "dynamic legitimacy" of temporal rules in use. To conduct the examination, this research focuses primarily on how adjudicators under the WTO dispute settlement system interpret and apply temporal rules. In principle, the WTO adjudicators shall follow the means of interpretation of VCLT Article 31, which requires them to interpret legal provisions by virtue of the ordinary meaning of the words in their context and in light of the object and purpose of the treaty. If the meaning is still ambiguous or obscure or leads to a manifestly absurd or unreasonable result, they may recourse to supplementary means of interpretation of VCLT Article 32. In this regard, three interpretative approaches to establish shared understandings of temporal rules are identified in WTO practice, which are: (1) explicit temporal rules, (2) implicit temporal rules, and (3) no temporal rule by default.

First, adjudicators usually rely on the ordinary meaning of the words to interpret *explicit temporal rules* to confirm their scope or intention applied in particular cases (*e.g.*, temporal application of legal rules, temporal scope of measures, or temporal requirement of procedures). In terms of the confirmation of the scope, adjudicators may refer to the plain wording of temporal rules to prescribe the precise dates, to clarify their legal characters in context (as mandatory, exceptional, or indicative), or to determine the consistency of relevant legal provisions. In terms of the confirmation of the intention, adjudicators may consider the underlying reasons for their explicit expressions, for example, to draw a clear line for applying legal rules, to provide certainty for the outcome of procedures, or to prevent circumvention of the proceedings.

Second, *implicit temporal rules* are not expressly stated in legal texts and may be inferred in the course of interpretation from the relevant context, the object and purpose, or general principles of law. The relevant context refers to certain semantic terms in legal provisions containing intrinsic temporal meaning by definition (*e.g.*, continue, emergency, and unforeseen), which may be interpreted or elaborated by means of temporal rules. In addition, the object of purpose of legal provisions may also be acknowledged by adjudicators to derive the implied temporal limitation of procedures in consideration of their nature, such as to ensure the comprehensiveness and reliability of the data or the prompt settlement of the dispute. As for general principles of law, adjudicators may have a margin of discretion to place time constraints or grant permission for time in line with the principle of due process, aiming to balance the interests of the parties in the course of the proceedings. They may also hold legitimate expectations that the parties will act in a timely manner, in accordance with the principle of good faith to prevent abuse of the proceedings.

Third and finally, temporal rules may be left out intentionally in legal texts, which means there is *no temporal rule by default* in some particular cases (*e.g.*, temporal application of legal rules, temporal scope of measures, temporal requirement of procedures, or temporal reference for factual determination). In those cases, adjudicators may be cautious and reluctant to make an *a priori* choice during their interpretation. They may also read the temporal possibilities broadly and openly, viewing them as having no limitations or additional requirements, and offering no decisive rules or specific guidance.

TABLE 6.2 Making and applying temporal rules in WTO Law

| Making temporal rules | Applying temporal rules |
|---|---|
| **(1) As a Benchmark for Calculation or Evaluation**<br>– *Calculation (amount)*:<br>fixed point or duration (specific);<br>most recent and/or representative period (general and static)<br>– *Evaluation (fact)*: given period<br>**(2) As a Means of Regulating the Proceedings**<br>– *Objective*: speed modifier (prompt)<br>– *Predictability and Control*:<br>fixed period (time-limit)<br>– *Balancing the Needs of the Parties*:<br>reasonable period<br>**(3) As a Means of Balancing the Interests of the Measures**<br>– *Consultation*: sufficient time<br>– *Publication to Entry into Force*:<br>reasonable interval<br>– *Imposition*: for such period of time as may be necessary (general); fixed period (specific)<br>– *Review*: after a reasonable period of imposition; at request of the parties<br>– *Termination*: on a date not later than a fixed period; effective extension<br>**(4) As a Facilitator of Transparency and Notification**<br>– *Notification*: speed modifier (prompt)<br>– *Delay Avoidance*: as far in advance as practicable; before the measure is applied<br>– *Recurring Notification*: fixed frequency<br>**(5) As a Tactic of Special and Differential Treatment**<br>– *Transitional Period*: fixed period<br>– *Implementation Date*:<br>prescribed date (self-designated) | **(1) Explicit Temporal Rules**<br>– *Application of Legal Rules*:<br>intend to draw a clear line<br>confirm precise dates<br>– *Scope of Measures*:<br>clarify in context:<br>straightforward and mandatory? any exception? effective treaty interpretation?<br>establish inconsistency of legal provisions<br>– *Requirement of Procedures*:<br>provide certainty regarding the outcome<br>ascertain the rights of Members<br>prevent circumvention of the proceedings<br>be read as indicative only (time-limit)<br>**(2) Implicit Temporal Rules**<br>– *Intrinsic Meaning by Definition*:<br>*e.g.*, continue, emergency, remain, and unforeseen<br>– *Implied Limitation in the Nature of Procedures*:<br>*e.g.*, to ensure comprehensiveness, reliability, promptness, and effectiveness<br>– *Discretion under the Due Process Principle*:<br>strike a balance of interests<br>place time constraints<br>grant permission for time<br>– *Expectation under the Good Faith Principle:*<br>prevent an abusive exercise<br>legitimate expectation<br>**(3) No Temporal Rule by Default**<br>– *Application of Legal Rules*:<br>remain open<br>– *Scope of Measures*:<br>no limitation<br>a lack of decisiveness<br>no indication or guidance |

TABLE 6.2 Making and applying temporal rules in WTO Law (*cont.*)

| Making temporal rules | Applying temporal rules |
|---|---|
| – *Short Extension* (less than a fixed period): upon early warning<br>– *Long Extension*: upon request<br>**(6) As a Facilitator of Implementation**<br>– *Specification*: prescribed period<br>– *Periodic Review*: fixed frequency<br>– *Under Surveillance*: after a fixed period<br>**(7) As a Response to Change in Law**<br>– *Transition to New Institutional Frameworks*: prescribed period (co-existence); prescribed date (termination)<br>– *Exception/Exemption for New Legal Rules*: on the date of the Agreement (historical preferences); prior to entry into force of the Agreement (predated advantages) | – *Requirement of Procedures*:<br>no limitation on rights<br>no additional/amplified requirement on obligations<br>no preclusion of evidence<br>– *Reference for Factual Determination*:<br>not decisive for proper reasoning<br>not appropriate to make an *a priori* choice or find a correlation |

Section 6.3 addresses the contribution of temporal rules to the theoretical framework of legalization, positioning temporal rules as foundational to legalization. It refers back to the four-dimensional framework of legalization discussed at the beginning of this book (Section 1.4): the *strength* of IL (*i.e.*, precision, obligation, and delegation) and the *effect* of IL (*i.e.*, implementation). It relies on the overall observations and results in the preceding Chapters to draw a closer connection between the temporal rules and each of the four dimensions of legalization in the context of WTO Law. In doing so, it illustrates how temporal rules are relevant to the theoretical framework of legalization.

In terms of the *strength* of WTO Law, at the theoretical level, temporal rules may be perceived as "internal standards" in WTO Law to orderly arrange legal events by signaling *when, how long*, and *how often* the events should exist or happen. At the practical level, they may be further developed as temporal "indicators" in line with the characteristics and elements established in the existing literature on indicators as standard-setting instruments for global governance. To link the idea of temporal "indicators" with each of the three dimensions concerning the *strength* of WTO Law, this research proposes its contributions as follows: (1) the dimension of *precision*: to name temporal rules for the purpose of producing knowledge (*e.g.*, six categories of temporal rules in Chapter 3), and then be able to simplify them as "default rules of guidance;" (2) the dimension of *obligation*: to establish an ordinal structure for a set of rules or commitments for the purpose of making a comparison within or across different legal regimes (*e.g.*, temporal events association in Chapter 4), and then be able to evaluate the recurring elements for future considerations; and (3) the dimension of *delegation*: to identify the relevant authorities involved in establishing, modifying, and elaborating temporal rules (*e.g.*, systemic mechanisms in Chapter 5), and then be able to reflect on their credibility and impartiality for creating or applying these rules in dynamics.

In terms of the *effect* of WTO Law, at the theoretical level, temporal rules may serve as important elements to "improve compliance" with legal rules. At the practical level, they may enhance the effectiveness of WTO Law by striking a balance between "supporting structure" and "adaptive fluidity" in the legal system. To link temporal rules to the dimension of *implementation* concerning the *effect* of WTO Law, this research firstly draws attention to the broader understanding of the concept of "compliance" (*i.e.*, not limited to legal consequences), and argues in theory that temporal rules *per se* may have the potential to "improve compliance" with WTO Law, owing to their traits as secondary rules of law (Section 6.1) and their functional uses in application (Section 6.2). Secondly, in practice, temporal rules may enhance the "effectiveness" of WTO Law by facilitating the balance between "supporting structure" and "adaptive fluidity" in the legal system. Amid the modern phenomenon of social acceleration and the concept of "dynamic stabilization," maintaining a balance between "supporting structure" and "adaptive fluidity" has become a critical issue for ensuring the effectiveness of a legal system. Accordingly, this research observes the potential capacity of temporal rules to strike the balance within the legal system, which are: (1) *supporting structure*: the potential effect of temporal rules to stabilize expectations or create stickiness on legal events by temporal ordering or structuring (Chapter 4); and (2) *adaptive fluidity*: the systemic mechanisms supporting the development of temporal rules to ensure flexibility and adaptability to new conditions by reshaping temporal order or structure (Chapter 5).

CHAPTER 7

# Conclusion

While recognizing the rising interest in temporal issues (or "time") in the WTO, most of the existing discussions seem to center around the challenges and *problem-solving* strategies in WTO practice, such as the problem of delay, the lack or conflict of time regulation, and the innovation of time management. However, from a *purpose-finding* perspective, this book maintains that the ever-present time elements in legal texts (*i.e.*, temporal rules) still pass unnoticed from a systematic or theoretical point of view (Section 1.1). For this reason, this book carefully *observes* and *classifies* temporal rules in the twenty agreements of WTO Law (Section 1.2). The aim is to explore the universe of temporal rules in WTO Law by defining and investigating their existence and formation to raise sufficient awareness of the intellectual theme on the role of time in law (Section 1.3). Most importantly, this book provides a brand-new angle of thinking about the theoretical framework of legalization in the field of IL/IR (Section 1.4).

Before proceeding to the main course of this book, the topic of the "Time and Law" in Chapter 2 draws upon the disciplines of (1) law, (2) IL/IR, and (3) computer science (natural language processing) to establish a special research territory. As a result of the integration of diverse literature in different disciplines, this book positions itself to the following three research tactics: First, it explores the role of time in WTO Law through one of the four lenses of legal studies, *i.e.*, how law *uses* time to regulate legal events (*cf.*, the other three lenses: law *embedded* in time, law *explained* in time, and law *makes* time) (Section 2.1). Second, it investigates temporal rules not only statically within WTO legal texts but also dynamically in WTO practice (Section 2.2). Third, it develops a temporal-event taxonomy in the (international) legal domain by systematically extracting and categorizing temporal rules and related events from WTO legal texts through careful and close reading (Section 2.3). In addition to these three research tactics, WTO Jurisprudence provides useful guidance to generate an initial blueprint for the identification of temporal rules in WTO Law (Section 2.4). Generally speaking, this book posits that the broad effort to systemically observe and classify temporal rules in legal texts and practice can be crucial for building up a system of thought in the underexplored research territory of "Time and Law."[1]

1 As Bowker and Star stated, "[p]eople often cannot see what they take for granted until they encounter someone who does not take it for granted." Geoffrey C Bowker and Susan Leigh Star, *Sorting Things Out: Classification and Its Consequences* (The MIT Press 2000), 291.

 | DOI:10.1163/9789004745629_008

As for the main course of this book, referring back to its initial orientation in Section 1.5, this book aims to examine (1) how temporal rules (Chapter 3) and their associated legal events (Chapter 4) can be categorized in order to provide a preliminary temporal-event taxonomy for the (international) legal domain; (2) how temporal rules are subject to change and interpretation over time in practice (Chapter 5) in order to acknowledge their fluidity in balancing static expectation with dynamic adaptation in the legal system; and (3) how temporal rules are designed and applied in order to understand their potential significance in laying the foundations for the theoretical framework of legalization (Chapter 6).

## 7.1 Temporal-Event Taxonomy in the (International) Legal Domain

Chapter 3 sets out a taxonomy for six categories of temporal rules in WTO Law (Section 3.1), namely, *point in time, timing, frequency in time, period in time, sequence in time, and conceptual expression in time*. In addition to the "numerical expressions" of temporal rules with a *fixed* value (*e.g.*, 1 January 1995, annual, or five years), this book draws special attention to the "non-numerical expressions" of time in legal texts. These "non-numerical expressions" of temporal rules can be varied and expressed by (1) a *prescribed* or *unspecified* value (*e.g.*, "the date to be determined by Ministers" or "the date of entry into force"); (2) the *moment* or *possibility* of an event (*e.g.*, "upon acceptance" or "at any time"); (3) a *consecutive* or *simultaneous* order (*e.g.*, "after" or "at the same time"); and (4) a *speed* or *degree* modifier (*e.g.*, "immediate" or "temporary").

Apart from the categorization of temporal rules, this book conducts quantitative reseach (Section 3.2) and finds that the overall density of temporal rules to be about 2 % (*i.e.*, one temporal rule within 50 words of the legal texts), and about a quarter of them are *period in time* (25.1 %). Besides, the results suggest that the WTO agreements with a higher density of temporal rules tend to contain more *period in time*. This may be due to the fact that *period in time* does not often stand alone and usually conjoins with several other temporal rules to form a complex temporal events nexus in legal context. Last but not least, the high proportion of "non-numerical expressions" of temporal rules cannot be neglected, prompting further inquiry into the relevant *legal events* and the *authorities* involved in shaping legal content.

Drawing on the above observations of temporal rules in WTO Law, Chapter 4 takes a step further to construct a 2-D model with the intention of capturing the "temporal events association" in WTO legal texts, namely, the association among temporal rules, main events, and supporting events. This 2-D model may serve as a valuable analytical tool for revealing the role of time in relation to WTO legal content (Section 4.1), Despite the ambitious and diverse nature of WTO Law, it is still possible to classify legal events into sixteen distinct *event-types* listed as follows:

- Eight types of substantive events:
  DEFINITION, METHOD, OBJECTIVE, INSTITUTION, SUBSTANCE, ORDER, APPLICATION, and EFFECT (Section 4.2)
- Eight types of procedural events:
  DISCUSSION, NOTIFICATION, EXPRESSION, ACCEPTANCE, REVIEW, DECISION, IMPLEMENTATION, and MODIFICATION (Section 4.3)

In sum, the effort to frame temporal rules alongside sixteen *event-types* introduces a 2-D model for conceptualizing the "temporal events association" inherent in WTO Law. Through this 2-D model, analysis can progress from examining the complex nature of legal content to a more straightforward assessment of the quantitative distribution of the "temporal events association" across various agreements (Section 4.4). Section 4.5 presents *a 16 × 16 matrix* which captures the overall temporal events association in the twenty agreements of WTO Law (Table 4.20). It offers a preliminary prototype for establishing a temporal-event taxonomy within the (international) legal domain.

## 7.2 Fluid Temporal Rules in Practice

Following the construction of a *static* 2-D model representing the "temporal events association" embedded in WTO legal texts, Chapter 5 demonstrates how temporal rules can also be *dynamic* and subject to change in WTO practice.[2] This book identifies nine systemic mechanisms for change in the WTO (Figure 5.1), namely: *negotiation, accession, waiver, amendment, decision, recommendation, rules of procedure* (or *working procedures/working practices*), *dispute settlement report*, and *declaration* (or *mutual agreement/joint request of the parties*). It should be noted that this book does not examine in detail the issues typically associated with the legal effects of each mechanism under varying circumstances. Instead, it focuses on how *fluid* or *dynamic* the six categories of temporal rules could be in real cases (Sections 5.1 to 5.6). It provides a systemic overview to enhance understanding of the "organic or incremental change" of rules within the WTO legal system over time. To be more specific, this book highlights thirty-three representative cases that have contributed

2 As Slaughter also argued, "[b]est practices are never static; they are instead subject to constant improvement through experimentation." Anne-Marie Slaughter, *A New World Order* (4th edition, Princeton University Press 2005), 193.

to the establishment, modification, and elaboration of temporal rules in WTO Law (Figure 5.2). Section 5.7 provides a summary of all the modalities of fluid temporal rules over time, and argues that temporal rules can be relevant not only because of the *static* expectations established in WTO legal texts (*i.e.*, the 2-D temporal events association). The relevance of temporal rules also stems from their fluid character, which enables *dynamic* adaptation to the changing environment in WTO practice (*i.e.*, the 3-D systemic infrastructure).

## 7.3 Temporal Rules as the Foundations of Legalization

Putting the static 2-D temporal events association and the dynamic 3-D systemic infrastructure together, Chapter 6 proposes a new angle for approaching the theoretical framework of legalization in IL/IR (Figure 6.1). It explores the implications of temporal rules within a broader process, including: (1) *making* temporal rules: seven strategic assumptions for their rational design in WTO legal texts; (2) *applying* temporal rules: three interpretative approaches in relation to establishing dynamic legitimacy in WTO practice; and (3) the contribution to *the theoretical framework of legalization*: the role of temporal rules in regards to the *strength/effect* of WTO Law.

First, in terms of *making* temporal rules (Section 6.1), temporal rules can be viewed as operating as "secondary rules of law." They establish specific temporal criteria that serve as one of the "appropriate" means to determine the primary rules governing actions or behaviors. In this regard, this book identifies seven strategic assumptions concerning the rational design of temporal rules in WTO Law, which may be of interest to future studies within single or multiple treaty regimes (Table 6.2).

- As a benchmark for calculation or evaluation
- As a means of regulating the proceedings
- As a means of balancing the interests of the measures
- As a facilitator of transparency and notification
- As a tactic of special and differential treatment
- As a facilitator of implementation
- As a response to change in law

Second, in terms of *applying* temporal rules (Section 6.2), this book relies on the notion that shared understandings of temporal rules can be built upon in WTO practice. It sheds light on the "dynamic legitimacy" of temporal rules in use. Especially, this book outlines three interpretative approaches employed by WTO adjudicators in accordance with the rules of interpretation set forth in the VCLT (Table 6.2), which are:

- *Explicit temporal rules*: They are often interpreted by relying on the ordinary meaning of the literal words to ascertain their scope or intent.
- *Implicit temporal rules*: They may be inferred from the relevant context, the object and purpose, or general principles of law (*i.e.*, the principle of due process or the principle of good faith).
- *No temporal rule by default*: It may be read as intentional and be interpreted openly with caution.

As a result, temporal rules are not merely seen as a matter of strategical design in WTO legal texts. Through application and interpretation in WTO practice, adjudicators may further establish the legal relevance of temporal rules beyond the static wording of legal texts.

Third, in terms of the contribution to *the theoretical framework of legalization* (Section 6.3), this book integrates the findings on temporal rules from the earlier Chapters into the four-dimensional framework of legalization in IL/IR, concerning the *strength/effect* of WTO Law. It demonstrates how temporal rules may lay the foundations for legalization under each of its four dimensions:

*The* ***Strength*** *of WTO Law*
- *Precision*: One may *name* temporal rules as the internal "indicators" of law to produce knowledge in analyzing particular temporal criteria for relevant conducts (*e.g.*, six categories of temporal rules in Chapter 3), and then be able to *simplify* them as "default rules of guidance."
- *Obligation*: One may establish an *ordinal structure* for a set of rules or commitments to make a comparison within or across different legal regimes (*e.g.*, the 2-D temporal events association in Chapter 4), and then be able to *evaluate* the recurring elements of legal content in various (international) legal settings.
- *Delegation*: One may identify the relevant *authorities* involved in establishing, modifying, and elaborating temporal rules (*e.g.*, the 3-D systemic infrastructure in Chapter 5), and then be able to reflect on the *credibility* or *impartiality* of the relevant authorities to confront different changes in the (international) legal system.

*The* ***Effect*** *of WTO Law*
- *Implementation*: One may regard the traits of temporal rules as "secondary rules of law" (Section 6.1) and acknowledge their broad interpretative space in practice (Section 6.2). In doing so, one may further consider the role of temporal rules to "improve compliance" with WTO Law, and then be able to direct the attention to the "effectiveness" of WTO Law. This book argues for the potential of temporal rules to strike

> a balance between (1) *supporting structure*: to stabilize expectations or create stickiness on legal events by temporal ordering or structuring (Chapter 4); and (2) *adaptive fluidity*: to ensure flexibility and adaptability to new conditions by reshaping temporal order or structure through diverse systemic mechanisms (Chapter 5).

Taken together, this book puts forward a sophisticated analysis of the ways in which temporal rules can influence and support all dimensions of the legalization framework. It lays the theoretical and empirical groundwork for the studies of IL/IR, combining insights from the disciplines of (1) law, (2) IL/IR, and (3) computer science (*i.e.*, natural language processing). This book will close by turning to the broader relevance of the current findings in this research. Although this research is specific to WTO Law, its findings would have implications for a large variety of IL. In other words, although this groundwork research on temporal rules focuses only on WTO Law, it would provide theoretical value beyond the specific international trade regime. Especially, it has built up a common analytical model for the categorization of temporal rules and their associated legal events. It widens our understanding of temporal rules by identifying their strategic assumptions under rational design as well as tracking their establishment, modification, and elaboration via diverse systemic mechanisms leading to different legitimate outcomes. This book refines the theoretical framework of legalization and makes a valuable contribution to enhancing our understandings of time elements in law.

For future research, more methodological work is required on how to robustly capture temporal rules and events across different legal regimes. Could the manual identification of regular temporal rules in this book be applied on machine-learning tools? In other words, would these current findings be relevant or be useful for the development of machines for the (international) legal domain?[3] Moreover, the limitations of analyzing temporal rules in a specific issue area on international trade are that the implications provided here may be greater in some issue areas than in others. From a perspective of procedural

3 *E.g.*, Megan Ma and others, 'Deconstructing Legal Text: Object-Oriented Design in Legal Adjudication' (2020) MIT Computational Law Report, 11, https://law.mit.edu/pub/deconstructinglegaltext/release/1 (last visited 5 June 2025). ("In this futuristic construct, lawmakers would only be required to set general policy objectives. Machines would bear the responsibility to examine its application in all possible contexts, creating a depository of legal rules that best achieve such an objective. The legal rules generated would then be converted into micro-directives that subsequently regulate how actors should comply with the law.") *See also* Anthony Casey and Anthony Niblett, 'The Death of Rules and Standards' (2017) 92 Indiana Law Journal 1401.

rules, as Rosa found, some processes are more "speedable" or can easily be accelerated in time (*e.g.*, economic transactions, scientific progress, and technological innovations) than others (*e.g.*, the workings of political democracy and cultural reproduction).[4] For this reason, since the notion of temporal rules is established in the context of WTO Law, would the current findings be more *rationalist-oriented* towards time due to the nature of the specific issue of trade? Last but not least, in the issue area of human rights, there is an urge to reconceptualize human rights as "procedural norms" (or the so-called "proceduralization") to be applied in a more specific manner.[5] In this regard, would temporal rules be one of the important elements to be reckoned in the "proceduralization" of human rights? That is, would temporal rules also be one of the topical issues for the discussions on time and international human rights law?[6] These and other interesting questions remain to be studied in greater detail.

---

4 Hartmut Rosa, 'De-Synchronization, Dynamic Stabilization, Dispositional Squeeze: The Problem of Temporal Mismatch' in Judy Wajcman and Nigel Dodd (eds), *The Sociology of Speed: Digital, Organizational, and Social Temporalities* (Oxford University Press 2016), 35–36.

5 Jan Klabbers, *International Law* (2nd edition, Cambridge University Press 2017), 127. (To construe a set of procedural obligations, "the court does not need to take a stand on the great and controversial moral issues involving life.")

6 *See generally* Kathryn McNeilly and Ben Warwick (eds), *The Times and Temporalities of International Human Rights Law* (Bloomsbury Publishing 2022). ("The book explores how time and its diverse forms can be understood to operate on, and in, this area of law; how time manifests in the theory and practice of human rights law internationally; and how specific areas of human rights can be understood via temporal analyses.")

# Appendix 1. Temporal Cases in WTO Jurisprudence

**1. Temporal Connotation (Chapter 2, Section 2.4)**

| # | Type | Article | Case | Interpretation |
|---|---|---|---|---|
| 1 | Grammatical tense | AG Art. 4.2: the timing to convert measures into ordinary customs duties | AB, *Chile—Price Band System*, para. 206 | Present perfect tense: "have been required;" impose obligations that came into being in the past, but may continue to apply at present |
| 2 | Grammatical tense | SCM Art. 6.2: the relationship between the subsidy and the effect | AB, *US—Upland Cotton*, para. 477 | Present perfect tense: "has not resulted;" some time may have passed between the granting of the subsidy and the demonstration of the absence of its effects |
| 3 | Grammatical tense | TBT Art. 2.4: the usage of relevant international standards as a basis | PR, *EC—Sardines*, para. 7.74 | Present tense: "exist;" oblige to use relevant international standards that currently exist |
| 4 | Grammatical tense | SG Art. 2.1/ GATT Art. XIX:1(a): the timing of the increase in imports | AB, *Argentina—Footwear* (*EC*), para. 130 | Present tense: "is being imported;" necessary to examine "recent" imports |
| 5 | Grammatical tense & Temporal rule | SG Art. 2.1/ GATT Art. XIX:1(a): following the interpretation of "recent" imports in AB, *Argentina—Footwear* (*EC*), para. 130 | PR, *US—Line Pipe*, para. 7.204 | "not long past; that happened, appeared, began to exist, or existed lately;" imply some form of retrospective analysis |
| 6 | Temporal rule: point in time | AG Art. 13(b)(ii): grant support in excess of that decided during "the 1992 marketing year" | Panel Report, *US—Upland Cotton*, para. 7.442 | Define the marketing year for the relevant products as beginning on 1 July and ending on 30 June of the following year |

 | DOI:10.1163/9789004745629_009

(*cont.*)

| # | Type | Article | Case | Interpretation |
|---|---|---|---|---|
| 7 | Temporal rule: timing | DSU Art. 5.3: good offices, conciliation or mediation may be requested and take place "at any time" | AB, *China—HP SSST (Japan) / China—HP SSST (EU)*, fn. 59 | The disputing party suggested a "procedural possibility" to voluntarily participate in a short informal meeting |
| 8 | Temporal rule: timing | DSU Art. 15.2: hold a further interim review meeting "at the request of a party" | PR, *Canada—Continued Suspension*, para. 6.2 | Not for the panel to decide whether holding an interim review hearing would be useful |
| 9 | Temporal rule: timing | GATT Art. XXI:(b)(iii): essential security interests ... taken "in time of" war or other emergency | PR, *Russia—Traffic in Transit*, para. 7.70; PR, *US—Steel and Aluminium Products (Turkey)*, para. 7.155 | Connote a chronological concurrence; create a temporal link between the action and the circumstances |
| 10 | Temporal rule: frequency | CV Art. 5.1(a)(i) and (ii): the commissions "usually" paid, the additions "usually" made, the "usual" costs of transport | PR, *Thailand—Cigarettes (Philippines)*, para. 7.347 | Not necessarily be tied to a particular unit price for the sale |
| 11 | Temporal rule: frequency | SG Art. 7.4: the liberalization of the safeguard measure "at regular intervals" | PR, *Ukraine—Passenger Cars*, para. 7.362 | "recurring or repeated at fixed times, recurring at short uniform intervals;" at equal intervals over the period of application |
| 12 | Temporal rule: period | GATS Art. XX:1(d): the "time-frame" for implementation of commitments | PR, *Mexico—Telecoms*, paras. 7.366 and 7.368 | "a period of time especially with respect to some action or project;" not open-ended |
| 13 | Temporal rule: period | SCM Annex I(j): the "long-term" operating costs and losses of export credit guarantee or insurance programmes | PR, *US—Upland Cotton*, para. 7.832 | Undertake an overall appraisal of the programme over a sufficiently long period of time |

(*cont.*)

| # | Type | Article | Case | Interpretation |
|---|---|---|---|---|
| 14 | Temporal rule: period | ADP Art. 10.6(ii): the injury is caused by massive imports "in a relatively short time" | PR, *US—Hot-Rolled Steel*, para. 7.168 | Massive imports that were not made in *tempore non suspectu* |
| 15 | Temporal rule: period | GATT Art. XI:2: "a previous representative period" for allocation of quota | PR, *EU—Poultry Meat* (*China*), para. 7.349 | "no general rule that applies in all cases regarding the selection of the reference period" |
| 16 | Temporal rule: period | SPS Art. 5.7: review the provisional SPS measure "within a reasonable period of time" | AB, *Japan—Agricultural Products II*, para. 93 | Case-by-case basis |
| 17 | Temporal rule: period | DSU Art. 23.2(b): the reasonable period of time to implement DSB recommendations and rulings | PR, *US—Section 301 Trade Act*, para. 7.38 | "It is for the WTO or both of the disputing parties, through the procedures set forth in Article 21—not for an individual WTO Member—to determine the reasonable period of time for the Member concerned to implement DSB recommendations and rulings" |
| 18 | Temporal rule: period | ADP Art. 2.2.1: provide the recovery of all costs "within a reasonable period of time" | PR, *EC—Salmon* (*Norway*), para. 7.277 | Equivalent to the period of investigation; equated by definition under the express terms |
| 19 | Temporal rule: period | ADP Art. 6.8 and Annex II(1): submit information "within a reasonable period/time" | AB, *US—Hot-Rolled Steel*, para. 84 | Case-by-case basis; a degree of flexibility |
| 20 | Temporal rule: period | SCM Art. 12.7: submit information "within a reasonable period" | PR, *US—Anti-Dumping and Countervailing Duties* (*Korea*), para. 7.351 | Case-by-case basis; a time-limit imposed by an investigating authority does not *ipso facto* constitute a "reasonable period" in all circumstances |

(*cont.*)

| # | Type | Article | Case | Interpretation |
|---|---|---|---|---|
| 21 | Temporal rule: period | DSU Art. 21.3(c) "reasonable period of time" for implementation of the recommendations and rulings; should not exceed "15 months" from the date of adoption of a report | ARB, *US—Washing Machines* (*Article 21.3(c)*), para. 3.7; ARB, *US—Offset Act* (*Byrd Amendment*) (*Article 21.3(c)*), para. 41 | "as short a period as possible when immediate compliance is not practicable;" as "a 'guideline', expressed as a maximum period, and does not represent an average, or usual, period" |
| 22 | Temporal rule: sequence | CV Art. 13: the "final" determination of customs values | PR, *Thailand—Cigarettes* (*Philippines*), para. 7.1034 | Drafters' intention to distinguish final actions from provisional actions |
| 23 | Temporal rule: sequence | DSU Art. 9.3: "harmony the timetable" for the panel process | AB, *EC—Bananas III* (*Article 21.5—Ecuador II*) / *EC—Bananas III* (*Article 21.5—US*), para. 192 | "harmony" does not require that elements coincide exactly in time; not require adoption of identical timetables in multiple proceedings |
| 24 | Temporal rule: sequence | ADP Art. 2.4: compare sales at "as nearly as possible the same time" | PR, *US—Stainless Steel* (*Korea*), para. 6.122 | No obligation to use multiple averaging periods |
| 25 | Temporal rule: sequence | SG Art. 4.2(b): factors other than increased imports are causing injury to the domestic industry "at the same time" | AB, *US—Lamb*, para. 179 | "[Determination] only be made if the injurious effects caused by all the different causal factors are distinguished and separated" |
| 26 | Temporal rule: conceptual expression | DSU Art. 21.3: if it is impracticable to comply "immediately" with the recommendations and rulings | ARB, *US—Offset Act* (*Byrd Amendment*) (*Article 21.3(c)*), para. 40 | "reasonable period of time" for implementation is not available unconditionally |

*(cont.)*

| # | Type | Article | Case | Interpretation |
|---|---|---|---|---|
| 27 | Temporal rule: conceptual expression | SG Art. 12.1: "immediately" notify the Committee on Safeguards | AB, *US—Wheat Gluten*, para. 105 | "a certain urgency;" the degree of urgency or immediacy required depends on a case-by-case assessment |
| 28 | Temporal rule: conceptual expression | GATT Art. X:1: "prompt" publication of trade regulations | PR, *EC—IT Products*, para. 7.1074 | "not an absolute concept, i.e. a pre-set period of time applicable in all cases" |
| 29 | Temporal rule: conceptual expression | GATT Art. X:3(b): "prompt" review and correction of administrative action | AB, *Thailand—Cigarettes* (*Philippines*), para. 203 | "a quick and effective manner and without delay" |
| 30 | Temporal rule: conceptual expression | DSU Art. 21.1: "prompt" compliance with recommendations or rulings of the DSB | ARB, *Chile—Alcoholic Beverages* (*Article 21.3(c)*), para. 38 | "a certain element of flexibility in respect of time is built into the notion of compliance" |
| 31 | Temporal rule: conceptual expression | SCM Art. 4.7: withdraw the prohibited subsidy "without delay" | AB, *Brazil—Taxation*, para. 5.446 | Case-by-case basis; the nature of the measure(s) and the domestic procedures available |
| 32 | Temporal rule: conceptual expression | TRIPS Art. 41.2: procedures concerning the enforcement of intellectual property rights shall not entail "unwarranted delays" | PR, *Canada—Patent Term*, para. 6.117 | "the delays, which are not tied to any valid reason related to the examination and grant process" |
| 33 | Temporal rule: conceptual expression | DSU Art. 12.2: sufficient flexibility while not "unduly delaying" the panel process | AB, *Thailand—Cigarettes* (*Philippines*), para. 150 | a balancing of various interests, including systemic interests as well as those of the parties, and both general and case-specific considerations |
| 34 | Temporal rule: conceptual expression | SPS Annex C(1)(a): undertake and complete approval procedures "without undue delay" | AB, *Australia—Apples*, para. 437 | "not involve periods of time that are unwarranted, or otherwise excessive, disproportionate or unjustifiable" |

(*cont.*)

| # | Type | Article | Case | Interpretation |
|---|---|---|---|---|
| 35 | Temporal rule: conceptual expression | DSU Art. 4.9: a request for the panel to "accelerate" the proceedings | PR, *Canada—Patent Term*, para. 1.5 | "accelerate ... to the greatest extent possible;" "due to other demands on its Members' time, it could not accelerate the timetable prior to the first substantive meeting" |
| 36 | Temporal rule: conceptual expression | DSU Art. 22.8: the suspension of concessions or other obligations shall be "temporary" | AB, *Canada—Continued Suspension*, para. 310 | "an abnormal state of affairs that is *not meant to remain indefinitely"* |
| 37 | Temporal rule: conceptual expression | GATT Art. XI:2(a): export prohibitions or restrictions "temporarily" applied | AB, *China—Raw Materials*, para. 323 | "lasting or meant to last for a limited time only; not permanent; made or arranged to supply a passing need" |
| 38 | Temporal rule: intrinsic concept | SG Art. 4.1(b): serious injury that is clearly "imminent" | AB, *US—Lamb*, para. 125 | "a high degree of likelihood that the anticipated serious injury will materialize *in the very near future*" |
| 39 | Temporal rule: intrinsic concept | ADP Art. 3.7: the dumping would cause material injury must be clearly unforeseen and "imminent" | PR, *US—Softwood Lumber VI*, para. 7.58. | Evaluate "how the future will be different from the immediate past" |
| 40 | Temporal rule: intrinsic concept | TRIPS Art. 50.3: the infringement of the applicant's rights is "imminent" | PR, *India—Solar Cells*, para. 7.260 | "'impending, soon to happen;" pass a higher threshold than one of mere possibility |

## 2. Making Temporal Rules (Chapter 6, Section 6.1)

| # | Type | Article | Case | Interpretation |
|---|---|---|---|---|
| 1 | Benchmark | AG Art. 13(b)(ii): the reference period for the *de minimis* level of domestic support measures | PR, *US—Upland Cotton*, para. 7.438. | "during the 1992 marketing year;" "a very specific limitation on the establishment of the benchmark" |

(*cont.*)

| # | Type | Article | Case | Interpretation |
|---|---|---|---|---|
| 2 | Benchmark | AG Annex 3, para. 9: the reference period for calculation of the fixed external reference price | AB, *Korea—Various Measures on Beef*, paras. 117–118 | "the years 1986 to 1988" |
| 3 | Benchmark | AG Annex 5: the reference period for the price gap calculation for tariff equivalents | ARB, *EC—The ACP-EC Partnership Agreement, paras. 82–83.* | "the most recent representative reference period;" "minimize the need for ad hoc adjustments to be made to the data and corresponds as closely as possible to the trade regime as applied" |
| 4 | Benchmark | Paragraph 6 of *Understanding on Art. XXVIII*: the reference period for calculation of future trade prospects | PR, *EU—Poultry Meat* (*China*), para. 7.272 | the most recent period/year preceding "the initiation of the negotiations" rather than "the conclusion of the negotiations;" "[the] use of a continually moving benchmark as the basis for negotiations could perpetuate negotiations indefinitely" |
| 5 | Benchmark | ADP Art. 2: the reference period for determination of dumping | AB, *EC—Tube or Pipe Fittings*, para. 80 | "the standardized reliance on a [period of investigation], although not fixed in duration by the [Anti-Dumping Agreement], assures the investigating authority and exporters of a consistent and reasonable methodology for determining present dumping" |
| 6 | Benchmark | SCM Art. 2.1(c): the reference period for the determination of *de facto* specificity | PR, *US—Countervailing Measures* (*China*) (*Article 21.5—China*), para. 7.272 | "the length of time during which the subsidy programme has been in operation;" as a safeguard that keeps in check the flexibility |

(*cont.*)

| # | Type | Article | Case | Interpretation |
|---|---|---|---|---|
| 7 | Benchmark | SPS Art. 6.3: the assessment of the effectiveness of the control measures of a disease | PR, *Russia—Pigs (EU)*, para. 7.411; AB, *Russia—Pigs (EU)*, paras. 5.83 and 5.86 | "One useful element for the assessment of the effectiveness of these control measures, to the extent it is available, is data regarding the actual spread of a disease within a given time frame." |
| 8 | Proceedings | DSU Art. 3.3: the principle of "prompt" settlement of disputes | *e.g.*, AB, *US—Upland Cotton (Article 21.5—Brazil)*, para. 246 | the objective of the DSU to promote "prompt settlement" |
| 9 | Proceedings | ADP Art. 5.10: the time-limit for investigation | PR, *Pakistan—BOPP Film (UAE)*, para. 7.471 | "in no case more than 18 months;" preserve predictability |
| 10 | Proceedings | ADP Art. 6.1.1, first sentence/ SCM Art 12.1.1: the time-limit for questionnaire responses | AB, *US—Hot-Rolled Steel*, para. 73 | "in the interest of orderly administration investigating authorities do, and indeed must establish such deadlines" |
| 11 | Proceedings | ADP Annex II(6): the time-limit for submission of explanations | PR, *Egypt—Steel Rebar*, para. 7.282 | "within a reasonable period;" balance the need to provide an adequate period |
| 12 | Proceedings | ADP Art. 6.8: the time-limit for submission of necessary information | AB, *US—Hot-Rolled Steel*, para. 77 | "if information is, in fact, supplied 'within a reasonable period', the investigating authorities cannot use facts available, but must use the information submitted by the interested party" |

(*cont.*)

| # | Type | Article | Case | Interpretation |
|---|---|---|---|---|
| 13 | Proceedings | SCM Art. 12.1.1: the time-limit for questionnaire responses | PR, *US—Anti-Dumping and Countervailing Duties (Korea)*, para. 7.351 | "the mere fact that information is provided after the expiry of such time-limits does not, without more, establish that the information was not provided within a 'reasonable period' under Article 12.7 of the SCM Agreement" |
| 14 | Measure | SG Art. 12.3: sufficient time for prior consultation of safeguard measures with Members affected | AB, *US—Wheat Gluten*, para. 136 | "sufficient information and time to allow for the possibility, through consultations, for a meaningful exchange on the issues identified" |
| 15 | Measure | TBT Art. 2.12: a reasonable interval between publication and entry into force of technical regulations | AB, *US—Clove Cigarettes*, para. 274 | "carefully balances the interests of. … the exporting Member whose producers might be affected by a technical regulation and … the importing Member that wishes to pursue a legitimate objective through a technical regulation" |
| 16 | Measure | TRIPS Art. 33: the duration of the patent protection | AB, *Canada—Patent Term*, para. 92 | "[t]he opportunity to obtain a twenty-year term must be a readily discernible and specific right, and it must be clearly seen as such by the patent applicant when a patent application is filed" |

*(cont.)*

| # | Type | Article | Case | Interpretation |
|---|---|---|---|---|
| 17 | Measure | ADP Art. 11.2: the timing to review the need for the continued imposition of the anti-dumping duty | AB, *Mexico—Anti-Dumping Measures on Rice*, para. 314 | "(i) the passage of a reasonable period of time since imposition of the definitive duty; and (ii) the submission by the interested party of 'positive information' substantiating the need for a review" |
| 18 | Transparency | GATT Arts. X:1 and X:2: prompt publication of new measures | AB, *US—Countervailing and Anti-Dumping Measures (China)*, para. 4.65; AB, *US—Underwear*, p. 21 | "traders ... have time to become acquainted with, and to adapt to, the new measures;" "have a reasonable opportunity to acquire authentic information about [the new] measures" |
| 19 | Transparency | GATT Art. XIX:2: the timing of notification for safeguard measures | PR, *Dominican Republic—Safeguard Measures*, paras. 7.433 and 7.438 | "as far in advance as may be practicable;" before the measure is applied but not necessarily before it is adopted |
| 20 | S & DT | SPS Art. 14: delay application of the provisions of the SPS Agreement | AB, *EC—Hormones*, fn. 99 | "where such application is prevented by lack of technical expertise, technical infrastructure or resources" |
| 21 | Implementation | GATS Art. XX:1(d): the specification of the time-frame for implementation of commitments | PR, *Mexico—Telecoms*, para. 7.368 | not "allow a window of discretion with regard to temporal aspects of these commitments that could erode the practical value of a commitment" |
| 22 | Implementation | GATT Art. XVIII:12(c)(ii): the conformity with the legal provisions "within a specified period" | PR, *India—Quantitative Restrictions*, para. 5.227 | provide "for a period of time to be granted to the Member in order to implement the requirement to remove or modify the inconsistent measures" |

(*cont.*)

| # | Type | Article | Case | Interpretation |
|---|---|---|---|---|
| 23 | Change | GATT Art. V:6: maintain pre-existing direct consignment commitments | PR, *Colombia—Ports of Entry*, para. 7.466 | "existed in 1947 (when commitments among Members were negotiated) without violating the obligation in the first sentence" |

**3. Applying Temporal Rules: Explicit Temporal Rules (Chapter 6, Section 6.2.1)**

| # | Type | Article | Case | Interpretation |
|---|---|---|---|---|
| 1 | Application of Legal Rules | ADP Art. 18.3: the Anti-Dumping Agreement in general, Arts. 9.3 and 11.3 in particular (investigations and reviews of existing measures) | PR, *US—DRAMS*, para. 6.14 | "on or after the date of entry into force;" only "post-WTO reviews" |
| 2 | Application of Legal Rules | SCM Art. 32.3: the SCM Agreement in general, Art. 21.3 in particular (investigations and reviews of existing measures) | AB, *Brazil—Desiccated Coconut*, p. 18 | "on or after the date of entry into force;" avoid uncertainty, unpredictability, and unfairness |
| 3 | Application of Legal Rules | SCM Art. 27.2(b): the end date of transitional period for developing countries to apply Art. 3.1(a) | PR, *India—Export Related Measures*, para. 7.39 | "eight years from the date of entry into force;" "running from 1 January 1995 to 1 January 2003" |
| 4 | Application of Legal Rules | TRIPS Art. 65.4: the end date of transitional period for developing countries to apply the provisions on product patent protection of Section 5 of Part II | PR, *India—Patents (US)*, para. 7.27 | "five years from the entry into force of the WTO Agreement" as to "1 January 2000;" "an additional period of five years" as "until 1 January 2005" |
| 5 | Scope of Measures | TRIPS Art. 33: the term of protection of a patent | AB, *Canada—Patent Term*, paras. 85 and 95 | "twenty years;" very little interpretative difficulty; straightforward and mandatory |

(*cont.*)

| # | Type | Article | Case | Interpretation |
|---|---|---|---|---|
| 6 | Scope of Measures | SCM Arts. 17.3 and 17.4: apply provisional measures | PR, *US—Softwood Lumber III*, para. 7.100 | not be applied "sooner than 60 days" after initiation and their application shall be limited to maximum "four months;" unambiguous and non-retroactive |
| 7 | Scope of Measures | SCM Art. 20.6: retroactively apply definitive duties | PR, *US—Softwood Lumber III*, para 7.97 | allow for the retroactive application; the principle of effective treaty interpretation |
| 8 | Scope of Measures | GATT Art. XIII:3(b): quota allocation | PR (GATT), *EEC—Restrictions on Imports of Dessert Apples—Complaint by Chile*, L/6491–36S/93, para. 12.26 | quotas "during a specified future period;" no backdated quota |
| 9 | Scope of Measures | SPS Annex B(2); (5)(a), (b), and (d): publication and entry into force of SPS regulations | PR, *India—Agricultural Products*, paras. 7.758, 7.784, 7.790, and 7.796 | failure to comply: "a reasonable interval" between publication and entry into force; notification "at an early stage;" allow "reasonable time" for comment |
| 10 | Requirement of Procedures | SCM Art. 11.11: the time-limit for investigation | PR, *Mexico—Olive Oil*, para. 7.121 | "in no case more than 18 months;" clear and unequivocal; no prolongation |
| 11 | Requirement of Procedures | ADP Art. 5.10: the time-limit for investigation | PR, *Pakistan—BOPP Film (UAE)*, para. 7.471 | "in no case more than 18 months;" preserve predictability |
| 12 | Requirement of Procedures | DSU Art. 4.7: consultation before the request of the panel establishment | PR, *Turkey—Textiles*, para. 9.24 | "60 days;" ascertain whether the period has lapsed |

(*cont.*)

| # | Type | Article | Case | Interpretation |
|---|---|---|---|---|
| 13 | Requirement of Procedures | DSU Art. 16.4 the time-limit for the adoption or appeal of the panel report | AB, *EC—Sardines*, para. 147 | "60 days;" reject the conditional withdrawal and the new notice of appeal |
| 14 | Requirement of Procedures | DSU Arts. 12.8, 12.9, and 20: the time-limits for dispute settlement proceeding | PR, *US—Section 301 Trade Act*, para. 7.31 | "six months", "nine months", "12 months", etc.; minimum time-limits without ceilings or maximum time-limits that are indicative only |

**4. Applying Temporal Rules: Implicit Temporal Rules (Chapter 6, Section 6.2.2)**

| # | Type | Article | Case | Interpretation |
|---|---|---|---|---|
| 1 | Definition | ADP Art. 11.2: "continued" imposition of anti-dumping duties | PR, *US—DRAMS*, para. 6.27 | "a temporal relationship between past and future" |
| 2 | Definition | GATT Art. XIX:1(a): "unforeseen" development for the increase in imports | AB, *Argentina—Footwear (EC)*, para. 96 | development must have been unforeseen "at the time when the concession was negotiated" |
| 3 | Definition | SCM Art. 21.1: countervailing duties "remain in force" only as long as necessary | PR, *Japan—DRAMS (Korea)*, para. 7.350 | "as imposing disciplines regarding the 'continued application' of countervailing duties, which apply 'after the imposition' thereof" |
| 4 | Definition | SPS Art. 5.7: "insufficiency" of relevant scientific evidence | AB, *Canada—Continued Suspension*, para. 679 | "not a perennial state, but rather a transitory one;" until such time as allowing the performance of a more objective assessment of risk |

(*cont.*)

| # | Type | Article | Case | Interpretation |
|---|---|---|---|---|
| 5 | Nature of Procedures | SCM Art. 15.1 the reference period for determination of injury | PR, *Mexico—Olive Oil*, para. 7.267 | no unlimited discretion; "ensure the comprehensiveness and reliability of the data used as the basis for an injury determination" |
| 6 | Nature of Procedures | SCM Art. 15.2: the reference period of data collection for determination of injury | PR, *EC—Countervailing Measures on DRAM Chips*, para. 7.341 | "the data on which the injury analysis is based should be sufficiently recent in order for this data to be relevant and probative such as to constitute positive evidence of injury caused by subsidized imports" |
| 7 | Nature of Procedures | DSU Art. 9.2: request for separate reports | AB, *US—Offset Act (Byrd Amendment)*, paras. 315–316 | no unlimited discretion; "ensure the 'prompt settlement' of disputes" |
| 8 | Nature of Procedures | SCM Art. 32.6/ADP Art. 18.5: the timing of notifications for countervailing duty/anti-dumping legislation | PR, *US—Customs Bond Directive*, para. 7.283 | within a reasonable time; "in order for any notification to be effective" |
| 9 | Nature of Procedures | SCM Art. 21.2: the reference period for reviewing the need for the continued imposition of the duty | AB, *US—Carbon Steel (India)*, para. 4.530 | include present, retrospective, as well as prospective analysis; the purpose to determine "whether the injury would be likely to continue or recur" |

(*cont.*)

| # | Type | Article | Case | Interpretation |
|---|---|---|---|---|
| 10 | Nature of Procedures | SPS Art. 5.1: conduct risk assessment | PR, *EC—Approval and Marketing of Biotech Products*, para. 7.3030 | "both a risk assessment carried out before the adoption of a particular safeguard measure and a risk assessment carried out after its adoption could 'sufficiently warrant', or 'reasonably support', the maintenance of that measure" |
| 11 | Nature of Procedures | SPS Annex C(1): the relevant period for SPS measures to check and ensure their fulfilment | AB, *Australia—Apples*, para. 436 | measures exist prior to the operation, undertaking or completion of, the relevant procedures; to "check and ensure fulfilment of SPS measures" |
| 12 | Nature of Procedures | SG Art. 4.2(a): evidence for determining a threat of serious injury | AB, *US—Lamb*, para. 137 | evidence from the most recent past; "provide the strongest indication of the likely future state of the domestic industry" |
| 13 | Nature of Procedures | DSU Art. 22.6: assessment of the level of nullification and impairment | ARB, *US—Tuna II (Mexico) (Article 22.6—US)*, para. 4.14 | past practice; usually the period that follows the end of the reasonable period of time |
| 14 | Due Process | DSU Art. 10.2: request to participate as a third party | PR, *EC—Export Subsidies on Sugar* (*Australia*), para. 2.2 | "the DSU leaves panels a margin of discretion to deal, always in accordance with due process, with specific situations that may arise in a particular case and that are not explicitly regulated" |

(*cont.*)

| # | Type | Article | Case | Interpretation |
|---|---|---|---|---|
| 15 | Due Process (constraint) | DSU Art. 7: the timing of objection to the panel's jurisdiction | AB, *US—1916 Act*, para. 54 | "be raised as early as possible and panels must ensure that the requirements of due process are met" |
| 16 | Due Process (constraint) | DSU: the timing for the submission of evidence | AB, *Thailand—Cigarettes (Philippines)*, para. 149; PR, *China—Rare Earths*, para. 7.27 | "at an early stage in panel proceedings;" "could have been submitted earlier and in a manner consistent with due process" |
| 17 | Due Process (constraint) | DSU Art. 13: the timing for filing *amicus curiae* briefs | AB, *EC—Seal Products*, para. 1.15 | deemed the brief inadmissible due to its late filing; "given an adequate opportunity fully to consider any written submission filed with the Appellate Body" |
| 18 | Due Process (constraint) | ADP Art. 6.1.1, second sentence: the extension of the time-limit for questionnaire responses | AB, *Mexico—Anti-Dumping Measures on Rice*, para. 282 | "cannot extend indefinitely;" "limited by the investigating authority's need to 'control the conduct' of its inquiry and to 'carry out the multiple steps' required to reach a timely completion of the proceeding" |
| 19 | Due Process (constraint) | CV Art. 16: the timing for explanation in writing | PR, *Thailand—Cigarettes (Philippines) (Article 21.5—Philippines)*, para. 7.432 | deemed a late explanation to be inconsistent; "an important transparency and due process objective" |
| 20 | Due Process (permission) | DSU Art. 6.2: the temporal qualification of the specific measures at issue identified by the complainant | AB, *US—Zeroing (Japan) (Article 21.5—Japan)*, para. 121 | "the measures enacted subsequent to the establishment of the panel may, in certain limited circumstances, fall within a panel's terms of reference" |

(*cont.*)

| # | Type | Article | Case | Interpretation |
|---|---|---|---|---|
| 21 | Due Process (permission) | DSU Art. 12.3: the timetable for the panel process | AB, *US—Steel Safeguards*, para. 5.3 | the calendar may be changed; due to "a heavy burden on parties in terms of their obligations to make submissions" |
| 22 | Due Process (permission) | DSU Art. 15.1: the time-limit for comments on the descriptive sections of panel's draft report | PR, US—Clove Cigarettes, para. 6.3 | "within a period of time set by the panel;" decided to accept some of the requests for changes to ensure the accuracy of the description of the facts |
| 23 | Due Process (permission) | ADP Art. 2.1: evidence underlying the dumping determination | PR, *Pakistan—BOPP Film (UAE)*, para. 7.59 | "temporal scope [of evidence] is not, alone, dispositive", "must assess the authority's choice ... in light of all the relevant circumstances surrounding the authority's decision at the time" |
| 24 | Due Process (permission) | SCM Art. 7.10: evidence for quantifying the adverse effects determined to exist | ARB, *US—Large Civil Aircraft (2nd complaint) (Article 22.6—US)*, para. 6.65 | took into account post-reference period evidence; "to place as accurate a value as reasonably possible on the adverse effects" |
| 25 | Due Process (permission) | SCM Art. 4: new evidence or allegations | PR, *Canada—Aircraft*, para. 9.74 | "no reason why any such new allegation should necessarily be rejected by the panel as a matter of course, simply because it is submitted after the first substantive meeting with the parties" |

(*cont.*)

| # | Type | Article | Case | Interpretation |
|---|---|---|---|---|
| 26 | Good Faith | DSU Art. 3.10: not withhold arguments until the interim review stage | PR, *US—1916 Act* (*EC*), para. 5.18 | "should not withhold until the interim review stage arguments that they could be legitimately expected to have raised at a much earlier stage of the proceedings" |
| 27 | Good Faith | DSU Art. 3.7: exercise judgement for fruitful action | AB, *EC—Export Subsidies on Sugar*, para. 312 | covers "the entire spectrum of dispute settlement, from the point of initiation of a case through implementation" |
| 28 | Good Faith | SPS Annex C(1)(a): undertake and complete approval procedures "without undue delay" | PR, *EC—Approval and Marketing of Biotech Products*, para. 7.1498 | "essentially as a good faith obligation requiring Members to proceed with their approval procedures as promptly as possible" |

## 5. Applying Temporal Rules: No Temporal Rule by Default (Chapter 6, Section 6.2.3)

| # | Type | Article | Case | Interpretation |
|---|---|---|---|---|
| 1 | Application of Legal Rules | SPS in general, SPS Arts. 5.1 and 5.5 in particular | AB, *EC—Hormones*, para. 128; PR, *EC—Hormones (US)*, para. 8.26 | apply to measures which were enacted before 1995 but which continue to be in force thereafter |
| 2 | Application of Legal Rules | TBT in general | PR, *EC—Sardines*, para. 7.76; AB, *EC—Sardines*, para. 2.11 | apply to technical regulations which were already in force prior to the entry into force of the TBT Agreement |
| 3 | Application of Legal Rules | SCM Art. 5: the causing of adverse effects | AB, *EC and certain member States—Large Civil Aircraft*, para. 686 | apply to the continuing situation of causing adverse effects through the use of the subsidy |

(*cont.*)

| # | Type | Article | Case | Interpretation |
|---|---|---|---|---|
| 4 | Scope of Measures | GATS Art. XVI:2: the temporal qualification inscribed in the market access column of the Schedule | PR, *Mexico—Telecoms*, paras. 7.358 and 7.361 | "temporal elements are not part of the substantive elements that can be market access limitations under [the Article]" |
| 5 | Scope of Measures | GATT Art. III:2: the temporal qualification of "internal charges" | AB, *China—Auto Parts*, para. 162 | "the time at which a charge is collected or paid is not decisive" |
| 6 | Scope of Measures | GATT Art. XIII:4: the timing of quota reallocation | PR, *EU—Poultry Meat* (*China*), para. 7.478 | no specific guidance of "any time frame as to when or how often such reallocation would have to take place, or based on the occurrence of which events" |
| 7 | Requirement of Procedures | DSU Art. 18.2: the timing of the disclosure of written submission available to the public | PR, *Argentina—Poultry Anti-Dumping Duties*, para. 7.15 | nothing in this provision which would impose any limits on rights accruing to Members |
| 8 | Requirement of Procedures | SG Art. 3.1: the timing of publication for investigation report | PR, *Ukraine—Passenger Cars*, para. 7.440 | improper to read a word "promptly" into the text that would add to, and amplify, the basic publication requirement |
| 9 | Requirement of Procedures | DSU Art. 11: evidence to a panel by a party to the dispute | e.g., AB, *Argentina—Textiles and Apparel*, para. 79; AB, *EC—Selected Customs Matters*, para. 188 | no precise deadlines for the presentation of evidence; "A panel is not precluded from assessing a piece of evidence for the mere reason that it pre-dates or post-dates its establishment" |

(*cont.*)

| # | Type | Article | Case | Interpretation |
|---|---|---|---|---|
| 10 | Requirement of Procedures | TBT Art. 2.1: evidence pre-dating the establishment of a panel | AB, *US—Clove Cigarettes*, para. 206 | "Nothing in Article 2.1 enjoins panels from taking into account evidence pre-dating the establishment of a panel to the extent that such evidence informs the panel's assessment of the consistency of the measure at that point in time" |
| 11 | Factual Determination | ADP Art. 3: the reference period for the determination of injury | PR, *Egypt—Steel Rebar*, para. 7.130 | "neither [ADP Arts. 3.1 and 3.5], nor any other provision of [the Anti-dumping Agreement], contains any specific rule as to the time periods to be covered by the injury or dumping investigations, or any overlap of those time periods" |
| 12 | Factual Determination | ADP Art. 11.3: the reference period for the determination of the likelihood of continuation or recurrence of injury | AB, *US—Oil Country Tubular Goods Sunset Reviews*, para. 364 | "determination of injury can be properly reasoned and rest on a sufficient factual basis even though the time-frame for the injury determination is not explicitly mentioned" |
| 13 | Factual Determination | SCM Art. 5: the reference period for the determination of adverse effects | PR, *EC and certain member States—Large Civil Aircraft*, para. 7.1694 | "in the absence of any specific guidance on this issue, the Panel should avoid making an a priori choice of reference period" |

(*cont.*)

| # | Type | Article | Case | Interpretation |
|---|---|---|---|---|
| 14 | Factual Determination | SCM Art. 6.3(c): the reference period for determination of the significant price suppression effect of the subsidy | AB, *US—Upland Cotton (Article 21.5—Brazil)*, para. 392 | "can also be assessed on the basis of a long-term perspective that focuses on how the subsidy affects decisions of producers to enter or exit a given industry" |
| 15 | Factual Determination | SG Art. 5.1: the reference period for calibrating level of safeguard measures | PR, *EU—Safeguard Measures on Steel (Turkey)*, para. 7.257 | "not require that the time periods that are used for setting the level of the safeguard be the same as the period that is used for the injury analysis" |

# Appendix 2. Non-denoted Temporal Information in WTO Law

| Agreements | Non-denoted temporal information |
|---|---|
| MAR | – the General Agreement on Tariffs and Trade *1994* ("GATT *1994*")<br>– the General Agreement on Tariffs and Trade, *dated 30 October 1947* ("GATT *1947*") (Art. II:4)<br>– the *annual* budget (Art. VII:1); the *annual* review (Art. IX:4)<br>– the Convention on the Privileges and Immunities of the Specialized Agencies, approved by the General Assembly of the United Nations *on 21 November 1947* (Art. VIII:4) |
| GATT | – the General Agreement on Tariffs and Trade *1994* ("GATT *1994*")<br>– the General Agreement on Tariffs and Trade, *dated 30 October 1947* ("GATT *1947*")<br>– the Protocol of *Provisional* Application<br>(Para. 1(a) of GATT 1994; GATT Arts. XXIV:1, XXXII:1, Ad Art. 1:1)<br>– Document MTN/FA of *15 December 1993*; MTN/FA/Corr.6 of *21 March 1994*<br>(Fn. 1 of GATT 1994)<br>– the decision … taken *on 26 March 1980* (BISD 27S/24)<br>(Art. 8 of GATT's Understanding on Art. II:1(b))<br>– the questionnaire on state trading adopted *on 24 May 1960* (BISD 9S/184–185)<br>(Art. 3 of GATT's Understanding on Art. XVII)<br>– the Ministerial Decision on Notification Procedures adopted *on 15 April 1994*<br>(Fn. 1 of GATT's Understanding on Art. XVII)<br>– the Declaration on Trade Measures Taken for Balance-of-Payments Purposes adopted *on 28 November 1979* (BISD 26S/205–209, … the '*1979* Declaration')<br>(Preamble of GATT's Understanding on Art. BOP)<br>– the procedures for consultations on balance-of-payments restrictions approved *on 28 April 1970* (BISD 18S/48–53) (Art. 5 of GATT's Understanding on Art. BOP) |

 | DOI:10.1163/9789004745629_010

(*cont.*)

| Agreements | Non-denoted temporal information |
| --- | --- |
| | – the simplified procedures approved *on 19 December 1972* (BISD 20S/47–49) (Art. 8 of GATT's Understanding on Art. BOP) |
| | – *interim* agreement(s) (GATT's Understanding on Art. XXIV) |
| | – the guidelines adopted *on 10 November 1980* (BISD 27S/26–28) (Art. 4 of GATT's Understanding on Art. XXIV) |
| | – "Procedures for Negotiations under Article XXVIII" adopted *on 10 November 1980* s(BISD 27S/26–28) (Art. 2 of GATT's Understanding on Art. XXVIII; Art. 6 of MAR Protocol) |
| | – the screen *time* (GATT Art. IV) |
| | – the Decision of *23 March 1965* (GATT Fns. 2, 3, 5, and 6) |
| | – an *interim* agreement (GATT Art. XXIV:5) |
| | – the Protocol Modifying Part II and Article XXVI of the General Agreement on Tariffs and Trade, *dated September 14, 1948* (GATT Annex I, Ad Art. 1, Para. 1 and Ad Art. II, Para. 2(a)) |
| | – in the *early* stages of development (GATT Art. XVIII:1 and 4(a)) |
| | – in an *early* stage of processing (GATT Annex I, Ad Art. XI, Para. 2(c)) |
| | – the Economic and Social Council in its resolution 30 (IV) of *28 March 1947* (GATT Annex I, Ad Art. XX:(h)) |
| AG | – the *Mid-Term* Review (of the Uruguay Round) (Preamble) |
| | – the "*Annual* and Final Bound Commitment Levels" (Arts. 1(h)(i), 6.1 and 6.3) |
| | – the "*Current* Total AMS" (Arts. 1(h)(ii), 6.2, 6.3, and 6.4) |
| | – GATT *1994* (Arts. 3.1, 5.1, 5.8, 12.1, 13, 19, and 21) |
| | – GATT *1947* (Fn. 1) |
| | – the *Mid-Term* Review Agreement (Art. 6.2) |
| | – the Food Aid Convention *1986* (Art. 10.4(c)) |
| | – *early*-warning systems (Annex 2, Para. 2(b)) |
| | – (*"the base period"*) (Annex 5, Para. 1(a)) |
| SPS | – GATT *1994* (Preamble; Arts. 2.4, 3.2, and 11.1) |
| TBT | – GATT *1994* (Preamble; Art. 14.1) |
| | – the sixth edition of the ISO/IEC Guide 2: *1991* (Annex 1) |

(*cont.*)

| Agreements | Non-denoted temporal information |
|---|---|
| TRIMS | – GATT *1994* (Arts. 2–4, 6.1, 6.3, and 8; Annex)<br>– the Declaration on Trade Measures Taken for Balance-of-Payments Purposes adopted on *28 November 1979* (BISD 26S/205–209) (Art. 4)<br>– the Understanding Regarding Notification, Consultation, Dispute Settlement and Surveillance adopted *on 28 November 1979* (Art. 6.1)<br>– the Ministerial Decision on Notification Procedures adopted *on 15 April 1994* (Art. 6.1) |
| ADP | – GATT *1994* (Arts. 1, 2.7, 3.1, 4.3, 5.2, and 18.1; Fn. 24)<br>– *provisional* (or *final*) measures (Arts.5.7, 6.14, 7, 8.1, 8.6, 10, 12.2, and 17.4)<br>– *preliminary* (or *final*) determinations (Arts. 6.8, 6.14, 7, 10, 12.2, and 13)<br>– *provisional* duty (Arts.7.2 and 10.3)<br>– *final* assessment (Art. 9.3.1)<br>– *final* liability (Art. 9.3.1; Fn. 21)<br>– *preliminary* or *final* (anti-dumping) actions taken (Arts. 16.4 and 17.4)<br>– the *semi-annual* reports (Art. 16.4) |
| CV | – GATT *1994* (Preamble; Arts. 7.1 and 12)<br>– the *usual* costs of transport and insurance (Art. 5.1(ii))<br>– the procès-verbal of rectification of *23 September 2014* (WT/Let/986) (Fn. 1)<br>– the *final* determination of such customs value (Art. 13)<br>– the Agreement on Implementation of Article VII of the General Agreement on Tariffs and Trade done on *12 April 1979* (Arts. 20.1 and 20.2)<br>– a *sequential* order of application/in a *sequence*/the normal order of the *sequence* (Annex 1, Sequential Application of Valuation Methods, Paras. 1–3)<br>– *usual* profit and general expenses (Annex 1, Use of Generally Accepted Accounting Principles, Para. 2; Note to Art. 5, Para. 9)<br>– *usual* pricing policies (Annex 1, Note to Art. 6, Para. 5)<br>– the *final* instance to appeal (Annex 1, Note to Art. 11, Para. 1)<br>– a *provisional* agenda for each session (Annex 2, Para. 12)<br>– the reversal of the *sequential* order (Annex 3, Para. 3) |

(*cont.*)

| Agreements | Non-denoted temporal information |
|---|---|
| PSI | – GATT *1994* (Preamble; Arts. 2.2, 2.6, 7, and 8; Fn. 4)<br>– the *final* documents (Art. 2.16)<br>– a *preliminary* verification of price (Art. 2.17) |
| RO | – GATT *1994* (Preamble; Arts. 1.1, 1.2, 2(g), 3(e), 7, and 8; Fn. 2; Annex II, Paras. 2, 3(c))<br>– the *last* substantial transformation (Art. 3(b) and 9.1(b)) |
| LIC | – GATT *1994* (Preamble; Arts. 1.2, 1.10, and 6)<br>– the Agreement on Import Licensing Procedures done *on 12 April 1979* (Fn. 5)<br>– GATT *1947* document L/3515 of *23 March 1971* (Fn. 7) |
| SCM | – GATT *1994* (Arts. 1.1, 5, 10, 11.2, 15.1, 16.4, 20.6, 25, 26.1, 27.9, 30, and 32.1; Fns. 1, 12, 13, 18, 36, 56, and 59; Annex 1, Para. (l))<br>– the *regular* meeting of the Committee (Arts. 8.4, 26.1 and 26.2)<br>– *provisional* (or *final*) measures (Arts. 11.7, 12.12, 13.3, 17, 18.1, 18.6, 20, 22.4, and 22.5)<br>– *preliminary* (or *final*) determinations (Arts. 12.7, 12.8, 12.12, 13.3, 17, 18.2, 19.1, 20, 22.3, 22.4, and 23; Fn. 44)<br>– *provisional* countervailing duties (Art. 17.2)<br>– *final* legal assessment (Fn. 51)<br>– *preliminary* or *final* actions (Art. 25.11)<br>– *semi-annual* reports (Art. 25.11)<br>– *subsequent* crediting of the tax; *succeeding* stage of production (Fn. 58)<br>– *prior*-stage cumulative indirect taxes (Annex 1, Para. (g); Annex II, Section I)<br>– the *long-term* operating costs and losses of the programmes (Annex 1, Para. (j))<br>– the *final* product (Annex II, Section II, Para. 3) |
| SG | – GATT *1994* (Preamble; Arts. 1, 8.1, 8.2, 11.1, and 14; Fns. 1 and 3)<br>– a *preliminary* determination (Art. 6)<br>– *provisional* measure (Arts. 6 and 7.3)<br>– GATT *1947* (Art. 10)<br>– a *provisional* safeguard measure (Art. 12.4)<br>– the results of *mid-term* reviews (Art. 12.5) |

(*cont.*)

| Agreements | Non-denoted temporal information |
|---|---|
| TFA | – the Decision of the Doha Work Programme adopted by the General Council on *1 August 2004* (WT/L/579) (Preamble)<br>– GATT *1994* (Preamble; Arts. 6.1.1, 7.8.2(d), 20, and 24; Fns. 4 and 23)<br>– an *advance* ruling (Art. 3)<br>– a *second* test/the *first* test (Art. 5.3)<br>– *advance* lodging of documents (Art. 7.1.2)<br>– *final* determination of customs duties, taxes, fees, and charges (Art. 7.3)<br>– the *Time* Release Study of the World Customs Organization (Art. 7.6.1)<br>– such average release *time* measurement (fn. 6)<br>– *expedited* shipments (Art. 7.8)<br>– the *July 2004* Framework Agreement (WT/L/579) (Art. 13.1)<br>– the *first* meeting of the Committee/ the *first* Committee meeting (Art. 18.5) |
| GATS | – GATT *1994* (Fn. 4)<br>– the decision of the arbitrator shall be *final* (Art. XXII:3)<br>– *permanent* residence (Art. XXVIII:(k))<br>– the *final* report of the Negotiating Group on Maritime Transport Services<br>(Annex on Negotiation on Maritime Transport Services, Para. 1(b))<br>– the *real-time* transmission of customer-supplied information (Annex on Telecommunications, Para. 3(b))<br>– the *final* report of the Negotiating Group on Basic Telecommunications<br>(Annex on Negotiation on Basic Telecommunications, Para. 1(b) |
| TRIPS | – GATT *1994* (Preamble; Art. 31bis, Paras. 3 and 4; Art. 64)<br>– the Paris Convention (*1967*) (Arts. 1.3, 2.1, 3.1, 15.2, 16.2, 16.3, 22.2(b), 39.1, 62.3, and 63.2; Fn. 2)<br>– the Stockholm Act of this Convention of *14 July 1967* (Fn. 2)<br>– the Berne Convention (*1971*) (Arts. 1.3, 3.1, 4(b), 9.1, 10.1, 14.3, 14.6, and 70.2; Fn. 2)<br>– the Paris Act of this Convention of *24 July 1971* (Fn. 2)<br>– the International Convention for the Protection of Performers, Producers of Phonograms and Broadcasting Organizations, adopted at Rome *on 26 October 1961* (Fn. 2) |

(*cont.*)

| Agreements | Non-denoted temporal information |
|---|---|
| | – the Treaty on Intellectual Property in Respect of Integrated Circuits, adopted at Washington *on 26 May 1989* (Fn. 2)<br>– the Decision of *28 November 1979* on Differential and More Favourable Treatment Reciprocity and Fuller Participation of Developing Countries (L/4903) (Art. 31bis, Para. 3)<br>– a judicial authority of *final* administrative decisions (Art. 41.4)<br>– *preliminary* and *final* determinations (Art. 43.2)<br>– *provisional* measures (Arts. 50, 55)<br>– *provisional* relief (Art. 53.2)<br>– a *provisional* judicial measure (Art. 55)<br>– *final* administrative decisions (Art. 62.5)<br>– *final* judicial decisions (Art. 63.1) |
| DSU | – GATT *1947* (Arts. 3.1, 3.11, and 8.1)<br>– the *first* objective of the dispute settlement mechanism/the *last* resort (Art. 3.7)<br>– the Decision of *5 April 1966* (BISD 14S/18) (Art. 3.12)<br>GATT *1994* (Arts. 4.11 and 26; Fns. 4 and 10; Appendix 2)<br>– the roster of non-governmental panelists established *on 30 November 1984* (BISD 31S/9) (Art. 8.4)<br>– the *first* meeting of the panel (Art. 10.3)<br>– *first* submission/*sequential* arrangements/*subsequent* written submissions (Art. 12.6)<br>– the *final* (panel) report (Arts. 12.8, 15.2, and 15.3; Appendix 3, Para. 12(j) and (k))<br>– *interim* report (Art. 15.2; Appendix 3, Para. 12(g))<br>– the *interim* review stage (Art. 15.3)<br>– the *current* "Services Sectoral Classification List" (Art. 22.3(f)(ii))<br>– the arbitrator's decision as *final*/a *second* arbitration (Art. 22.7)<br>– *final* settlement of the dispute (Art. 26.1(d))<br>– the Decision of *12 April 1989* (BISD 36S/61–67) (Art. 26.2)<br>– *first* substantive meeting (of the panel) (Appendix 3, Paras. 4–7 and 12)<br>– *second* substantive meeting of the panel (Appendix 3, Paras. 7 and 12)<br>– *first* written submissions of the parties (Appendix 3, Para. 12(a))<br>– the *final* report (of the expert review group) (Appendix 4, Para. 6) |

(*cont.*)

| Agreements | Non-denoted temporal information |
|---|---|
| TPRM | – the Decision of *19 July 1989* (BISD 36S/406–409) (Para. D)<br>– GATT *1994* (Para. E) |
| CA | – Ministers *on 12–14 September 1973* agreed the Tokyo Round of Multilateral Trade Negotiations (Preamble)<br>– *final* resolution of these issues (Art. 8.7)<br>– *provisional* accession (Art. 9.1.2)<br>– the *1992, 1996 and 2002* versions of the Harmonized Commodity Description and Coding System (Preamble of Protocol (2001))<br>– the Protocol (*1986*) Amending the Annex to the Agreement on Trade in Civil Aircraft (Para. 1 of Protocol (2001)) |
| GPA | – a *fixed-term* contract (Art. II:8)<br>– *final* judgments (Art. VIII:4(d))<br>– a *first* good or service (Art. XIII:1(f))<br>– *regular* suppliers (Art. XIII:1(g))<br>– *interim* measures (Art. XVIII:7(a))<br>– the Protocol Amending the Agreement on Government Procurement, adopted *on 30 March 2012* (Art. XXII:7) |

# Appendix 3. The Distribution of Temporal Rules in WTO Law

| Agreement (Number of Temporal Rules) | 1. Period 25.1 % (940) | | | 2. Sequence 21.0 % (784) | | 3. Timing 19.6 % (734) | | 4. Point 18.0 % (674) | | | 5. Concept 12.3 % (459) | | 6. Frequency 4.0 % (150) | |
|---|---|---|---|---|---|---|---|---|---|---|---|---|---|---|
| | F | P | U | C | S | M | P | F | P | U | S | D | F | U |
| 1. SG | 49.0 % | 3.9 % | 47.1 % | 96.6 % | 3.4 % | 100 % | 0.0 % | 10.0 % | 20.0 % | 70.0 % | 33.3 % | 66.7 % | 75.0 % | 25.0 % |
| (138) | (25) | (2) | (24) | (28) | (1) | (10) | (0) | (2) | (4) | (14) | (8) | (16) | (3) | (1) |
| 2. DSU | 57.7 % | 14.6 % | 27.7 % | 95.6 % | 4.4 % | 86.7 % | 13.3 % | 0.0 % | 26.7 % | 73.3 % | 45.5 % | 54.5 % | 20.0 % | 80.0 % |
| (341) | (75) | (19) | (36) | (65) | (3) | (52) | (8) | (0) | (12) | (33) | (15) | (18) | (1) | (4) |
| 3. LIC | 39.3 % | 10.7 % | 50.0 % | 90.0 % | 10.0 % | 90.9 % | 9.1 % | 0.0 % | 5.9 % | 94.1 % | 55.6 % | 44.4 % | 100 % | 0.0 % |
| (78) | (11) | (3) | (14) | (9) | (1) | (10) | (1) | (0) | (1) | (16) | (5) | (4) | (3) | (0) |
| 4. AG | 67.0 % | 22.7 % | 10.2 % | 98.1 % | 1.9 % | 100 % | 0.0 % | 28.4 % | 1.5 % | 70.1 % | 12.5 % | 87.5 % | 92.3 % | 7.7 % |
| (255) | (59) | (20) | (9) | (52) | (1) | (26) | (0) | (19) | (1) | (47) | (1) | (7) | (12) | (1) |
| 5. TPRM | 50.0 % | 25.0 % | 25.0 % | 100 % | 0.0 % | 100 % | 0.0 % | 0.0 % | 50.0 % | 50.0 % | 33.3 % | 66.7 % | 63.6 % | 36.4 % |
| (28) | (2) | (1) | (1) | (5) | (0) | (3) | (0) | (0) | (1) | (1) | (1) | (2) | (7) | (4) |
| 6. RO | 68.4 % | 10.5 % | 21.1 % | 95.7 % | 4.3 % | 90.0 % | 10.0 % | 42.9 % | 0.0 % | 57.1 % | 93.8 % | 6.3 % | 77.8 % | 22.2 % |
| (104) | (13) | (2) | (4) | (22) | (1) | (27) | (3) | (3) | (0) | (4) | (15) | (1) | (7) | (2) |
| 7. TFA | 53.1 % | 10.9 % | 35.9 % | 96.3 % | 3.8 % | 98.0 % | 2.0 % | 0.0 % | 69.2 % | 30.8 % | 57.1 % | 42.9 % | 33.3 % | 66.7 % |
| (310) | (34) | (7) | (23) | (77) | (3) | (48) | (1) | (0) | (36) | (16) | (32) | (24) | (3) | (6) |

 | DOI:10.1163/9789004745629_011

(*cont.*)

| Agreement (Number of Temporal Rules) | 1. Period 25.1 % (940) | | | 2. Sequence 21.0 % (784) | | 3. Timing 19.6 % (734) | | 4. Point 18.0 % (674) | | | 5. Concept 12.3 % (459) | | 6. Frequency 4.0 % (150) | |
|---|---|---|---|---|---|---|---|---|---|---|---|---|---|---|
| | F | P | U | C | S | M | P | F | P | U | S | D | F | U |
| 8. GPA | 42.0 % | 25.0 % | 33.0 % | 87.5 % | 12.5 % | 97.9 % | 2.1 % | 11.9 % | 31.0 % | 57.1 % | 73.3 % | 26.7 % | 81.8 % | 18.2 % |
| (259) | (37) | (22) | (29) | (35) | (5) | (47) | (1) | (5) | (13) | (24) | (22) | (8) | (9) | (2) |
| 9. ADP | 41.9 % | 1.6 % | 56.5 % | 91.1 % | 8.9 % | 98.2 % | 1.8 % | 0.0 % | 6.1 % | 93.9 % | 74.3 % | 25.7 % | 80.0 % | 20.0 % |
| (246) | (26) | (1) | (35) | (51) | (5) | (54) | (1) | (0) | (2) | (31) | (26) | (9) | (4) | (1) |
| 10. CA | 66.7 % | 0 % | 33.3 % | 91.7 % | 8.3 % | 100 % | 0.0 % | 52.2 % | 4.3 % | 43.5 % | 72.7 % | 27.3 % | 60.0 % | 40.0 % |
| (67) | (2) | (0) | (1) | (11) | (1) | (13) | (0) | (12) | (1) | (10) | (8) | (3) | (3) | (2) |
| 11. SCM | 64.6 % | 10.6 % | 24.8 % | 94.9 % | 5.1 % | 96.3 % | 3.7 % | 6.5 % | 3.2 % | 90.3 % | 69.6 % | 30.4 % | 77.8 % | 22.2 % |
| (409) | (73) | (12) | (28) | (75) | (4) | (78) | (3) | (4) | (2) | (56) | (39) | (17) | (14) | (4) |
| 12. GATT | 51.3 % | 24.3 % | 24.3 % | 96.9 % | 3.1 % | 88.4 % | 11.6 % | 41.0 % | 16.5 % | 42.6 % | 47.8 % | 52.2 % | 57.1 % | 42.9 % |
| (664) | (59) | (28) | (28) | (154) | (5) | (99) | (13) | (77) | (31) | (80) | (33) | (36) | (12) | (9) |
| 13. TRIMS | 100 % | 0 % | 0 % | 80.0 % | 20.0 % | 100 % | 0.0 % | 0.0 % | 0.0 % | 100 % | 0.0 % | 100 % | 100 % | 0.0 % |
| (25) | (9) | (0) | (0) | (4) | (1) | (3) | (0) | (0) | (0) | (4) | (0) | (2) | (2) | (0) |
| 14. PSI | 71.4 % | 0 % | 28.6 % | 90.9 % | 9.1 % | 91.7 % | 8.3 % | 22.2 % | 33.3 % | 44.4 % | 70.6 % | 29.4 % | 100 % | 0.0 % |
| (58) | (5) | (0) | (2) | (10) | (1) | (11) | (1) | (2) | (3) | (4) | (12) | (5) | (2) | (0) |
| 15. TRIPS | 60.0 % | 6.7 % | 33.3 % | 100 % | 0.0 % | 94.2 % | 5.8 % | 13.0 % | 0.0 % | 87.0 % | 60.7 % | 39.3 % | 100 % | 0.0 % |
| (238) | (36) | (4) | (20) | (49) | (0) | (49) | (3) | (6) | (0) | (40) | (17) | (11) | (3) | (0) |
| 16. MAR | 45.0 % | 25.0 % | 30.0 % | 100 % | 0.0 % | 100 % | 0.0 % | 22.2 % | 33.3 % | 44.4 % | 50.0 % | 50.0 % | 50.0 % | 50.0 % |
| (73) | (9) | (5) | (6) | (13) | (0) | (23) | (0) | (2) | (3) | (4) | (2) | (2) | (2) | (2) |

(*cont.*)

| Agreement (Number of Temporal Rules) | 1. Period 25.1 % (940) | | | 2. Sequence 21.0 % (784) | | 3. Timing 19.6 % (734) | | 4. Point 18.0 % (674) | | | 5. Concept 12.3 % (459) | | 6. Frequency 4.0 % (150) | |
|---|---|---|---|---|---|---|---|---|---|---|---|---|---|---|
| | F | P | U | C | S | M | P | F | P | U | S | D | F | U |
| 17. TBT | 22.2 % | 11.1 % | 66.7 % | 94.7 % | 5.3 % | 89.6 % | 10.4 % | 25.0 % | 0.0 % | 75.0 % | 87.5 % | 12.5 % | 75.0 % | 25.0 % |
| (109) | (4) | (2) | (12) | (18) | (1) | (43) | (5) | (1) | (0) | (3) | (14) | (2) | (3) | (1) |
| 18. GATS | 69.0 % | 17.2 % | 13.8 % | 100 % | 0.0 % | 97.1 % | 2.9 % | 0.0 % | 31.0 % | 69.0 % | 80.0 % | 20.0 % | 33.3 % | 66.7 % |
| (143) | (20) | (5) | (4) | (29) | (0) | (34) | (1) | (0) | (9) | (20) | (12) | (3) | (2) | (4) |
| 19. CV | 47.6 % | 19.0 % | 33.3 % | 86.5 % | 13.5 % | 90.5 % | 9.5 % | 0.0 % | 16.7 % | 83.3 % | 43.8 % | 56.3 % | 50.0 % | 50.0 % |
| (140) | (10) | (4) | (7) | (32) | (5) | (38) | (4) | (0) | (2) | (10) | (7) | (9) | (6) | (6) |
| 20. SPS | 27.3 % | 9.1 % | 63.6 % | 100 % | 0.0 % | 90.5 % | 9.5 % | 0.0 % | 0.0 % | 100 % | 45.5 % | 54.5 % | 0.0 % | 100 % |
| (56) | (3) | (1) | (7) | (7) | (0) | (19) | (2) | (0) | (0) | (3) | (5) | (6) | (0) | (3) |
| Total | 54.5 % | 14.7 % | 30.9 % | 95.2 % | 4.8 % | 93.6 % | 6.4 % | 19.7 % | 18.0 % | 62.3 % | 59.7 % | 40.3 % | 65.3 % | 34.7 % |
| (3741) | (512) | (138) | (290) | (746) | (38) | (687) | (47) | (133) | (121) | (420) | (274) | (185) | (98) | (52) |

# Bibliography

## Journal Articles and Conference Papers


Abbott KW and others, 'The Concept of Legalization' (2000) 54 International organization 401.

Allen JF, 'Maintaining Knowledge about Temporal Intervals' (1983) 26 Communications of the ACM 832.

Allott P, 'The Concept of International Law' (1999) 10 European Journal of International Law 31.

Alschner W, Pauwelyn J and Puig S, 'The Data-Driven Future of International Economic Law' (2017) 20 Journal of International Economic Law 217.

Altwicker T and Diggelmann O, 'How Is Progress Constructed in International Legal Scholarship?' (2014) 25 European Journal of International Law 425.

Barrozo P, 'Law in Time: Legal Theory and Legal History' (2021) 31 Yale Journal of Law and the Humanities 316.

Basra H, 'Increased Legalization or Politicalization? A Comparison of Accession under the GATT and WTO' (2012) 46 Journal of World Trade 937.

Bender A and Beller S, 'Mapping Spatial Frames of Reference onto Time: A Review of Theoretical Accounts and Empirical Findings' (2014) 132 Cognition 342.

Borgen CJ, 'Resolving Treaty Conflicts' (2005) 37 George Washington International Law Review 573.

Britton-Purdy J and others, 'Building a Law-and-Political-Economy Framework: Beyond the Twentieth Century Synthesis' (2020) 129 Yale Law Journal 1784.

Burley A-MS, 'International Law and International Relations Theory: A Dual Agenda' (1993) 87 American Journal of International Law 205.

Callender C, 'Is Time an ILLUSION?' (2010) 302 Scientific American 58.

Casey A and Niblett A, 'The Death of Rules and Standards' (2017) 92 Indiana Law Journal 1401.

Cohen J, 'A Coefficient of Agreement for Nominal Scales' (1960) 20 Educational and Psychological Measurement 37.

Copelovitch MS and Putnam TL, 'Design in Context: Existing International Agreements and New Cooperation' (2014) 68 International Organization 471.

Czapnik B, 'The Unique Features of the Trade Facilitation Agreement: A Revolutionary New Approach to Multilateral Negotiations or the Exception Which Proves the Rule?' (2015) 18 Journal of International Economic Law 773.

d'Aspremont J, 'The Idea of "Rules" in the Sources of International Law' (2014) 84 British Yearbook of International Law 103.

D'Amato A, 'Groundwork for International Law' (2014) 108 The American Journal of International Law 650.

Davey WJ, 'The Case for a WTO Permanent Panel Body' (2003) 6 Journal of International Economic Law 177.

Djeffal C, 'International Law and Time: A Reflection of the Temporal Attitudes of International Lawyers Through Three Paradigms' (2014) 45 Netherlands Yearbook of International Law 93.

Dowty DR, 'The Effects of Aspectual Class on the Temporal Structure of Discourse: Semantics or Pragmatics?' (1986) 9 Linguistics and Philosophy 37.

Duffield JS, 'The Limits of "Rational Design"' (2003) 57 International Organization 411.

Dyson K, 'The Evolving Timescapes of European Economic Governance: Contesting and Using Time' (2009) 16 Journal of European Public Policy 286.

Ehlermann C-D, 'The Workload of the WTO Appellate Body: Problems and Remedies' (2017) 20 Journal of International Economic Law 705.

Elsig M, 'Legalization in Context: The Design of the WTO's Dispute Settlement System' (2017) 19 The British Journal of Politics and International Relations 304.

Elsig M and Eckhardt J, 'The Creation of the Multilateral Trade Court: Design and Experiential Learning' (2015) 14 World Trade Review 13.

French RR, 'Time in the Law' (2001) 72 University of Colorado Law Review 663.

Gordon G, 'Engaging an Infrastructure of Time Production with International Law' (2021) 9 London Review of International Law 319.

Greenhouse CJ, 'Just in Time: Temporality and the Cultural Legitimation of Law' (1989) 98 Yale Law Journal 1631.

Grimmer J and Stewart BM, 'Text as Data: The Promise and Pitfalls of Automatic Content Analysis Methods for Political Texts' (2013) 21 Political Analysis 267.

Gruber RP, Montemayor C and Block RA, 'From Physical Time to a Dualistic Model of Human Time' (2020) 25 Foundations of Science 927.

Haskell J and Rasulov A, 'International Law and the Turn to Political Economy' (2018) 31 Leiden Journal of International Law 243.

Helfer LR, 'Exiting Custom: Analogies to Treaty Withdrawals' (2010) 21 Duke Journal of Comparative & International Law 65.

Higgins R, 'Time and the Law: International Perspectives on an Old Problem' (1997) 46 The International and Comparative Law Quarterly 501.

Hoffmann S, 'The Study of International Law and the Theory of International Relations' (1963) 57 *Proceedings of the American Society of International Law at Its Annual Meeting (1921–1969)* 26.

Howse R and Nicolaidis K, 'Enhancing WTO Legitimacy: Constitutionalization or Global Subsidiarity?' (2003) 16 Governance 73.

Hulme M, 'Preambles in Treaty Interpretation' (2016) 164 University of Pennsylvania Law Review 1281.

Johannesson L and Mavroidis PC, 'The WTO Dispute Settlement System 1995–2016: A Data Set and Its Descriptive Statistics' (2017) 51 Journal of World Trade 357.

Jørgensen SW, 'Events as Grammatical Objects. The Converging Perspectives of Lexical Semantics and Syntax.' (2001) 24 Nordic Journal of Linguistics 241.

Kaplow L, 'Rules versus Standards: An Economic Analysis' (1992) 42 Duke Law Journal 557.

Kennedy M, 'Why Are WTO Panels Taking Longer? And What Can Be Done About It' (2011) 45 Journal of World Trade 221.

Kessler O, 'The Same as It Never Was? Uncertainty and the Changing Contours of International Law' (2011) 37 Review of International Studies 2163.

Khan LA, 'Temporality of Law' (2009) 40 McGeorge Law Review 55.

Knight B, Ma J and Nissan E, 'Representing Temporal Knowledge in Legal Discourse' (1998) 7 Information & Communications Technology Law 199.

Kolikipogu R and others, 'A Novel Model for Timed Event Extraction and Temporal Reasoning In Legal Text Documents' (2011) 2 International Journal of Computer Science and Engineering Survey 39.

Koremenos B, 'Contracting around International Uncertainty' (2005) 99 The American Political Science Review 549.

Koremenos B, Lipson C and Snidal D, 'Rational Design: Looking Back to Move Forward' (2001) 55 International Organization 1051.

Koremenos B, Lipson C and Snidal D, 'The Rational Design of International Institutions' (2001) 55 International Organization 761.

Koremenos B and Nau A, 'Exit, No Exit' (2010) 21 Duke Journal of Comparative & International Law 81.

Koskenniemi M, 'Histories of International Law: Significance and Problems for a Critical View' (2013) 27 Temple International and Comparative Law Journal 215.

Kryvoi Y and Matos S, 'Non-Retroactivity as a General Principle of Law' (2021) 17 Utrect Law Review 46.

Lascarides A and Asher N, 'Temporal Interpretation, Discourse Relations and Commonsense Entailment' (1993) 16 Linguistics and Philosophy 437.

Lawrence TB, Winn MI and Jennings PD, 'The Temporal Dynamics of Institutionalization' (2001) 26 Academy of Management Review 624.

Marsic G, 'Syntactically Motivated Task Definition for Temporal Relation Identification' (2012) 53 Traitement Automatique des Langues 23.

Mawani R, 'Law as Temporality: Colonial Politics and Indian Settlers' (2014) 4 UC Irvine Law Review 65.

Meltzer J, 'State Sovereignty and the Legitimacy of the WTO' (2005) 26 University of Pennsylvania Journal of International Law 693.

Meyer T, 'How Compliance Understates Effectiveness' (2014) 108 AJIL Unbound 93.

Moens M and Steedman M, 'Temporal Ontology and Temporal Reference' (1988) 14 Computational Linguistics 15.

Mortenson JD, 'The Travaux of Travaux: Is the Vienna Convention Hostile to Drafting History?' (2013) 107 American Journal of International Law 780.

Murphy L, 'Varieties of Effectiveness: What Matters?' (2014) 108 AJIL Unbound 99.

Murphy SD, 'Temporal Issues Relating to BIT Dispute Resolution' (2022) 37 ICSID Review—Foreign Investment Law Journal 51.

Naik. MV, Guda V and Srujana I, 'Reasoning in Legal Text Documents with Extracted Event Information' (2011) 28 International Journal of Computer Applications 8.

Navas-Loro M and others, 'TempCourt: Evaluation of Temporal Taggers on a New Corpus of Court Decisions' (2019) 34 The Knowledge Engineering Review 1.

Navas-Loro M and Santos C, 'Events in the Legal Domain: First Impressions', *Proceedings of the 2nd Workshop on Technologies for Regulatory Compliance co-located with the 30th International Conference on Legal Knowledge and Information Systems (JURIX 2017) (TeReCom)* (Zenodo 2018).

Neumayer E, 'Strategic Delaying and Concessions Extraction in Accession Negotiations to the World Trade Organization: An Analysis of Working Party Membership' (2013) 12 World Trade Review 669.

Núñez R and Cooperrider K, 'The Tangle of Space and Time in Human Cognition' (2013) 17 Trends in Cognitive Sciences 220.

O'Neal Taylor C, 'Beyond Retaliation' (2017) 38 Northwestern Journal of International Law & Business 55.

Orford A, 'On International Legal Method' (2013) 1 London Review of International Law 166.

Orlikowski WJ and Yates J, 'It's about Time: Temporal Structuring in Organizations' (2002) 13 Organization Science 684.

Padelford NJ, 'Review of Politics among Nations: The Struggle for Power and Peace' (1949) 64 Political Science Quarterly 290.

Panizzon M, 'Fairness, Promptness and Effectiveness: How the Openness of Good Faith Limits the Flexibility of the DSU' (2008) 77 Nordic Journal of International Law 275.

Pauwelyn J and Pelc K, 'Who Guards the "Guardians of the System"? The Role of the Secretariat in WTO Dispute Settlement' (2022) 116 American Journal of International Law 534.

Pauwelyn J, Wessel RA and Wouters J, 'When Structures Become Shackles: Stagnation and Dynamics in International Lawmaking' (2014) 25 European Journal of International Law 733.

Pierson P, 'Increasing Returns, Path Dependence, and the Study of Politics' (2000) 94 The American Political Science Review 251.

Qian M, '"Reasonable Period of Time" in the WTO Dispute Settlement System' (2012) 15 Journal of International Economic Law 257.

Schilder F and McCulloh A, 'Temporal Information Extraction from Legal Documents', *Annotating, Extracting and Reasoning about Time and Events. Dagstuhl Seminar Proceedings* (2005).

Schuster MM, 'Is the Flow of Time Subjective?' (1986) 39 The Review of Metaphysics 695.

Singh C, 'The Concept of Time in Law: Basis of Laws of Limitation and Prescription' (1990) 32 Journal of the Indian Law Institute 328.

Steinbach A, 'The Treatment of Confidential Information in WTO Dispute Settlement Proceedings' (2014) 24 American Review of International Arbitration <https://aria.law.columbia.edu/issues/24-4/the-treatment-of-confidential-information-in-wto-dispute-settlement-proceed ings-vol-24-no-4/>.

Steinberg RH, 'Judicial Lawmaking at the WTO: Discursive, Constitutional, and Political Constraints' (2004) 98 The American Journal of International Law 247.

Uruena R, 'Temporariness and Change in Global Governance' (2014) 45 Netherlands Yearbook of International Law 19.

Valenzuela J and Alcaraz Carrión D, 'Temporal Expressions in English and Spanish: Influence of Typology and Metaphorical Construal' (2020) 11 Frontiers in Psychology 1.

Vidigal G, 'Hidden Meanings: Evolutionary Interpretation Between Norm Application and Progressive Development' (2021) 24 Journal of International Economic Law 203.

Wheatley N, 'Law and the Time of Angels: International Law's Method Wars and the Affective Life of Disciplines' (2021) 60 History and Theory 311.

## Books and Book Chapters

Abbott A, *Time Matters: On Theory and Method* (University of Chicago Press 2001).

Alter KJ, 'Delegation to International Courts and the Limits of Recontracting Political Power' in Darren G Hawkins and others (eds), *Delegation and Agency in International Organizations* (Cambridge University Press 2006).

Aristotle, *Politics: A Treatise on Government* (CreateSpace Independent Publishing Platform 2015).

Barnes B, Bloor D and Henry J, *Scientific Knowledge: A Sociological Analysis* (University of Chicago Press 1996).

Beynon-Jones SM and Grabham E (eds), *Law and Time* (Routledge 2019).

Bilder RB, *Managing the Risks of International Agreement* (University of Wisconsin Press 1981).

Bilder RB, 'Beyond Compliance: Helping Nations Cooperate' in Dinah Shelton (ed), *Commitment and Compliance: The Role of Non-binding Norms in the International Legal System* (Oxford University Press 2003).

Binder C and Hofbauer J, 'The Temporal Scope of Application of Investment Treaties and the Effects on General International Law' in Christian Tams, Stephan Schill and Rainer Hofmann (eds), *International Investment Law and General International Law* (Edward Elgar Publishing 2023).

Bowker GC and Star SL, *Sorting Things Out: Classification and Its Consequences* (The MIT Press 2000).

Brunnée J and Toope SJ, *Legitimacy and Legality in International Law: An Interactional Account* (Cambridge University Press 2010).

Butterfield J (ed), *The Arguments of Time* (Oxford University Press 2006).

Carey H (Chip) and Mitchell SM, 'Introduction: Re-Conceptualizing Legalization—The Positive and Negative Uses and Effects of International Law' in Henry (Chip) Carey and Stacey M Mitchell (eds), *Legalization of International Law and Politics: Multi-Level Governance of Human Rights and Aggression* (Springer International Publishing 2023).

Comrie B, *Aspect: An Introduction to the Study of Verbal Aspect and Related Problems* (Cambridge University Press 1976).

Cook G, 'The Illusion of "Evolutionary Interpretation" in WTO Dispute Settlement' in Georges Abi-Saab and others (eds), *Evolutionary Interpretation and International Law* (Hart Publishing 2019).

Craven M, Fitzmaurice M and Vogiatzi M (eds), *Time, History and International Law* (Brill Nijhoff 2007).

Davis KE, Kingsbury B and Merry SE, 'Introduction: Global Governance by Indicators' in Kevin Davis and others (eds), *Governance by Indicators: Global Power through Quantification and Rankings* (Oxford University Press 2012).

Dunoff JL and Pollack MA (eds), *Interdisciplinary Perspectives on International Law and International Relations: The State of the Art* (Cambridge University Press 2013).

Felski R, *Doing Time: Feminist Theory and Postmodern Culture* (NYU Press 2000).

Franck TM, *Fairness in International Law and Institutions* (Oxford University Press 1998).

Fuller LL., *The Morality of Law* (14th edition, Yale University Press 1977).

Gadamer H-G, *Philosophical Hermeneutics* (University of California Press 2008).

Grabham E and Beynon-Jones SM, 'Introduction' in Siân M Beynon-Jones and Emily Grabham (eds), *Law and Time* (Routledge 2019).

Grisot C, 'The Linguistic Expression of Temporal Reference', *Cohesion, Coherence and Temporal Reference from an Experimental Corpus Pragmatics Perspective* (Springer International Publishing 2018).

Guzmán AT, *How International Law Works: A Rational Choice Theory* (Oxford University Press 2008).

Haas PM, 'Choosing to Comply: Theorizing from International Relations and Comparative Politics' in Dinah Shelton (ed), *Commitment and Compliance: The Role of Non-binding Norms in the International Legal System* (Oxford University Press 2003).

Hansel M, 'Feminist Time and an International Law of the Everyday' in Susan Harris Rimmer and Kate Ogg (eds), *Research Handbook on Feminist Engagement with International Law* (Edward Elgar Publishing 2019).

Hart HLA, *The Concept of Law* (Oxford University Press 1972).

Hassan R, *Empires of Speed: Time and the Acceleration of Politics and Society* (Brill Nijhoff 2009).

Hom A and others (eds), *Time, Temporality and Global Politics* (Bristol: E-International Relations 2016).

Howse R, 'Adjudicative Legitimacy and Treaty Interpretation in International Trade Law: The Early Years of WTO Jurisprudence' in Joseph HH Weiler (ed), *The EU, the WTO, and the NAFTA: Towards a Common Law of International Trade?* (Oxford University Press 2001).

Hutchings K, *Time and World Politics: Thinking the Present* (Manchester University Press 2008).

Kahn PW, *The Cultural Study of Law: Reconstructing Legal Scholarship* (University of Chicago Press 1999).

Kennedy D, 'The Mystery of Global Governance' in Jeffrey L Dunoff and Joel P Trachtman (eds), *Ruling the World?: Constitutionalism, International Law, and Global Governance* (Cambridge University Press 2009).

Klabbers J, *International Law* (2nd edition, Cambridge University Press 2017).

Kolb R, 'Evolutionary Interpretation in International Law: Some Short and Less than Trail-Blazing Reflections' in Georges Abi-Saab and others (eds), *Evolutionary Interpretation and International Law* (Hart Publishing 2019).

Le Poidevin R, 'The Experience and Perception of Time' in Edward N Zalta (ed), *The Stanford Encyclopedia of Philosophy* (Summer 2019, Metaphysics Research Lab, Stanford University 2019).

Livermore MA, Rockmore DN and Badawi AB (eds), *Law as Data: Computation, Text, & the Future of Legal Analysis* (The Santa Fe Institute Press 2019).

Luhmann N, *Law as a Social System* (Oxford University Press 2008).

Matsushita M and others, *The World Trade Organization: Law, Practice and Policy* (3rd edition, Oxford University Press 2015).

McNeilly K and Warwick B (eds), *The Times and Temporalities of International Human Rights Law* (Bloomsbury Publishing 2022).

Pöppel E, 'Time Perception' in SM Anstis (ed), *Perception (Handbook of Sensory Physiology)*, vol 8 (Springer International Publishing 1978).

Puşcaşu G and Mititelu VB, 'Annotation of WordNet Verbs with TimeML Event Classes' in Nicoletta Calzolari and others (eds), *Proceedings of the Sixth International Conference on Language Resources and Evaluation (LREC'08)* (European Language Resources Association (ELRA) 2008).

Raftopoulos E, *International Negotiation: A Process of Relational Governance for International Common Interest* (Cambridge University Press 2019).

Rakoff TD, *A Time for Every Purpose: Law and the Balance of Life* (Harvard University Press 2002).

Rosa H, 'De-Synchronization, Dynamic Stabilization, Dispositional Squeeze: The Problem of Temporal Mismatch' in Judy Wajcman and Nigel Dodd (eds), *The Sociology of Speed: Digital, Organizational, and Social Temporalities* (Oxford University Press 2016).

Rosa H and Trejo-Mathys J, *Social Acceleration: A New Theory of Modernity* (Columbia University Press 2013).

Rothstein S, 'Verb Classes and Aspectual Classification', *Structuring Events: A Study in the Semantics of Lexical Aspect* (John Wiley & Sons, Ltd 2004).

Ruggie JG, 'Foreword' in Thomas G Weiss and Ramesh Thakur (eds), *Global Governance and the UN: An Unfinished Journey* (Indiana University Press 2010).

Salojärvi JM, 'Human Rights in Time: Temporalization of Human Rights in Historical Representation' in Klara Polackova Van der Ploeg, Luca Pasquet and León Castellanos-Jankiewicz (eds), *International Law and Time: Narratives and Techniques* (Springer International Publishing 2022).

Schilder F, 'Event Extraction and Temporal Reasoning in Legal Documents' in Frank Schilder, Graham Katz and James Pustejovsky (eds), *Annotating, Extracting and Reasoning about Time and Events* (Springer International Publishing 2007).

Schilder F, Katz G and Pustejovsky J (eds), *Annotating, Extracting and Reasoning about Time and Events* (Springer International Publishing 2007).

Schramm BK, 'Interstellar Justice Now: Back to the Future of International Law' in Klara Polackova Van der Ploeg, Luca Pasquet and León Castellanos-Jankiewicz (eds), *International Law and Time: Narratives and Techniques* (Springer International Publishing 2022).

Shelton D, 'Law, Non-Law and the Problem of "Soft Law"' in Dinah Shelton (ed), *Commitment and Compliance: The Role of Non-binding Norms in the International Legal System* (Oxford University Press 2003).

Slaughter A-M, *A New World Order* (4th edition, Princeton University Press 2005).

Soave T, 'The Politics of Time in Domestic and International Lawmaking' in Klara Polackova Van der Ploeg, Luca Pasquet and León Castellanos-Jankiewicz (eds), *International Law and Time: Narratives and Techniques* (Springer International Publishing 2022).

Šubrt J, *The Sociology of Time: A Critical Overview* (Springer International Publishing 2021).

Sunstein CR, *Simpler: The Future of Government* (Simon and Schuster 2013).

Trindade AAC, 'Time and Law Revisited: International Law and the Temporal Dimension', *International Law for Humankind: Towards a New Jus Gentium* (Brill Nijhoff 2020).

Van Damme I, 'Understanding the Choice for Evolutionary Interpretation' in Georges Abi-Saab and others (eds), *Evolutionary Interpretation and International Law* (Hart Publishing 2019).

Van den Bossche P, 'Is There Evolution in the Evolutionary Interpretation of WTO Law?' in Georges Abi-Saab and others (eds), *Evolutionary Interpretation and International Law* (Hart Publishing 2019).

Van den Bossche P and Zdouc W, *The Law and Policy of the World Trade Organization: Text, Cases and Materials* (4th edition, Cambridge University Press 2017).

Van der Ploeg KP and Pasquet L, 'The Multifaceted Notion of Time in International Law' in Klara Polackova Van der Ploeg, Luca Pasquet and León Castellanos-Jankiewicz (eds), *International Law and Time: Narratives and Techniques* (Springer International Publishing 2022).

Vanhullebusch M, 'China, Confucian Time and International Law: A Normative and Behavioral Account' in Klara Polackova Van der Ploeg, Luca Pasquet and León Castellanos-Jankiewicz (eds), *International Law and Time: Narratives and Techniques* (Springer International Publishing 2022).

Werner WG, 'Regulating Speed: Social Acceleration, and International Law' in Moshe Hirsch and Andrew Lang (eds), *Research Handbook on the Sociology of International Law* (Edward Elgar Publishing 2018).

Wyler E and Whelan A, 'Lawyers as Creators of Law's Temporal Reality: A Pragmatic Approach to International Law' in Klara Polackova Van der Ploeg, Luca Pasquet and León Castellanos-Jankiewicz (eds), *International Law and Time: Narratives and Techniques* (Springer International Publishing 2022).

Zappalà S, 'Can Legality Trump Effectiveness in Today's International Law?' in Antoni Cassese (ed), *Realizing Utopia: The Future of International Law* (Oxford University Press 2012).

## Other Resources

Bacchus J, 'The World Trade Organization: Myths versus Reality' (*Cato Institute*, 26 September 2023) <https://www.cato.org/publications/world-trade-organization-myths-versus-reality>.

Chittaro L and Combi C, 'Extending the Event Calculus with Temporal Granularity and Indeterminacy' [2000] AAAI Technical Report WS-00-08 53.

Duranti G and Di Prata O, 'Everything Is about Time: Does It Have the Same Meaning All over the World?', *PMI® Global Congress 2009—EMEA, Amsterdam, North Holland, The Netherlands. Newtown Square, PA: Project Management Institute* (2009).

Ferro L and others, 'TIDES 2005 Standard for the Annotation of Temporal Expressions' <https://www.ldc.upenn.edu/sites/www.ldc.upenn.edu/files/english-timex2-guidelines-v0.1. pdf>.

Ma M and others, 'Deconstructing Legal Text: Object-Oriented Design in Legal Adjudication' [2020] MIT Computational Law Report <https://law.mit.edu/pub/deconstructinglegaltext/release/1>.

Neufeld N, 'The Long and Winding Road: How WTO Members Finally Reached a Trade Facilitation Agreement' [2014] WTO Staff Working Papers <https://www.wto.org/english/res_e/reser_e/ersd201406_e.htm>.

Saurí R and others, 'TimeML Annotation Guidelines Version 1.2.1' <https://nilsreiter.de/assets/2017-10-01-howto-annotation/timeml-1.2.1.pdf>.

'The Intertemporal Problem in Public International Law' (Institut de Droit International 1975) <https://www.idi-iil.org/en/publications/i-le-probleme-intertemporel-en-droit-international-public/>.

# Index

www.ingramcontent.com/pod-product-compliance
Lightning Source LLC
LaVergne TN
LVHW010658300926
849161LV00005B/1163